Freedom, Trauma, Continuities

Studies on Contemporary South Asia

A joint publication series
with South Asian Studies Association (SASA)
&
South Asian Research Unit (SARU)
Curtin University of Technology

General Editors: Peter Reeves, John McGuire and Jim Masselos
Administrative Editors: Terry Richards and Bruce Watson

Freedom, Trauma, Continuities

Northern India and Independence

Edited by

D.A. Low
and
Howard Brasted

<u>Studies on Contemporary South Asia No. 2</u>

ALTAMIRA
PRESS

WALNUT CREEK • LONDON • NEW DELHI

Sponsored by the South Asian Studies Association and the South Asian Research Unit.

For information address:

AltaMira Press
A Division of Sage Publications, Inc.
1630 North Main Street, Suite 367
Walnut Creek, CA 94596

SAGE Publications Ltd.
6 Bonhill Street
London EC2A 4PU
United Kingdom

SAGE Publications India Pvt. Ltd.
M-32 Market
Greater Kailash I
New Delhi 110 048 India

Printed in New Delhi, India

Library of Congress Cataloging-in-Publication Data

Freedom, trauma, continuities : Northern India and independence/
 edited by D.A. Low and Howard Brasted.
    p. cm.—(Studies in contemporary South Asia : v. 2)
  Includes bibliographical references and index.
  ISBN 0–7619–9225–1 (alk. paper).—ISBN 0–7619–9226–x (pbk.:
alk.paper)
   1. India—Politics and government—1947– I. Low, D.A. (Donald
Anthony), 1927– . II. Brasted, Howard, 1945– . III. Series.
       DS480.84.F74 954.04—dc21   1997 97—32071

Interior Design and Production by Curtin University Press, Perth
Cover Design by FACET

CONTENTS

ACKNOWLEDGMENTS

Most of the chapters in this volume were first prepared as papers for a workshop in December 1993 at the Nehru Memorial Museum and Library in New Delhi, a workshop which was arranged by the Director, Professor Ravinder Kumar, with his customary generosity and care. The contributors are greatly indebted to him and the staff at the NMML for making the workshop a memorable occasion.

Guest edited by Professor D.A. Low these papers subsequently appeared in a special issue of *South Asia* (Vol. XVIII) in 1995, under the title: 'North India: Partition and Independence'. Such was the interest generated in this volume that it was decided to republish it as number two in the SASA-SARU series: 'Studies on Contemporary South Asia', through Sage Publications. With a degree of revision and two extended chapters by Dr Gyanesh Kudaisya replacing his single original paper, the collection re-emerges here as *Freedom, Trauma, Continuities: Northern India and Independence.* We would like to thank not only Terry Richards for his editorial assistance in preparing camera-ready copy, but also Sage for their useful suggestions and considerable patience.

D.A. Low and Howard Brasted

CONTRIBUTORS

Swarna Aiyar   London, UK
Sarah Ansari   Royal Holloway, University of London
Dipesh Chakrabarty   University of Chicago, Illinois
Ian Copland   Monash University, Victoria
Vinita Damodaran   Sussex University, UK
Gyanesh Kudaisya   National University of Singapore, Singapore
Medha Malik Kudaisya   Nanyang Technological University, Singapore
D.A. Low   Research School of Pacific and Asian Studies, ANU,
                        Canberra
Andrew J. Major   National University of Singapore, Singapore
Ian Talbot   Coventry University, UK
Tan Tai Yong   National University of Singapore, Singapore

Digging Deeper: Northern India in the 1940s

D. A. Low

In August 1947 India became independent and was partitioned into the two separate states of India and Pakistan. The immensity of these historical developments has understandably engrossed the historiography of South Asia for the 1940s and a rich literature of scholarly and other interpretations and an abundant harvest of published documents has resulted. The former began with a raft of quasi-official accounts, of which the more important were V.P. Menon, *The Transfer of Power in India* (1957), H.V. Hodson, *The Great Divide: Britain-India-Pakistan* (1969), and C.M. Chaudhuri, *The Emergence of Pakistan* (1973). There were as well from the British side some notable personal accounts such as A. Campbell-Johnson, *Mission with Mountbatten* (1951) and P. Moon, *Divide and Quit* (1962), and several attempts to capture a popular audience, of which L. Collins and D. Lapiere, *Freedom at Midnight* (1982) was amongst the most widely read.

As the archives came to be opened up, scholars sought to add to these earlier versions with such studies as B. R. Tomlinson, *The Political Economy of the Raj, 1914-1947: The Economics of Decolonization in India*, R.J. Moore, *Churchill, Cripps and India, 1939-45* (1979) and *Escape from Empire. The Attlee Government and the Indian Problem* (1983), M.N. Das, *Partition and Independence of India* (1982), A.I. Singh, *The Origins of the Partition of India, 1936-1947* (1987). Of major importance have been Professor Nicholas Mansergh's twelve magisterial volumes of edited British documents on *Constitutional Relations between Britain and India. The Transfer of Power. 1942-1947*, (London 1970-1983). These have come to have a dominating influence upon scholarly discussion of the events of the 1940s over most of the time since they were first published. They have been counterpointed by *The Collected Works of Mahatma Gandhi* (1958-73), by *The Selected Works of Jawaharlal Nehru* (1972-) edited by Professor Gopal, by *Sardar Patel's Correspondence, 1945-50* (1971-4) edited by D. Das, and by *Dr Rajendra Prasad. Correspondence and Select Documents*, (1983-) edited by V. Chaudhary; and *Quaid-i-Azam Mohammad Ali Jinnah Papers* (1993-) edited by Z.H. Zaidi. It can now be expected that they will be significantly supplemented by the publication of the principal volumes of the Indian Council of Historical Research's series of Indian documents for the period, *Towards Freedom* (of which the first volume for 1937 appeared in 1985), and in due course by the Quaid-i-Azam Academy's series of *Muslim League Documents 1900-1947*, edited by Professor Sharif al Mujahid.

Fifty years on there is no lack of information about the bitter controversies, soul-wrenchings, persistent uncertainties, and protracted negotiations that preceded and accompanied the advent of Independence and Partition in the sub-continent. Until recently indeed almost the only other occurrence during the 1940s to have engaged subtantial scholarly attention was the 1943 famine in Bengal.[1] Even Ayesha Jalal's arresting study of *The Sole Spokesman: Jinnah, The Muslim League and the Demand for Pakistan* (1985), which provides the only significant revisionist interpretation of any aspect of the previously conventional story, stands firmly upon the same scholarly terrain. The sheer teleology to the climax in August 1947 when British power was formally 'transferred' has all but monopolised the scene.

With the fiftieth anniversary of these great events the time has come when scholars, and especially younger scholars, are starting to give attention to a variety of other occurrences and developments in the 1940s; some of which were no less portentous, and many of which had consequences that have been as least as long lasting, several of which were intimately connected with the high level politics, which have hitherto preoccupied attention yet have rarely been given the attention which is their due.

As an aid to this process a Workshop was held at the Nehru Memorial Museum and Library in New Delhi in December 1993 at the instance of its ever generous Director, Professor Ravinder Kumar, to whom, and to the staff of the Nehru, all of those who attended are deeply indebted. They are especially indebted to his own invariably arresting contributions to the discussions. The chapters which are published here cannot be anything more than a selection of the papers which were presented there (or in two cases would have been presented there if their authors had in the end been able to attend). Some of the others have been separately published in other forms,[2] while those included here have been revised in the the light of the discussions which took place. These chapters were first published as a Special Issue of *South Asia*, Volume XVIII, (1995), and with some alterations, are now republished here for a wider readership.

As was proposed at the outset of the Delhi Workshop, the issues for consideration broadly divide into those which relate to a number of the deep, and not infrequently terrible disruptions which occurred in association with the major political developments of that time, while others concern the strong continuities which can be discerned through all the upheavals with which India and the new Pakistan were so cruelly plagued during the 1940s.

Among the upheavals – aside from and never forgetting the Bengal famine – none was more substantial during the early 1940s than the 'Quit India' movement. Since 1988 we have had Professor Gyan Pandey's invaluable collection on the incidence of the movement in different parts of India (G.Pandey, ed., *The Indian Nation in 1942*). There remains, however, both a persistent debate about its character, together with a growing – and one may guess still unfinished – collation of insights into its prevening circumstances, its time span, and its aftermath. The former is canvassed in Vinita Damodaran's contributions in which the earlier conclusions by first Max Harcourt and then Stephen Henningham are substantially queried, and a further interpretation is advanced. The latter begin with the recognition that when the Congress ministries in the Provinces resigned office late in 1939, by contrast with other occasions when Congress changed its tactics (from 'office acceptance' to nationalist agitation and back again), it was for much of the next three years very much at a loss as to exactly what it should do next.[3] This was all the more so since it was always clear that should there be another Congress-led mass agitation, the British would clamp down upon it as hard as they had done previously in 1932. Gandhi's 'Individual *Satyagraha*' movement of 1940-41 took the form that it did precisely to obviate that eventuality. By August 1942, however, as Gandhi in some growing despair came to recognise, the widespread propensity towards a further nationalist agitation had become impossible to check, and it accordingly exploded to a degree that he could not control. (His 'epic' fast early in 1943 was plainly a determined move to reassert his authority over the nationalist movement so as to bring it back onto the non-violent course that he held so dear).

There are three further aspects of the 1942 movement on which new light has lately been shed. In the first place, during the intervening years since late 1939, more attention was given by Congress supporters to the formation and systematic training of Congress cadres than ever before (and one is inclined to say 'or since').[4] To a degree that has still to be fully elucidated these constituted the organising sinews in the ensuing convulsion so soon as the more prominent Congress leadership was so extensively swept into jail. Then there is Indivar Kamtekar's seminal argument that, especially in what was shortly to be the heartland of the revolt, there had come to be by mid 1942, as a consequence of the momentous Japanese military successes since the beginning of the year in Southeast Asia and more especially in Burma, a profound and widespread belief, represented by all manner of stockpiling, that the British *raj* was upon its last legs and that only a sudden popular eruption would be needed to topple it over. The essential point here is that that belief proved in very short order to be grievously mistaken. Because of the preparations the British were making to throw the Japanese back out of Burma, they had more troops at this very moment at their command in India than ever before, and they were in no mood to permit a popular outburst to frustrate their plans. That was made clear within days of the August outbreak. Once the British called out the army (fifty-seven and a half battalions were mobilised) large parts of the revolt very quickly petered out.[5] To this must be added Gyanesh Kudaisya sustained evidence that ever since 1857 the British had been preparing for just such an outburst as occurred in August 1942, and were accordingly unusually well primed to suppress it.[6]

There have been important accounts of how in places the revolt nonetheless trickled on until the end of the war.[7] Perhaps the more important point is the very paradox in the aftermath. On the one side the message had gone out in India that even on its last legs the British coercive machine was by no means undone; it had indeed been substantially reinforced since 1939 by the extensive new recruiting of armed auxiliary police.[8] This not only helps to explain the fact that Congress leaders on their release from jail in 1944 put a further nationalist agitation quite out of their minds. It helps to explain why, in spite of Sir Stafford Cripps' announcement early in 1942 that India would be granted independence as soon as the war was over, there was such relatively little distancing in the latter years of the war of Indian subordinate administrators from their imperial masters (of which the British had been so fearful in 1931-33). It also illuminates the widespead belief that notwithstanding the precise terms of the Cripps declaration the British could not possibly have meant what they said. At the same time, however, the very fact that the British had been able to suppress the 'Quit India' movement in 1942 served to ensure that they would in fact be as good as their word. For it was quite clear that with the defeat of the Japanese in 1945, and the demobilisation of large numbers of British troops which then inevitably ensued, the British would not again have available to them the overwhelming forces that would be needed to suppress any recurrence of the 1942 movement, let alone, as would have been more than likely, something far more explosive. For this reason, if for no other, and there were others, the British did not make the mistake which both the Dutch and the French made (neither of whom had had a similar preceding experience during the war) of attempting, quite fatally, to withstand the post-war resurgence of nationalism in their Asian colonies with armed force. In India considerations arising from their differing experiences of the 'Quit India' movement cooled minds upon both sides.

In the first half of the 1940s there were further serious disruptions of a more pervasive if less dramatic kind which are no more than touched on here, but are beginning to be discussed elsewhere. In particular it seems clear that the wartime exigencies created all kinds of supply problems, especially of food (quite apart from the Bengal famine), that were coupled with increased government regulations, inflation, and substantial transfers of land particularly through resumption and foreclosure.[9] The full implications of all this turmoil have still to be traced out, but they were evidently very substantial.

For all that, nothing that occurred during the early 1940s matched the depth of horrendousness and disruptiveness of so many of the major events of the late 1940s across the length and breadth of northern India. With limited exceptions most of these did not afflict southern India, and it is that distinction which warrants the focus of attention here upon northern India. They turned, of course, on the quadrapartite partition which created there two new international borders, and four new states where two provinces had existed before.

The immense disruptions which now occurred began with the appalling Hindu-Muslim communal killings that erupted upon an unprecedented scale from 1946 onwards. There are still considerable difficulties in accounting for the grotesque animosities that suddenly came to be displayed between peoples who hitherto had frequently dwelt in relatively amicable harmony with each other, even if from time to time sudden conficts and even serious riots could break out between them. It seems clear that the waves of killings in different areas which now erupted sprayed out upon each other, and that at their core all were deeply poisoned with the same miasmic venom. Four shafts of light upon the whole horrendous story point to some particular contingencies in four different places which made for certain marked differences in their character amid the wider carnage they all displayed in common.

As Suranjan Das has explained, the 'Great Calcutta Killings' of August 1946 were to a large degree at least an elite-propelled battle between Hindu and Muslims for control of this key city (whose disposition in any end-game for the Pakistan movement was quite particularly uncertain), in which both sides unabashedly patronised *goonda* gangs in the city; 'an umbrella term used to denote a broad spectrum of social groups', Das explains, 'ranging from various marginalised elements to habitual criminals'. The outbreak, he writes, 'was political in nature and directly connected with developments in institutional politics': '*goonda* links with the world of organised politics was clear'; 'it was this section of society...who emerged as the organizers of violence'.[10] That was a very different circumstance from that which was witnessed in the scarcely less notorious communal killings in Noakhali and Tippera in East Bengal. Here the conflict saw a powerful strain of Muslim tenant-peasant revolt against their Hindu landlords and moneylenders. In East Bengal it began, so Das writes (and Sugata Bose has very much the same story) with an attack upon 'the establishments of the two richest Hindus in the locality', and in short order led on to 'a general Muslim rising against the Hindu populace of the district'.[11]

The subsequent bloodbaths in Bihar had a particular character that differed again. Here, by and after the end of the war, there had been a revival of the bitter agrarian disputes which had marked the late 1930s (with the so-called Bakasht movement), but which had then been overlaid by the principally nationalist revolt which had been so substantial in Bihar in 1942. While the grave discontents that were prevalent here could be variously expressed in nationalist and agrarian terms, they could also, it seems, be expressed in communal terms, and, as Vinita Damodaran shows, there is striking evidence that in consort with the inherently corrosive communal division, it was by 1946 possible for landowners to douse down a potential agrarian revolt by transmuting what was essentially a 'horizontal' agrarian upheaval into a 'vertical' communal conflict.

None of these factors lay behind the major massacres at the time of independence in 1947 which occurred so notoriously in the Punjab. These were neither focussed upon a major battle for a single city, nor marked by goonda free-for-alls;neither were they impelled by a peasant upthrust against landlords and merchants, nor were they fuelled by a deliberately contorted peasant insurgency.

The Punjab massacres of 1947 are part of the stock-in-trade of anyone with any interest at all in the Indian and Pakistani stories, let alone their historians. This self-assured knowledge is, however, for the most part insubstantial. For the details, the distinctive character, the endless ramifications are scarcely ever followed through. Following upon some much earlier and variously problematic official accounts, a major beginning has now been made here by Swarna Aiyar,[12] of which her chapter below offers a preliminary account of some key aspects of the whole story.

It seems clear that the riots of March 1947, which were largely confined to the western districts of the Punjab, need to be very precisely distinguished from the partition massacres of August-September, which among other things were province-wide. The former took their thrust from the outrage of so many Muslims that, despite their preponderant numbers in the province, the provincial government, following the elections of 1946, was made up of a coalition of Congress-Unionist Party-Sikh members to the total exclusion of the largest political party, the Muslim League. Muslims despaired that unless this situation was speedily righted, this key province, or at all events the preponderant part of it, which was crucial to the very viability of the Pakistan idea, would elude their grasp. As a consequence of the Muslim-inspired disturbances in March, the coalition government in the Punjab was toppled. That immediately emboldened, however, the province's already widespread advocates of *force majeure*. It was replaced, moreover, by 'governor's rule', which left the ultimate political control of the province open to seizure by the most resolute in the land.

In these earlier disturbances the Sikhs in particular had found themselves off-guard and suffered accordingly. They were absolutely determined that that should never happen again. In the supercharged atmosphere which ensued, when the disposition of different districts between the soon impending different states of India and Pakistan was to begin with quite uncertain, and then with the announcement of the decisions of the Boundary Commission in August 1947 which caused bitter heartburnings upon all sides, the whole province exploded into murderous frenzy. The deep irony here was that the very province which throughout most of the proceding two decades had, superficially at least, shown itself to be more committed through its predominant support for the tri-communal Unionist Party (rather than the Congress, let alone the Muslim League) to communal cooperation than any other in India, now broke apart into three furiously raging communities to wreak the most perfervid communal carnage of all upon each other.

This, as Swarna Aiyar (and others) have shown, was principally made many times worse because of the unique prevalence in mounting the slaughter in the Punjab of trained ex-soldiers (and sometimes not always ex-) in what for several decades had been the British Indian Army's preeminent recruiting ground. One in three Punjabi men of recruitable age had at one point or another in their adult lives served in the army. In this total picture it remains to be determined why, aside from the appalling killings of upwards of 2000 Muslims at Garmukteswar in November 1946[13] and some other episodes too, the United Provinces seemingly saw at this time fewer communal conflicts than either of its two immediate neighbours. Given, however, the virtual absence of many trained soldiers in Bengal it becomes the more understandable that, despite Calcutta and Noakhali, Bengal did not collapse into quite the scale of communal killings in 1947 that convulsed the Punjab.

Whilst Swarna Aiyar gives details of some of the sequence of killings in the Punjab, in railway carriages, in foot convoys, and in other contexts elsewhere, one hitherto understandable consequence of the horrific character of the mass killings and traumatic disruptions which occurred has been that a great many people have apparently shrunk from detailing them in retrospect. This is despite millions of them having been marked for life by the experiences which they passed through. As a consequence the human agonies which they suffered are, in the standard accounts, often buried away. Often they are neglected altogether. Only now, it seems, and very late in the day, is much oral history being attempted.

Two further contributions help, however, to pull the veil a little aside. Significantly, in seeking the most explicit, still available descriptions of what occurred, Ian Talbot finds these not in any oral or memoir accounts, nor in any studies resting upon them, but in literature, where direct personal experience is on many occasions very evidently drawn upon. The fictionalised narrative apparently furnishes a more bearable medium for explicit descriptions of unnerving horrors than raw accounts by victims and survivors can provide even now.

One particular aspect of those horrors has begun to be described elsewhere, and Andrew Major here takes the story a step further. In 1947-8 both the Pakistani and the Indian governments were deeply perturbed about the mass abduction of women, and both mounted operations to secure their restoration to their families. Yet, as he details, the embroilment here ran so deep that even the profoundly solicitous intentions of governments very often never touched the core of what was entailed. And there is here the unspoken implication which nowadays is perhaps rather more difficult to unearth: that women were at least abducted; had they been men they would, more often than not, have been slain.

The depths of the human morass of the Partition massacres are never likely to be fathomed to the full, but at least some beginings are now being made. These years also saw the outcomes to many other disjunctures, several of which upon any ordinary scale of human upheaval were immensely disruptive as well. Estimates vary but it seems as if during the course of 1947 and into 1948 something like 5.5 million Hindus and Sikhs crossed over from West Pakistan to the new India, while something like 5.8 million Muslims managed to travel in the opposite direction. Estimates for the migrations to and from East Bengal seem impossible to compile, both because they extended over a considerably longer period, and because they were essentially far more episodic. However, they must be counted in millions. Gyanesh Kudaisya first provides here a striking account of how, amidst the immense confusion of mass migration and resettlement, the opportunity was taken to effect a well nigh uniquely effective land reform in East Punjab, and then in a further chapter recounts the very different, long protracted, and all but totally disastrous story of refugee settlement in eastern India.[14]

Supplementing this theme is Sarah Ansari's account of the great difficulties involved in settling the Muslim *muhajirs*, as they came to be called, mostly from north central India in Sind and more particularly in Karachi, a story, which as she very appositely underlines, lives on to this day, in seemingly ever aggravated form.[15] Her contribution is alas the only one offered here which in any way touches upon what by any account must be seen as one of the most considerable consequences of the immense disruptions which plagued the partition process in 1947. This lies in the fact that in so many ways almost all the major cities right across the old pre-partition northern India bear to this day the character of refugee cities. If, as she emphasises, this is true of Karachi, it is true as well of Lahore, Delhi, Calcutta and Dacca, to mention the most obvious but by no means the only cases. One of the major *lacunae* indeed in twentieth century South Asian historiography lies precisely in the absence of major studies of what has happened to these cities in the second half of the twentieth century. Unfortunately it has not proved possible to make many amends here.[16]

However, one further commentary is provided. In all this highly-wracked upheaval there was in addition to all the killings, migrations and resettlements that occurred, the great distress that many people felt that all the old familiar sights, sounds and associations had been left behind. Dipesh Chakrabarty provides a threnody upon this still profoundly haunting theme.

That there were other considerable disruptions as a consequence of South Asian independence and partition beyond all these is neatly illustrated by Ian Copland's account of what happened to Princely India – one third after all of the whole sub-continent. Emphasis in the conventional accounts is placed on the relatively smooth transition in 1947 in the subcontinent as a whole, despite the argument and the anguish and the accompanying massacres, from colonial rule to independence. These, however, overlook the many political upheavals at this time in the princely states, along with the major step towards their complete destruction which the advent of independence set on foot. This story has been hitherto historiographically marginalised. That was not how Sardar Patel, the most forceful of independent India's first central government ministers, saw it. For him at the moment of independence the future of India's Princely states topped the agenda. It is well to be reminded of that here.[17]

There was a superabundance of often exceedingly grave disruptions in the South Asian body politic at the moment of independence and partition. These were soon to be followed by others: the abolition of *zamindari*, the Kashmir, Hyderabad and other consequential crises, such as over Punjabi Suba and the Khalistan campaign. Nevertheless, there were also some critically important continuities through the 1940s, not all of which figure as strikingly as they should in the customary teleological accounts of these years. Two that are not detailed here, though their existence goes far to explain a great deal of what did and more especially what did not happen, were simply that there was no anti-colonial war in India in the late 1940s, as there was in Vietnam and in effect in Indonesia; nor was there any revolution of the kind that happened either in the one or in the other.[18] In India in 1947 the striking fact is that in so many respects the existing state trundled on.

It is important in this connection to distinguish carefully between the authority of the colonial state and the authority of the Indian state. As Gyanesh Kudaisya has shown in some detail for U.P., the former was steadily undermined during the 1930s and into the 1940s. This was in large part due to the effect of nationalist propaganda, but it stemmed too from the extensive recourse by the British in the early 1930s, and again in the early 1940s, to quite exceptional legal and coercive measures to uphold their position against the onslaughts of the Congress. By resorting to such extraordinary powers they succeeded in maintaining their hold over India, but at the expense of a severe erosion in the authority they had previously possessed there. That erosion was still further deepened by the subtle shifts the Congress effected in the allegiance of the subordinate Indian bureaucracies and police during the years 1937-9 when they exercised executive control in the Provinces.[19] Kudaisya and Kamtekar have then begun to map out 'the crisis of the colonial state' in its final years, when there were obvious crises over: managing food supplies, over ensuring the 'loyalty' of the navy, over the bungled move in 1945-6 to arraign leaders of the Indian National Army, and much else besides.

By 1946 the Viceroy, Wavell, was thus understandably deeply perturbed as to whether the ultimate hold of the *raj* could be sustained very much longer. In the following year there can be no doubt too that the embryonic government of the new state of Pakistan was in an exceedingly parlous state as independence and partition suddenly burst upon it. However, for all that, as Swarna Aiyar argues, even in the Punjab amidst all the huge disruption of the partition massacres and the accompanying migrations, the collapse of state power was quite extraordinarily short-lived. Within a few short weeks of independence and certainly by early 1948 state authority on both sides of the new border, such was its deeply ingrained resilience, was firmly re-installed in the saddle.[20]

In parallel with all of this there were other important continuities as well. Vinita Damodaran rehearses in her chapter below how upon its return to government in Bihar in 1946, the right-wing dominated Congress drew upon its previous, often disconcerting, experience in office in 1937-39 to propel it in the direction of an often high-handed suppression of anything that smacked of disruptive forces in the state, whether as a consequence of agrarian conflicts, or by the police. No longer neophytes in the business of government, the state Congress leadership was now as a consequence of its earlier experience a group of battle-hardened politicians who would have no truck with their opponents. 'Broken Promises', she has characterised their consequential policies.

In the Punjab there were two important contuinuities too. In the harsher areas of the eastern Punjab during the earlier decades of the century, the hardworking, agricultural Hindu *jats* had developed a political cohesion under the dynamic leadership of Sir Chhotu Ram. He had propelled them into the multi-communal Unionist Party, led by successive, essentially non-Muslim League, leaders, rather than into the urban-dominated Punjab Congress. Following the death of Chhotu Ram and as a consequence of the growing communal fission, the Punjab's Hindu *jats* then threw most of their support at the elections in 1946 behind the Congress.[21]

Thereafter they have remained, as the Haryana *jats*, a remarkably cohesive voting bloc, ready to switch their allegiances behind their leaders as the exigencies of a changing political scene seem to advise.

More portentous that even this is Tan Tai Yong's pathbreaking account of the extent to which, and uniquely in pre-Partition India, the provincial administration of the (undivided) Punjab had become increasingly 'militarised' in the preceding decades from at least the First World War onwards. This stemmed from its prime importance as the principal recruiting ground of that ultimate bulwark of the British *raj* in India, the Indian Army. It was then still further propelled in this direction by the continuing special demands placed upon the Punjab during the Second World War. In the manner that he indicates, upon Independence this singular development provided the administrative sinews that enabled the exiguous Pakistan state to survive its armed conflict with India, and thereafter made the ensuing transition in (originally West) Pakistan to 'the state of martial rule' all the more explicable. A remarkably straight line runs through the continuing turbulances upon the surface.[22]

There are other continuities which need to be noticed too. Medha Malik Kudaisya outlines one whose importance would seem to become all the more important as the ensuing decades pass by. There have long since been several accounts of the activities of Indian capitalists in the interwar period.[23] By focusing upon the most remarkable of these men, G.D. Birla, she elucidates a new theme. Whenever they looked to his leadership India's capitalists clove closely to the Congress, and were cautious in countering the socialist tendencies of some of its leaders, Jawaharlal Nehru in particular. Birla's objective, as she describes it, was an independent India, shorn of its Muslim parts if need be, if they threatened to undermine its need for a strong central government, that in the context of a government-constructed infrastructure would be committed to the development of a Hindu capitalist state. This vision was well exemplified in the titles of the two influential publications which he owned: the *Hindustan Times* and the *Eastern Economist*. The foundations for the outcome were first laid in the industrialists' Bombay plan of 1944, and then following the collapse of the Cabinet Mission Plan of 1946 (which gravely threatened their demand for a strong centre) in the creation of a strongly centralised state in India held together by the overwhelmingly 'broad-church' Congress party. Birla's more particular ambitions might have been more vigorously pursued had Sardar Patel (with whom he was closely associated) lived on into the 1950s and 1960s rather than Jawaharlal Nehru. Yet from the perspective of the 1990s they would seem to have very extensively achieved.[24]

As these lines were being written a newly published book highlighted not so much another continuity as a striking political revival that came with independence and partition.[25] The day had been when the Bengali (largely Hindu) *bhadralok* had dominated the politics of Bengal. Since 1926, however, their primacy had been superseded by that of Bengal's Muslims – not least with the support of the British. Earlier on, between 1905 and 1912, Bengal had been partitioned by the British, to the fury of the *bhadralok*, in a machiavellian effort to reduce their power.[26] Paradoxically (or so one may suggest) by the 1940s the *bhadralok* were campaigning for the partition of Bengal once again so that they should once more predominate politically at least in its western parts. India's partition in 1947 gave them what they wanted. It is a nice question whether Bengal might have been partitioned as they wished even if India had not been partitioned. As it was that issue never came to a head. With Dr B.C.Roy's premiership in a Congress government in West Bengal from 1947 onwards *bhadrolok* primacy was restored there once again.[27]

There remains a great deal more to be learnt about the hinge years of the 1940s. Yet at least these studies, and the larger accounts of which several here are no more than a foretaste of what has yet to come, are starting to widen the perspectives upon the momentous events of the 1940s, particularly across northern India, where the major political decisions of the time had a much more tumultuous impact than elsewhere. That in turn promises to advance the cause of historical writing about the post-independence years which hitherto has largely been the scholarly preserve of professional economists and political scientists. In that sense the chapters which follow serve to underscore the fact that a new generation of historians is saddling up to cross the pre-existing historiographical frontier, and ride out across the terrain of South Asia's post-independence history. The upshot will be interesting to behold.

Notes

1   P.R.Greenhough, *Prosperity and Misery in Modern Bengal: The Famine of 1943-44* (Delhi, 1982).

2   E.g. R. Vasudevan, 'Dislocations: The Cinematic Imagining of a New Society in 1950s India', *The Oxford Literary Review*, Vol. 16, nos 1-2 (1994), pp. 93-124.

3   V. Damodaran, *Broken Promises. Popular Protest, Indian nationalism and the Congress Party in Bihar, 1935-1946* (Delhi 1992), Ch. 3 'Marking Time: Congress in a Quandary, 1939-42'.

4   G.Kudaisya, 'State Power and the Erosion of Colonial Authority in Uttar Pradesh, India, 1930-42' (PhD thesis, Cambridge Univ., 1992), pp. 240-45

5   I. Kamtekar, 'The Crisis of the Colonial State' (PhD thesis, Cambridge Univ., 1988), Chs. 1-2

6   Kudaisya, 'State Power', Chs.2 & 5.

7   E.g. V. Damodaran, 'Azad Dastas and Dacoit Gangs: The Congress and Underground Activity in Bihar, 1942-44', *Modern Asian Studies*, Vol. 26, no. 3 (1992), pp.417-50.

8   Kudaisya, 'State Power', pp. 227-35.

9   Kamtekar, 'Crisis of the Colonial State', Ch.3 et seq.; Damodaran, *Broken Promises*, pp.248-57, 288-95; Kudaisya, 'State Power', pp.235-40.

10 S. Das, *Communal Riots in Bengal 1905-1947* (Delhi, 1991), pp.161-92.

11 *Ibid.*, pp.192-203; Sugata Bose, *Agrarian Bengal Economy, Social Structure and Politics, 1919-1947* (Cambridge, 1986), pp. 223-32.

12 S Aiyar, 'Violence and the State in the Partition of Punjab: 1947-48' (PhD thesis, Cambridge Univ.,1994).

13 For a summary account see Ian Stephens, *Pakistan. Old Country/New Nation* (Harmondsworth, 1964), p. 137.

14 For a preliminary account see G.Kudaisya, 'Divided Landscapes, Fragmented Identities: East Bengal Refugees and their Rehabilitation in India, 1947-79', *Singapore Journal of Tropical Geography*, Vol. 17, no. 1 (1996), pp. 24-39.

15 See also Sarah Ansari, 'The Movement of Indian Muslims to West Pakistan after 1947', in Judith Brown and Rosemary Foot (eds), *Migration. The Asian Experience* (New York, 1994), pp.149-68.

16 Among other things this matter will begin to be tackled in Tan Tai Yong and Gyanesh Kudaisya, *The Aftermath of Partition in South Asia* (forthcoming).

17 See more generally I.F. Copland, *Unwanted Allies. The Princes of India in the Endgame of Empire* (Cambridge, 1997).

18 For ease of reference see A.J.S. Reid, *The Indonesian National Revolution, 1945-50* (Melbourne, 1974), and E.J. Hammer, *The Struggle for Indochina, 1940-1955* (Stanford, 1954).

19 Kudaisya, 'State Power', Part II.

20 Aiyar, 'Violence and the State', pp. 154 *et seq.*

21 P Chowdhury, 'The Congress Triumph in South-East Punjab: Elections of 1946', *Studies in History*, Vol. II, no. 2 (1980), pp. 81-110.

22 Tan Tai Yong, 'The Military and the State in Colonial Punjab, 1900-1939' (PhD thesis, Cambridge Univ., 1992). See also 'Maintaining the Military Districts: Civil-Military Integration and District Boards in the Punjab, 1919-1939', *Modern Asian Studies*, Vol. 28, no. 4 (1994), pp. 833-74. See also D.A.Low (ed.), *The Political Inheritance of Pakistan* (London 1991), and Ayesha Jalal, *The State of Martial Rule:*

the Origins of Pakistan's Political Economy of Defence (Cambridge, 1991).

23 E.g. C. Markovits, *Indian Business and Nationalist Politics, 1931-39: The Indigenous Capitalist Class and the Rise of the Congress Party* (Cambridge, 1985).

24 Medha Maik Kudaisya, 'The Public Career of G.D. Birla, 1911-1947' (Ph.D thesis, Cambridge Univ., 1992).

25 Joya Chatterjee, *Bengal Divided: Hindu Communalism and Partition, 1932-1947* (Cambridge, 1994).

26 J.H. Broomfield, *Elite Conflict in a Plural Society. Twentieth Century Bengal* (Berkeley, 1968).

27 Chatterjee, *loc. cit.*

'August Anarchy':
The Partition Massacres in Punjab, 1947 [*]

Swarna Aiyar

The advent of independence on 15 August 1947 simultaneously saw the division of the Indian sub-continent into two new states. The exhilaration and excitement heralding independence in some areas of the sub-continent was however surpassed in intensity by the exceptionally savage massacres that gripped other areas. The province most affected by this dark side of independence was the Punjab which was caught in a maelstrom of unprecedented violence. These massacres claimed thousands of lives. While it is almost impossible to arrive at even approximate figures, the most conservative estimates put the death toll at roughly 180,000,[1] while G. D. Khosla, an Indian High Court Judge, who examined the question closely put the total number of casualties at about 200,000-250,000 non-Muslims and an equal number of Muslims.[2] As for the loss of property the Indian government estimated that the Hindus and Sikhs who left West Punjab lost Rs. 500 crores, while similar estimates for the loss to Muslims who left East Punjab was put at Rs. 100 crores.

The effects of partition were far-reaching. One of the largest ever processes of forced migration was set off,[3] with an estimated four and a half million Sikhs and Hindus moving from West Punjab into the eastern areas that became part of India, and an estimated five and a half million Muslims moving in the opposite direction. This transformed the demographic profile of the region quite dramatically.[4]

This mass migration, the bulk of which took place within a period of three to four months after independence and partition, was conducted against a backdrop of immense brutality and violence and in an atmosphere inflamed with passions. Yet, curiously enough, considering the magnitude of the changes, both in terms of the sheer cost to human lives, and in the challenge posed by this violence to the authority and legitimacy of the state, especially given the changing nature of that state, little research has been done on this aspect of the transformation of the Punjab in this time of trauma.

Partition and independence have played a major part in studies of the 1940s that have been devoted to the end-of-empire. But while nearly all such studies

[*]   I am grateful to Prof. D.A. Low and Dr J. Majeed for their valuable comments on earlier drafts of this paper.

refer to the violence and the migrations, the actual massacres and migrations themselves have remained seriously neglected. Political, socio-economic, cultural, financial and communal explanations for the partition have been provided. However while explanations for partition abound, the catastrophic events accompanying partition have met with relative silence. This is true even of studies of the Punjab, which for this period, tend to concentrate by and large on the shifts in the fortunes of political parties. Given the widespread ramifications of the partition and its effects on the lives of millions of people, and on the nature of the state and its impact on inter-state relations between India and Pakistan, this silence is all the more remarkable.[5]

Against the backdrop of the wider socio-economic and political ramifications of partition, this essay seeks to document some of the violence that accompanied partition in the Punjab in August 1947. The first section will examine in detail the massacres which occurred on trains. It will discuss the planning involved and the methods employed in these killings.[6] The second will consider the role played by the large numbers of demobilised soldiers in determining the nature of the violence. It will examine the relationship between the involvement of these soldiers and the scale, magnitude and brutality of the violence.

Before proceeding to discuss the violence during partition in any detail, it is important to set it in its context. Not only was it qualitatively different from that in any other province, it was also substantially different from the previous rioting in the Punjab in the 1920s and 1930s. While those riots had revolved around religious issues – cow *qurbani*, the playing of music before mosques, the performance of *arti* or *namaz*, proselytisation and the defilement of religious symbols and institutions – the partition violence occurred in the context of the transfer of power. While not underestimating the importance of cultural and socio-economic factors in Punjab in this period, the violence at this time had a definite political orientation and was closely connected with the question of independence and partition.

At the beginning of 1947 the issue which had a direct bearing on the future of Punjab, namely the Pakistan question and the possibility of the partition of Punjab, still hung in the balance. The Muslim League despite winning the election in March 1946 had been unable to form the government. The announcement on 20 February by the British that the transfer of power would take place by June 1948 heightened the urgency of the need to gain political ground. Frustrated, the League felt compelled to seek other means by which to express its grievances. The League thus resorted to violence as the desperate response in what it perceived to be a situation lacking in alternatives. These developments were followed by major riots in March 1947.

It was only as late as 3 June 1947 that partition became a certainty and even then the precise boundaries in Punjab were left to the Boundary Commission which did not announce its decision until after the transfer of power had taken place. In all of this the Punjab bore the brunt of the disruption of partition although it was, paradoxically, among the last to subscribe to the idea of Pakistan. The political build up of the last decade and more importantly of the last year and its attendant instability and uncertainty made the situation very volatile, and provided the reasons for the outbreak of the violence.

The riots in March may be described as the first phase of violence in that year. It lasted about three weeks at its peak intensity. Its spread was largely confined to West Punjab and it was characterised by large scale arson and destruction of property with comparatively smaller loss of life. The rural areas were affected for the first time. The second phase between April and July was a period of uneasy calm characterised by sporadic outbursts of rioting. This phase saw organised raiding and stabbing in both cities and villages but was carried out on a 'cloak and dagger' basis with no mass uprisings. There was almost no urban rioting although the rural areas were tense.[7]

After the plan outlining the transfer of power and partition was announced on 3 June 1947 and as the date for independence drew nearer, the situation in Punjab steadily and rapidly deteriorated. Every fresh outburst of trouble saw a hitherto undisturbed area going up in flames, so that when the August massacres happened not a single district, city or village in the province was unaffected. As an illustration of the intensity of the violence, the methods of attack, the targets and the composition of the attackers this discussion will consider the relatively novel and most notorious feature of the partition violence: the killing of refugees travelling by train.[8]

The timing of the violence – which peaked around 13 to 19 August – coincided with two major events: the advent of independence and the announcement of the Boundary Award on 16 August. While independence was ushered in with great ceremony in the rest of the country, Punjab was ablaze. The dissatisfaction with the Boundary Award found expression in the mass murders that took place not only around these dates but continued for some weeks to come. The Sikhs, who not only stood to lose their lands, livelihoods and shrines but faced the risk of their community being split by partition, had been threatening reprisals if the award was not to their liking. It was no coincidence, therefore, that Sikh violence escalated after the announcement of the Boundary Award. When the violence began it started in the central districts of Punjab: Lahore, Amritsar, Ferozepur, Ludhiana, Sheikhupura, Gurdaspur, Sialkot, Montgomery, Lyallpur, Gujranwala, and the Jullundur Doab, where the Sikhs were spread out.[9] This is not to apportion blame, or to suggest that the sole responsibility for the violence rests principally either with the Sikhs or any one particular community. All sides were equally guilty of the atrocities, and no real purpose is served by covering the familiar ground of much of the existing polemical literature.

In the context of the violence which occurred this discussion employs the overarching categories of Hindus, Muslims and Sikhs seemingly unproblematically. It has been possible to do so not because intra-community divisions did not exist, but because in moments of violence during the course of the partition massacres each community perceived itself and was perceived by others as being homogenous.

II

Although the first of the numerous train incidents, which became so infamous, occurred at the end of July,[10] the first actual sabotage of a train occurred on 9 August. Until then the only incidents involving trains had been stoppages and attempted derailments (so far unsuccessful). On 9 August a Pakistan Special train, carrying Pakistani government employees and their families from Delhi to Karachi, was derailed about a quarter of a mile outside the state of Patiala, about fifteen miles west of Bhatinda in East Punjab. Six carriages were derailed, casualties were about ten people injured, and one woman and her baby were killed in the crash, but no attack was made. The tracks ran over a mine. The mine exploded and blew up eleven feet of track. Gun cotton had been placed under the rails and connected by three hundred feet of cable to a battery detonator.[11] The material recovered from the spot was three pounds of gelignite, massed together, a cigarette tin with sand in it, a length of cable wire, a large high tension battery, two metal hooks with stick holds and cables attached, and seventeen empty .450 revolver cartridge cases.[12]

Just a few days previously, on 5 August 1947, G.R. Savage of the Punjab CID Control had reported the arrest of a man named Kuldip Singh, 'who was a bomb maker and incendiarist and had done a lot of successful work. He was probably involved in six bomb-throwing cases and *had specialised in train wrecking*' [emphasis added]. This man stated that the Sikhs were planning to blow up a Pakistan Special with remote control firing apparatus. The remarkable similarity of the description with the actual incident is striking.[13] If further confirmation was necessary, this was provided two days later by Major General D.C. Hawthorn, who received a report from General Rees, the Commander of the Punjab Boundary Force, attributing the derailment to the Sikhs, as the Jeep containing the saboteurs was chased by the Force and disappeared into Faridkot State territory.[14] The meticulous planning that had so obviously gone into the derailment incident will be discussed further below.

In Lahore city retaliation from the Muslims was swift. In addition to derailments, attacks and stabbing of passengers in trains began. Between 12 and 18 August – the dates around independence and the announcement of the Boundary Award – Lahore railway station became a veritable death trap as the non-Muslim population, driven by riots in the city, accumulated at the station in an attempt to leave. By 13 August it became impossible for passengers to reach the station because they were attacked *en route*.[15] Trains on their way to Lahore were attacked by Muslims, spreading panic among the passengers waiting to leave.[16] On 14 August thirty-five Sikhs were stabbed at Lahore railway station.[17] On 14 and 15 August the railway station became a scene of wholesale carnage and according to one witness there was a continuous rain of bullets there. By 15 August the NWR (North West Railway) had stopped running trains except mails, expresses and military mails. No goods trains were running as the crews did not report for duty.[18]

Trouble soon spread; radiating outwards from Lahore and Amritsar to the neighbouring districts. On 13 August, forty-three non-Muslims were stabbed in the Mughalpura Railway Workshops.[19] On the night of independence – 15/16 August – the pilot engine of a Pakistan Special train was derailed six miles north-west of Amritsar.[20] Sialkot district witnessed two derailments between 14 and 17 August.[21] Three trains were held up in the Wazirabad-Sialkot area by Muslim mobs.[22] On 15 August a train was held up near Wazirabad and the casualties were estimated at one hundred killed and two hundred wounded by stabbing.[23] The Rawalpindi area witnessed two attacks on trains as a reprisal for the Sikh activities in the Lahore and Amritsar area.[24] By 15 August the rail service in the Punjab was seriously disturbed following the killings in Lahore station.

Trains running between Lahore and Lyallpur were attacked from 21 August onwards, particularly at Sheikhupura railway station, where large scale stabbing took place.[25] Between Ferozepur and Bhatinda, Sikhs methodically held up and attacked a passenger train on 21 August, looting its passengers and then butchering those who refused to leave the train.[26] By 22 August – the end of 'independence week' – General Rees called for the restricted running of trains, and warned GHQ Delhi that the Boundary Force could not accept any Pakistan Specials without secret and adequate warning (a minimum of twenty-four hours notice).[27] On 24 August two trains, the Frontier Mail and the Karachi Mail, were attacked in Lahore city, and one hundred and fifty non-Muslims were reported slain on the Karachi Mail.[28] On that day rail travel was officially declared unsafe throughout east and west Punjab.[29] Services were disrupted and remained infrequent until the Refugee Specials were arranged in September. Even then conditions of travel did not improve as we shall see below.

Soon the trouble spread from the cities to the rural areas.[30] Villages started emptying out, and people headed towards railway stations, often camping there, while awaiting the next train they could board. Nearly every east bound train passing through the districts of Montgomery and Lahore was stopped at some stage of its journey.[31]

Unavoidable in any journey, as both the entry point for one set of refugees and the exit point for another, stations formed particularly vulnerable and easy targets. As the refugee traffic on the stations swelled the conditions on the stations worsened. The condition of Amritsar railway station, for example was, in the middle of September, as a British army officer touring Punjab put it, 'indescribable'. 'Hindu and Sikh evacuees are everywhere, and the front porch and the whole station stinks of human excreta and urine. Masses of flies are carrying infection from the filth all round to the food the evacuees are eating, as they sit in this scene of "Disgrace Abounding".'[32] This could be taken as representative of the conditions on railway stations in general all over Punjab during these weeks.

West Punjab districts were not the only scene of carnage. Across the border in East Punjab conditions were just as bad if not worse. Revenge and retaliation were the key sentiments expressed by all communities as each side swore to get 'an eye for an eye'. A British railway officer, travelling over the Narnaul (a railside town in Patiala State) and Mahendargarh area by night train on 10 September, described with horror the stoppage of trains and the slaughter of Muslims between stations all through the Sikh-dominated area. He saw a succession of bodies of about fifteen Muslims being thrown from a first class carriage adjacent to his own. This included infants and women.[33] Another account by a British army officer described a west-bound Muslim refugee train in Amritsar on 12 September, which by the time it arrived there had already been derailed twice, first about four miles west of Kapurthala, and again just before reaching Jullundur. The evacuees were harassed at every stage by being searched by the police and the military. They were refused food and water and medical supplies. 'There were dead and dying in every rail truck, and their beddings were covered by bile and excreta. The smell was almost unbearable.'[34] Police reports stated that the train had arrived in Jullundur with one hundred and forty-five dead, of whom one hundred had been killed, and the rest had died of thirst or starvation. There was no respite for the passengers further down their journey. When the train arrived in Amritsar a further one hundred and twenty were killed. A British army officer reported that except for the timely intervention of the Royal Garhwal Rifles (Gurkhas) the passengers on this train would have been wiped out by the Sikhs.[35]

While in August the attacks took place on trains that were on regular schedules, by September the Refugee Specials organised by the governments of East and West Punjab had become operative. Paradoxically this facilitated the killings as it meant that the attacks could then be specifically directed at such trains. These trains generally carried members of one community only, who were headed in the opposite direction and provided ideal targets. The wholesale slaughter which occurred on trains now became more frequent on these Refugee Specials.

A British officer travelling with a Dogra Company (Hindus) on a Military Special from Razmak in West Punjab to Lucknow in UP gave a graphic account of the typical conditions of travel prevailing all along the route on trains and stations on both sides of the border. His account also serves to illustrate the tactics and methods employed in the derailments and in the attacks on trains at this time.

> On 11th September [he wrote] we mounted a guard over 650 Hindu refugees who were brought to Mari-Indus for onward despatch to Mianwali where a refugee camp had been established. While at Mari-Indus the non-Muslim shopkeepers in the camp repeatedly requested us to smuggle them away in our train as they considered themselves unsafe in present conditions. This sense of fear was further increased by the arrival in Mari-Indus of the Guides Cavalry (a Pakistani unit) on their way to Dera Ismail Khan, who openly declared that they would one day "cut them up for meat".
> On 13th September we entrained for Rawalpindi...We arrived in Rawalpindi on 14th September...
> On 20th September we left Rawalpindi on a military special for Delhi...
> The train was detained overnight at Lahore (20th/21st September). The railway station was a mass of human beings, presumably Muslim refugees awaiting onward despatch.

On 21st September the train did not leave Lahore as was intended because a report had been received that a Muslim mob had gathered at Harbanspura and was waiting to attack any train passing that way from Lahore.

From a conversation with a Muslim V.C.O. at Lahore station, it appeared that it was the confirmed opinion of all Muslims that the Sikhs were wholly and solely responsible for the trouble in the Punjab. He declared that not a single Sikh was left in Lahore and it was the intention that not a single Sikh would ever enter Lahore again...This V.C.O. described in some detail the horrible outrages performed by Sikhs against Muslim women and children...

On 22nd September the train left Lahore at 11.30 am. At Harbanspura we saw the results of the previous night's attack on a refugee train – dead bodies were lying on the railway track. Locals at Attari informed us that about 1,500 non-Muslims had been killed in the attack on the train and that the Muslims had been working all night to remove the bodies so as to show no trace of the attack. When we passed the place about 30-40 bodies were lying on the track and they were being removed under military supervision. The smell in the area was dreadful. At Attari, the first railway station on the Indian border, the train was given a rousing welcome by the local Sikhs. Food and water were distributed freely amongst all, including the troops. We were looked upon as martyrs who had been imprisoned by the Pakistan Government and had only just been set free. The main topic of conversation was the previous night's attack on the refugee train at Harbanspura. The population were infuriated and declared that not a single Muslim refugee train would enter Pakistan – everyone would be attacked and the occupants killed.

At Khasa railway station (about 10 miles from Amritsar) the train was again detained owing to the line ahead having been tampered with. The locals openly admitted that they had tampered with the line and that their intention was to stop the up Muslim refugee train and slay every individual in it by way of revenge against the Harbanspura incident. Troops report that at about 5.30 am on 23rd September a body of Sikhs passed the station on their way home with their spears smeared in blood. It was rumoured that every Muslim on that train was killed and that the attack was organised as a minor military operation, with covering fire from L[ight] M[achine] G[un]s and rifles for those who went in with knives and spears. All that remained in evidence of the attack when we passed through were empty boxes and torn clothing and patches of blood.

The train left Amritsar at 3 pm. The smell from the dead bodies on these stations was unbearable. The bodies were on some back platform and could not be seen...

At Jullundur I spoke to a respectable Sikh gentleman and he said that the Sikhs would now only let a refugee train go through to Pakistan unmolested provided one came from there unmolested. This he said equally applied to road and foot convoys.[36]

The savage brutality with which these attacks were made and the use of military tactics in carrying these out is clearly described in this account, which can be taken as typical of the conditions on the Refugee Specials. Since this was also an account of a train that travelled through the territories of both West and East Punjab, it reveals that the attitudes of the communities on both sides of the border were mirror images of each other, whether it concerned the grim declarations of revenge or of the refusal to grant provision of food and water.

The methodical and systematic manner in which these train attacks took place point to a high degree of planning and organisation. Sikhs on railway platforms would observe Muslims entraining, and enter the same carriages. After the train's departure, they would single out the Muslims and push them out of the carriages, or throw them out of the windows, at pre-decided spots, like railside telegraph poles that were marked with a white flag. There gangs of killers waited to complete the killing. Often the gangs conducting this operation had their couriers on trains who pulled the communication cord between stations, and the killer gangs then operated throughout the train.[37] As the above account reveals, the attacks were organised often with military precision, with one half of the gang providing covering fire while the others entered the train to kill.

However, the actual methods of attack employed on all trains were by and large crude. Stoppages were much more common than derailments or sabotages on any sophisticated level. Very often trains were stopped by laying a boulder or tree trunk across the railway line, or else the lines were tampered with by damaging fish plates. The drivers would stop the train and out of fear would frequently abandon the train, which would then be set upon, and its passengers dragged out and killed, and their luggage looted. A British police officer recalled one such instance while travelling by train through Amritsar district:

> All along the way from Amritsar for a distance of about ten to fifteen miles numerous groups of Sikhs with spears and swords and knives could be seen converging on a small railway station where a refugee-filled train was standing with no engine. It appears that the engine driver, having come to hear of the impending attack, detached his engine from the train and started for Amritsar. We actually did pass a lone engine on the up line making for Amritsar.[38]

Trains would usually be attacked when passing through the countryside, which provided ideal cover for the mobs stopping the trains, as they could lie in wait in the nearby fields of standing crops of sugarcane or maize, and vanish with equal ease once the looting and killing were completed.[39] For the same reasons attacks were generally carried out at night or in the early hours of the morning.[40] Again, the train attacks were carried out where there was inadequate protection. One report described an attack on a train with sixty guards who were effectively useless.[41] In another situation a mob making a determined attack on a train near Amritsar was held off by a military picket. But the picket soon ran out of ammunition and had to withdraw. By the time reinforcements arrived on the scene, the mob had overpowered the escorts, shot two of them and injured five others, and had succeeded in attacking the passengers in the train and killing several of them.[42] Auchinleck, the Supreme Commander for the Joint Defence Council, reported that seventy per cent of the attacks were conducted in areas outside the jurisdiction of the Punjab Boundary Force.[43]

It very soon became evident that the effectiveness of guards depended more on their composition than their numbers. Refugee trains that were sent from either side under the control of mixed armed guards were seldom attacked. But the trains, both the ordinary as well as the Specials, sent by the East Punjab government either without arrangement with Movement Control or with guards drawn from a single community were attacked. Where the guards were not mixed the chances of them being communal and therefore unreliable were very high. The East Punjab government soon decided not to send refugee trains without the knowledge of Movement Control and without intimation to the West Punjab government.[44]

Not surprisingly then, Military Specials were the only trains that were relatively safe from attacks as these trains transported military personnel who were ordinarily well armed and able to defend themselves with ease. A trainload of such passengers would, for obvious reasons, not be easy prey. However, since civilians could not travel on these trains Military Specials were of little use to them.

The systematic organisation and the high degree of planning that was involved in the sabotage and stoppage of trains suggests at least some degree of complicity by officials, among the staff of the civil administration generally, and the railway staff in particular. The gangs attacking trains often had sufficient if not detailed information about train schedules and time-tables both of the regular trains and of the Refugee Specials. Intelligence reports regarding the derailment of the Pakistan Special on 9 August clearly stated that Tara Singh, the leader of the Akalis, was in possession of information regarding train time-tables and planned to keep himself updated by means of a wireless.[45]

The potentially hazardous journey for those travelling by the Refugee Specials was made even worse by the intolerable overcrowding in these trains. Most trains carried on average three thousand to four thousand passengers.[46] A successful massacre on one such train carrying two thousand to two thousand five hundred passengers, left one thousand people killed and the rest (except for about one hundred) injured.[47] One British officer who had been captured by the Japanese and had worked on the Siam Railway during the war remarked, 'I thought the Japs knew how to pack a train of P.O.W.s to the limit, but this beats them hollow'.[48] The discomfort of travelling in such conditions was exacerbated by the fact that there was little or no food or water available to those on the refugee trains, so that those who escaped being killed or injured often died of hunger or thirst and this included women and children. Of the twenty-one who died in a derailment on 14 September in Amritsar, one account stated, only two had died as the result of the derailment; the rest mostly old men, women and children had died of sun-stroke, starvation, thirst and dehydration.[49] This shortage was not always due to short supply of water in the stations. Often water was deliberately denied to passengers. The civil authorities were no more co-operative, and in many stations did nothing in the way of organising medical aid, food or water.

Passengers, it appears, were not the only target. Goods trains headed in the opposite direction were equally subject to destruction. One train headed for Pakistan bearing Pakistani government goods and records from Delhi was looted in Rewari. In trains for several destinations the Pakistani wagons had been clearly marked out and wherever they were side-tracked only those wagons were looted and no others.[50]

The particularly heavy monsoon in 1947 added to the general disruption in travel conditions. Although late that year, it resulted in serious floods, which caused considerable damage, destroying railway bridges and tracks across rural areas, thus assisting the task of those intent on killing.

From early in August to late in September trains were attacked nearly every, or every other, day. Towards the end of September attacks began to decline and gradually petered out by the middle of October. It may be confidently asserted that very few trains in the interim, whether Refugee Specials or regular trains, made a complete journey without being subject to an attack (whether successful or not) at least once (and on many occasions more than once) along the route. A British army officer touring Punjab at this time captured the ordeal of train travel for the hapless refugees when he wrote:

> Some of the events such as murder, brutality, looting, ill-treatment of women and small children in evacuee trains, the results of vicious hatred and communal fury, have outdone even Belsen and other bestialities created by the warped Nazi mind.'
> 'I do not think I have ever witnessed such cold-bloodedness by any human beings as I witnessed last night...[with reference to a specific refugee train killing]...In every carriage without exception the dead and dying were mixed up with the wounded – it was certainly a train of death...'[51]

However by the third week of October, the situation had stabilised and the authorities were able to report movement of refugees by train without incident. On some routes foot columns of refugees and trains even managed to pass alongside each other peacefully.[52] For the marauding gangs out to kill, the 'trains of death' had served their purpose. For the refugees who attempted to journey to safety and security, the price could not have been higher.

III

The exceedingly brutal and gruesome nature of the violence during this period is clear from any account of the partition. But in Punjab the highly militarised nature of the society gave the character of the violence a distinctiveness that was both extraordinary and unparalleled anywhere else in India.[53] The violence at this time was not so much a matter of 'crowds' or 'collective action', as it was about campaigns conducted in a military style. While not denying the importance of studies of crowd violence, it may be pointed out that in the partition massacres crowds formed as much the victims as the aggressors. Much of the violence was directed against the crowds fleeing towards safety and security, by small and well organised bands. Notwithstanding the moral, social, economic, and cultural explanations for the pattern of violence, it was this military quality that is central to an understanding of the violence accompanying partition in Punjab.

The pivotal role of the Punjab as the cornerstone of the *raj*'s military establishment has by now been well established.[54] At the beginning of the second world war the Punjab contributed roughly forty-eight per cent of men to the army.[55] In sheer numbers the province supplied a hefty 715,184 men to the army, with new recruits numbering 633,228, and the Princely States providing another 90,000.[56] Of Punjabi men who were fit to serve in the army and were of recruitable age (between the ages of seventeen and thirty years), approximately one man in three served in the army in the second world war.[57] Rawalpindi District alone – the leading recruiting area in the province – could boast of one man in every two as having served in the war, and 1420 persons were recorded as having sent three or more sons to the army.[58] These figures show that in terms of manpower, the proportion of Punjabi men in the army far exceeded that of other provinces.

Furthermore, the socialisation of the majority of Punjabi males involved what might be described as 'a quasi-military initiation ceremony', which incorporated (and even exalted) the values that the army instilled into men. This helps to explain the extraordinary group solidarity and willingness to die for a cause which was prevalent amongst them. While this was generally true of all soldiers this was particularly noticeable among the Sikh *jathas* who presented a striking example of this kind of solidarity and acquired a reputation among the others who were themselves soldiers.

Soldiers recently back from the war-front were a conspicuous presence in the violence. Their participation meant that the violence took on for a time the characteristics of civil war. Ordinary crowd violence usually involves actual physical confrontation, and generally crude weapons, if any. Professional techniques such as ambush and modern sophisticated weapons that the ex-soldiers used made for quite a different kind of impact, carrying the violence to an altogether new and different plane. Military campaigns are designed to be sustained over long periods of time and the stamina of soldiers, able to endure long periods of fighting under adverse circumstances, is well known. It was the professional training of such soldiers that gave to the violence its distinctive stamp and its especially brutal edge over ordinary street fighting by crowds not trained as professional fighters.

The Sikh *jathas* were especially notable in this respect. Reputed to be particularly efficient and thorough,[59] military training was clearly visible in their functioning. The preparation, training and organisation of these *jathas* (as much as the other private armies such as the National Guards and the RSS) in the preceding months was now put to very efficient use in the first three weeks of August as the Sikh *jathas* led the Punjab Boundary Force on a merciless chase through the villages of central Punjab.[60] The military aspect of the Sikh religion has been the subject of much research.[61] Nowhere did this appear more in evidence than in Punjab. The unique nature of the Sikh religion combined with military training to make the *jathas* a dreaded force to contend with. Even in peacetime it was not uncommon to see *jathas* marching in military formation from one *gurudwara* to another singing militant songs. In their religious garb and all of them carrying *kirpans*, the sight of these religious processions was comparable to soldiers marching into battle. In August 1947, the *jathas* seemed to be playing out the Sikh prayer, 'First of all I worship thee, O sword'.

Every gang that was formed usually had a 'nucleus' of trained members [frequently ex-servicemen], 'armed and skilled in the use of modern lethal weapons'.[62] The *jathas* would often assemble outside a village *gurudwara* and would be briefed by their leaders before setting out on their mission.[63] They could be formed at very short notice and were well 'organised into units and sub-units'.[64] Their size depended on their mission. They could range from twenty or thirty to formations as large as a few thousand people.[65] The *jathas* were given shelter by the villagers in the area of their operation. If the mission was an attack on trains, neighbouring villages or refugee convoys on foot, local villagers would join in and 'then disperse to their homes'.[66] Large *shahidi jathas* (suicide squads) attacked isolated Muslim villages and pockets throughout the areas of Amritsar, Tarn Taran Tehsil and Majitha. In Amritsar and its vicinity well organised armed Sikh bands of considerable strength carried out raids on Muslim majority villages at the rate of three or four each night.[67] The *jathas* would first throw bombs or use fire-arms on one side of the village to drive the people onto another party waiting on the other side of the village armed with spears and swords. All the inhabitants would be massacred. The dead bodies were then collected and heaped in piles of fifty to one hundred and were either set on fire, or buried, so as to obliterate any trace of evidence.[68] Once the butchery was over, the *jathas* would loot the village and set it on fire. The *jathas* and their targets were carefully controlled by a central organisation reputedly run by Sikh personnel of the INA, Mohan Singh and Naranjan Singh Gill, who were strongly suspected of employing military tactics for organising the killings. A regular War Room with maps and targets marked off for *jathas* to deal with was available. In order to use their arms and ammunition most effectively activities were restricted to one or two districts at a time until all the East Punjab districts were hit, and Muslims either killed or driven into refugee camps.[69]

> There were... leaders, H.Q.s (which shifted); and systems of messengers travelling on foot, or on horseback, or by M.T. [military transport].[70]

Communication systems had been set up 'with a certain amount of signalling equipment'.[71] 'The method of attack most used was the ambush';[72] and this was especially evident in the train hold-ups as noted above where even the general tactics used reveal the mark of military training.[73]

The confidence as well as the familiarity with the handling of aircraft that military training had provided, led some groups to organise their own defence arrangements. 'The Muslim Ahmadiya sect's headquarters at Qadian, east of Amritsar, had organised a local volunteer defence force of its own, with a system of signalling, and also two light aircraft whose pilot was reported to be an ex-officer of the INA'.[74] In addition, 'two light aircraft, formerly of a local flying club', were pressed into service.[75] These aircraft served the dual purpose of reconnaissance and refugee transport.[76] In addition the armed bands that conducted nightly raids on villages often included mounted men who were used as scouts to reconnoitre for a favourable opportunity.[77]

The dominance of the Punjabis in all sections of the army and especially artillery made access to arms and ammunition easy.[78] Military intelligence reported as early as mid-1942 that armed desertions were frequent.[79] For example, of the total of fifteen men who deserted in January 1943, twelve took riles, pistols or bayonets.[80] Proportionately this amounts to seventy-five per cent of those deserting doing so with arms. By January 1944 an alarming amount of arms and ammunition was finding its way into Punjab's villages. The process was assisted by the fact that until 1945 there were no search regulations for troops returning home on leave. In the last years of the War thefts of grenades and ammunition had increased sharply.[81] Many of these weapons were being sold in the bazaars by hawkers. Reports mention the case of a Pathan 'charwallah' approaching a British soldier with a view to buying a pistol and ammunition. The army believed that there was money to made in such traffic, especially as the value of arms in tribal areas such as the NWFP was high.[82]

The aftermath of the riots in March 1947 had produced a spurt of applications for arms licences.[83] By August these arms were very much in evidence. In the villages of Punjab 'the country-made weapons, often forged from farm tools ... hatchets, battle axes of all shapes and sizes, and spears', knives, and *lathis*, were supplemented with modern weapons, including German, Italian and Japanese arms.[84] Military expertise had assisted in making some of these weapons and this in turn increased their effectiveness and the likelihood of casualties. A retired police officer recalled conducting raids on illegal arms production centres (producing largely crude weapons) in and around Rawalpindi district.[85] Country-made firearms and home-made mortars were used to attack the Punjab Boundary Force.[86] The attacking gangs in Punjab were often armed with 'efficient hand grenades', '.303 rifles', 'shotguns', 'twelve bore guns', 'revolvers', as well as the 'most modern tommy gun and light machine-gun'.[87] In villages with a predominantly soldier population, attackers used sophisticated war weapons. A British officer describing the appearance of a refugee train after it had been attacked wrote that it was riddled with bullets, which appeared to be mostly Sten gun and rifle bullet holes, and the all shutters and windows had been smashed.[88] While the country-made implements contributed to the savage nature of the killings, the modern weapons made the killings efficient and quick. Both kinds had their uses depending upon the situation the killers found themselves in.

The presence of ex-INA men, employed 'both as leaders and among the rank and file', added yet another military dimension.[89] Field Marshall Auchinleck reported the involvement of ex-INA personnel in the violence.[90] The Home Secretary of the Punjab, A. A. Williams, recalled that there 'were cases of known Indian Army officers on leave organising mass attacks (when) the entire village could take part in the wholesale slaughter of those of the opposite religion'.[91]

However, partiality among the rank and file was more common than among officers. After the movement of refugees began, Sikh military personnel, who were permitted to visit their relatives in Lyallpur district and the Colonies areas and help them to evacuate, were alleged to have become a menace to the local Muslim population.[92] In the Montgomery district the Dogras, under a Sikh Major, were reported to have shot dead two Muslims, one of whom was a Municipal Commissioner. The Chief Secretary of the Punjab noted partiality among the Sikh, Mahratta, and Dogra troops in the Montgomery, Multan, and Lahore districts.[93]

In the post-war climate of unemployment and food and cloth rationing, many ex-soldiers retained their uniforms and continued to wear them. Many of the members of the gangs were thus dressed in uniform – either their own old ones or those brought back by ex-servicemen.[94] This gave the attackers a military appearance. There were even instances of attackers posing as soldiers or military men to gain greater legitimacy. In early August, such 'bogus military created terror amongst the Muslims in Amritsar district'.[95] Bristow, a senior British officer, reported seeing large groups of Sikhs in uniform on the streets of Jullundur city. He recognised one Sikh who had served with him on active service as a *havildar*, brandishing a *kirpan* on the streets, who admitted to him that he was 'hunting Muslims'.[96]

Military training was discernible in the skilful sabotage of trains and canal headworks that took place at this time. The manner in which this was executed and the material recovered from the spot not only pointed to a high degree of planning and organisation but also access to military equipment and stores. The derailment of the Pakistan Special on 9 August (discussed above) suggested that the leading culprits were men who had either served in the army (possibly in the engineering unit) or had been trained in guerrilla warfare. The report of the Addl. Deputy Commissioner, Ferozepur, suggested that the derailment was conducted by ex-army men but also very possibly by men still serving in the army. He based his conclusions on the fact that the materials used such as gelignite (which was supplied exclusively to military stores), new cable wires, a new battery, a telephone, .450 revolver rounds and a khaki coloured jeep were found at the spot.[97]

It is no wonder then that the Punjab Boundary Force found itself facing a formidable task. Quite apart from the other difficulties involved, it faced 'accurate sniping, bombing, and rifle and automatic fire'.[98] One of General Tuker's staff officers observed that in the early days of the Force's life, the Sikh *jathas* did not question the Force's authority or resent the army doing its job. His anxiety that this situation might change, and *jathas* would start retaliating by ambushing and attacking isolated trucks, and thereby force the army to use larger numbers of personnel in the escort of small parties, was not misplaced as such confrontations did occur.[99] However, street gangs would ordinarily be expected to hesitate before challenging the troops. Such a challenge would have had to come from either army or ex-army men as indeed they did, especially in the cities of Lahore and Amritsar, where the Force encountered tough street fighting from both individuals and gangs.[100] In Sheikhupura district, a two thousand strong Sikh *jatha* using hand grenades clashed with the troops.[101] In the districts of Amritsar, Hoshiarpur, Jullundur, and Ludhiana the *jathas* were aggressive in action against the Force and in one instance even ambushed troops of an MT patrol, inflicting casualties.[102] Auchinleck reported *jathas* resisting troops and fighting back. The troops captured mortars, tommy guns and rifles, and the Sikh bands were armed with light machine guns.[103] Experienced in war, these were men who were not easily overawed. The Boundary Force was challenged and resisted by ex-army men or those who had at the very least undergone similar training. This was what made it especially difficult for the army to impose its control on the situation as effectively as it could otherwise have done. A militarised society had turned in on itself. The price paid by Punjabi society for the long-standing British policy of making it the main recruiting ground of the army was high indeed.

IV

This essay has focused on the nature of partition violence in the Punjab. However, in the disruption and upheaval of partition it was not only society that was splintered. The state machine was being divided too. While speaking of the 'state' in August/ September it is important to stress that there were in fact three different states. The outgoing British state was handing power over to the two successor states – India and Pakistan. In considering the breakdown of order during this period, it is therefore necessary to keep in mind the context in which such a breakdown was occurring. The transfer of power and the division of resources and the general disarray that ensued with the dismantling of the existing colonial state was followed by the efforts of the two new states to build up viable alternatives. An analysis of the nature of partition violence in the crucial province of Punjab can therefore also help us to understand the transitional period during which the colonial state's resources were being divided between the two successor states.

It has been argued that the events of partition led to the collapse of the state in Punjab.[104] It is true that the violence in the Punjab in particular constituted a major challenge to the viability of the two new states. However, the responses of the successor states to this violence reveals the resilience of the structures inherited by them from the departing colonial state, and shows how both these structures and the resources upon which they depended were inherited and modified. In fact, a closer examination reveals that at no time was there a complete collapse of either the colonial state or the successor states, during this period.

The state at this time was officiating over a society convulsed by cataclysmic events. To restore the morale of a people shocked and traumatised by the recent upheavals, while at the same time bolstering the existing state apparatuses and structures of authority to make them more responsive as well as resilient to the demands of society at such a time, was an awesome task. As is clear from the above account, the military-style violence conducted by the demobilised soldiers amounted to an extremely serious and quite unusual challenge to the authority and legitimacy of the two nascent successor states at the very moment that they were coming into existence. Moreover, in a period of transition where two new states were in-the-making, these very soldiers would ordinarily have formed part of the pool of manpower from which the new states would seek to recruit their strength.[105] This added to the problems of the new states in their attempts to regain legitimacy and authority, as it placed the soldiers in a twilight zone between the legitimate arm of the state and the renegades. As ex-soldiers of the outgoing colonial state these men had participated in the violence and soon after in the changed situation they could well form the manpower of the newly formed states.

The magnitude of the task of evacuation and rehabilitation coupled with the unexpectedness of it and the consequent lack of preparation on the part of the state made matters even more difficult. The new province of East Punjab was as yet barely a week old when it faced the first slide in of the avalanche. It had scarcely come to terms with the fact of partition, seen by many Punjabis as an amputation, when it was engulfed by the rush of refugees. The environment of hostility, suspicion, insecurity and violence in which all of this took place opened up an abyss.

However, once the border had been defined and the two new governments had been installed, it became possible more quickly than might have seemed feasible whilst the massacres were at their worst, to impose order on to the situation. On both sides of the new border India and Pakistan soon moved into action to secure control. In the short space of three and a half months after August 1947, nearly five to six million people were moved under the auspices of the two new states.[106] The evacuation process was facilitated by the fact that the similarity of the foundations of the two new states enabled them to set up structures that mirrored each other. Resettlement was never easy, but it was nonetheless not unsuccessfully effected. That the two new states were successful in this endeavour says quite as much about the resilience of the structures of the colonial state as it does about the capabilities of the new states themselves. The violence and its ramifications highlight the shifting contours of the outgoing colonial state and those of the two emerging successor states, which were being built on the foundations of the outgoing colonial state's resources.[107] The response of the successor states to this violence is useful in charting their recapturing of authority and legitimacy as viable entities. The task of restoring order, arranging for the evacuation and migration of those on the move, and organising resettlement successfully, serves to emphasise that the state, although traumatised and temporarily weakened, did not collapse.[108]

Notes

1   See P. Moon, *Divide and Quit* (London, 1961), pp.269, 293.

2   See G.D. Khosla, *Stern Reckoning, A Survey of the Events Leading up to and Following The Partition Of India* (London, 1950 and reprinted New Delhi, 1989), pp.298-9.

3   *After Partition*, Ministry of Information and Broadcasting (Delhi, 1948), p.50. If Bengal and Punjab were taken together, then an estimated 12.5 million people (i.e. about 3 per cent of undivided India's population) were uprooted as a result of partition. See also Penderel Moon, *Divide and Quit*, pp.269, 293, and 'Migration and Population in W. Punjab' in *Sikhs in Action: Showing the Sikh Plan in actual operation,* pamphlet issued by the Government of Pakistan (Lahore, 1948), London, India Office Library (hereafter IOL), Mudie Collection, Mss Eur., F164/47.

4   In Punjab in 1941, the Muslims comprised some 58 per cent the Hindus 26 per cent and the Sikhs 13 per cent of the population. Government of India *Census of India, 1941,* 1, pp.98-100, quoted in R.A.Kapur, *Sikh Separatism; The Politics of Faith* (London, 1986), p.208. By 1951, 61 per cent of all Punjabis in Eastern Punjab were Hindus and 35 per cent were Sikh. Government of India *Census of India, 1951,* paper no. 1 1951, Religion and Livelihood Classes by Educational Standards of Reorganised State, pp.7-8, quoted in R.A.Kapur, *Sikh Separatism,* p.208.

5   Some exceptions to the general trend may be mentioned here. However, these too formed part of the general body of official sources. The Indian Government survey was represented by G. D. Khosla, *Stern Reckoning.* The Pakistani Government issued its version in five pamphlets entitled: *Note on the Sikh Plan: an account of the secret preparations of the Sikhs; The Sikhs in Action: Showing the Sikh Plan in actual operation; The Rashtriya Swayam Sevak Sangh: or the activities of the secret terrorist Hindu organisation in the Punjab; Tribal Repercussions or what led the tribal Pathans of the north-west frontier to come to the aid of the people of Kashmir; Kashmir Before Accession: showing why the people of Kashmir rebelled against the Maharaja's government, what he did to suppress them and why he acceded to India.* The only other studies include Kirpal Singh, *Partition of Punjab* (Patiala, 1972) and Satya Rai, *Partition of Punjab: A Study of Its Effects on the Politics and Administration of the Punjab (I) 1947-56* (London, 1965). However, Rai concentrates on the processes of partition rather than the violence itself. Ayesha Jalal has recently undertaken a study of the post-partition developments in Pakistan. See Jalal, *The State of Martial Rule: Pakistan's Political Economy of Defence* (Cambridge, 1990). More recently Talbot has examined crowd activity and its contribution to the emergence of Pakistan. See Ian Talbot, 'The Role of the Crowd in the Muslim League Struggle for Pakistan', *The Journal of Imperial and Commonwealth History,* Vol. XXI, no. 2 (1993), pp.307-33. Following upon e.g. Moon, *Divide and Quit* and Ian Stephens, *Pakistan: Old Country/New Nation* (Harmondsworth, 1964) the role of soldiers and ex-soldiers in Punjab massacres has been more lately discussed by I. Kamtekar, especially on pp.143-148 of his thesis cited in Fn.53 below.

     Fictional recreations provide dramatised accounts of the partition. Some of the best known works in this area are: Saadat Hasan Manto, *Kingdom's End and Other Short Stories* (Translated from Urdu by Khalid Hasan) (New Delhi, 1987). Among his best known short stories that focus directly upon the partition violence and its horrific impact are, 'Toba Tek Singh', 'Cold as Ice' and 'The Black Shalwar'. Other writers include Ismat Chugtai, *The Quilt and Other Short Stories,* Khushwant Singh, *Train to Pakistan* (New York, 1961), Bhisham Sahni, *Tamas* (New Delhi, 1988) (first published in 1974). For a discussion of partition from this perspective see Ian Talbot essay.

Moreover, there is nothing for the period comparable to the documentation of the riots in Delhi in 1984 following the assassination of Indira Gandhi. See Uma Chakravarti and Nandita Haksar, *The Delhi Riots; Three Days in the Life of a Nation* (New Delhi, 1987). Post independence riots too have been documented better. See Asghar Ali Engineer (ed.), *Communal Riots in Post-Independent India* (Hyderabad, 1984); Veena Das (ed.), *Mirrors of Violence: Communities, Riots and Survivors in South Asia* (New Delhi, 1990], (see her article) and V. Das (ed.), *The Word and the World: Fantasy, Symbol and Record* (New Delhi, 1986); M. J. Akbar, *Riot after Riot: Reports on Caste and Communal Violence in India* (New Delhi, 1988); A. Hussain, 'The Karachi riots of December 1986: crisis of state and civil society in Pakistan', in V. Das (ed.), *Mirrors of Violence*; and F. Shaheed, 'The Pathan-Muhajir Conflicts, 1985-6: A National Perspective', in V. Das (ed.), *Mirrors of Violence*. However even Veena Das, in one of the most recent and valuable collections on communal and ethnic violence, fails to include a discussion of the partition violence in the historical section. See Das, *Mirrors of Violence*.

[6]   The massacres were however not confined to trains. People driven out of their homes set forth towards their destinations on equally if not more perilous journeys on foot. The road convoys, and long foot columns, and the killings of the people in these columns, is another aspect of the partition massacres which has been discussed elsewhere. For an elaboration of this aspect of the violence see Swarna Aiyar, 'Violence and the State in the Partition of Punjab, 1947-48' (Ph.D. thesis, Univ. of Cambridge, 1994), pp.129-32.

[7]   The total number of casualties in 1947 up to 2 August 1947 were approximately 4632 killed, and 2573 seriously injured. Compiled from Memorandum from Jenkins to Mountbatten (4 Aug. 1947), IOL, L/P&J/8/663.

[8]   Considerations of space prevent a detailed discussion of the total spread and intensity of the violence, other characteristic features, the differences between the urban and rural areas, the wide ranging methods of attack or the various choices of targets. For a fuller discussion of these and other aspects of the violence, see S. Aiyar, 'Violence and the State', pp.104-16, 132-5.

[9]   The Doab comprised the districts of Jullundur and Hoshiarpur. It was about sixty miles long and wide. Hoshiarpur District covered the north and east of it, Jullundur District the centre and south, and the Sikh Princely State of Kapurthala the west. Population-wise however these districts did not show a pronounced bias in favour of any particular community. They merely indicate a territorial distribution. The western districts were predominantly Muslim and the eastern districts predominantly non-Muslim.

[10] On 22 July, Lahore Railway Station and Moghalpura Railway Station were attacked by Hindus and Sikhs. On 23 July, a workmen's train was held up by Muslims near Harbanspura and non-Muslims were murdered, while another train was held up near Gurdaspur. Jenkins to Mountbatten (30 July 1947), IOL, L/P&J/5/250.

[11] Report of D.W. McDonald, Addl. Deputy Commissioner, Ferozepore (10 Aug. 1947), on the 'Derailment of the Pakistan Special near Giddarbaha on the night of 9th August 1947', Appendix VI, Mudie Collection, IOL, Mss Eur., F164/47. See also Abell to Governor's Secretary, Sind (10 Aug. 1947), N. Mansergh and P. Moon (eds),*Constitutional Relations Between Britain and India: The Transfer of Power 1942-7* [henceforth *TP*], Vol. XII, *The Mountbatten Viceroyalty: Princes, Partition and Independence, 8 July-15 August 1947* (London, 1983), , p.648, and Report on

the Punjab Boundary Force [hereafter PBF], IOL, L/MIL/17/5/4319, pp.7-8.

12 Report of D.W. McDonald, Addl. Deputy Commissioner, Ferozepore (10 Aug. 1947), on the 'Derailment of the Pakistan Special near Giddarbaha on the night of 9th August 1947', Appendix VI, Mudie Collection IOL, Mss Eur., F164/47.

13 See the account of the Punjab CID by G R Savage, Police Collection, IOL, Mss Eur., F161/6. See also Viceroy's Interview no. 178 (5 Aug. 1947), IOL, Mountbatten Collection, Mss Eur., F200/193.

14 Note by General D.C. Hawthorn (11 Aug. 1947). The note summarised a report received by telephone from Rees, the Commander of the Punjab Boundary Force, on the same day, *TP* XII, p.667. The Punjab Boundary Force was set up to maintain law and order. It was in operation during the month of August, and covered an area of 12 of the 14 civil districts which were declared disturbed. For details see Report on the PBF, IOL, L/MIL/17/5/4319. See also R. Jeffrey, 'The Punjab Boundary Force and the Problem of Order, August 1947', *Modern Asian Studies* [hereafter *MAS*], 8, 4 (1974), p.497.

15 Khosla, *Stern Reckoning*, p.122.

16 An attack on the Sind Express killed 9 and injured about 30 non-Muslims. Jenkins to Mountbatten, 13 August 1947, IOL, Mountbatten Collection, Punjab, Situation in, Part II (b), Mss Eur., F200/127.

17 G.R. Stevens, *The History of the Fourth Indian Division,* 1948, p.408, See also Report on the PBF, IOL, L/MIL/17/5/4319, p.8.

18 'Note on Situation in the Punjab Boundary Force Area for Joint Defence Council on 16 August 1947', by Field Marshal Auchinleck (15 Aug. 1947), *TP* XII, pp.734-7.

19 Report on the PBF, IOL, L/MIL/17/5/4319, p.8.

20 *Ibid.,* p.11.

21 Khosla, *Stern Reckoning*, pp.143-44.

22 Report on the PBF, IOL, L/MIL/17/5/4319, p.8.

23 'Note on Situation in the Punjab Boundary Force Area for Joint Defence Council', by Field Marshal Auchinleck (15 Aug. 1947), *TP* XII, pp.734-7.

24 Jenkins to Mountbatten (14 Aug. 1947), *TP* XII, p.732.

25 Khosla, *Stern Reckoning*, p.128.

26 Report on the PBF, IOL, L/MIL/17/5/4319, p.13.

27 *Ibid.* pp.15, 23.

28 Report on the PBF, IOL, L/MIL/17/5/4319, p.16.

29 *The Times,* 25 Aug. 1947, where Harrington Hawes, Secretary to the Agent for the Punjab States, gives an account of the derailment of a refugee train. Cited in Jeffrey, 'The Punjab Boundary Force', p.504.

30 In the rural areas of far flung districts such as Multan and Lyallpur (if one were to take central districts like Lahore as the focal point) the disturbances were to begin later. In August these areas were merely subject to disrupted communications and the trains ran infrequently. It was only in September that the train killings spread to the rural areas of Multan and there were five attacks on trains in the district during this month.

31 Khosla, *Stern Reckoning*, pp.164-5.

32 Lieut.-General Sir Francis Tuker, *While Memory Serves* (London, 1950), p.482.

33 Described in letter by Gilbert Waddell, I.G. Railway Police, Ajmer and Rajasthan (27 Sept. 1947), Police Collection, IOL, Mss Eur., F161/3.

34 Report by a British army officer (14 Sept. 1947), Tuker, *While Memory Serves*, p.480.

35 *Ibid.,* p.480.

[36] Tuker, *While Memory Serves*, pp.485-88.
[37] From Gilbert Waddell, I.G. Railway Police, Ajmer and Rajasthan (27 Sept. 1947), IOL, Police Collection, Mss Eur., F161/3, Item 78.
[38] Tuker, *While Memory Serves*, pp.486-7.
[39] Khosla, *Stern Reckoning*, p.203, See also letter to Gandhi from unknown sender, Bulletin no. 1 from Mamdot Villa, Lahore (21 Sept. 1947), IOL, Punjab, Situation in, Part III (b), Mountbatten Collection, Mss Eur., F200/129.
[40] Sender and Receiver unknown. Bulletin no. 3, from Lahore (11 Sept. 1947), Punjab, Situation in, Part III (b), IOL, Mountbatten Collection, Mss Eur., F200/129.
[41] The train was brought to a halt by threatening the driver. The marauders poured in, creating panic among the refugees, who in turn poured out. In the ensuing confusion, the guards, usually in a compartment at the back of the train, were unable to do their work and the attackers completed their job successfully. Letter to Gandhi from unknown sender, Bulletin no. 1 from Mamdot Villa, Lahore (21 Sept. 1947), Punjab, Situation in, Part III (b), IOL, Mountbatten Collection, Mss Eur., F200/129.
[42] Account of a Muslim Refugee train by a British Army officer (23 Sept. 1947), Amritsar, Tuker, *While Memory Serves*, p.483.
[43] Note prepared by Supreme Commander for the Joint Defence Council on the Future of the Punjab Boundary Force (29 Aug. 1947), Punjab, Situation in, Part III (a), IOL, Mountbatten Collection, Mss Eur., F200/128.
[44] Sender and receiver unknown but presumed to be an Indian official posted in Lahore, letter (11 Sept. 1947), Lahore, Punjab, Situation in, Part III (b), IOL, Mountbatten Collection, Mss Eur., F200/129.
[45] Record of an interview between Mountbatten, Jinnah, L. A. Khan, Patel and Captain Savage, Viceroy's Interview no. 178 (5 Aug. 1947), IOL, Mountbatten Collection, Mss Eur., F200/193; Jenkins to Abell (4 Aug. 1947), 'Punjab Security Arrangements for Partition', IOL, Mountbatten Collection, Mss Eur., F200/130; Mountbatten to Jenkins (6 Aug. 1947), IOL, Governor's Correspondence, Mountbatten Collection, Mss Eur., F200/185; and Mountbatten to Listowel, (8 Aug. 1947), IOL, Mountbatten Collection, Mss Eur., F200/176.
[46] Report of the Deputy Chief Liaison Officer (11 Sept. 1947), PSA, EPLA Records, LVII/22/8-B.
[47] Tuker, *While Memory Serves*, p.484.
[48] *Ibid.,* p.482.
[49] Report of the Deputy Chief Liaison Officer (11 Sept. 1947), PSA, EPLA Records, LVII/22/8-B.
[50] Letter (27 Sept. 1947), By G. Waddell, I.G. Railway Police, Ajmer and Rajasthan, IOL, Mss Eur., F161/3, Item 78.
[51] A British army officer in Notes (15 Sept. and 23 Sept. 1947), quoted in Tuker, *While Memory Serves*, pp.481, 484.
[52] Reports for the weeks ending 23 Oct. 1947, 30 Oct. 1947 and 7 Nov. 1947, IOL, Mountbatten Collection, Weekly Summaries, Mss Eur., F200/190.
[53] The militarised society has been remarked upon not only by students of the military history of the Punjab like T. Tai Yong and Clive Dewey, but the wider ramifications of the military in the polity and society of Punjab has been commented upon by others as well. Among earlier writings are the works of Penderel Moon, *Divide and Quit*, Ian Stephens, *Pakistan: Old Country/New Nation*, Alan Campbell-Johnson, *Mission with Mountbatten* to cite only a few. For more recent works see Imran Ali, *Punjab Under Imperialism 1885-1947* (Princeton, 1988), Prem Chowdhry, 'Social

Support Base and Electoral Politics: The Congress in Colonial Southeast Punjab',
in *MAS*, 25, 4 (1991), 811-31, I. Kamtekar, 'The End of the Colonial State in India,
1942-47' (Ph.D thesis, Univ. of Cambridge, 1989), and the writings of I. Talbot
cited earlier.

54 See for example Tan Tai Yong, 'The Military and the State in Colonial Punjab, 1900-
1939' (Ph.D thesis, Univ. of Cambridge, 1992); Clive Dewey, 'The Rural Roots of
Pakistani Militarism', in D. A. Low (ed.), *The Political Inheritance of Pakistan* (London,
1991) pp.255-83; Stephen P. Cohen, *The Indian Army:Its Contribution to the
Development of a Nation* (Berkeley, 1971); and S.P. Cohen, *The Pakistan Army*
(Berkeley, 1984) and Imran Ali, *Punjab Under Imperialism*, to name only a few.

55 Of these approximately 23 per cent were Muslims, 13 per cent Hindus and 12 per
cent Sikhs. 'Annual Return Showing the Class Composition of the Indian Army,
Indian State Forces, etc., on 1 January 1942', Class Composition of the Army in
India, IOL, L/WS/1/456. These figures were invariably estimates as different
calculations showed different figures and precise numbers were in any case
unavailable. See also 'Recruitment, Indian Army, 1939-45', IOL, L/MIL/17/5/2153.

56 Calculated from the figures in *Recruiting for the Defence Services in India* (New
Delhi, 1946), Appendix H, pp.140-42. See also Darling, *At Freedom's Door* (Oxford,
1946), p.336.

57 Calculated from the figures in *Recruiting for the Defence Services*, Appendix H, pp.140-2.

58 File 16, Khizar Papers, cited in Talbot, 'The 1946 Punjab Elections' in *MAS*, 14,1
(1980), p.75. British policy also contributed to the strength of the military in Punjabi
society. As a reward for military service, the British had adopted the policy of making
land grants to ex-servicemen. This had begun with awards or leases of wastelands
and later, of land in the canal irrigated colonies. The scale of allocation was such
that ex-soldiers came almost to expect it as their right and soldier settlement in the
canal colonies was much enlarged. For a detailed discussion of the militarisation of
the canal colonies see Imran Ali, *Punjab Under Imperialism*, Chapter IV.

59 Although the Muslim gangs were equally well armed and worked in the same ways
as did the Sikh *jathas* – a hard core to gangs out on the warpath – in the early stages,
they did not achieve the same degree of organisation as the Sikhs.

60 The growing fear of civil war over the last year before independence had led to the
build up of private armies. While the Muslim League mobilised Muslim public opinion
through the Muslim League National Guards (MLNG), the Hindu Mahasabha and its
militant front, the Rashtriya Swayamsevak Sangh (RSS) sought to rally Hindu popular
opinion. Both the MLNG and the RSS formed their own armies which were constantly
being expanded and trained. See 'Volunteer Organisations: MLNG Constitution and
Rules of', National Archives of India (NAI), Home (Poll.) (28 Apr. 1946), 'Punjab
Public Safety Ordinance', draft proposals, from the Secretary to the Governor Punjab,
C.M. Brander, to the Secretary to the Governor General (Public), Simla (21 Sept.
1946), NAI, Home (Poll.) 6/2/46, Correspondence from the Governor of Punjab to the
Secretary of State for India, *TP* IX, pp.556-66, and Jenkins to Wavell, Fortnightly
Report for 2nd Half of January, 1947, IOL, L/P&J/5/250.

61 The literature on the subject is vast, however to give only a few examples see Richard
Fox, *Lions of the Punjab: Culture in the Making* (Berkeley, 1985); Ruchi Ram
Sahni, *Struggle for Reform in the Sikh Shrines* (ed. Ganda Singh), (Amritsar, n.d.);
W.H. McLeod, *The Evolution of the Sikh Community* (Oxford, 1976); W.H. McLeod,
Who is a Sikh: The Problem of Sikh Identity (Oxford 1989); W.H. McLeod, *The
Sikhs: History, Religion and Society* (New York, 1989); Mark Jurgensmeyer, *Sikh*

Studies: Comparative Perspectives in Changing Tradition (Berkeley, 1979); Mohinder Singh, *The Akali Movement* (Delhi, 1974); Fauja Singh Bajwa, *The Military System of the Sikhs* (Delhi, 1964); Khushwant Singh, *History of the Sikhs* (Princeton, 1963); A.E. Barstow, *The Sikhs: An Ethnology* (Delhi, 1985), [originally published as *Handbook for the Indian Army, Sikhs*, 1928, and revised at the request of the Government of India).

[62] Report on the PBF, IOL, L/MIL/17/5/4319, p.7. See also Brigadier R.C.B. Bristow, *Memories of the British Raj: A Soldier in India* (London, 1974), p.147.

[63] Brig. Bristow reported witnessing *jathas* assembling in such a manner from the air. Bristow, *Memories of the British Raj*, p.162.

[64] Report on the PBF, OIOC, L/MIL/17/5/4319, p.22. See also p.7.

[65] *Ibid.*, pp.9, 21.

[66] *Ibid.*

[67] There were Muslim bands organised for a similar purpose in Lahore. But these were apparently fewer in number, less well organised and smaller in size. See Mountbatten to the Secretary of State of India (16 Aug. 1947), Viceroy's Personal Report, no. 12, IOL, Mountbatten Collection, Mss Eur., F200/187. See also 'Note by Major General D.C. Hawthorn' (11 Aug. 1947), *TP* XII, pp.667-8.

[68] One witness on the staff of the Commander of the Boundary Force reported having come across such piles of corpses in the Tarn Taran area. Sikhs in Action', Part II, IOL, Mudie Collection, Mss Eur., F.164/47, p.36.

[69] 'Sikhs in Action', Part II, IOL, Mudie Collection, Mss Eur., F.164/47, p.37.

[70] Report on the PBF, IOL, L/MIL/17/5/4319, p.21.

[71] *Ibid.,* p.22. Khushwant Singh's *Train to Pakistan* provides a fictional account of the massacres on trains. The planning involved and the signalling system used by attackers in such operations is vividly brought out.

[72] Report on the PBF, IOL, L/MIL/17/5/4319, p.20-22, see also 'Sikhs in Action', Part II, IOL, Mudie Collection, Mss Eur., F.164/47, p.31.

[73] See the account above by a British officer on a train attack where the attack was organised a minor military operation.

[74] Report on the PBF, OIOC, L/MIL/17/5 4319, p.16. The aircraft were eventually grounded by the Boundary Force's commander.

[75] *Ibid.*, p.22.

[76] Report on the PBF, IOL, L/MIL/17/5/4319, p.22.

[77] Mountbatten to the Secretary of State of India (16 Aug. 1947), Viceroy's Personal Report, no. 12, IOL, Mountbatten Collection, Mss Eur., F200/187.

[78] Just before the First World War figures show that Punjabis accounted for 66 per cent of all cavalrymen in the Indian Army, 87 per cent in the artillery, and 45 per cent in the infantry. See Annual Caste Returns Showing Class Composition of the Indian Army, January 1910, IOL, L/MIL/14/226. This pattern did not change in the next War and Punjabis (especially Muslims) were prominent in all artillery brigades of the Army.

[79] In May and June 1942, intelligence reported that there had been an 'abnormal number of Sikh desertions with arms particularly from the Eastern Army.' General HQ, India (6 Nov. 1942), 'Note on Sikhs', Appendix A, IOL, L/WS/2/44. September 1942 saw the same pattern with Punjabi Muslims. Weekly Summary no. 46 (18 Sept. 1942), Military Intelligence Summaries, India, Internal, IOL, L/WS/1/1433.

[80] Weekly Summary no. 77 (23 Apr. 1943), Military Intelligence Summaries, India, Internal, IOL, L/WS/1/1433. Darling likewise observed that, 'many soldiers' were reported as having 'brought back pistols and revolvers from the war, and some... rifles

from across the Frontier.' Darling, *At Freedom's Door*, p.37, and see also pp.29-30.

81 'Report on activities directed against the armed forces in the Punjab.' Appendix C, Military Intelligence Summaries, India, Internal, IOL, L/WS/1/1433. That these thefts had begun earlier is confirmed by a report of such an incident in June 1942 in the 10/ 16th Punjab Regiment. See General HQ, India (6 Nov. 1942), 'Note on Sikhs', Appendix A, IOL, L/WS/2/44.

82 Weekly Summary no. 43 (28 Aug. 1942), Military Intelligence Summaries, India, Internal, IOL, L/WS/1/1433.

83 Deputy Commissioner of Multan, File 4, A. J. V. Arthur Papers, Cambridge, SAS.

84 Report on the PBF, IOL, L/MIL/17/5/4319, pp.21-22. See also pp.7, 20.

85 Interview with IG Police (retd), Mr. Gurbax Singh, Chandigarh (1990).

86 Report on the PBF, IOL, L/MIL/17/5/4319, p.22.

87 *Ibid.,* pp.7, 21. See also 'The Sikhs in Action', IOL, Mudie Collection, Mss Eur., F.164/47 Part II, p.17.

88 Tuker, *While Memory Serves*, p.484.

89 'The Sikhs in Action', Part X, IOL, Mudie Collection, Mss Eur.F., 164/47 Part II, p.37-38 See also Report on the PBF, IOL, L/MIL/17/5/4319, p.21.

90 'Note on Situation in the Punjab Boundary Force Area for Joint Defence Council on 16 August 1947', by Field Marshal Auchinleck (15 Aug. 1947), *TP* XII, pp.734-7.

91 Memoirs of A. A. Williams, IOL, Mss Eur., F.180/70, fol.19.

92 'The Sikhs in Action', IOL, Mudie Collection, Mss Eur., F.164/47, p.49.

93 Undated report quoted in *ibid.*, p.35.

94 Report on the PBF, IOL, L/MIL/17/5/4319, p.25 and 'Sikhs in Action', IOL, Mudie Collection, Mss Eur., F.164/47 Part II, p.30.

95 Statement recorded by Muhammad Said, Terminal Tax Superintendent in Amritsar, 'The Sikhs in Action', IOL, Mudie Collection, Mss Eur., F.164/47, p.22.

96 Brigadier Bristow, *Memories of the British Raj*, pp.152-3.

97 Report of D.W. McDonald, Esq., Addl. Deputy Commissioner, Ferozepur, to the Chief Secretary to the Government Punjab (10 Aug. 1947), on the derailment of the Pakistan Special on 9 August 1947, Appendix 6 to 'The Sikhs in Action', IOL, Mudie Collection, Mss Eur., F164/47, p.xxxvi.

98 Report on the PBF, IOL, L/MIL/17/5/4319, p.21.

99 Tuker, *While Memory Serves*, Report from an unnamed officer (23 Sept. 1947), p.492.

100 Report on the PBF, IOL, L/MIL/17/5/4319, p.6.

101 'The Sikhs in Action' (3 Sept. 1947), Sheikhupura district, IOL, Mudie Collection, Mss Eur., F164/47 Part II, p.48.

102 Report on the PBF, IOL, L/MIL/17/5/4319, p.15.

103 'Note on Situation in the Punjab Boundary Force Area for Joint Defence Council on 16 August 1947', by Field Marshal Auchinleck (15 Aug. 1947), *TP* XII, pp.734-7.

104 See for example I. Kamtekar, 'End of the Colonial State in India, 1942-47', (Ph.D Thesis, Univ. of Cambridge, 1989).

105 Jenkins reported cases of many ex-soldiers who were being recruited to the Punjab Additional Police. Jenkins to Mountbatten (13 Aug. 1947), Mountbatten Collection, Governor's Correspondence, IOL, Mss Eur., F200/185.

106 'Evacuation Plan', Brig. Command, Military Evacuation Organisation [hereafter MEO], India and HQ MEO, Pakistan (10 Oct. 1947), Punjab State Archives (hereafter PSA), East Punjab Liaison Agency Records (hereafter EPLA Records), File No. LV/18. See also 'Joint Evacuation Movement Plan', 20 October 1947, sd. H.M. Mohite, Brig, Command MEO, India, and F.H. Stevens Brig. Command. MEO,

Pakistan, PSA, EPLA Records, File No. LV/18. In addition a large number (an estimated 2,100,000 Muslims and 2,000,000 Muslims) had already moved of their own volition, before the formal state machinery got into action. *Ibid.*

[107] The experience of succession however was by no means identical for both the new states. Despite the common foundations the crisis of succession was, in many ways, deeper for Pakistan. For a more nuanced and detailed investigation of state-building in Pakistan see Ayesha Jalal, *The State of Martial Rule*.

[108] A discussion on the state and manner in which it coped with disruption during this period is a story that merits much greater attention than is possible here. For a more detailed inquiry into this theme see S. Aiyar, 'Violence and the State'.

Literature and the Human Drama of the 1947 Partition

Ian Talbot

Independence brought forth a bitter harvest in the north Indian region of the Punjab. The grim reaper claimed at least a million lives, while a further ten million people were uprooted from their ancestral homes. The Partition, related massacres and migrations, represented an unfolding human tragedy of enormous proportions. Nevertheless, historical studies have tended to focus on the causes of Partition rather than its impact.[1] Sustained treatment of its consequences has largely been limited to accounts whose main purpose is to apportion blame for the related massacres.[2] In this great human event, human voices are strangely silent.[3]

Yet the sheer scale of the turmoil justifies its examination, if a serious distortion is not to enter into the historical discourse. Moreover, valuable clues to the future circumstances of North India may be lost by the failure to address the human dimension of Partition. It should not be forgotten that in this, the century of the displaced person, India's Partition still remains one of the greatest social upheavals.

This chapter explores the human dimension of Partition through the physical and psychological impact of the four experiences of violence, abduction, migration and resettlement. It deploys a fresh range of source materials including autobiographical accounts. The most sustained use however is made of literary 'representation'. Before turning to the insights which can be derived from works of fiction, it is necessary to consider the range of such sources and the problems associated with their utilisation.

Novelists, unlike historians have fully addressed the human agonies which accompanied Partition. Hundreds of novels, short stories and plays have taken these as their theme. Much of this outpouring has been cathartic as the writers relate their own experiences. While many of the works lack artistry, some of the greatest pieces of literature from the subcontinent have also been produced. The contributions in English of Khushwant Singh[4] and Chaman Nahal,[5] of Kartar Singh Duggal[6] in Punjabi, of Bhisham Sahni[7] in Hindi and Saadat Hasan Manto,[8] Rajinder Singh Bedi[9] and Intizar Hussain[10] in Urdu spring readily to mind. Historians of Indian independence have been much more reluctant than their colleagues in other fields to utilise such creative outpourings as source material. There are of course methodological problems in the use of literature,[11] but it is curious that standard historical accounts of Partition have not seized on this rich vein of material to begin to uncover the human dimension of the experience.

II

The most immediate physical and psychological impact of Partition was the brutal violence which it brought. Before examining autobiographical and literary accounts of its impact, it is necessary to understand, firstly how creative writers have responded to this phenomenon and secondly to differentiate between the Partition related massacres and earlier episodes of 'communal' conflict.

Such novelists as Manto[12] have derived much black humour from the Partition violence. Others such as the progressive[13] author Krishan Chander[14] have attempted to underline the moral that all communities were equally guilty. Another common theme is the role of politicians in inciting hatred to serve their own purposes. This is addressed with considerable subtlety and power by Bhisham Sahni[15] in his award winning work, *Tamas*[16], which is based on his experiences during the time of Partition. Novelists have also commented on the brutalising effects of violence on its perpetrators and on its elemental ferocity. Especially with regard to this latter point, art closely mirrors reality.

Kirpal Singh in his recently published compilation, *Partition of the Punjab, 1947*[17] provides a graphic account of the impact of violence on non-Muslims by reproducing the evacuation reports of the District Liaison Officers. Similar material can be drawn from the private papers of the West Punjab Governor, Sir Francis Mudie, to build up a Muslim perspective. What emerges from such accounts is the ferocity and cold bloodedness of the violence. This had a severe traumatic effect on survivors which has not been adequately researched and can only be glimpsed in autobiographical and literary accounts. The violence in the Punjab in 1947 was in fact of a different character to earlier 'communal riots' and should be treated in a distinct category.

Attacks on refugee trains, and minority villages for example were often carried out with a military precision which was not surprising given the role played by ex-servicemen from both the Indian Army and the INA.[18] Light tanks were even deployed in the attack against the heavily fortified Harnoli *mandi* in the Mianwali district in which three thousand inhabitants were massacred.[19] Moreover, while revenge and bloodlust were motives, Punjabi

Muslims and Sikhs alike turned to violence to ensure 'ethnic cleansing'.[20] Force was also of course used in boundary demarcation in the Frontier and Bengal. During the Noakhali riots, one British observer spoke of a 'determined and organised' Muslim effort to drive out all the Hindus.[21] But the Partition-related violence should not be treated as merely an extreme variant of earlier 'communal' outbreaks, although it shared similar features: attacks on mosques, temples, attempts at forced conversion and endeavours to 'dishonour' the 'other' community by molestation of females.[22]

This section will examine the impact of violence on both its victims and perpetrators through the insights of autobiographical sources and fictional 'representation'. The authors will be allowed to speak for themselves once the background to the text has been explained. We shall turn first to the horrific picture of violence painted by the novelist Bapsi Sidwa[23] in her compulsive work, *Ice-Candy Man*. The book's heroine, Lenny, a young Parsee girl growing up in Lahore, is drawn from the author's own experience. Similarly, the sub-plot Ranna's Story given in extract below is based on the childhood recollections of one of her friends.

> The attack came at dawn. The watch from the mosque's single minaret hurtled down the winding steps to spread the alarm. The panicked women ran to and fro snatching up their babies, and the men barely had time to get to their posts. In fifteen minutes the village was swamped by Sikhs – tall men with streaming hair and thick biceps and thighs, waving full-sized swords and sten-guns roaring, 'Bohal so Nihal! Sat Sri Akal!' They mowed down the villagers in the mosque with the sten-guns. Shouting 'Allah-o-Akbar' the peasants died of sword and spear wounds in the slushy lanes and courtyards... Ranna awoke with a start. Why was he on the floor? Why were there so many people about in the dark? He felt the stir of men getting to their feet. The air in the room was oppressive: hot and humid and stinking of sweat. Suddenly Ranna remembered where he was and the darkness became charged with terror... Suddenly the noon light smote their eyes... Ranna saw his uncles beheaded, his older brothers, his cousins. The Sikhs were among them like hairy vengeful demons, wielding bloodied swords, dragging them out as a sprinkling of Hindus, darting about at the fringes, their faces vaguely familiar, pointed out and identified the Mussulmans by name. He felt a blow cleave the back of his head and the warm flow of blood... Later in the evening he awoke to silence. At once he became fully conscious. He wriggled backwards over the bodies and slipping free of the weight on top of him felt himself sink knee-deep into a viscous fluid. The bodies blocking the entrance had turned the room into a pool of blood.[24]

This account brings out clearly the ferocity and suddenness of the violence in the rural Punjab in August 1947. Standard historical accounts tend to overlook this altogether. Its counterpart written from the non-Muslim perspective is the equally harrowing account of the attack on the Sikh minority of Sayyedpur contained in *Tamas*.[25] This reaches a climax with the mass suicide of the Sikh women in the village well. Common to both accounts is the elemental violence let loose by communal animosity and the coming together of past and present hatreds. Interestingly, Sahni has the Sikhs of Sayyedpur call their attackers 'Turks' although they were near neighbours.

Such fictional 'representations' of the bloodshed in rural Punjab minimises rather than exaggerates it. The real life equivalent of Sayyedpur was the episode at Harnoli in the Mianwali district where hundreds of women jumped into wells or threw themselves into burning houses to escape being molested.[26] An equally chilling actual episode this time in East Punjab is contained in Mashkur Hassan's autobiography, *Azadike caragh*.[27] The writer recalls that his Hissar home was attacked on 29 August. When the police were called, they joined in the assaults. Like the 'fictional' character Ranna, Hassan was an injured witness to the death of his family and friends. Parched by the heat of a fire elsewhere in the building he licked the blood which was flowing from the victims. Twelve hours elapsed before he was able to stagger from the building's shattered remains.

The following extract from Bhisham Sahni's *Tamas* focuses on the cold-blooded stray stabbings which were a marked feature of urban violence in North India during the Partition period. This aspect has been similarly overlooked by historians. The passage must be read in the context of Sahni's general belief that violence resulted from the manipulation of simple people by the power-hungry to serve their selfish ends. A Hindu communalist, Master Devbrat has trained a group of young school boys to kill their Muslim 'foe'.

> The four warriors in the squad were spoiling for action. Stationed on the roof they felt like gallant Rajputs waiting for the Muslim foe down in the Haldi Ghati.
> Being rather short Ranvir liked to believe he was like that other great short-statured hero Shivaji... Sometimes he wished he were wearing a long Rajput coat, a saffron turban on his head and a long sword hanging from a cummerbund round his waist. To take part in a fierce fight in loose pyjamas, an ill-fitting shirt and worn out chappals didn't seem right; it was not the dress of a fighting man... There was not a moment to be lost. He must decide and decide quickly. This man was a Muslim and a stranger to the place, carrying a heavy load of bags. He could neither flee nor protect himself. And he looked so tired. Everything was in favour of attacking. Ranvir's eyes met Inder and he signalled his decision...
> Inder was very composed. He kept walking steadily, his hand firmly gripping the knife in his pocket, his eyes fixed on the perfume seller's waist. Even Arjuna who had killed a bird by looking at its reflection in a receptacle of oil would have envied Inder his concentration. As they walked past the tap Inder's energy suddenly concentrated in his right hand, his mind measuring each step as they walked together.
> 'In the bazaar there is greater demand for cotton swabs while in the lanes I sell more bottles of oil and perfume,' the old man said. Suddenly Inder lunged. The old man saw the boy's left hand move swiftly. Something bright flashed in the air. Before he could stop and feel his bag to see if anything had been taken, he felt a sharp agonising pain in his stomach. Inder twisted the knife he had plunged into the man's belly as he had been taught. then leaving it where it was he ran.[28]

The artistic power of the extract lies of course in the contrast it presents between the romanticised view of violence which Master Devbrat has inculcated in his acolytes and Inder's futile murder of the helpless old man. The reader is left to ponder whether the boys themselves should not be viewed as victims.

The effect of violence on its perpetrators is a constant theme of Partition literature. Chaman Nahal in *Azadi* for example excels in his depiction of the moral disintegration of Abdul Ghani, the hookah maker and neighbour of the novel's main protaganist, Lala Kanshi Ram. Saadat Hassan Manto's short story, *Thanda Gosht* remains, however, the most notable work on this theme. Iswar Singh's impotence following his rape of a dead Muslim girl provides a compelling symbol of the loss of human sensibilities during the miasma of terror and violence in August 1947.

Some may argue that little is to be served by cataloguing the horrors brought by the massacres of 1947. All that will be achieved is the reopening of old wounds. Indeed this argument was used to try to prevent the broadcasting of *Tamas* by

Doordarshan. Yet to bury away these agonies is to deny the experience of countless people. In the name of both justice and truth, victims should be given their voice. Furthermore, it could be argued that a nation's maturity can be gauged by its ability to confront unpleasant aspects of its historical past. The more it does this the less likely they are to be repeated. By denying the horrors of the 1947 massacres, the courage and humanity which was displayed during them is also neglected. There were many who like the fictional character Jugga Singh in *Train to Pakistan* risked their own lives to save others. We shall conclude this section with three brief quotations from interviews conducted by Miriam Sharma and Urmila Vanjamij among Hindu *jat* refugees from the Multan district. The story they tell is, however, not confined to their community.

> The Muslims of our area were the ones who warned us to leave or we would be slaughtered. They were Rajputs before who had become Muslims in the old times and they had a certain amount of sympathy for us.
> A lot of people came to our village and I saw this happen – killings and murders with my own eyes. Actually many of the big land-holding Muslims were very helpful. They gave us shelter and tried to protect us from the others, from the small Muslim-like have-nots who wanted to push us out kill us off and take our land.
> The five fingers are not the same. Some people want to trouble you and others want to help you. The Muslims were like that too... There was a Muslim man. He said, no matter what happens I will let nothing happen to these people. He was an officer on the Pakistan side. He made sure that we left safely. There were others who helped us. Like in our own village, there were people who extended hands of help to us and wouldn't let any harm come to us.[29]

III

The break up of families through abduction and abandonment is a second largely untold aspect of the Partition experience. The increasing incidence of abductions and attacks on women in 1946-7 undoubtedly reflected attempts to expose the most protected aspect of the 'other's' honour and self-identity.[30] Like other gender aspects of Partition, the experience of women as both victims and survivors of violence is absent from the standard historical account. All we are given are the bald statistics that by October 1952 just over eight thousand women and children had been rehabilitated from Pakistan, while twice this number had been recovered from India.[31] These tell us nothing of the physical and psychological scars left by the experience of abduction. Did women, as in other victim circumstances, blame themselves for their sufferings rather than the male perpetrators of the violence against them? The comparative oral history project on women's experience of Partition is beginning to address this question. Ritu Menon and Kamla Bhasin began the publication of the project's findings in an article in the *Economic and Political Weekly* in April 1993.[32]

Creative writers also provide some clues for the historian in the recovering of this neglected aspect of the reality of Partition. Amrita Pritam in her novel

Pinjer, through the character Pooro-Hamida, explores the theme of abduction.[33] Bapai Sidhwa in the following extracts from *Ice-Candy Man* approaches this through the sufferings of Lenny's Hindu *ayah*. The first gives a vivid account of her forcible abduction, next there is a description of the home for rehabilitated women near to Lenny's house and finally there is the picture of the devastated *ayah* who has been married to one of her Muslim captors.

They move forward from all points. They swarm into bedrooms, search the servants' quarters, climb to the roofs, breach locks and enter our godowns and the small store-rooms near the bathrooms.

They drag Ayah out. They drag her by her arms stretched taut, and her bare feet – that want to move backwards – are forced forward instead... Her violet sari slips off her shoulder, and her breasts strain at her sari-blouse stretching the cloth so that the white stitching at the seams shows. A sleeve tears under her arm.

The men drag her in grotesque strides to the cart and their harsh hands, supporting her with careless intimacy, lift her into it. Four men stand pressed against her, propping her body upright, their lips stretched in triumphant grimaces.

The mystery of the women in the courtyard deepens. At night we hear them wailing, their cries verging on the in-human... One cold night I am awakened by a hideous wail. My teeth chattering, I sit up. I must have dozed off, because Hamida is still sitting by my bed...

'Why do they wail and scream at night?' I ask. It is not a subject I have broached till now, mindful of Hamida's sensibilities.

'Poor fate-smitten woman,' says Hamida, sighing. 'What can a sorrowing woman do but wail?...

My heart is wrung with pity and horror. I want to leap out of my bed and soothe the wailing woman and slay her tormentors. I've seen Ayah carried away – and it had less to do with fate than with the will of men... I tell (Godmother) of my conversation with Hamida.

'Hamida was kidnapped by the Sikhs,' says Godmother seriously... 'She was taken away to Amritsar. Once that happens, sometimes, the husband – or his family – won't take her back.'

'Why? It isn't her fault she was kidnapped!'

'Some folk feel that way – they can't stand their women being touched by other men.' It's monstrously unfair: but Godmother's tone is accepting.

'So!' whispers Godmother, blinking and nodding impishly. 'He has christened our *ayah* Mumtaz!'

'Lenny baby, aren't you going to embrace my bride?' Ice-candy-man asks.

And Ayah raises her eyes to me.

Where have the radiance and the animation gone? Her vacant eyes are bigger than ever: wide-opened with what they've seen and felt... 'I want to go to my family.' Her voice is harsh, gruff: as if someone has mutilated her vocal cords...

'Isn't he looking after you?'

Mumtaz nods her head slightly.

'What's happened has happened,' says Godmother. 'But you are married to him now. You must make the best of things.'...

'I will not live with him.' Again that coarse rasping whisper... 'I cannot forget what has happened.'

'That was fated daughter. It can't be undone. But it can be forgiven... Worse things are forgiven. Life goes on and the business of living buries the debris of our pasts... That's the way of life.'
'I am past that,' says Mumtaz. 'I'm not alive.'
'What if your family won't take you back?' (Godmother) asks.
'Whether they want me or not, I will go.'[34]

I wish to conclude this brief examination by citing two male writers who have provided the historian with sensitive insights into the impact of abduction on ordinary people. We shall turn respectively to the work of Rajinder Singh Bedi[35] and Saadat Hassan Manto.

Bedi's short story *Lajwanti*[36] which is set in the Partition period is rightly regarded as an Urdu classic. The plot revolves around Sunder Lal and his wife Lajwanti who has been abducted. 'Sunder Lal had abandoned all hope of finding Lajwanti,' Bedi tells his readers. 'He had made his loss a part of the general loss. He had drowned his personal sorrow by plunging into social service.'[37] He daily led processions and remonstrated with those who refused to take back their abducted women. This existence was turned upside down by Lajwanti's unexpected return. Her Muslim style of dress disgusted him when he first saw her at the police station, but unlike the other men he takes her in.

The story concludes, however, on a poignant, rather than joyful note. For Sunder Lal refuses to allow Lajwanti to unburden her experiences. He treats her instead with an over-exaggerated respect calling her *devi*. She had been rehabilitated but not accepted. Lajwanti is as much a victim in her own home as she was at the time of her abduction. But Sunder Lal has also been diminished.

Manto's short story, *Khuda ki Qasim*[38] also reflects on the emotional trauma of abduction. It too provides valuable insights which have surprisingly been ignored by historians. The narrator is a liaison officer involved in the recovery of abducted women. During his work he encounters an old Muslim woman who is searching for her daughter with increasing desperation. She refuses to return to Pakistan with him, as she is convinced that her daughter is still alive.

'Why?' I asked her.
'Because she is so beautiful – so beautiful that no one would dare kill her – no one will slap her even' she replied to me.

The old woman is so distressed at the time of their final meeting in Freed Chowk Amritsar that the Liaison Officer decides to get her admitted to a lunatic asylum. Just at that moment a 'sharp-faced' young Sikh walks by accompanied by a veiled woman. The Sikh whispered to the 'goddess of beauty', 'Look – your mother.' The young woman looks for a moment then averts her eyes and walks away. The old Muslim woman in that moment recognises her daughter and shouts after the Liaison Officer, 'I have just seen her, just seen her.' He firmly replies, fully aware of what is happening, 'By God, I do not lie, By God she is dead.'[39] At that instant the old woman collapses to the ground.

Manto's ending to the story is not only artistically powerful, but reveals perhaps better than anything else that Partition involved the death of family ties as well as of individuals. The character of the old woman, moreover, articulates the uncertainties and anxieties of many relatives waiting to hear of loved ones. Such fears overcame any personal relief at safely crossing the great divide of 1947.

IV

Migration was the single most important human agony which attended the transfer of power. It brought in its wake a sense of hopelessness and uprootedness. Around ten million people in all were forced to flee from their homes. Delhi and Karachi took on the character of refugee cities which they have never lost. The subsequent historical development of large areas of the Indo-Pakistan subcontinent has been profoundly shaped by the migration experience. *Muhajirs* have played a crucial role, some might add a divisive one, in Pakistan's post-independence history.[40] And much of post-1947 Sikh history and of the Indian Punjab has been shaped by the need to recover the physical and psychological losses brought by the Partition.

Yet despite the magnitude of the migration and its long term consequences, comparatively little has been written about this human aspect of Partition. The aim of this section is to illustrate how historians could obtain fresh insights into the experience of migration by the use of both literary and autobiographical material. There will be an attempt to examine its psychological effects as well as its more immediate physical dangers and hardships.

Kartar Singh Duggal's[41] novel, *Twice-Born. Twice-Dead*[42] centres around the physical hardships of those who were forced to flee their homes by communal violence. The main character Sohne Shah and his adopted Muslim daughter Satbharai wander from the Rawalpindi district to Lahore and thence to Lyallpur where they once again are driven out. Duggal draws on first-hand material to depict the refugees' plight. Towards the close of the novel he provides the following poignant picture of a refugee column which is unmatched in Punjabi literature and is of inestimable value to the historian concerned with understanding the partition experience 'from beneath'.

A caravan of Muslim evacuees was on the move. Whenever such a caravan was to pass, the police usually clamped down a curfew. ...Policemen lined both sides of the road to prevent incidents. Still the Hindu shopkeepers and their children poked fun at the cowed, miserable, hungry and emaciated evacuees.
The caravan was moving. Bullock carts were loaded with boxes, trunks and spinning wheels. On the top were *charpoys*, bedding and sacks. On the sacks were old men and women, carrying fowls, cats and lambs. From the bullock carts hung hubble-bubbles, baskets, prayer mats, odds and ends. Holding onto the bullock carts for imaginery support walked women with babies at their breasts. Muslim women nurtured behind seven veils ran the gauntlet of hostile glances. The men were wounded they had seen their relatives hacked to pieces with *kirpans*. There was not a single young man in the column.. There were small boys, bare-footed, bare-headed, walking fast or slowing

down to cast a longing glance at the hot *jalebies* in the sweet shops. The most yearning look however was cast at the running tap.. No Muslim dared to take a drop of water from the Hindu tap. Men, women and children looked beseechingly at the water flowing from the tap and moved on.[43]

Those who migrated by train were spared such physical deprivations. But they faced a terrifying ordeal in that refugee trains were frequently attacked and their passengers murdered or abducted. The tense atmosphere which accompanied such journeys is powerfully recalled in the extract below. This is taken from an autobiographical account of the train ride from Delhi to Pakistan given by an educated Muslim women, Dr. Zahida Amjad Ali.

All passengers were forced into compartments like sheep and goats. Because of which the heat and suffocating atmosphere was intensified and it was very hard to breathe. In the ladies compartment women and children were in a terrible condition.. Women tried in vain to calm down and comfort their children.. If you looked out the window you could see dead bodies lying in the distance.. At many places you could see corpses piled on top of each other and no one seemed to have any concern. At one place we saw the dead bodies of innocent children, and in such condition that even the most stone-hearted person would draw breath for a moment if he saw them.. These were the scenes that made your heart bleed and everybody loudly repented their sins and recited verses asking God's forgiveness.. Every moment seemed to be the most terrifying and agonising.[44]

Migration brought not only constant danger, but the emotional trauma of uprootedness and broken identities. Historians have totally neglected this aspect of Partition, yet it lay at its very heart and still continues to exert a profound psychological effect. Saadat Hassan Manto explores this theme in his classic short story, *Toba Tek Singh*.[45] He approaches the subject through an allegory, which concerns the exchange of lunatics after independence. The plot increasingly centres around an aged Sikh inmate by the name of Bishan Singh. He is known to everyone as Toba Tek Singh because of his large landholdings there. Bishan Singh becomes obsessed with the question whether Toba Tek Singh is in India or Pakistan. His insistence flusters a neighbour Fazal Din who visits him with the result that his reply is ambiguous. Bisha Singh only discovers the truth that Toba Tek Singh is in fact in Pakistan when he is awaiting evacuation at the border. He then refuses to cross to India and is left standing on a spot midway between the boundary lines.

Just before dawn, an ear-splitting cry issued from Toba Tek Singh's silent throat. Officials ran from both sides and discovered that the man who had remained upright on his legs for fifteen years was now lying on his face. On one side behind the barbed wire was India; Pakistan was behind the barbed wire on the other side. Between them, stretched on the ground of no-man's land, lay Toba Tek Singh.[46]

Manto makes the character Bishan Singh reflect the sense of confusion and uprootedness which faced many refugees. They were attached to their ancestral villages not out of mere sentimentality, but as the allegory reveals because it was there that the core of their identity resided. Chaman Nahal in *Azadi* makes a similar point through the chief protagonist Lala Kanshi Ram, a grain merchant who is forced to flee his native Sialkot. He arrives safely in Delhi with his family, but has suffered serious emotional loss, in addition to his extensive property which will never be restored.

> Lala Kanshi Ram would forgive the English and the Muslims all their sins, if only he could return. Return and die here and be cremated by the side of the river Aik! To be carried shoulder high on a bier through the streets of Sialkot, through all the streets in each of which somewhere sat a friend. Then at the last moment, for his spirit to look at the Aik and the land of Sialkot from above, from the sky, or to come down and roll in the dust of the fields - that would be the very pinnacle of his delight.[47]

The sense of alienation brought by partition is explored with great subtlety by the Urdu writer Intizar Husain.[48] In the story *Sirhiyan*[49] he focuses on the loss of meaning and identity through the character Saiyid who has been robbed of his memory. He has also become unable to dream and subconsciously retrieve it in this way. One summer evening he is depicted lying on his *charpoy* along with three friends, Akhtar, Basher Bhai and Razi. Basher Bhai is interpreting a dream that Razi has related. It is suffused with past memories of a small town somewhere in east UP. When Razi mentions the *imambara*, a series of past memories and events are triggered in Saiyid's mind. He regains his power to dream and with it his wholeness and sense of identity and his past is again part of his present.

This strong feeling for the flow of Indian Muslim history and the sense that Partition has sundered the past is further explored in Intizar Husain's short story, *Akhri Mom Bati*.[50] The Pakistani narrator returns to visit his aunt in the UP. He notices that everything in the village has changed and that his widowed aunt has suddenly grown old. On the eve of *muhurram*, he remembers how his aunt and his cousin Shamina who is now living in Karachi used to decorate the *imambara* and receive visitors. When he returns from a stroll to the railway station, the *imambara* is illuminated and Shamina is there to his amazement. His aunt, however laments that this will be the last such occasion. The narrator lies awake listening to the worship. When he falls asleep he dreams that all the candles except one have been extinguished and through it he can hear the sound of religious songs.

The mournful feeling of the work is impossible to capture in translation, but Intizar Husain's message is clear. He returns to the past, not to worship it, but to help understand the present. Only when this has happened, as for the character Saiyid, can the present be comprehended. Intizar Husain provides an illuminating insight into *muhajir* emotions. He articulates not only their sense of loss, but maintains that this is not self-indulgent. For in effect what he is saying is that a truly Pakistani ethos and sensibility can only emerge after a reassessment has taken place of past Indian Muslim cultural identity.

Intizar Husain's elegies harmonise with much autobiographical writing. The sense of loss and uprootedness is especially striking in the following two quotations from Shahid Ahmad and A. Hameed. Both men are renowned writers[51] in Pakistan. They reflect the feelings of the North Indian Muslim professional class which migrated in 1947. Shahid Ahmad briefly returned to Delhi just six months after Partition. He was at first struck by the physical changes which had resulted from the refugee influx; the congested streets and markets, the pavements crammed with migrants selling their wares on trays. In the midst of all this bustle, he became acutely aware of a deeper feeling of loss, of sundering links with the past. He poetically describes this as follows in his autobiography.

> I came to my mother's lap with a broken heart and come back with a dead heart. I saw mother's widowhood, her widow's tears. I saw the Shah Jehan mosque in beautiful moonlight, and thought that mother had lifted her hands to the heavens in prayer. And like Mary her heart is full of flames. This vision has been engraved in such a way that I cannot forget. And repeatedly these questions come to my mind, 'Mother have you lost the happiness of your marriage for good?'[52]

For Shahid Ahmad, Delhi has been lost and widowed as earlier were such Muslim cities as Cordoba and Granada. Like them it will continue to haunt Muslims as a memorial to their vanished glory. A. Hameed has expressed similar feelings when he recalls his former Amritsar home.

> In fact Amritsar for me is Jerusalem, separated from me and I am her 'wailing wall.' Amritsar is circulating in my body, within my blood. I see Amritsar, before I go to sleep, and the first thing I see when I get up in the morning is Amritsar. When I walk Company Garden accompanies me. When I sit, the trees of Saktari Garden shadow me. When I speak, I hear the call for prayer from the mosques and when I am silent, I hear the hissing sound of flowing water in the canals of Amritsar, as if very close to my ears. When I look at one of my hands, I see the sleeping lanes and paths of the place (where I lived).[53]

Hameed visits in his imagination such places as Hal Bazaar, Chowk Farid, Katra Safaid and Company Garden, but finds them sad and desolate.

> Even the ruins of Muslim culture were not visible. Mosques seemed to be reciting an elegy. Hindu women were once plastering the walls which formed the rendez-vous for Kashmiris.. In the dust of Amritsar's mosques are hidden the prints of prostrations of my ancestors and its lanes are with the blood of martyrs... O Spain! You are the trustee of the blood of Muslims. You are very sacred in my eyes. In your dust are hidden the prints of the prostrations and silent calls for prayer can be heard in your morning breeze.[54]

Spain is of course a popular symbol for Muslim writers concerned with past Islamic glories. But what we have here is something more than literary convention. It is an expression of deep pain and sense of loss and longing. This lies at the heart of the Partition experience for many South Asian Muslims. It is of course part of a wider emotional current in Muslim society which Akbar Ahmed has termed the Andalus syndrome. He sees it existing wherever a great Muslim civilisation has been lost and its descendants face an uncertain future. Akbar Ahmed's view is that it constitutes an unhealthy neurosis in which there is permanent perplexity and trauma.[55]

V

At the end of difficult and frequently terrifying journeys, migrants had to re-establish their lives in a strange environment. This brief examination of the human impact of Partition will conclude by focusing on the experience of resettlement. Refugee experiences on arrival in their new homeland varied enormously. Some had relatives to smooth their paths and were soon able to pick up their old occupations. The less fortunate had to make their own way and faced both short term exploitation and months of demoralising inactivity in refugee camps. Amir Abdullah Khan Rokri, for example, provides evidence in his autobiography, of bureaucrats and landlords feathering their nests at the refugees' expense. Pakistan government officials, in connivance with local Muslim and Hindu businessmen, sold goods on the black market which had been donated to refugees in the transit camp at Pathankot.[56] Shahid Ahmad recalls how he was fleeced by coolies and *tonga* drivers on his arrival in Lahore, when they heard him speaking Urdu.[57]

Kartar Singh Duggal, whose Muslim wife Ayesha worked among the refugees in Jullundur, has painted an especially vivid picture of refugee life in his novel *Twice Born. Twice Dead*. The first extract brings home the extent of the larger camps, while the second evokes the often desperate struggle for survival in the transit camps.

> The camp was like a small township. As far as the eye could see there were...tents. Living quarters, bathrooms, offices, hospitals, schools, gurdwaras, temples, the post office and shops were all housed in tents. Roads, lanes and by lanes criss-crossed...Children were crying, men and women were shouting, there was uproar all around. Sohne Shah remembered the peace and quiet of his village. He could walk miles there without meeting anyone.[58]
>
> Every instant flocks of refugees on bullock carts and trucks came to the camp under the protection of the army. Day and night the process continued... No one dared to set foot outside the gates. Those who had gone outside without protection never returned. A few used to go out of the camp with the police. It transpired that a black market was flourishing - flour at ten rupees a seer and salt at a rupee. People were exchanging gold ornaments for bicycles, tongas and even camel coaches.[59]

Qudrat Allah Shahab's short story, *Ya Khuda*[60] is less well known than Kartur Singh Duggal's work, but provides similar insights into the hardships of refugee life, this time from the Muslim perspective. Dilshad a *maulvi*'s daughter arrives dishonoured and penniless in Lahore where she encounters indifference and contempt. Life is equally tough for her friend Zubeida who has to disregard her modesty to keep alive her son Mahmood during the bitter Lahore winter. The local shopkeeper meanwhile stockpiles blankets and sanctimoniously recites Iqbal's poetry.

Dilshad is tricked into going to the house of Mustafa Khan who claims to know the whereabouts of her beloved Rahim Khan who has disappeared during the journey from the East Punjab. Mustafa Khan makes sexual advances towards Dilshad as soon as they are alone, prompting the narrator to comment with bitter irony on the relationship between the *muhajirs* and their *ansar* helpers.

> Lahore was not Lahore it was Medina, the people of Lahore were not of Lahore, they were the *ansars* of Medina offering help to the Holy Prophet. Here for Dilshad a new Rahim Khan was being born. For Zubeida a new grandfather was born daily, for daughters new fathers, for sisters new brothers, the relationship of flesh was meeting flesh and blood with blood.[61]

Not all Muslim refugee experiences were as painful. In Hyderabad even *tonga* drivers were found residing in the luxurious homes once occupied by Hindu businessmen. The first Muslim arrivals in the West Punjab canal colony areas vacated by Sikhs found the fields almost ready for harvesting, millet and rice crops provided the migrants with food, while cotton could be sold for cash. Shahid Ahmad encountered generosity as well as exploitation. When his refugee train reached the first station in Pakistan, hundreds of people were waiting and descended on the carriages with gifts of bread, lentils and pickles.[62] There were many on both sides of the Punjab border like Amir Abdullah Khan Rokri who moved out of their houses to provide temporary accommodation for refugees. Moreover, for some Muslims the migration experience was viewed in terms of *hijrat* which transcended human sufferings. Looking back four decades later on her flight from Nikodar in East Punjab, Hurmat Bibi expresses this understanding on behalf of many other migrants.

> I had lost everything, forty people of our family were martyred, but the happiness I found when I saw the Pakistan flag flying at the Pakistan border, is still living in every cell of my body.[63]

Non-Muslim refugees could not of course seek a similar religious solace for their material losses. These were frequently greater than those of their Muslim counterparts as the Hindu and Sikh population of the West Punjab was far wealthier than the Muslims of the East. It owned the bulk of the businesses and factories and urban property in the 'Pakistan' areas. Non-Muslim farmers also cultivated around 6.7 million acres of land. This not only exceeded the land left by Muslims, but contained superior soil and irrigation facilities.[64] The fictional character, Lala Kanshi Ram's futile endeavours to secure compensation for his lost property, during his prolonged sojourn in a Delhi refugee camp is representative of the resettlement experience of many Punjabi non-Muslims.

Chaman Nahal, however, also makes his character express a sense of pride in the independent India which he has struggled so hard safely to reach. The novel closes with this short description following Gandhi's assassination.

> What impressed Lala Kanshi Ram was the pride with which the men stood.. He thought of pre-independence days... An Indian leader dying and the crowd feeling openly for him? Today the men stood in pride... Lala Kanshi Ram raised his head with pride and stretched back his shoulders. He was unrestricted now, he was untramelled.[65]

Three themes emerge strongly from this brief exploration of literary representations of the human dimension of Partition in North India. The first is that of the searing reality of the agony of the Partition massacres and migrations. The emotional and physical pain of innumerable ordinary men and women is represented by such fictional characters as Lala Kanshi Ram. It is frequently forgotten that significant sections of the subcontinent's population entered the new era of independence severely traumatised. The social and political implications of this reality have been largely neglected.

The second theme is that of the conflicting human emotions evoked by Partition. National pride and religious fulfilment mingled with a sense of loss and bewilderment. The primary concern was for immediate family and kin. The loss of her daughter meant far more to the old woman in Manto's story *Khuda ki Qasim* than the establishment of Pakistan or for that matter even her own life. Novelists repeatedly point to the reality of how violence from outside intruded itself into harmonious family and community relationships destroying that which it claimed to uphold.[66]

Third, there emerges a strong sense of the uprootedness brought by migration. The demented character Toba Tek Singh merely caricatures the fact that separation from ancestral home threatened the core of many migrants' identity. Such varied authors as Duggal, Nahal, Intizar, Husain and Manto reflect on an emotion which affected all communities. Shahid Ahmad in his autobiographical account articulates the same feeling on behalf of many Muslim *muhajirs* in a classic Urdu poetical convention. The Lahore educationist Dr Prem Kirpal in his autobiographical poem, 'Spirit's Musings' expresses similar emotions for the non-Muslims whose familiar home had suddenly become a foreign land.

> My beloved city of Lahore still standing not far from Delhi, within quicker reach by air or train, suddenly become a forbidden land guarded by a sovereign state of new ideologies, loves and hates. Homes were lost and hearts were bruised in both unhappy parts of Punjab.[67]

Historians have neglected the sense of loss and uprootedness brought about by Partition. Such emotions cut across community identity. They lie at the very heart of the human impact of Partition. To omit this dimension is not only to distort the historical discourse, but to lose an important key to understanding social and political developments in the decades which have followed North Indian independence.

Notes

[1] A notable exception is Chapter Thirteen of C.M. Ali, *The Emergence of Pakistan* (New York, 1967). See also, the recollections of the East Punjab refugee Rehabilitation Commissioner, M.S. Randhwa, *Out of the Ashes* (Jullundur, 1954) and J. Nanda, *Punjab Uprooted* (Bombay, 1948).

[2] See for example, Pakistan Government, *Note on the Sikh Plan* (Lahore, 1948).

[3] In an attempt to remedy this situation, a recent study of the demographic consequences of the Partition in the Punjab concludes with sixty-two personal accounts of people caught up in the disturbances. R.S. Corruccini & S.S. Kaul, *Halla: Demographic Consequences of the Partition in the Punjab, 1947* (Lanham, 1990), pp.60-93.

[4] K. Singh, *Train to Pakistan* (New York, 1956).

[5] C. Nahal, *Azadi* (London, 1976).

[6] K.S. Duggal (J. Ara trans.), *Twice Born, twice Dead* (New Delhi, 1979).

[7] B. Sahni (J. Ratan trans.), *Tamas* (New Delhi, 1990). Also (J. Ratan trans.), *We have Arrived in Amritsar and other stories* (London, 1990).

[8] S.H. Manto (C.M. Naim and R.L. Schmidt trans), *Thanda Gosht Journal of Asian Literature*, 1 (1965), pp.14-19. Also (R.B. Haldane trans.), *Toba Tek Singh Journal of South Asian Literature*, 6 (1970), pp.19-23 (M. Ali trans.), *Khuda qi Qasim Pakistan Review* (13 Apr. 1965), pp.33-4.

[9] R.S. Bedi (K. Singh trans.), *Lajwanti* in R. Mathur and M. Kulasrestha (eds), *Writings on India's Partition* (Calcutta, 1976), pp.126-135.

[10] J. Hussain, 'Akhri Mom bati' in *Kankary* (Lahore, 1987), pp.90-104. See also, 'Ek bin likhi razmiyah' in *Gali Kuce* (Lahore, 1952), pp.193-221.

[11] The novelist's art is subjective by its very nature. All literary sources must therefore be treated circumspectly by historians. It must be remembered that they have been produced by tiny élites in 'traditional' societies. The great writers can of course transcend their own experiences and echo the feelings of other classes and communities. But lesser novelists lack this empathy and produce merely stereotypes and stylised emotional responses.

[12] The collection *Siyah Hashiye* is particularly noted for its irony and black humour. The short story entitled *Karamat* is typical. The miracle of the sweet water in a village well is really to be explained by the fact that a man drowned in it, while trying to hide a looted bag of sugar.

[13] The Progressive Writers' Movement was launched in London in 1934 before being established at Lucknow in April 1936. Krishan Chander was its General Secretary for a number of years. For further details see, H. Malik, 'The Marxist Literary Movement in India and Pakistan', *Journal of Asian Studies*, xxvi, 4 (Aug. 1967), pp.649-64.

[14] See especially his noted short story *Peshawar Express* translated in Mathur and Kulasreshtha *op. cit.*, p.69 & ff.

[15] Bhishan Sahni was born in 1915 in Rawalpindi. He was brought up in a devout middle class Arya Samajist family. He taught for a number of years at Delhi University College following Partition before spending time working as a translator in the Soviet Union. He has written widely in Hindi.

[16] *Tamas* was first published in 1974, the following year it received the prestigious Sahitya Akademi award. In 1988 it was dramatised for Indian television.

[17] K. Singh (ed.), *Partition of Punjab 1947* (Delhi, 1991).

[18] For the role of ex-INA men in organising Sikh *shahidi jathas* see *The Sikh Plan*, pp.17-29.

[19] *Ibid.*, (18) Report of Work in Mianwali District, L.A.R. File No. Lic/7, p.677.

[20] The *akali* leader Master Tara Singh emphasised that territory which contained Sikh religious places and property should not be included in Pakistan at any cost. *The Sikh Plan*, 26-7.

[21] S. Das, *Communal Riots in Bengal 1905-1947* (Delhi, 1991), p.199.

[22] Bapsi Sidhwa, *Ice-Candy Man* (London, 1989), p.199 & ff.

[23] Bapsi Sidhwa was born in Karachi, but brought up by her Parsee parents in Lahore. She has published a number of novels and has lectured in America. In 1975 she represented Pakistan at the Asian Women's Congress.

[24] B. Sidhwa, *Ice-Candy Man* (London, 1989), p.199 & ff.

[25] B. Sahni, *Tamas* (New Delhi, 1990), p.193 & ff.

[26] *Ibid.* (18), p.677.

[27] M. Hassan, *Azadike Caragh* (3rd ed., Lahore, 1986).

[28] Sahni, *Tamas*, p.137 & ff.

[29] M. Sharma and U. Vanjani, 'Remembrances of Things Past. Partition Experiences of Punjabi villagers in Rajasthan.', *Economic and Political Weekly*, 4 Aug. 1990, p.1731.

[30] See S. Das, *Communal Riots in Bengal 1905-1947* (Delhi, 1991), p.198.

[31] C.M. Ali, *The Emergence of Pakistan* (Lahore, 1973), p.274.

[32] R. Menon and K. Bhasin, 'Recovery, Rupture, Resistance. The Indian State and Abduction of Women during Partition', *Economic and Political Weekly*, 24 Apr. 1993, WS2-WS17.

[33] The novel centres around the abduction of Pooro by a young Muslim farmer who is avenging his own 'dishonour'. The novel was published in Punjabi in 1950. It has been translated by Khushwant Singh, *The Skeleton* (Delhi, 1984).

[34] Sidhwa, *op. cit.*, pp.183, 212-15, 260-62.

[35] Bedi was born into a lower middle class Punjabi family. He began his literary career in the 1930s and was associated with the progressive Writers' Movement, although he never fully conformed to its ideology.

[36] See (10) above.

[37] *Ibid.*, p.127.

[38] Muhammid Ali has rendered this into English in *Pakistan Review*, 13 (Apr. 1965), pp.33-4.

[39] *Ibid.*, p.34.

[40] The *muhajirs* dominated politics during the early years of Pakistan, more recently they have institutionalised claims to be Pakistan's fifth nationality through the MQM. See, T.P.Wright, 'Indian Muslim refugees in the politics of Pakistan' *Journal of Commonwealth and comparative Politics*, Vol XII (1975).

[41] Duggal is a leading author in Punjabi. He moved to Delhi from the Rawalpindi district at the time of Partition and is married to a Muslim.

[42] K.S. Duggal (trans. J. Ara) *Twice-Born. Twice-Dead* (New Delhi 1979).

[43] Duggal, *op. cit.*, pp.136-7.

[44] K. Iftikhar, *Jab Amritsar jal raha tha* (9th ed., Lahore 1991), pp.259-61.

[45] This has been translated into English by R.B. Haldane in the *Journal of South Asian Literature*, Vol 6 (1970), pp.19-23.

[46] *Ibid.*, p.23

[47] Nahal, *op. cit.*, pp.148-9.

[48] Intizar Husain was born in the Bulandshahr district of UP. and migrated to Pakistan in August 1947 cutting short his college career in Meerut.

[49] This is summarised in M.U. Menon, 'Partition Literature: A study of Intizar Husain', *Modern Asian Studies*, Vol. 14, no. 3 (1980), pp.377-410.

50 This is included in Husain's collection entitled, *Kankary* (Lahore 1987), pp.90-104.

51 Shahid' Ahmad was a member of the Progressive Writers' Movement who migrated to Pakistan in 1947. He has left behind a valuable autobiographical account of this period entitled, *Dihli ki Bipti.*

52 S. Ahmad, 'Dilhi Ki Bipta' in M.Shirin (ed.), *Zulmat-i-Neem Roze* (Karachi 1990), p.169.

53 A. Hameed, Foreword in Iftikhar, *op. cit.,* p.35.

54 *Ibid.,* pp.42-43.

55 A.S. Ahmed, *Discovering Islam: Making sense of Muslim History and Society* (London 1988), pp.159-60.

56 A. Abdullah Khan Rokri, *May awr Mera Pakystan* (2nd ed., Lahore 1985), p.76.

57 Shirin, *op.cit.,* p.157.

58 Duggal, *op.cit.,* pp.143 &136.

59 *Ibid.,* p.130.

60 This is found in the collection edited by Mumtaz Shirin, *op. cit.,* pp.315-52.

61 Shirin, *op.cit.,* p.339.

62 *Ibid.,* p.339.

63 These sentiments were expressed during the course of an interview with the researcher Tahima Farhi Manazar. This was published in M.M. Mirza and S. Bakht (eds), *Azadi ki Mwjahyd* (Lahore 1989), p.16.

64 For further details see, K Singh, *The Partition of Punjab* (Patiala 1972), p.151 & ff.

65 Nahal, *op.cit.,* p.368.

66 See, for example, K.S. Duggal (trans. J. Ara), *Twice Born. Twice Dead* (New Delhi 1979), p.11 & ff.

67 Prem Kirpal, *Spirit's Musings* quoted in P. Nevile, *Lahore. A Sentimental Journey* (New Delhi 1993) p.18.

'THE CHIEF SUFFERERS': ABDUCTION OF WOMEN DURING THE PARTITION OF THE PUNJAB*

Andrew J. Major

The insensate communal fury that engulfed the punjab at the time of the province's partition in August 1947 produced a human tragedy of almost unimaginable proportions. Starting with armed attacks on villages in the Multan and Rawalpindi districts in March, the violence escalated to a province-wide orgy of violence and plunder and a massive upheaval and evacuation of populations in August and September.[1] Although dedicated and courageous efforts were made by numerous agencies and individuals to stem the fury, it is difficult to deny Satya Rai's claim that this was a time when 'communal passions swept the whole Punjab community clean of all decency, morality and sense of human values'.[2]

The suddenness and ferociousness of the violence deranged the minds of many who witnessed it, embittered relations between the new Dominions of India and Pakistan and brought about a virtual, though temporary, collapse of government in the two new Punjabs. For these reasons the exact scale of the tragedy is highly debatable and probably will never be known. Estimates of the number killed and of those made refugees have differed widely, but a safe guess would seem to be around half a million and eleven millions respectively.[3] Even if there was general agreement on the validity of these two figures, however, it needs to be pointed out that the partition holocaust inflicted other, equally traumatic, human agonies that are at best mentioned but in passing in the standard accounts of 1947. It is, of course, undeniable that virtually all sections of Punjabi society could count among their kinsmen those who were uprooted, plundered, assaulted and murdered. And yet – as is so often the case in civil wars that are driven by ethnic or religious hatred and fear – it was women who were frequently singled out for especially humiliating treatment at the hands of men of the rival community: molestation, rape, mutilation, abduction, forcible conversion, marriage and death (the latter sometimes also inflicted by their own menfolk in order to save the 'honour' of women who were about to be maltreated). As Jawaharlal Nehru candidly observed to an Indian women's conference in December 1947, 'The last few months have seen terrible happenings in northern India and women have perhaps been the chief sufferers'.[4]

This essay looks at the abduction of women in the Punjab in 1947 and at the efforts made by the Indian and Pakistani governments during and after the partition

---

* The research for this paper was assisted by a grant from the Indian Council of Historical Research.

to recover and rehabilitate them. Some of the specialised accounts of the period, written shortly thereafter, touch on aspects of this topic, but only briefly and in a somewhat raw manner.[5] After several decades of silence, however, a more frank and sympathetic appraisal of women's suffering in 1947 is emerging. Not surprisingly, this has so far taken the form of a feminist reconstruction which contrasts the experiences of abducted women (as recorded in official and personal accounts) and the aims and expectations of a patriarchal Indian state determined to effect an honourable, post-partition reconstitution of the moral order.[6] Significant, too, is the recent publication of a compilation of partition stories, many of which – although fiction – clearly draw upon personal knowledge of abduction experiences.[7] As the half-centennial of partition approaches, it is possible that a more general catharsis of the public mind of today's two Punjabs will occur, resulting in the liberation of other, long-suppressed memories and information that will further augment the present historical record on the horrors of 1947.

II

Systematic communal outrages on women began in March 1947 in Rawalpindi district. There a number of Sikh villages were attacked over an eight-day period and, in addition to large-scale murder and looting, many cases of rape and abduction were reported.[8] In one village some ninety women committed suicide by throwing themselves into a well, while at another place thirty-two women were put to the sword by their own men when their capture by Muslim attackers was seen to be imminent.[9] Although a cross-communal Peace Committee was quickly established in Rawalpindi city to restore order, the violence only spread to the neighbouring Attock and Jhelum districts. All this, however, was only a curtain-raiser to the wholesale abuse of women that would occur throughout the province five months later.

At the height of the war of extermination (August and September), when the vast majority of rapes and abductions occurred, mob fury knew no bounds. Consider this account of the attack on the non-Muslim residents of Harnoli, a rich market town in Mianwali district, in September:

> More than half the population (being 6000 men and women and children) were massacred and burnt alive. Children were snatched away from their mothers' arms and thrown into the boiling oil. Hundreds of women saved their honour by jumping into wells or throwing themselves into burning houses... Girls of 8 to 10 years of age were raped in the presence of their parents and then put to death mercilessly. The breasts of women were cut and they were made to walk all naked in rows of five in the bazaars of Harnoli. About 800 girls and women were abducted and small kiddies were wandering without a cover in the jungles and were kidnapped by the passers-by.[10]

There is no reason to suspect that this report was exaggerated, or to think that it describes a one-off occurrence, because there are official and eyewitness reports of similar atrocities in many other districts.[11]

Apart from abductions that took place in the course of a mob attack on a village or targeted suburb, there was also the taking of women on a planned basis, particularly in situations where large numbers of refugees – disorientated and inadequately protected –were assembled or on the move. For instance, in Jhelum district women were separated from their menfolk and distributed among groups of Pathans, while in Gujrat district, where the number of abducted women was estimated at four thousand, women were openly taken from refugee trains.[12] And here is the statement of an observer who watched the progress of a refugee column marching out of East Punjab:

> I saw a long column of Muslim men, women and children proceeding from Kapurthala to Jullunder. The column was guarded by a few military sepoys. It was ten or twelve deep, the women and children walking in the centre, flanked on either side by men. Groups of armed Sikhs stood about in the fields on either side of the road. Every now and again one of these groups would make a sudden sally at the column of Muslims, drag out two or three women and run away with them. In the process they would kill or injure the Muslims who tried to resist them. The military sepoys did not make a serious attempt to beat off these attacks. By the time the column arrived at Jullunder almost all the women and young girls had been kidnapped in this manner.[13]

Where the Sikh *jathas* (war bands) did allow Muslim women to pass over to West Punjab, they frequently stripped them naked before releasing them.[14]

How are we to explain this widespread and horrific abuse of women? Since time immemorial, rape has been a prominent – seemingly inevitable – feature of war, a conscious process of maximising intimidation in a conquered people.[15] And in situations of civil war, where nearly every man is a soldier fighting for his homeland, women can come to be seen as 'territory' to be 'occupied'.[16] In such a context revenge can become a powerful motive (or excuse) for abuse of women. Yet it would seem to be quite wrong to regard the rape and abduction of Punjabi women in 1947 as a product merely of the anomie of the times, as an abnormal occurrence in a society undergoing severe temporary dislocation, for that would be to ignore the fact that violence against women is embedded in everyday relationships in this society. Recent studies have confirmed that 'power rape' – the raping of women in order to demoralise and defeat rival men in a patriarchal society – is particularly common in northern India.[17] Abduction is also conspicuous in the history of inter-clan rivalry in the Punjab: speaking of the turbulent Jat villages near the India-Pakistan border, a former Chief Justice asserted that 'thefts, dacoities, murders and abductions have always constituted the normal spare-time activity of the inhabitants'.[18] Referring to one Jat Sikh villager's raping of many Muslim refugee women in 1947, the same author writes that the rapist 'was not impelled by anger or a desire for revenge. For him it was a God-given occasion to do something he heartily enjoyed'.[19]

It should not be assumed from this that all Punjabi men seized the opportunity in 1947 to commit offences against women, for we have ample evidence of quite ordinary men risking their lives to rescue women who were in danger of being violated or killed. To give just one of several examples, Anis Kidwai, who was a social worker in the refugee camps in Delhi at the time, recalls an old Hindu Jat rescuing a Muslim girl in the face of hostility from his fellow villagers.[20] Nor should it be assumed that peasants were the only, or the worst, offenders, for men from all social classes were involved in rape and abduction. A former Liaison Officer who helped recover abducted women in Pakistan wrote of abductors, 'They did not belong to any single class. The rich as well as the poor were well represented'.[21] Ordinary villagers were certainly involved. Frequently this was just part and parcel of general looting – women being regarded as men's property. Thus in Bahawalpur state the Muslim peasantry was, according to Penderel Moon, generally less interested in blood than 'the quiet enjoyment of Hindu property and Hindu girls'.[22] Sometimes retaliation was a motive: for instance, in Sialkot district, women were abducted by refugee men whose own women had been taken by Sikhs in East Punjab[23], while Sikh leaders asserted that Sikh atrocities upon Muslim women and children were revenge attacks.[24] And where there existed a long-standing rivalry between clans, as between the Hindu Jats and Gujars and the Muslim Meos of the Gurgaon region, on the outskirts of Delhi, large-scale abduction and sale of girls seems to have been part of a systematic process of 'ethnic cleansing'.[25]

Men of influence, like deputy commissioners and police officials, often worked hard to prevent abductions or rescue the victims.[26] But, equally, such men often abused their authority to connive at, or participate in, the crimes. One Muslim member of the Legislative Assembly was said to have five hundred girls in his possession in West Punjab, while an abducted Muslim girl from a well-known family was reported to be with the Maharaja of Patiala.[27] In West Punjab police officials, members of the Muslim League and landed magnates were involved.[28] So too were the criminal elements, generally referred to as the *goondas* and *badmashes*. Describing the massacre of refugees at Kamoke, in Gujranwala district, on 24 September 1947, an Indian official wrote,

> The most ignoble feature of the tragedy was the distribution of young girls amongst the members of the Police Force, the National Guards and the local goondas. The S.H.O. [Station House Officer] Dildar Hussain collected the victims in an open space near Kamoke Railway Station and gave a free hand to the mob. After the massacre was over, the girls were distributed like sweets.[29]

Armed Pathans, operating in bands, were perhaps the worst offenders in West Punjab, especially in the districts of the Rawalpindi division (where they were concentrated), for it was they who systematically preyed upon the refugee trains and convoys, carrying off women to be sold for as little as Rs 10 or 20 to Muslim men.[30] Non-Muslim women from Kashmir also were offered for sale in West Punjab, sometimes ending up as 'slave girls' in factories.[31] A report from Sargodha district claimed,

The Pathans brought a very large number of abducted women and children from the Kashmir front and they had been selling these like cattle and chattel. There were cases in which a woman had been sold thrice or four times. The Pathans had made this a regular trade.[32]

By early 1948 the Pathans were getting so out of hand that they were even abducting Muslim women for sale, and special camps for them had to be opened by the Pakistan government.[33]

In East Punjab 'large scale' abduction of Muslim women was blamed on the Sikh *jathas* and on refugees from the west.[34] But here, too, the local police and military frequently participated in the abduction and distribution of women.[35] Anis Kidwai, later recalled what generally became of these women:

The better 'stuff' would be distributed among the police and army while the 'small coin' would be given to the rest [of the attackers]. After this the girls would go from one hand to another, and after being sold four or five times, would become showpieces in hotels, or they would be kept in 'safe-custody' in a house for the enjoyment of police officials.[36]

How many women and girls were abducted? The incompleteness and unreliability of the data make this a question impossible to answer accurately. Nehru, addressing India's Constituent Assembly on 29 November 1947, observed,

Women have been abducted by the thousands, not a few cases. Nobody knows the exact figures, but if you know the estimated figures, both for West Punjab and East Punjab, you will be staggered at the number ... thousands have been rescued, but tens of thousands still remain.[37]

Leonard Mosley, summarising the collective costs of the partition, writes of '100,000 young girls kidnapped by both sides, forcibly converted or sold on the auction block'.[38] But he does not give any source. At one time the Indian government thought there were 33,000 Hindu and Sikh women abducted in Pakistan, while Pakistan estimated that there were 50,000 Muslim women abducted in India; however, Gopalaswami Ayyangar (who headed the Indian delegation to the inter-Dominion conferences) later called these 'rather wild figures.'[39] In the next section of this essay a more realistic figure will be inferred from the data on reported recoveries of abducted women.

III

The understandable public indignation that was aroused by abductions demanded prompt and decisive action by the new, and already overburdened, governments of India and Pakistan. Nehru (whose private correspondence bag in the months of August to October 1947 was full of letters from people whose relatives were missing[40]) asserted in January 1948 that recovery of women was 'one of the most urgent' of the many problems being faced[41]; and his government declared 16-22 February 1948 to be Rehabilitation of Abducted Women and Children Week to give momentum to the task.[42] Leading political figures and their wives in both India and Pakistan appealed for public cooperation in this matter, and in May 1948 the two governments decided to use radio campaigns, mobile publicity vans attached with loudspeakers, and the assistance of the various religious authorities like *sajjada-nashins, maulvis, pandits* and *granthis* to spread the recovery message to the masses.[43]

Even earlier than this, however, the two governments had agreed on a common policy and a combined administrative effort regarding victims of abduction. Following one of their joint tours through the most riot-torn districts of the Punjab in early September 1947, Nehru and his Pakistani counterpart, Liaquat Ali Khan, declared that their governments would refuse to condone abductions or recognise the legality of forced marriages and conversions effected after 1 March 1947.[44] This declaration was ratified by an Inter-Dominion Conference in December which further established recovery procedure. The Central Recovery Offices of both countries were to compile the claims of relatives who had crossed the new border and send lists of names to the opposite side. There the local police were to have the prime responsibility for locating abducted women.[45] However, the police were to be assisted by District Liaison Officers (DLOs) appointed by the Liaison Agency of the opposite Punjab government to coordinate refugee evacuation, by social workers and by a limited number of 'guides' (relatives of abducted women). District transit camps for recovered women were to be established in both Punjabs with a central camp for non-Muslim women at Lahore and a similar camp for Muslim women at Jullundar. The Indian and Pakistani Military Evacuation Organisations (MEOs), which had been established following the disbandment of the Punjab Boundary Force, were to provide guards in transit camps and escorts for recovered women being transferred to their respective Dominions. Finally, on the Indian side, a steering committee made up of representatives of the various agencies involved would plan and review recovery work.[46]

Nehru's government was convinced that cooperation between the widest possible range of agencies and individuals, and not military force, was the key to speedy recovery.[47] For this reason the role of volunteer women social workers – among them close associates of Mahatma Gandhi, like Mridula Sarabhai, Rameshwari Nehru, Anis Kidwai and Dr Sushila Nayar – and welfare organisations was stressed. A squad of over one hundred women workers was organised to assist with recovery work, and many of these women operated in West Punjab. Volunteers from organisations like the National Council of Women, the International Red Cross and the Friends Service Unit were also involved.[48] Until September 1948 Pakistan also employed a small number of Muslim women social workers at district transit camps in East Punjab.[49]

However, this careful planning did not yield the anticipated results. Whereas the MEOs had completed the large-scale evacuation of refugees by mid-December 1947, the recovery of abducted women was painfully slow. Nehru commented in

January 1948: 'Neither side has really tried hard enough to recover them'.[50] And the Indian Chief Liaison Officer noted in April that 'very little work is being done in connection with the recovery of abducted women and girls throughout West Punjab. [The 13 Indian women workers posted there] along with their transport are, therefore, being practically wasted'.[51] What had gone wrong?

One problem was that Hindu and Sikh refugees in India, mistakenly believing that far more of their women had been abducted in West Punjab than Muslim women had been taken in the east, and that the Indian government was more concerned with the return of Muslim women to Pakistan than of non-Muslim women to India, mounted a public campaign to persuade Nehru's government to take a tougher line towards Pakistan on this matter, specifically by holding back recovered Muslim women as hostages.[52] Nehru firmly rejected this suggestion, arguing that it would likely be counter-productive.[53] Nevertheless, the two governments agreed in May 1948 to stop making public mention of the estimated figures of abducted women remaining unrecovered, with a view to cooling public passions.[54]

Rivalry between the new Dominions was another factor contributing to the slowness of recovery. When cooperation between the two Central Recovery Offices petered out, the Pakistanis claimed it was because of a widespread refusal of non-Muslims in India to take back their abducted women on the grounds that they had been 'defiled'.[55] Nehru acknowledged and denounced, in characteristically blunt terms, this 'objectionable and wrong attitude'[56] of some of his countrymen. But his government also accused the Pakistani authorities of being uncooperative.[57] In January 1948 Pakistan rejected the earlier proposal that MEOs be associated with recovery work, and barred the entry of Indian officials to those West Punjab districts that adjoined the disputed Kashmir territories.[58]

In the districts the recovery officials faced many problems. Exceptionally heavy rains, which caused deep floods over wide areas of West Punjab, hampered recovery work.[59] Locating and rescuing abducted women was sometimes relatively easy, in that the disapproving families of the abductors informed on them, or the women themselves made a dash for freedom when the recovery parties made an appearance. But, equally, sympathisers in the village could warn the abductors of the approach of the rescuers; and, for this reason, small children playing outside the village were often a great asset in recovery work.[60] On rare occasions recovery work could be downright dangerous. In May 1948 a Sikh police constable, searching for abducted Muslim women in a village near Amritsar, unwittingly took shelter in the house of a landowner who had several abducted women with him, and in the night the constable was murdered by the landowner out of fear that his own case be exposed.[61]

Even when the whereabouts of an abducted woman was known, rescuing her was often difficult. In West Punjab abducted women were frequently moved about (so that several 'raids' had to be made to recover a single victim) or were sent to tribal areas or districts from which Indian officials were banned.[62] Another widespread complaint of Indian officials was that abductors who possessed influence were being shielded by the local police. For example, the DLO at Multan reported of one 'landed magnate' who had led the abduction of many women and children, 'I have moved for his arrest but for political considerations he is not being touched'.[63] The Chief Liaison Officer also reported :

> The general feeling amongst the Muslims in West Punjab is against the recovery of women and children who are with Muslims. Police officers in various districts have openly declared that it is their duty to see that proper regard is paid to public opinion.[64]

Even in Delhi, where the bureaucracy was supposedly more rigorous in recovering abducted women, the police were for a long time reluctant to search the homes of the rich and influential, and most women recovered were rescued from poor non-Muslim families.[65]

But perhaps the most perplexing problem of all was the reluctance of many abducted women to be rescued.

> A girl said to the D.L.O., 'How can I believe that your military strength of two sepoys could safely take me across to India when a hundred sepoys had failed to protect us and our people who were massacred?' Another said, 'I have lost my husband and have now gone in for another. You want me to go to India where I have got nobody and of course you do not expect me to change husbands every day'. A third said, 'But why are you particular to take me to India? What is left in me now – religion or chastity [?]'[66]

In East Punjab the majority of a group of one hundred and seventy-five Muslim women recovered from Patiala state refused to leave their new homes and threatened to commit suicide if they were forcibly repatriated; forty-six of them escaped from the transit camp in which they were being held.[67]

Such reluctance to be rescued and repatriated was a far from simple thing. No doubt some of these women were influenced by the fear of rejection by their families; many non-Muslim women would seem to have been told by Pakistani authorities that they would be murdered by their own people if they went to India.[68] Others must have been burdened by a personal sense of shame and guilt that we can only imagine. They had been raped (often by more than one man). They had often been impregnated or inflicted with venereal diseases[69]. Once their recovery became a strong possibility, hundreds of them had been tattooed on their hands or chests with slogans like 'Pakistan Zindabad' (Long live Pakistan) or, in the case of Muslim women, the names of their abductors and the dates of their abduction (the abductor's final insult, perhaps, to the opposite community).[70]

But others had clearly adjusted to their new, and often materially better, life or, having become mothers, did not wish to abandon their children. A small percentage of abductors, it must be said, were lovers and protectors, rather than bestial rapists. 'This type of affection', reported a former Liaison Officer, 'has been reciprocated by the girls and some of them fell in love with their abductors. Their sobs even after the third day of their recovery are still a nightmare'.[71] Since the two governments were committed to restoring all abducted women to their 'rightful' (communally-defined) homeland, recovery work thus sometimes involved breaking up happy families and relationships. On the Indian side this in turn produced a sharp difference of opinion among women social workers, in particular between Rameshwari Nehru (who saw forcible recovery as state-sponsored re-abduction) and Mridula Sarabhai (who believed that the Indian state had a moral duty to recover every single abducted woman).[72] In the end, and after public concern had been raised on the matter, especially the problem of children abandoned by repatriated women, the Indian and Pakistani governments agreed in 1954 that such women should not be forcibly repatriated.[73]

Between 6 December 1947 and 27 April 1948 some 3,912 non-Muslim women and children were recovered from West Punjab, with an estimated 11,430 more still to be recovered. The number of Muslim women recovered from East Punjab during the same period was 7,495.[74] To June 1948 the numbers of women recovered from Pakistan and India were 5,270 and 8,344 respectively.[75] This painfully slow rate of recovery continued until 30 November 1948 when the East Punjab Liaison Agency was closed, along with the Central Recovery Office associated with it. Thereafter the recovery work was conducted by the external affairs ministries of India and Pakistan. In 1949 the Indian parliament passed the Abducted Persons (Recovery and Restoration) Act which remained in force until 30 September 1957.[76] By 31 October 1952 the numbers of abducted women and children recovered from Pakistan and India stood at 8,326 and 16,545 respectively; by 30 September 1957 they had risen to 10,007 and 25,856.[77]

Thus by 1957 a total of 35,863 abducted women and children had been recovered. A few of these were persons abducted from areas lying outside the Punjab, and some – perhaps one-quarter – were children who had been abducted along with their womenfolk or had been born after the abduction of their mother. However, we also have to take into account the at least equivalent number of women who were reported or assumed murdered but in fact were abducted and never recovered, were privately rescued by their families, or were unwilling to be recovered. In the end, therefore, the total number of women abducted during the partition riots in the Punjab in 1947 probably stands at 40-45,000, with roughly twice as many Muslim women as Hindu and Sikh women having been taken. The East Punjab government claimed that the higher figures for recovered Muslim women represented the greater diligence and honesty of rescue work in East Punjab.[78] But this is clearly not a complete explanation, especially in view of the military precision with which the Sikh *jathas*, equipped with rifles and automatic weapons, attacked the Muslim refugee trains and columns in August and September 1947.[79]

The great majority of rescued women were, it would seem, fairly quickly re-united with their families and gladly welcomed by them, contrary to earlier propaganda. Understandably, most meetings between fathers and daughters or husbands and wives were extremely emotional, with many girls breaking down in tears. But not all, as a former Liaison Officer reported:

> The less sensitive ones ... started prattling as soon as they met, the girl complaining to her husband against the abductors as if they were his next-door neighbours who had misbehaved during his absence in the fields and who should now be brought to book.[80]

To attend specifically to the needs of women and children whose relatives had all been killed or could not be traced, the Indian government set up a women's section of the Ministry of Relief and Rehabilitation (under the honorary directorship of Rameshwari Nehru, until her resignation in July 1949 over the issue of forcible recovery), and between 1947 and 1953 some twelve homes and infirmaries were opened for the rehabilitation of these women who, being mostly illiterate and unskilled, represented 'the most helpless victims of the tragedy of partition'.[81]

Because the records of India's Ministry of Relief and Rehabilitation have yet to be opened to independent scholars, we have little idea of the experiences that abducted women had either in transit camps before their restoration to their families or in homes and infirmaries before their possible re-integration into society. All that we do have, with the exception of the standard and dry, semi-official accounts[82], are some fragmentary and depressing references to women in transit camps being treated like criminals or untouchables (and, in consequence, behaving as such)[83], being re-abducted and given away for marriage[84], or being raped by their guards (who, in at least one instance, were their co-religionists[85]). At one time Hindu, Sikh and Muslim recovered women were kept together in the same camp and, according to Mridula Sarabhai, found mutual understanding in their shared experiences.

> It was a heart-rending experience to hear them talk to each other. Whether they were Hindus or Muslims or Sikhs it did not matter. They talked as woman to woman, baffled, humiliated, stunned and full of doubts for the future. Why had they been made victims of brute force was the question that puzzled them. Their common suffering created greater understanding.[86]

IV

The experience of abducted women was typified in the following accounts.

> On the 18th August, 1947, I came to the village Babakwal with my father and other relations, for fear of life. On the 24th/25th August night about 20,000 Muslims attacked Babakwal with the help of the Muslim Military. They killed about 3,000 Hindu and Sikh residents of the town and abducted 200 Hindu and Sikh ladies. I was one of them. Myself, Lilawanti, daughter of Labha Shah, and Parkash, daughter of Dayal Chand, along with nine others were taken by Fateh, and he kept us in his house. He kept us there for 12 days. After that he sold us off to different persons. He sold me to Ghulam Mohd. of village Karaul. Ghulam Mohd. kept me for 1 months. I was put to great insult and hardship. Being tired of life I sent a message to Bawa Singh of Rattanpura. Bawa Singh, who had become a Muslim, paid Rs. 140 to Ghulam Mohd. and brought me to his house. About 8-9 days ago he brought me to his house with the aid of Military (Hindu). Bawa Singh brought me to Sir Ganga Ram Hospital day before yesterday, i.e., 19-10-1947. I was brought to D.A.V. College Camp. As I was confined to bed I was spared badfeli [rape]. The other girls were badly raped in my presence. The treatment is most horrible to remember.[87]

My father was a teacher at Mirpur. We had left our village and had gone to Mirpur to seek shelter from the disturbances which had started in March last. When the raiders came we, the people of Mirpur, ran and at Akalgarh the Muslim Military surrounded us and they sorted out young girls. Abdur Rahman captured me and took me to Sakhrana, Tahsil Kahuta. I was married to him at Sakhrana and lived with him as his wife for one month. The police visited Sakhrana and found me out and took me to Rawalpindi Camp. I was lodged in the camp at Rawalpindi for a month and ten days, when I was brought to Lahore with Pandit Nihal Chand. There are 48 girls in the Camp at Rawalpindi. The Muslims who visited the camp to meet the girls to whom they are married usually threatened them that if they go to India they would be killed by the Sikhs and Hindus and thus warned them that they should not express their willingness to be evacuated.[88]

During the partition riots of 1947 a large number of women were abducted in both West and East Punjab. Forcibly separated from their menfolk, and often raped before their eyes, these unfortunate women were then taken away to be kept by their abductors or sold and married to other men. A few of these women were well treated, and in some cases even voluntarily surrendered, by their abductors; but for most the entire experience was one of pain and humiliation. Even when they reached the relative security of the transit camps, they could be subjected to the further shame of molestation by their guards.

Although *goondas*, Pathans and members of Sikh *jathas* played a significant role in the abduction and sale of women, they were not the only participants in this sordid business: all classes of Punjabi men would appear to have been involved. The widespread collapse of law and order in 1947 was attended by a collapse of moral values, or perhaps in some cases an intensified expression of normal, immoral behaviour, so that large numbers of men – from illiterate peasants and artisans to landlords and political leaders – lost their sense of humanity and deliberately trampled on the virtue of women whose only 'crime' was that they belonged to a different religious community.

Recovery of abducted women was an urgent task for the new governments of India and Pakistan. They moved quickly to declare a joint policy and establish administrative machinery for recovery. Rising tensions between the new Dominions, especially over the status of Kashmir, undermined this combined firmness of purpose, however. Meanwhile, in the districts, recovery officials were impeded and frustrated by a number of difficulties. As a result, recovery of abducted women was painfully slow and incomplete. How many women were not restored to their families is something we probably never will know.

Notes

1   Detailed (but one-sided) accounts of these events are given in Gopal Das Khosla, *Stern Reckoning* (rep. New Delhi, 1989) and Gurbachan Singh Talib (comp), *Muslim League Attack on Sikhs and Hindus in the Punjab 1947* (rep. New Delhi, 1991). Khosla's work draws upon material provided by the Fact Finding Commission established by the Indian government's Ministry of Relief and Rehabilitation in 1948. The Pakistani representative at the UN Security Council had charged India of genocide of Muslims in East Punjab, so the Commission was established to collect statements of refugees from West Punjab to prove that non-Muslims were maltreated there. Talib's work was compiled for the SGPC (the elected committee that oversees the management of historic Sikh temples) to refute Pakistani charges that the Sikhs had a plan for the annihilation of Muslims in the event of partition.

2   Satya M. Rai, *Partition of the Punjab* (London, 1965), p. 257.

3   Percival Spear, *A History of India*, Vol. 2 (Middlesex, Harmondsworth, reprint 1968), p.238.

4   S Gopal (gen. ed.), *Selected Works of Jawaharlal Nehru* [hereafter *SWJN*](2nd series, Vols 4-14, New Delhi, 1986-1993), Vol. 4, p. 660.

5   Both Khosla's *Stern Reckoning* and Talib's *Muslim League Attack* have accounts and incomplete figures on abduction; Rai's *Partition* has a brief section on the recovery and rehabilitation aspects.

6   Urvashi Butalia, 'Community, State and Gender: On women's Agency during Partition': *Economic and Political Weekly*, Vol. XXVIII, no. 17, 24 Apr. 1993 (see also *Oxford Literary Review*, Vol. 16, nos 1-2, 1994); Ritu Menon and Kamla Bhasin, 'Recovery, Rupture, Resistance: Indian State and Abduction of Women during Partititon' *Economic and Political Weekly*, Vol. XXVIII, no. 17, 24 Apr. 1993.

7   Alok Bhalla (ed.), *Stories About the Partition of India*, 3 Vols (New Delhi, 1994).

8   Khosla, *Stern Reckoning*, Appendix II: Tables and Statements, pp. 343-4.

9   S.P. Mookerjee Papers, 2nd instalment, no. 95, pt 1 Nehru Memorial Museum and Library [hereafter NMML], New Delhi ; Akhil Bharat Hindu Mahasabha Papers, M-17, 1947, NMML.

10 Report of K.C. Kalsa, District Liaison Officer Mianwali, n.d.: Kinpal Singh (ed.), *Select Documents on Partition of Punjab* [hereafter *SDPP*] (Delhi, 1991), 9 no.231.

11 Khosla, *Stern Reckoning*, SDPP, chap. IV. Penderel Moon, who was working in south-west Punjab at this time, heard numerous stories of 'sickening outrages' like mutilation and rape: *Divide and Quit* (London, 1962), p. 262.

12 Publications Division, Ministry of Information and Broadcasting, Government of India, *After Partition* (Delhi, 1948), pp. 45-6.

13 Quoted in Khosla, *Stern Reckoning*, p. 289. For another report on this incident, see an extract from sitrep. no. 248 from Chief Central Officer, Kotwali, Lahore, n.d., in Sir Francis Mudie Collection, Mss Eur., F 164/17, National Archives of India [hereafter NAI].

14 Lord Mountbatten Papers, File 129, Bulletin no. 4, 21 Sept. 1947, NMML.

15 Susan Brownmiller, *Against Our Will: Men, Women and Rape* (Toronto, 1975), chap.3.

16 Simona Sharoni, 'Every Woman is an Occupied Territory: The Politics of Militarism and Sexism and the Israeli-Palestinian Conflict', in *Journal of Gender Studies*, Vol. 1, no. 4, Nov. 1992.

17 Rehana Ghadially (ed.), *Women in Indian Society: A Reader* (New Delhi, 1988), pp.149, 196-200.

18 G.D. Khosla, *The Murder of the Mahatma: And Other Cases from a Judge's Notebook* (London, 1963), p.167.

19 *Loc. cit.*

20 Begum Anis Kidwai, *Azadi Ki Chhaon Men* (Hindi edn trans. from Urdu by Nur Nabi Abbasi, New Delhi, 1990), pp. 140, 309-11. (I am grateful to Gyanesh Kudaisya for assisting with the translation of this work); also interview with Mrs Subhadra Joshi, New Delhi, 3 May 1994. Mrs Joshi was a prominent Congress political worker who was among those who sought to protect Muslim life and property in Delhi in 1947.

21 Kulwant Virk, 'Recovering Abducted Girls in Pakistan', *The Tribune* (Lahore), 25 May 1948.

22 Moon, *Divide and Quit*, pp. 194, 262.

23 *SDPP*, no. 202.

24 Joint Statement by Master Tara Singh and Oodham Singh, n.d.: Mountbatten Papers, File 131 B, NMML.

25 Kidwai, *Azadi*, pp. 139, 309-10; S.P. Mookerjee Papers, 2nd instalment, no. 95, pt 1, NMML.

26 *SDPP*, nos 224, 232.

27 *SWJN*, Vol. 4, p. 76, n. 4; Vol. 8, pp. 154-5.

28 *SDPP*, nos 219, 224, 229.

29 Report of Chaman Lal Pandit, Fact Finding Officer, New Delhi, n.d.: *SDPP*, no.225.

30 *After Partition*, p. 46; SDPP, no. 219.

31 *Tribune*, 29 Dec. 1947.

32 Report of work in District Sargodha, no author, n.d.: *SDPP*, no. 232.

33 Cabinet Secretariat Circular No 314/C.F/49, 31 Dec. 1947: Mountbatten Papers, File 131 F, NMML; *Tribune*, 12 Jan. 1948, 6 Feb. 1948.

34 Telegram Foreign, Karachi to Foreign, New Delhi, 27 Aug. 1947: Mountbatten Papers, File 129, NMML; interview with Mrs Subhadra Joshi, New Delhi, 3 May 1994.

35 'Report on East Punjab Situation,' by Col. M. Sher Khan, Ad. H.Q. M.E.O. Pakistan, Amritsar, 24 Sept. 1947: Mudie Collection, Mss Eur., F 164/15, NAI.

36 *Azadi*, pp. 141-2; for a report on 'immoral traffic' in abducted and refugee women in Delhi hotels and restaurants, see Government of India, Ministry of Home Affairs, Police Section, File no. 8/22/48 - Police, NAI.

37 *SWJN*, Vol. 4, p. 196.

38 Leonard Mosley, *The Last Days of the British Raj* (London, 1961), p. 244.

39 *Tribune*, 16 Dec. 1949.

40 Khosla, *Stern Reckoning*, pp. 233-4.

41 *Hindustan Times* report, 17 Jan. 1948: *SWJN*, Vol. 5, p. 113.

42 Nehru's inauguration speech, 14 Feb. 1948, *ibid*, pp. 115-7.

43 *Tribune*, 8, 19, 20, 21 Feb., 7 May 1948.

44 Rai, *Partition*, p. 81.

45 *SDPP*, no. 174.

46 Rai, *Partition*, pp. 81-3; *SDPP*, nos 197, 204.

47 *SWJN*, Vol. 4, p. 196.

48 'Recovery of Abducted Women up to 15th July 1948', by Rameshwari Nehru (Director, Women's Section, Ministry of Relief and Rehabilitation, Government of India), n.d.: Rameshwari Nehru Papers, report no. 1, NMML; *SWJN*, Vol. 5, pp. 113, n. 2, 118, 122-3; Donald F. Ebright, *Free India: The First Five Years* (Nashville,

Tennessee, 1954).

49   *Tribune*, 21 Feb., 21 Nov. 1948.

50   Nehru to Rajendra Prasad, 22 Jan. 1948: *SWJN*, Vol. 5, pp. 113-4.

51   CLO (India) to Chief Secy, East Punjab, 29 Apr. 1948: *SDPP*, no. 219.

52   For example, Papers Relating to East Punjab Hindu Sabhas: copy of resolutions passed at General Meeting of Arya Samaj, Ferozepore, 17 July 1949: Akhil Bharat Hindu Mahasabha Papers, P 117, 1948-49, NMML; All India Refugee Conference, Delhi, 14 Dec. 1952, Resolution no. 15, 'Abducted Women': Delhi Police Special Branch (non-current records), 3rd instalment, no. 65, NMML; *SWJN*, Vol. 12, p.147, n.3.

53   Nehru to Mohanlal Saksena, 21 July 1949: *SWJN*, Vol. 12, p. 148.

54   *Tribune*, 22 May 1948.

55   Mosley, *Last Days*, p. 244, n. 1.

56   See n. 41 above.

57   For example, Nehru's cable to Liaquat Ali Khan, 3 Dec 1947: *SWJN*, Vol. 4, p. 358.

58   *SWJN*, Vol. 5, pp. 114, n. 3; 116, n. 4.

59   *SDPP*, nos 220, 230.

60   See n. 21 above; Kidwai, *Azadi*, p. 139.

61   *Tribune*, 10 May 1948.

62   *SDPP*, nos 219, 227.

63   Report of Kewal Krishnan, n.d.: *SDPP*, no. 229.

64   See n. 51 above.

65   Kidwai, *Azadi*, p. 308.

66   See n. 29 above; also Ebright, *Free India*, p. 52.

67   *SWJN*, Vol. 5, pp. 117-21.

68   See n. 29 above.

69   Out of 3, 577 Muslim women received at the Jullundar central transit camp. to July 1948, 135 were pregnant (29 virgin pregnancies) and 417 had V.D. Such cases were given 'medical care': 'Recovery of Abducted Women up. to 15th July 1948', n. 48 above. Anis Kidwai also believed that 'many girls have become victims of dreadful sexual diseases', and that some went insane: *Azadi* p. 319.

70   Kidwai, *Azadi*, pp. 156-7.

71   See n. 21 above. Kidwai tells several similar stories, *ibid*. See also Mridula Sarabhai, 'Abducted Women', *Tribune*, 16 Apr. 1948.

72   Menon and Bhasin provide a fuller treatment of this aspect : see n. 6 above.

73   *SDPP*, p. xxxiv.

74   See n. 51 above.

75   *After Partition*, p. 68.

76   *SDPP*, pp. xxxiii-iv.

77   Rai, *Partition*, pp. 86, 87, n. 46.

78   *Ibid.*, p. 87.

79   For correspondence on this between C.M. Trivedi, the governor of East Punjab, and Swaran Singh, the East Punjab Home Minister, see Mountbatten Papers, File 130 A, NMML. In Nov. 1947 Swaran Singh declared in the East Punjab Assembly that he wished to see 'a gun in every deserving hand in the East Punjab so that every Punjabee acts as a defender of this land of ours and uses his gun for protecting the honour of our sisters and daughters', *Tribune*, 5 Nov. 1947.

80   See n. 21 above.

81   Rai, *Partition*, pp. 87, 142-4.

[82]   For example, P.N. Luthra, *Rehabilitation* (Publications Division, Ministry of Information and Broadcasting, New Delhi, 1972) and U. Bhaskar Rao, *The Story of Rehabilitation* (Department of Rehabilitation, Ministry of Labour, Employment and Rehabilitation, Delhi, 1967).

[83]   Kidwai, *Azadi*, pp. 153-6.

[84]   In Sept. 1948 the Delhi Police intercepted the correspondence of the general secretary of the Gurdwara Parbandhak Commitee, Delhi Province, that suggested that Sikh girls in various Delhi transit camps were being abducted and married to Hindus: Delhi Police Special Branch (non-current records), 2nd instalment, no. 26, NMML.

[85]   *SDPP*, no. 224.

[86]   Sarabhai, 'Abducted Women', *Tribune*, 16 Apr. 1948.

[87]   Recorded Statement of a Hindu woman, reproduced in Talib (comp.) *Muslim League Attack*, appendix XIII.

[88]   Recorded Statement of a Hindu girl, aged 13, reproduced in ibid, appendix XX.

FROM DISPLACEMENT TO 'DEVELOPMENT': EAST PUNJAB COUNTRYSIDE AFTER PARTITION, 1947-67

Gyanesh Kudaisya

Introduction

In April 1951, more than three years after the traumatic events of partition, Diwan Chaman Lall, a pre-eminent public figure from Lahore and a parliamentarian and diplomat in independent India, was asked to speak on the subject of 'The Fate of the Punjabee Nation'. In his speech he declared:

> We have not only been uprooted – seven million of us – but all that we cherished has been destroyed, the sanctity and refuge of our homes, the little soil most of us owned, whitened in the past with the sacred bones of our ancestors, the tradition of the mohalla, the city, the village, the biradiri and the leadership – all things which were part and parcel of our existence, nay, which made our existence endurable and pleasant and happy – all that is finished for us. Like the fallen autumn leaves in the wind or bits of stray newspaper flying hither and thither in the blown dust, those who have come away safe in limb and mind are without any bearings and without any roots.[1]

His speech echoed the sentiments of loss and despondency which most Punjabis experienced after partition. His words, in particular, contained a ring of truth for the several million refugees who were faced with the challenge of rebuilding their lives and overcoming the diminished circumstances in which they found themselves. However, as these words were being spoken, processes of reconstruction and rebuilding were well underway to restore to the truncated province some of its lost glory. This chapter makes an attempt to study how these processes of reconstruction and resettlement worked in East Punjab in the years following partition. As the majority of the displaced persons were agriculturists, it provides an account of how the problem of rural rehabilitation was addressed and the manner in which the East Punjab countryside was resettled after the upheaval of partition.

Post-partition East Punjab countryside

Although communal violence began to intrude into the Punjab countryside several months before partition actually took place, and by March 1947 the scale of violence and its ferocity was such that several thousands in the Lahore and Rawalpindi districts were forced to leave their villages for refugee camps in towns, there was still very little talk of migration among the agricultural classes. To them the idea of leaving their hearths and homes appeared to be fantastic and incredible. From several accounts it becomes apparent that for most of the rural population which was displaced, the traumatic period of uncertainty of whether to go or not was relatively short and that the ultimate decision was often made abruptly. M. S. Randhawa, ICS, who in 1949 became the Director General of Rehabilitation in East Punjab, recalls that,

> the fatal decision was not delayed as the ring of death and destruction closed in from all sides....The hand that was sowing the seed in the fields in the morning was hurriedly packing in the afternoon...When at the time of evacuation the farmers yoked their bullocks to the carts which formed their miles long caravans they looked wistfully at their houses, granaries full of wheat, and orchards of oranges which they had planted with so much care.[2]

When their world turned upside down, the refugees, especially in the villages, were completely unprepared for the enormous calamity of displacement which had befallen them.[3]

To East Punjab they headed for safety and rehabilitation. But East Punjab was not well positioned to offer help and succour. Land for cultivation was in short supply in the recently truncated province, and there existed a wide disparity in its economic resources and those of West Punjab which made the problem of rural rehabilitation even more daunting. Partition left East Punjab with severe disabilities in the areas of irrigation, roads, commerce, etc.[4] Perhaps the most serious was the disadvantage it faced in irrigation.[5] West Punjab retained the prosperous canal colonies which included about seventy per cent of the fertile canal irrigation tracts of undivided Punjab and the huge revenue that accrued from these. West Punjab also retained fifty-five per cent of the population, sixty-two per cent of the area and controlled over sixty-nine per cent of the income of undivided Punjab. The best cotton and wheat producing areas of the canal colonies went to Pakistan and, in terms of food-grains alone, East Punjab was faced with an annual deficit of 35,000 tonnes. While the 'exchange of population' was almost even between the two parts of the Punjab, there remained a wide disparity in East Punjab in the land available for cultivation. As against the sixty-seven *lakh* acres of land abandoned by Hindu and Sikh landholders of West Punjab, only forty-seven *lakh* acres of evacuee land were available in Indian Punjab, including the princely states.[6] However, what was still worse from the point of view of East Punjab was the great disparity that existed in the quality of land and the lack of irrigation facilities there.[7] The Hindu and Sikh refugees had left behind forty-three *lakh* acres of irrigated land against only thirteen *lakh* acres of irrigated land evacuated by the Muslims of East Punjab.[8]

The rural refugee population which came from West Pakistan was made up of a number of groups and castes and it may be helpful to sketch the differentiated profile of each of the major groups. It was estimated that one out of every five rural refugees who migrated into East Punjab came from the canal colonies, while the other four came from other areas of West Punjab, Sind and the North West Frontier Province. Out of these four, two were self-cultivators, while two belonged to non-cultivating groups who possessed land. Among the refugees from the canal colonies included the Doaba Sikh Jats, the Kambohs, Dogras and, not the least, the Jat Sikhs who were traditionally regarded as industrious, sturdy and capable farmers. Among the non-canal colonists were the Jat Sikhs of the Manjha region, the Wirk Jats from Sheikhupura, the Manns from Gujranwalla, the Bawjas and Kehlons from Sialkot, the Rai Sikhs from Montgomery and the Sainis from Sialkot. A significant section of the refugees also came from the non-cultivating groups of Khattris and Aroras, who were scattered widely across the Punjab as shop-keepers and money-lenders.[9]

As we have seen, almost twenty per cent of the rural refugees came from the canal colonies. Here it may be worthwhile to briefly recall the story of the canal colonies in the years between 1885 and the 1940s when a massive expansion of agriculture took place in West Punjab due to the construction of canals in the districts of Lyallpur, Montgomery, Lahore, Multan and Sargodha.[10] This led to large-scale colonisation of land by the so-called 'martial races' and, in turn, to the creation of what Imran Ali calls 'a truly hydraulic society, whose patterns of dominance and subordination are pervaded by the fact that the water that sustains cropping comes not from the heavens but from human agency and human control'. This expansion of agriculture triggered a process of migratory settlement in the districts of West Punjab and provided 'a major demographic outlet' to the less fertile areas of East Punjab. From the 1890s onwards, in particular, large groups moved from East Punjab to the canal colonies to take advantage of the unprecedented growth in agricultural production in what became one of the largest irrigation systems in the world. Ali estimates that from 1885 till the end of British rule canal-irrigated areas, the bulk of which were situated in West Punjab, increased from under thirty *lakh* acres to around one hundred and forty *lakh* acres. He shows that between 1891 and 1941 the overall average rate of growth of population for the entire province was fifty-two per cent. However, in the case of the canal colonies, the rates of population increases were significantly higher. For instance, the population of Jhang, Multan, Shahpur and Sheikhupura districts rose by over one hundred per cent, while Montgomery's population rose by two hundred and nineteen per cent and Lyallpur district's by a massive two thousand two hundred and fifteen per cent.

The canal colonists thus had a history of migration and had proved their mettle as pioneers by breaking virgin soil and transforming it into what Malcolm Darling called 'one of the richest agricultural tracts in the whole of India, perhaps even in Asia'. Because large-scale migrations took place between the late-1880s and the 1920s, there remained a very large number among the partition refugees who had themselves been a part of the earlier wave of migrations or whose fathers had moved from East Punjab to the canal colonies. They had, therefore, been the great beneficiaries of the agricultural growth encouraged by irrigation. It was thus a great irony that they were in 1947 forced to abandon the prosperity for which they had worked hard, and found themselves returning to their ancestral villages in East Punjab as refugees.[11]

Early Relief Measures

Even while refugees were pouring into East Punjab in the latter part of 1947, it became apparent that the two-way migrations were going to be permanent. Initially, the contingency plans that were drawn up by administrators addressed problems of decongestion of relief camps, where most refugees were sheltered, and their dispersal not only within East Punjab but also in the surrounding provinces and princely states.[12] It was decided on 15 September 1947 that rural refugees should be temporarily settled on evacuee land and that each family be given a plough unit, regardless of its holdings in Pakistan.[13] It was also decided that refugees from particular districts of Pakistan should be settled together, as far as possible, in district-wise clusters. These steps, it was hoped, would avoid over-population in the border districts and moreover achieve a somewhat even distribution within the province. These measures were widely publicised. Even before a large number of refugees actually crossed the boundary line fixed at partition, they were told which particular district of East Punjab they should go to for temporary settlement. It thus became possible, at least temporarily, for displaced persons to be surrounded by their kinsmen and village folk, and this contributed in some measure to their 'psychological rehabilitation'.[14]

At the same time it was also decided that the temporary allotment of evacuee land should be done on the basis of groups of families, rather than single households or individuals.[15] During the migrations there had been a tendency among friends, relatives and kinsmen to collect together in small groups to cope with the prevailing insecurity and uncertainty. Relief administrators found it beneficial to deal with groups rather than individuals. Working in groups also created a sense of *biradari* and provided a semblance of security to the uprooted in their new and insecure surroundings. Moreover, it enabled individuals and families to pool together family labour, bullocks, ploughs and other agricultural implements.[16] This temporary allotment of evacuee land came as a measure of relief for the rural refugees. Its unique feature was that no discrimination was made between landholders and tenants, who were entitled to equal treatment. A large number of landless labourers and village artisans also got possession of land under this scheme, and this led to a certain levelling of hierarchies in rural society.

But mere allotment of land was not enough either for restoring the shattered agricultural economy of the Punjab or for rehabilitating the refugees. The cultivators who had been put on land still needed help. Their first need was to buy food which was no longer easily available in rural areas. Since it took almost six months for the raising of their first crops, they needed cash help to buy food. They were thus provided with food loans which were disbursed at the rate of Rs 3.5 per adult and Rs 2 per child per month. However, due to the dislocation of trade, conditions of scarcity widely existed in the countryside. Relief administrators, therefore, had to open retail shops in the larger villages for the supply of wheat. This help was provided till 1949 by when Rs. 8.2 million had been disbursed in the form of food subsidies. Finance was also provided for the purchase of bullocks for cultivation, and camels in the dry districts of Hissar and Gurgaon. In all over Rs 11 million were disbursed between 1947 and 1951 to enable the farmers to acquire livestock. Assistance was given too for the purchase of fodder for animals, and for seeds which were made available through government seed depots. Likewise, credit was provided for the purchase of agricultural implements, Persian wheels and well-gears. Artisans such as cobblers, carpenters, iron-smiths, weavers and leather workers received loans to enable them to re-establish their old trades and to restore the supply of goods produced by them.[17]

Help was also needed by the refugees in the area of housing. The partition disturbances had caused such extensive damage to houses, public buildings and wells that the authorities were forced to 'regard housing as a national problem of utmost urgency'.[18] It was estimated that thirty-four per cent of evacuee homes in East Punjab villages had been damaged beyond repair while only forty-seven per cent were intact. In the case of wells only sixty-two per cent were found to be in working order; loans and grants being given to villagers to undertake their repair as well as to reconstruct houses. In overall terms, all these measures went a long way towards rebuilding the rural economy of the Punjab.[19]

A field-survey undertaken in early 1948 in a village near Ludhiana provides us with a snapshot of the conditions that prevailed in the East Punjab countryside following the temporary allotment of land.[20] Conducted at Jamalpur village on the outskirts of Ludhiana city, the survey highlighted the enormous difficulties which the refugee settlers experienced in the new lands allotted to them. According to the survey, the village of Jamalpur had 2,536 acres of evacuee land, which was distributed under the group allotment scheme among one hundred and eighty-nine families, producing an average holding of 12.67 acres. However, as only 1,600 acres were of cultivable quality, in actual terms, the average size of holding per family came to only 8.4 acres. As each holding was typically made up of four types of land – *bet chachi, bet darani, budhi* and *dhatur* – it was of uneven quality and was scattered at several places. The survey further reported that group allotment created problems of cohesion and conflict of interest among the members. It also led to difficulties in the equitable distribution of work-loads and the sharing of responsibility. Further, the survey found a severe shortage of livestock which greatly hampered the cultivation effort.[21] In overall terms, it reported conditions of extreme hardship and urged the government to provide a fuller supply of livestock and agricultural implements and to evolve 'some effective machinery of self-administration within each group' to ensure the success of temporary allotment.

From the findings of this survey and from the thousands of petitions which it had received from the refugees, the government of East Punjab knew that the temporary allotment of land could only be a crisis response, and longer-terms measures for rehabilitation were urgently needed.[22] The government wanted to decongest the refugee camps which had sprung up in practically every town. Moreover, there existed the threat of a serious food crisis, especially at a time when the government was faced with the direct additional responsibility of providing for the several *lakhs* of refugees who were sheltered in its relief camps.

Government officials were naturally anxious that the fields abandoned by the Muslims in East Punjab should not lie uncultivated during the autumn and they, therefore, implemented the scheme of temporary allotment on a war footing.[23]

Towards Permanent Resettlement: 'Standard Acres' and 'Graded Cuts'

In the temporary settlement of refugees, no consideration had been given to their previous land-holdings, and it soon became clear that a revised scheme had to be formulated. In February 1948 the East Punjab government announced a new scheme aimed at a semi-permanent allotment of land.[24] This went some way towards meeting peoples' expectations that they would be given land according to the size of their former possessions in Pakistan. Most landholders were convinced that the extent of their earlier holdings must determine the future allotment of land. While a large number of refugees were in possession of evidence regarding their lands, the government had either no revenue records or incomplete records for most of the villages which had been evacuated during the partition massacres. In such a situation the only source of information on land ownership and claims to land were the refugees themselves who were invited to submit claims upon which a permanent scheme of resettlement could be drawn. The filing of these claims took place during March-April 1949, and in all 517,401 households or families submitted these.[25] Inevitably, in the absence of revenue records, these claims contained a certain amount of exaggeration. To get the true picture, it was decided to convene *panchayats* of particular villages. By a due process of enquiry, the revenue staff was finally able to obtain a fairly accurate picture of the precise extent of land ownership.[26] Radhawa , who was closely involved with the process of rural rehabilitation, recalls that 'in this work of verification of land claims, the *panchayats* played an extremely useful role' and 'displayed their traditional honesty and fearlessness'.[27]

By the middle of 1949 relief administrators in East Punjab had done the necessary groundwork to formulate the blueprint of a scheme of permanent rehabilitation.[28] The linchpin of the new scheme was the invention of the concept of the 'standard acre'.[29] Since people had to be settled across the whole of East Punjab where great diversity existed in terms of soil, irrigation, rainfall and productivity, there existed a compelling need to evolve a common measure to facilitate the allocation of land. It was with this in view that the concept was developed by Sardar Tarlok Singh of the Indian Civil Service, who was Punjab's first Director-General of Rehabilitation.[30] The 'standard acre' represented a unit of value based on the productivity of land. An acre which could yield ten to eleven *maunds* of wheat was given the value of sixteen *annas* and termed one 'standard acre'.[31] The physical area of the 'standard acre' thus varied and every piece of cultivable land in rural Punjab was given a valuation in *annas*, so that it could be measured easily in 'standard acre' terms.[32] In the dry districts of Hissar and Gurgaon where the valuation of one acre was only four *annas*, four physical acres went to make a 'standard acre', while in the canal-irrigated parts of the province where the value of an acre was full sixteen *annas*, an ordinary physical acre was the equivalent of a 'standard acre'.[33]

Another feature of the scheme was the attempt, as far as possible, to resettle persons from particular areas in Pakistan in specific districts. Many canal colonists who had originally migrated from East to West Punjab were able to return to their ancestral districts. Thus landholders from Lahore and Montgomery were settled in Ferozepur, while those from Rawalpindi, Sheikhupura and Gujranwalla were settled in Karnal. The refugees from Shahpur and Gujarat were allotted land in Ambala, while those from Multan were allotted land in the south-eastern districts of present-day Haryana. Those from Jhang found themselves being settled in Rohtak, while refugees from Dera Gazi Khan and Mianwali were given land in the dry district of Gurgaon. Similarly, provision of land for people from Sialkot was made in Hoshiarpur, Gurdaspur and Amritsar districts.

There was a great urge among the refugees to re-create their old village conditions and to revive the social ties which had bound them together. Although this demand for village-wise allotment was incorporated in the new scheme of permanent settlement, practical considerations nevertheless dictated that, as far as possible, those already settled on temporary allotments should not be disturbed. Administrative expediency dictated this freezing of temporary allotments which became a sort of a guiding principle in the new scheme.[34] While the refugees were broadly settled district-wise, and within these districts, as far as possible, village-wise, village communities, as they had existed before the partition, could never really be fully recreated and their disruption was a serious social and cultural loss to Punjab.

Another key feature of the new scheme was the concept of 'graded cuts'. Underlying this concept was the desire of resettlement administrators not so much to compensate the refugees, as to rehabilitate them economically and socially. They were inspired by the ideal of creating peasant proprietorship and encouraging the agriculturists to work hard to stand on their own feet. They thus formulated a scheme of 'graded cuts' incorporating the concept of the 'standard acre'.[35] According to this scheme, refugees were classified according to the size of their holdings in Pakistan expressed in 'standard acre' terms. Each category was then subjected to a scale of 'graded cuts', based on which the net entitlement of the refugee was arrived at. The scale of 'graded cuts' was worked out as follows:

Table I: Basis of Permanent Allotment of Land to Refugees

Grade (Standard Acres)	Rate of Cut (per cent)	Net Allotment (Standard Acres)
Up to 10	25	7.5
10 to 30	30	21.5
30 to 40	40	27.5
40 to 60	55	36.5
60 to 100	70	48.5
100 to 150	75	61
150 to 200	80	71

200 to 250	85	78.5
250 to 500	90	103.5
500 to 1000	95	128.5

Source: Randhawa, *Out of the Ashes*, p. 99.

By late 1949 the scheme of permanent allotment was ready for implementation, and in the winter months two hundred and fifty thousand allotment orders were issued. The relationship between the cultivator and his land is at the best of times an intense one and, not surprisingly, a very large number of applications were received containing appeals and requests for redress of grievances.[36] Efforts were made to consider these sympathetically, and this was followed by the revision of allotment orders and the actual delivery of land which was completed in early 1951.

Long-Term Effects

The gigantic scale upon which these land transfers took place had long-term repercussions for the rural society of the Punjab and Haryana region. According to Randhawa the innovation of 'graded cuts' only represented a compromise between extreme socialist views, which totally ignored the ownership of land and emphasised only the rehabilitation aspect, and the views of the displaced landholders themselves who desired full compensation for the land which they had been forced to abandon. Nonetheless, the changes which took place as a result of the massive land redistribution were very significant.

Among other things, they led to a levelling of large holdings and the eradication of absentee landlordism. Very large land-holdings in the East Punjab countryside were almost eliminated. A few examples of this may be considered. The largest landowner among the displaced persons was Mrs Vidyawanti who lost a total area of 11,582 acres in thirty-five villages in lieu of which she got an allotment of 835 acres in Karnal district, while Trilok Chand, another big landlord, left behind 5,328 acres in Lyallpur district for which he was given only 313 acres. Big landlords were thus substantially dispossessed of their large holdings.

The middle farmers also suffered, particularly with respect to the quality of land upon which they were settled. The planners of the scheme knew from their past experience that it was the middle farmer, with an average holding of ten to thirty 'standard acres', who represented the best skills of the Punjabi peasantry; and he, therefore, needed to be protected. On the resources of the small farmers the cuts worked very harshly. In overall terms the new scheme acted as a sort of 'shock therapy' to the agriculturists.[37] It forced the big farmers to take to cultivation themselves rather than live as absentee landlords, and made the middle and small farmers more industrious. At the same time, it provided an opportunity for mobility at the lower end of the spectrum, as efforts were made to give small plots to even the poorest rural households.[38]

In a technical sense, the rural refugees in East Punjab had been settled upon land on a permanent basis by late 1951, and we can conveniently conclude the Punjab story with that year.[39] However, these land transfers had far-reaching consequences which we must consider. What follows, therefore, is a survey in very broad terms of some of the developments of the 1950s and 60s.

Consolidation of Holdings

The immense scale of property transfers between 1947 and 1951 gave an irreversible impetus to another development which again had a far-reaching result – that of consolidation of agricultural holdings or *chakbandi*. Before partition agricultural holdings in the Punjab, as in other parts of the country, were scattered and fragmented.[40] A farmer owning a few acres of land may have his holdings scattered in ten or twelve tiny pieces. In some cases the plots were so narrow that, due to insufficient space, even bullocks could not be harnessed to plough them. Much land was also wasted in embankments and boundaries. Canal irrigation was impossible on scattered plots and wells could not be sunk due to their small size. Moreover, the laws of succession were such that, after each generation, further sub-division of holdings occurred. This process had gone on for several generations and had produced a severe fragmentation of agricultural holdings. Although the British had tried to promote consolidation for several decades, and in 1936 had even enacted the Punjab Consolidation Act, progress in this area had been extremely slow. By 1948 only about seven hundred thousand acres of land had been consolidated. However, the disruption caused by the partition and the pressing need to rebuild the rural economy of the Punjab necessitated that the work of consolidation of holdings be speeded up, and indeed undertaken on a war-footing.[41] As a result, the East Punjab Holdings: Consolidation and Fragmentation Act was enacted in 1948 which introduced an element of compulsion.[42] Thereafter, progress in consolidation work was rapid.[43] In 1951-52 alone over 1.7 *lakh* acres of land was consolidated, and by the year 1965-66 over 220.84 *lakh* acres of land had been consolidated across the Punjab.[44]

The manner in which consolidation of holdings transformed the Punjab countryside can be seen from Map I (page 85) which shows the changed landscape of a village before and after consolidation. From this map the advantages which consolidation offered are fairly obvious. It was reckoned that the increase in agricultural production due to consolidation alone, without involving any change in technology, was in the region of twenty-five per cent. In particular consolidation enabled a large area of waste land to be brought under cultivation which could be given to landless groups, Harijans and village artisans.[45] The most beneficial effect of consolidation was, however, that it enabled farmers to sink tube-wells on their holdings. In 1950 Punjab practically had no tube-wells, but by 1978 their number had risen to over 570,000. Thus consolidation of holdings led to significant changes in the pattern of irrigation as farmers were able to use sub-soil water for cultivation. They were also able to enjoy the benefits of canal irrigation. There occurred too a large increase in the total cultivated area which had previously been lost in embankments and field-bunds. All these changes provided a sound basis for the introduction of intensive agriculture in the Punjab. By 1969 both Punjab and Haryana had already achieved one hundred per cent targets in the consolidation of holdings of their cultivable land.[46]

New Irrigation Infrastructure

A parallel development which took place in the 1950s with far-reaching consequences for agriculture related to the building of the Bhakra-Nangal dam. The idea of the Bhakra project had a long history. In November 1908 Sir Louis Dane, the then Lieutenant Governor of Punjab, had felt that Nangal could be an ideal site for a dam. The first plan in this regard was made in 1911 and later revised in 1919. Following this, in 1927 an expert committee was set up to further examine the question but no real progress could be made. The idea of the Bhakra dam was then revived by the Unionist Party politician Chhotu Ram when South-East Punjab faced a severe drought in 1938, but again nothing eventuated. Then in 1945-46 detailed feasibility and design studies were carried out. Yet still the idea of the Bhakra dam, at least four decades old, had not taken off beyond the drawing board. It was only after partition and the consequent displacement of millions of people that it was felt that an ambitious multi-purpose project like the Bhakra dam could help mitigate the sufferings of refugees and facilitate the rehabilitation process.[47] After 1948 the implementation of the Bhakra project was, therefore, undertaken as an urgent task.[48] The construction of the dam, the second highest in the world, took fifteen years, and when in 1963 it was completed it had cost Rs. 2385 million.[49]

Let us briefly consider the tremendous impact which the Bhakra-Nangal project made on the agricultural economy of the region. It provided surface irrigation through canals to over three and a half million acres of land. But more importantly, it created the capacity to supply over 4,000 million units of electricity.[50] The power which became available as a result gave an impetus to the large-scale installation of tubewells in the whole of the Punjab and Haryana region. It is estimated that by 1990 there were about 7.5 million tubewells in the country, out of which the largest number was concentrated in Punjab and Haryana. Farmers found that tubewell irrigation based on the exploitation of ground-water had many advantages over surface irrigation, as it did not involve expenditure on storage of water and its transport. It avoided the loss of land needed to build canals and distributaries and saved costly and complicated systems of water distribution and drainage which are needed in canal irrigation. Tubewell irrigation also gave the farmer total control over the availability of water and he did not have to depend upon large bureaucracies. In addition, the rapid progress of rural electrification played a key role in transforming the economy of the Punjab region. It aided greater mechanisation of agriculture, with the farmers relying increasingly upon the use of pumping sets, threshers and fodder-cutters.

Punjab on the Threshold of Prosperity

From this survey it can be seen that by the early 1960s most rural refugees had not only settled in the Punjab and Haryana region but had also attained a certain level of prosperity.[51] The process of their rehabilitation had transformed the face of agriculture in the Punjab and led to what may be regarded as the earliest and most comprehensive land reforms in India after independence. The immense land transfers which took place due to partition gave rise to new patterns of land-holdings. The concepts of 'standard acre' and 'graded cuts' ensured that people ended up with economically viable holdings located at one site which could be used for intensive cultivation. Furthermore, the remarkable progress in the consolidation of fragmented holdings led to a substantial increase in agricultural productivity. The overall result was that most farmers ended up with sizes of holdings which permitted economies of scale. The sizes of their holdings also permitted the exploitation of sub-soil irrigation methods in an area of Punjab where canal irrigation was minimal. The Bhakra-Nangal scheme provided means of surface irrigation to an additional 3.5 million acres of land. But, more importantly, it generated electricity which the farmers were able to harness for energising their tubewells. All these developments firmly laid the foundations of intensive agriculture in the Punjab.

In this narrative of rural rehabilitation perhaps one last point needs to be made. This relates to the spirit of enterprise and energy displayed by the refugees in rebuilding their lives and restoring their shattered fortunes. Behind the transformation of agriculture in the Punjab lay the tremendous creative energy which the Punjabi farmers displayed after partition. P.N. Thapar, ICS, who as the Financial Commissioner of the Punjab Government was closely involved with rehabilitation work, observed in October 1951 that the newly-settled farmers 'are working harder and producing more than they were doing in West Punjab'. He added that 'a visit today to an average refugee tract fills us with deep admiration for the Punjab peasantry' whom he complimented for 'the robust common sense and the determination...to stand on their own feet again'.[52] Kusum Nair, who in 1958-59 conducted a field survey of agriculture, found great misery and poverty in the different states of India which she visited. However, in the Punjab she found that the refugee farmers were energetic and restless.[53] It was this restlessness, together with the risk-taking and innovative ability of the refugee farmers, which enabled them to make significant changes in their methods of irrigation and farming. Thus, when the 'miracle seeds' of the 'Green Revolution' arrived in India in 1966-67, it was in the Punjab that they found fertile fields and farmers with eager faces ready to sow them.

The story of the 'Green Revolution' is too well-known to be recounted here.[54] Basically, the production of wheat increased from 11.39 million tonnes in 1966-67 to 16.54 million tonnes in 1967-68 and by 1970-71 was 26.40 million tonnes. Production continued to increase throughout the 1970s and in 1978-79 stood at 30.58 million tonnes. So, once again, the Punjab had re-established itself as the bread-basket of the country, and the refugees who had settled there stood at the threshold of unprecedented rural prosperity.

Conclusion

In retrospect it would appear that the refugees who came into East Punjab could be settled on land with considerable success. The process of their settlement involved large-scale land transfers which led to the earliest and most comprehensive land reforms that took place in independent India. The reconstruction of the agricultural economy, the creation of an irrigation infrastructure and, not the least, the enterprise and energy shown by the refugee farmers laid the foundations of intensive agriculture in East Punjab and, in less than two decades, the region stood at the threshold of the unprecedented rural prosperity ushered in by the 'Green Revolution'.

It is perhaps important to recognise how distinctive were the developments that took place in East Punjab following partition. The achievements relating to reconstruction and resettlement in East Punjab appear even more remarkable when set against three contexts which were comparable but produced divergent outcomes. The first context relates to the challenge which West Bengal faced after partition in the area of refugee rehabilitation – a theme addressed in detail in another chapter which shows how official attempts to resettle the Bengali refugees failed appallingly. The second context is that of land reforms in independent India. The land redistribution measures implemented during the crisis situation which East Punjab faced after partition were unique. They stand in sharp contrast to attempts at land reforms in other states of India, most notably Bihar.[55] Several studies have shown that elsewhere in India the implementation of land reforms proved to be highly problematical and, in many instances, could never fully be carried out. The East Punjab experience of land redistribution and consolidation stands in sharp contrast to the rest of India in this regard. Last, but not least, it is worthwhile to take a look at the parallel experience of West Punjab, the 'twin' from which East Punjab was separated in 1947. The above discussion has shown how in the decades following partition, East Punjab was able to overcome the disadvantages it faced in natural and infrastructural resources and was substantially able to rebuild its rural economy. Recent research has shown that, in sharp contrast, West Punjab lagged behind in comparative agrarian performance and development.[56] In spite of the fact that West Punjab was more richly endowed at the time of partition, it was overtaken by East Punjab in almost all key respects such as the overall rate of agricultural growth, farm output, degree of mechanisation, per capita consumption patterns and literacy levels.[57] Undoubtedly, the foundations of the prosperity which East Punjab has enjoyed since the late 1960s were laid in the struggle against the hardships which had accompanied partition.

Map I: Consolidation of Agricultural Holdings in a Punjab Village

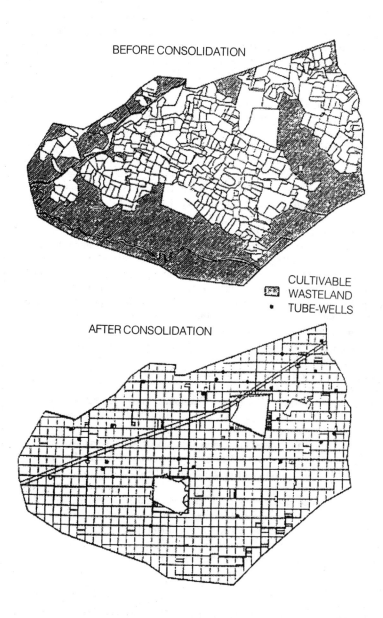

BEFORE CONSOLIDATION

CULTIVABLE
WASTELAND
• TUBE-WELLS

AFTER CONSOLIDATION

Courtesy: Indian Council of Agricultural Research, New Delhi

Notes

1   'The Fate of the Punjabee Nation', speech on 30 Apr. 1951, in Diwan Chaman Lall Papers, Subject File 1A 'Speeches', Nehru Memorial Museum & Library (NMML), New Delhi. Diwan Chaman Lall was born in 1892 and was educated at Oxford and qualified as a barrister from Middle Temple. He founded the All India Trade Union Congress in 1920. He was MLA (Central) 1924-31 and 1945-48; MLA, Punjab 1937-45; Member of the Constituent Assembly of India 1945-48; Indian Ambassador to Turkey 1949-50; and thereafter Member of the Rajya Sabha in the 1950s and 60s.

2   M S Randhawa, *Out of the Ashes , An Account of the Rehabilitation of Refugees from West Pakistan in Rural Areas of East Punjab* (Bombay, 1954), pp.25, 33.

3   For vivid accounts of the trauma and human tragedy that faced the refugees, see their numerous petitions available in several collections of private papers, e. g. Syama Prasad Mukherjee Papers, File nos 158, 183, 186A in NMML. Also see Margaret Bourke-White, *Halfway to Freedom: A Report on the New India in the Words and Photos of Margaret Bourke-White* (New York, 1949). Accounts of individual and family misfortunes are best reflected in Hindi, Urdu, Punjabi and Sindhi literature. For anthologies of these, see Mushirul Hasan (ed.), *India Partitioned: The Other Face of Freedom*, Vol. I (New Delhi, 1995) and Alok Bhalla (ed.), *Stories About the Partition of India*, Vols I-III (New Delhi, 1994).

4   In this discussion the area described as Punjab or East Punjab includes the province of East Punjab and PEPSU (the Patiala and East Punjab States Union) formed after partition in 1947. At the time of the linguistic reorganisation of the states in 1956 PEPSU and Punjab were merged, and thereafter in 1966 two separate states of Haryana and Punjab were formed. In other words, the term Punjab or East Punjab refers to the region constituting the present day Indian states of Punjab and Haryana.

5   Aloys Arthur Michel observes that, as a result of partition, 'each country was forced to devise a fundamental reordering of the irrigation system' of what was one of the largest integrated irrigation networks in the world. See A.A. Michel, *The Indus Rivers: A Study of the Effects of Partition* (Yale, 1967), p. 67.

6   A *lakh* is the equivalent of 100,000.

7   On these aspects, see V.V.S. Tyagi, 'Economic Impact of Partition on Indian Agriculture and Related Industries' (unpublished Ph.D Thesis, American Univ., Washington, 1958).

8   The precise figures are 2,711,386 hectares abandoned by Hindu and Sikh landholders in West Punjab as against 1,902,024 hectares evacuated by the Muslims of East Punjab and PEPSU. In terms of irrigated land, the precise figures are 1,022,044 hectares of land left behind by Hindus and Sikhs in Pakistan as against 308,990 hectares of irrigated land left behind by the Muslims in East Punjab. Also see C. N. Vakil, *Economic Consequences of Divided India: A Study of the Economy of India and Pakistan* (Bombay, 1950), especially chs II and III.

9   For a detailed description of the various communities and groups displaced from West Punjab, see Randhawa, *Out of the Ashes*, chs 4-5.

10   Imran Ali, *The Punjab Under Imperialism, 1885-1947* (Delhi, 1988), p.viii. This paragraph largely draws upon Ali's work.

11   For a narrative of how a family from one of the canal colonies was affected by displacement, see Darshan S. Tatla, 'The Sandal Bar: Memoirs of a Jat Sikh Farmer', paper presented in the Panel on Partition of Punjab and Bengal at the 14th European Conference on Modern South Asian Studies, Aug. 1996, at Copenhagen (mimeographed).

12 'A Skeleton Scheme for Rehabilitation' dated 3 Nov. 1947 by S K Kriplani, ICS, Secretary, Ministry of Relief and Rehabilitation, Government of India.

13 Tarlok Singh, 'Rural Resettlement in Punjab (I): The Background: A Transfer of Population', *Statesman* (New Delhi), 25 July 1950.

14 Randhawa, *Out of the Ashes*, p.5.

15 See Tarlok Singh, *Land Resettlement Manual for Displaced Persons in Punjab and Pepsu* (Simla, 1952),'especially ch.1.

16 However, group allotment did not enjoin individual allottees to cultivate their lands jointly. If an individual wanted to cultivate his share separately, he was given the right to do so.

17 See Randhawa, *Out of the Ashes*, especially pp.120-31 for details.

18 'A Plea for Improved Structures', Note by K. L. Luthra, 14 Jan. 1948, Diwan Chaman Lall Papers, Subject File 2B.

19 In all, rupees four *crores* and forty *lakhs* were disbursed by the government in the form of loans, grants and *taccavi* advances, Tarlok Singh, 'Restoring an Economy Dislocated by Partition – Changing Social Conditions', *Statesman*, 28 July 1950; also see his *Land Resettlement Manual*, pp.7 and 25-6.

20 'Settlement of Evacuees on Land', Note by K. L. Luthra, Research Officer, Economic Advisor's Office, Punjab, no date, Diwan Chaman Lall Papers, Subject File 2B.

21 Before partition Jamalpur village had 294 bullocks, whereas at the time of the survey, no more than 100 bullocks were found. Likewise, before partition there were 121 dry and 119 milch cows, whose number had now been reduced to only 25 milch cows.

22 'Rebuilding a New Punjab', *Tribune*, 1 Mar. 1948.

23 By Dec. 1947 as many as 190,155 families had been temporarily allotted 2,072,852 acres of cultivable evacuee land, and by February the number of beneficiaries had increased to 238,216 families who had been settled on 2,581,819 acres of land. Tarlok Singh, *Land Resettlement Manual*, p.5.

24 'Press Communiqué by the East Punjab government, 7 Feb. 1948', cited in Tarlok Singh, *ibid.*, pp 28-9. It was announced that land would be allotted under the new scheme only to those who were either owners, occupancy tenants and tenants. The intention of the government to impose 'graded cuts' was also made clear and the deadline of 31 May 1948 was set. Also see 'New Scheme of Rehabilitation in East Punjab', *Tribune*, 12 Mar. 1948 for details of the government's plans.

25 Severe penalties were imposed for making false claims. A person making a false or exaggerated claim was liable to punishment with rigorous imprisonment extending up to five years, or to a fine up to Rs 5000 or both.

26 The technical and procedural aspects involved in the exercise of land claims and their assessment and verification are described in great detail in Tarlok Singh, *Land Resettlement Manual*, pp.30-78.

27 Randhawa, *Out of the Ashes*, p.74.

28 In the mean time, the governments of East Punjab and West Punjab also took the steps to exchange copies of the surviving revenue records of the evacuee villages on both sides of the border. These provided some statistical basis for the formulation of the new scheme of rehabilitation in East Punjab.

29 See Tarlok Singh, 'The Standard Acre: Unit of Value for Land Allotment', *Statesman*, 26 July 1950.

30 Born in 1913 Tarlok Singh was educated at the London School of Economics and joined the ICS in 1937. In 1940 he conducted a field survey of nine villages of Hissar district, and in 1943 was posted as the Colonization Officer of Nilli Bar Colony in

West Punjab. Between 1944-46 he worked for the Finance Department of the Government of India, and thereafter served briefly as Private Secretary to the Interim Prime Minister during 1946-7. In 1945 he published *Poverty and Social Change: A Study in the Economic Reorganization of Indian Rural Society* (London, 1945). With such a background, he perhaps became a natural choice in 1947 for the newly-created position of Director General of Rehabilitation in the government of East Punjab. He continued in this position till December 1949 and then joined the Planning Commission where for the next 17 years he was involved in the formulation of several five-year national plans, first as a civil servant and then as a full-fledged Member.

[31] *Anna,* i.e. 1/16 fraction of an Indian rupee.

[32] See Tarlok Singh, 'Valuation of Fields: Methods of Allocation', *Statesman*, 27 July 1950.

[33] The characteristics and elements incorporated in the criteria adopted for the valuation of land are explained in Tarlok Singh, *Land Resettlement Manual*, ch. III. The details about the grading of land and its valuation in 'standard acres' for each tehsil are also provided in pp.283-304 of the *Manual*.

[34] On these issues, see Randhawa, *Out of the Ashes*, pp.109-18.

[35] See 'Principles of Allocation', pp.80-9 and pp.321-322 in Tarlok Singh, *Land Resettlement Manual* on the technical aspects of the scheme of graded cuts.

[36] In all over 100,000 applications were received requesting for revisions in allotments: out of these 33,000 requests were admitted and the necessary modifications made.

[37] Consider the change in the circumstances of Gobind Ram Sikka, a refugee from Sargodha. In a memorandum entitled: 'Miracles of the Punjab Re-habilitation in the Indian Republic', Sikka complained bitterly against the diminished circumstances in which he found himself. He claimed that, prior to partition, his family jointly owned 186 acres of agricultural land in West Punjab in lieu of which he had been allotted 99 acres on a quasi permanent basis in Ambala district. He previously had several wells in addition to non-perennial channels to irrigate his lands, but had now been given *barani, banjar jandid, banjar qadim* and even *ghair-mumkin* lands. Further, Sikka claimed that, while his family previously exercised full proprietary rights, such rights were denied now. To aggravate the situation, the land allotted to him belonged to evacuee Indian Muslims who contested possession and refused to relinquish their claims. See Memorandum by Gobind Ram Sikka, Mochpura Bazar, Ludhiana, no date, in S. P. Mookherjee Papers, File No. 161.

[38] See Tarlok Singh, 'Rural Resettlement in the Punjab after Partition' in his *Towards An Integrated Society: Reflections on Planning, Social Policy and Rural Institutions* (New Delhi, 1969), pp.213-35. Also see Randhawa, *Out of the Ashes*, pp.202-17.

[39] It is significant that by the early 1950s most refugee grievances in East Punjab related not to agricultural resettlement but to compensation for lost property, both movable and immovable. See, for example, Resolutions of the All India Refugees' Convention, Ludhiana, 3-4 June 1950, organised by Sharnarthi Sabha, Ludhiana, and the Resolutions of the All India Refugee Convention, 29-30 July 1950, Delhi, held under the Presidentship of Purshotam Das Tandon, S. P. Mookherjee Papers, File No. 37.

[40] On the benefits and consequences of land consolidation, see Jeffrey P. Bonner, *Land Consolidation and Economic Development in India, A Study of Two Haryana Villages* (New Delhi, 1987).

[41] 'Compulsory Consolidation of Holdings in East Punjab', *Tribune*, 12 Mar. 1948.

[42] See M. S. Randhawa, 'Consolidation of Holdings', June 1954, in *Kurukshetra, A Symposium on Community Development in India* (1952-55) (New Delhi, 1955), pp.124-30.

43 Under the 1948 Act village advisory committees were formed to advise on all matters concerning consolidation of land and, in particular, on the classification and valuation of fields and the preparation of village consolidation schemes.

44 See *Punjab on the March* (Chandigarh, 1967).

45 See *Resurgent Punjab* (n.p.p., 1956).

46 This was in sharp contrast to many other states such as Bihar where, as late as by 1969, only 6.77% of the total cultivable area had been consolidated. For details see F. Tomasson Jannuzi, *Agrarian Crisis in India, The Case of Bihar* (London, 1974).

47 'Demand for the Completion of Bhakra Dam', *Tribune*, 14 Mar. 1948

48 See K. N. Raj, *Some Economic Aspects of the Bhakra Nangal Project* (New Delhi, 1960). Raj observes: 'The considerations advanced in favour of the project were many. The most important of them were that it would assist in the drive to expand food production in the country, compensate to some extent for the loss of the irrigated areas of the Punjab as a result of the Partition, help to re-establish the refugees in this area, and promote the economic development of the whole of the region extending beyond the Punjab', p.2.

49 Vandana Shiva, *The Violence of the Green Revolution, Third World Agriculture, Ecology and Politics* (Goa, 1991), p.122.

50 K. N. Raj concluded his 1960 study with the observation: 'Apart from the desirability of promoting regional development, without going too much by calculations of costs and returns, the Bhakra Nangal project has given hope and confidence to the millions of people who were uprooted by the partition of India and had to be rehabilitated in this region', *Some Economic Aspects of the Bhakra Nangal Project*, p.125.

51 I am conscious that refugee rehabilitation in north India was not confined to the states of Haryana and Punjab. For instance, in the Terai region in Uttarakhand in Uttar Pradesh, large-scale agricultural colonization was undertaken to resettle Punjabi refugees. Constraints of space prohibit me from considering this story in detail and restrict my focus to the Punjab region where the main challenge of rehabilitation lay. For details of Terai colonization, see B. H. Farmer, *Agricultural Colonization in India Since Independence* (London, 1974).

52 P. N. Thapar, 'Foreword', in Tarlok Singh, *Land Resettlement Manual*, pp.ii-iii.

53 Kusum Nair, *Blossoms in the Dust, the Human Element in Indian Development* (London, 1961).

54 The literature on the 'Green Revolution' is fairly large. For an early view, see Francine R. Frankel, *India's Green Revolution, Economic Gains and Political Costs* (Bombay, 1971). M. S. Randhawa's *Green Revolution – A Case Study of the Punjab* (New Delhi, 1974) provides an optimist's view. The best introduction to the field is B. H. Farmer, 'Perspectives on the "Green Revolution" in South Asia' in *Modern Asian Studies*, Vol. 20, no. 1 (1986), pp.175-99. For analyses of changes brought about by the Green Revolution in different regional contexts, see Tim P. Bayliss-Smith and Sudhir Wanmali (eds), *Understanding Green Revolutions, Agrarian Change and Development Planning in South Asia, Essays in Honour of B. H. Farmer* (Cambridge, 1984).

55 On the problems which India has faced in the area of land reforms, see F. Tomasson Jannuzi, *India's persistent dilemma: the political economy of agrarian reform* (Boulder, 1994). More generally, on the crucial importance of land reforms for agricultural development, see Clifford T. Smith, 'Land reform as a pre-condition for Green Revolution in Latin America', in Bayliss-Smith and Wanmali (eds), *Understanding Green Revolutions*. The extreme case here is that of Bihar where

land reform measures have failed completely. Tom Jannuzi in his study of land reforms in Bihar observes: 'Nowhere in contemporary India is the gulf between articulated ideals with respect to agrarian reforms and accomplishment more conspicuous than in Bihar'. He further writes: 'Not only has Bihar failed to implement agrarian reforms, the misery and poverty of her landless labourers, share croppers and small farmers are extreme even in a country where per capita incomes are less than one hundred dollars per annum. To live at the margins of subsistence is the way of life for the majority of Bihar's peasantry. In real terms this means that some customarily need to consume undigested grain picked from the excrement of cattle as they struggle for survival'. See Jannuzi, *Agrarian Crisis in India, The Case of Bihar*, pp.7-9.

[56] In her study Holly Sims remarks: 'The Punjabs provide almost laboratory-like conditions of comparability, for they share virtually identical agro-ecological conditions, a common language and cultural traditions, and a legacy of institutions developed under colonial rule'. Holly Sims, *Political Regimes, Public Policy and Economic Development: Agricultural Performance and Rural Change in Two Punjabs* (New Delhi, 1988), p.18.

[57] Holly Sims shows that for two decades after partition, agricultural productivity was modest in both Punjabs and crop production grew by about 3 per cent annually. However, from the mid-1960s East Punjab showed a dramatic increase in growth rates: between 1965-66 and 1984-85 agricultural growth rates averaged 8.3 annually for East Punjab and only 4.3 for West Punjab. In the same period East Punjabi farmers reported significantly higher yields for major crops like wheat, rice sugarcane, gram and maize than their counterparts in West Punjab. Striking disparities also came to be noticed between the two Punjabs in literacy levels and a number of other social indices.

Partition, Migration and Refugees: Responses to the Arrival of *Muhajirs* in Sind During 1947-48

Sarah Ansari

Aproaching the end of the twentieth century, events of the 1940s can seem almost a world away from present day concerns. But in many ways Pakistan is still having to come to terms with the long-term implications of the political changes which bisected that decade. Indeed, the violence and unrest of recent years underline that the country has not yet been able to deal successfully with the task of reconciling the various interests brought together by independence and the migration which accompanied it. The emergence of the *muhajir* political movement in the cities and towns of Sind during the 1980s seems final confirmation of this for if refugees from the Muslim minority provinces of India, considered to be more committed than any other group to the Pakistan ideal, have felt it necessary to identify themselves as a separate ethnic category, then this suggests that Pakistan has fallen considerably short of its original aim of providing a homeland for the subcontinent's Muslims irrespective of their origins.

The term *muhajir*, of course, was part of Pakistan's political vocabulary from the outset. Its application to refugees from India during the late 1940s marked a conscious effort to rally support among those already living in what had become Pakistan behind the task of welcoming and then looking after the large numbers of people pouring across the border. But the general hardening of ethnic boundaries which has taken place in Pakistan has helped to tighten the definition of *muhajir*, to produce a revised category which incorporates Urdu-speaking Pakistanis above all, to the exclusion of other ethnic groups who were similarly uprooted at independence. That this narrower *muhajir* identity should have emerged, however, is not surprising. Within a few years of partition, differences between Pakistan's refugee communities were already becoming apparent as the distance began to grow between Urdu-speaking migrants and a Pakistani state which was increasingly associated with the province of the Punjab. Migrants from East Punjab, from being the epitome of those who constituted a 'refugee', gradually became labelled first and foremost as 'Punjabi' rather than *muhajir*, a description which was reserved more and more for refugees coming from northern India.

Fifty years on, it is interesting to look back to the late 1940s to examine responses to Pakistan's refugee communities as they made the difficult transition to their new homeland. The immediate post-1947 period reveals the complexity of relations between refugees arriving from India and the local populations of the places where they settled. In the case of somewhere like Sind where, prior to independence, there had already developed a deep sensitivity to the threat posed to Sindhi autonomy by 'outsiders', the arrival of so many refugees had swift repercussions as far as provincialism was concerned. Early interactions which took place between refugees arriving in Sind, the local Sindhi authorities and the central government, underlined the tricky nature of the refugee issue. How to handle the challenge of accommodating enormous quantities of uprooted people was more than simply an administrative problem which required solving. It posed dilemmas which confronted the very basis of Muslim solidarity upon which Pakistan had ostensibly been constructed, and it exposed the structural fragility of the political foundations that underlay the Pakistani state.

Large-scale, often involuntary, migration has been a feature of the twentieth century, generated by political conflict in many different parts of the world. On the whole, refugees caught up in these migrations have been forced to move to places over which they have little if any personal claim. In contrast, Muslims leaving India for Pakistan at partition perceived themselves to be migrating to a place of refuge which 'belonged' to them as 'Pakistanis' just as much as it did to the Muslims whom they found living there. This naturally complicated the whole issue of their resettlement. They presumed themselves to be there not by kind invitation but by right, and those who received them were equally expected to be bound by duty to make that reception as positive as possible. Against the backdrop of confusion and violence which accompanied partition has been projected a powerful image of Muslims solidifying behind a common cause, supporting each other in the traumatic crossing of a new border and as they arrived in a new land. What remains less clear is what actually happened to these refugees after they had made the all-important transition.

Undoubtedly, for many thousands of Muslims fleeing the threats which staying in India posed, there was some comfort to be drawn from the support which they received from fellow Muslims while *en route* and once they had arrived. This was their personal experience and it became a vital part of the process by which they came to terms with all that had happened to them and their families, influencing the way that they put down new roots. The days preceding partition coincided for Muslims with one of the holiest times of their religious year, the month of Ramadan, which, combined with drawing parallels between their own experiences and those of the original *muhajirs* who had accompanied the Prophet Muhammad to Medina, may have offered some compensation for their own sufferings and sacrifices. Under these circumstances, it was perhaps understandable that they should have seen the people already living in Pakistan as *ansars*, modern equivalents of the people of Medina who had welcomed so warmly the first set of Muslim migrants.[1]

Yet, the difficulty with this interpretation is that, while many of the encounters which took place between different Muslims in the aftermath of partition were supportive, others were less positive. What to do with so many refugees became a contentious issue and local politicians were quick to include the problem of coping with them in their list of complaints directed against the central government. This rapid politicisation of the refugee issue was a sign that all was not well with

Pakistan's political health. Put another way, issues connected to the resettlement of refugees provided ammunition for some of the first shots fired against each other by the central government of the new state and the provinces which comprised it. Thus, looking in particular at developments in Sind during 1947-48: the problem of the loss of non-Muslims from the province and how to regulate the entry of Muslims from India, the status of Karachi, and the reception of refugees arriving 'second hand' from the Punjab: can provide insights into the early stages of the drawn-out process of estrangement that has characterised the province's relationship with those who have controlled power at the centre.

Refugees Start Arriving in Sind

The magnitude of the refugee problem facing the authorities on both sides of the new border in August 1947 was very great. The number of refugees eventually generated by partition in time numbered some seven to eight million people moving in opposite directions, sixteen million in approximate total. Not all set off immediately. The crisis dragged on through into the 1950s with fluctuations affecting particular parts of India and Pakistan at different times. However, the initial figures were daunting enough and Indian and Pakistani government alike had to cope with huge numbers of destitute, traumatised people seeking material and psychological assistance and reassurance. By early September, 1.25 million people were estimated to have crossed from West into East Punjab and *vice versa*, while there were perhaps a million 'on the move' and the same number again still waiting to be moved.[2] The vast majority of the refugees heading for Pakistan arrived in West Punjab where naturally enough their presence posed grave difficulties for the new Pakistani government. Apart from the continuing communal problem and questions of transportation, the most pressing issues concerned food, clothing and medical supplies. Cholera quickly broke out in some areas leading to a heavy loss of lives. What particularly worried the authorities was the grave risk that West Punjab, recognised as the granary of what had become Pakistan, would lose its *kharif* crop. This loss would then be compounded if workers were not found before the start of the sowing time for the *rabi* crop, and the result would be serious famine. It was not a simple humanitarian problem but also a vitally important economic one.[3] These dangers to Pakistan's economic well-being were added to by the difficulty of feeding and housing the huge numbers of refugees. Having been in existence for only a few weeks and with many of its officials inexperienced and about forty per cent of its personnel and its most important files still in New Delhi, contemporary observers acknowledged the Pakistani administration as 'chaotic'.[4]

At first, compared with parts of Pakistan further north, Sind's experience of refugees moving in both directions was relatively limited. The vast majority of Muslim refugees who arrived straight after partition were East Punjabis who had headed for the nearest border crossing point which was into West Punjab. This meant that most of those refugees who arrived in Sind in the weeks following 14

August came either from places further east in India via railway connections between Jodhpur and Sind, or on ships from the coast of western India. In both cases, sooner or later, the focus for these new arrivals was Karachi, home to the new government of Pakistan and the country's foremost city, port, commercial and industrial centre. The pulling power of the new government was obviously great for it implied access to jobs and financial security. Many north Indian Muslim refugees came from families with a history of service in the bureaucracy. Likewise, many others from the towns and cities of the former United Provinces belonged to artisan families who sought the opportunities which Karachi offered their skills. Muslims from western India were often involved in trade and commerce, and had long-standing business and personal links with Karachi and the coastline which joined Sind to Gujarat and Bombay.

Sind, in comparison with the Punjab, was a haven of relative calm in the weeks leading up to and immediately following partition. Its population of some seventy-five per cent Muslims and twenty-five per cent Hindus and Sikhs, despite a growing sensitivity to communal issues, had maintained a fairly clean record. The low amount of communal tension in Sind meant that the level of violence associated with the movement of refugees was very much more restricted than in the Punjab. In Karachi there was enough tension to produce a curfew for the 'first time in living memory' in early September but this followed literally a handful of deaths not surprisingly attributed by locals to refugees newly arrived from India.[5] Despite these relatively calm beginnings, it was decided that the risk of escalating violence demanded that no more refugees be allowed into Karachi. Those who were on their way from places inland were to be detained at Hyderabad, those already there were to be relocated on land in the vicinity of the city rather than actually within it, for, apart from the economic aspects of a city that was 'overflowing' with excess people, there was always that constant danger of refugees helping to spark off further violence in the capital.[6]

These decisions finally 'culminated' in the promulgation of the Sind Maintenance of Public Safety Ordinance on 21 September. Although it was generally recognised that this drastic ordinance was needed to control the forces of potential lawlessness throughout Sind, for some it was more than a necessary evil. The most unfortunate of its features was virtual censorship over the local press which some commentators expected would thereafter be little more than official communiques of the government. While the authorities argued that this ordinance would serve to protect minority interests, there were non-Muslims who were fearful of its powers. Hindu-owned papers in Sind, for example, the *Daily Gazette* and the *Sind Observer*, had been considerably critical of the government and expected to suffer as a result of its imposition. Likewise, many non-Muslims felt that the ability to detain people without trial and prohibit meetings would furnish the authorities with arbitrary powers which could be used in an intolerable way against their communities. So, while the effectiveness of these measures from the law and order point of view can be gauged to some extent by the relative peace and quiet which followed[7], it is likely that the ordinance played a significant part in convincing many non-Muslims that they should in fact leave the province for India.[8]

Regulating Refugee Traffic In and Out of Sind

The changed reality highlighted by the communal violence of early September 1947 and the ordinance meant that shipping and airline offices were now besieged by non-Muslims wishing to leave as soon as possible. By mid-September, some fifty thousand non-Muslims had registered at local Congress organisations for aid in leaving Sind. Their departure from Karachi was initially limited to one thousand per day on the grounds that there were insufficient customs officials to check their baggage. But such a large increase in the number of non-Muslims leaving was viewed with considerable local (that is Sindhi Muslim) disquiet. Many of these refugees were vital contributors to the economic life of the city. Their departure, therefore, was viewed as scarcely a lesser crisis than the arrival of so many destitute Muslim refugees from India.[9]

Sindhi Muslim politicians found themselves in a quandary about how to react.[10] In the prevailing political climate, they could hardly fail to be supportive of the refugees arriving from India, even when this meant that non-Muslims bore the brunt of pent-up resentment at events far away. Yet they were already becoming doubtful about the extent to which the creation of Pakistan would benefit Sind, which led some of them to fear the long-term impact of so many non-Muslims leaving the province to be replaced by outsiders with far less proven attachment to the region.[11] In the decades preceding 1947, Sindhi Muslims had already grown to resent the arrival of outsiders in substantial numbers to take advantage of the commercial opportunities created by the extension of the irrigation system. Various Sindhi Muslim politicians had even talked about Sind's future as an independent state in the discussions which preceded independence and partition, in large part motivated by a desire to prevent Sind from being overwhelmed by larger Muslim-majority provinces such as the Punjab to the north.[12]

Thus, over the course of the later months of 1947, there was a shift in the way that the Sind government viewed its responsibilities towards the two sets of refugees – those arriving and those departing – with a move towards an apparently more conciliatory position *vis-à-vis* departing non-Muslim Sindhis and, at the same time, a more confrontational stance in relation to the central Pakistani authorities over the issue of refugees entering the province. The extent to which this had happened was exposed in the aftermath of a serious outbreak of communal violence in Karachi in January 1948 when a party of Sikhs from further inland were attacked by refugees on their way through Karachi. Karachi by then was heavily impregnated with refugees from Ajmer, where they had received severe punishment at the hands of non-Muslims. Following the September disturbances, the authorities had been trying to keep refugees, particularly from the Punjab, from coming to Karachi, but, in relation to the Ajmer arrivals, they felt that they had no alternative but to allow them to come to the city as the country north of there was overflowing with people still waiting to be settled.[13] Accordingly the authorities clamped down very hard, in the view of the refugees, who protested against the imposition of curfew and other law and order measures.

Almost immediately, the exodus of Hindus from Karachi intensified. Some twenty-one thousand left in the two weeks which followed the disturbances, with estimates of another forty thousand leaving by the end of the month, now accompanied for the first time by the large-scale departure of upcountry Hindus.[14] The impact on the economic life of the province was very great. Commercial firms and banks, which had already lost a very large part of their subordinate staff, were now handicapped by a shortage of employees and business virtually ground to a halt. Bank opening hours were limited to only one and a half hours a day with the likelihood of these being restricted to every other day and their work falling even further into arrears.[15]

The Sind authorities, under these worsening circumstances, began to take positive steps to try to slow down the outflow of non-Muslims. It was quite clear to Khuhro and his colleagues that Sind needed to retain as many Hindus as possible because it was on them that the efficient functioning of local business, education, and, to a large extent, agriculture depended. The Sind government's view, therefore, while not contradicting the outlook of the central authorities, did conflict with the latter's desire to admit the maximum possible number of refugees to Sind in order to relieve the pressure that was steadily mounting in the Punjab.

By January, Khuhro had stated that, although Sind had cheerfully accepted refugees from all sides, the stage had been reached when it had become imperative to check any further influx. In effect, it seemed to his ministry that the accelerating influx of Muslim refugees was incompatible with the retention of as many Hindus as possible. Although the Pakistani Minister for Refugee Relief and Rehabilitation, G.A. Khan criticised this statement as neither heartening nor encouraging, Khuhro proceeded to try to slow down the Hindu exodus, for example by issuing confidential orders to the district authorities in Upper Sind that no Hindu should be permitted to leave the district without a special permit from the District Magistrate.

In practice, this intervention proved futile. It failed to prevent a steady movement from Upper Sind to Karachi on the way to Bombay and Kathiawar, but also dislocated to some extent the normal internal movements of Hindus on business, giving rise to unfortunate incidents in which Hindu travellers were evicted from trains and allegedly maltreated. In addition, the Sindhi authorities sought to counteract efforts of the Indian High Commission to facilitate the departure of non-Muslims from Sind, contending with some justification that the widespread issue of free passages and provision of free transport and food amounted to incitement for people to leave Sind who otherwise would not have thought of moving.[16]

With the hope of reducing differences between themselves, the central authorities established a special committee, including the Sind premier, to examine the issue of refugee resettlement in Sind. Almost immediately, Khuhro announced that the government of Sind had reached a number of important decisions concerning the treatment of refugees which essentially limited the number able to settle in Karachi by proposing the removal of some of them from the city.[17] Pro-refugee newspapers such as *Dawn* seized on the contradiction inherent in the announcement of these decisions on the very day when the cabinet had formed its committee to examine the whole question. Leading articles condemned in no uncertain terms the 'provincialism' of the Sindhi authorities in their treatment of refugees.[18]

The Question of Karachi's Status: In or Out of Sind?

The growing ambivalence of official statements was demonstrated by the different stand taken by the Sindhi and the central Pakistani authorities over the issue of the future of Karachi. Again this round of decision-making was linked to the arrival of large numbers of refugees in the province. Antagonism had increased between the Sindhi Muslim community and Muslim refugees who now numerically threatened to outweigh the local inhabitants of Karachi, and this ill-feeling was revealed in 'violent reactions' to rumours circulating that the city was to be set aside as a separate capital for Pakistan with Sind's capital relocated elsewhere. The Sind government, not surprisingly, denied that any such move was contemplated but no authoritative statement was forthcoming from its Pakistani counterpart. It was not that Sindhis objected to Karachi being confirmed as the country's capital but that it would in the process be separated from the province. Eventually, on 22 May the Constituent Assembly resolved that Karachi would indeed become the country's permanent capital and a centrally-administered area. An important motivating factor was finance: that is, the extensive investments already made in Karachi by the government of Pakistan especially on accommodation, albeit mostly temporary, and the impossibility of finding either money or materials to begin constructing an alternative capital elsewhere.

Sindhi politicians immediately responded with complaints that Sind was being robbed and beheaded — and undoubtedly they were voicing the feelings of a large proportion of the local population, already jealous of the preponderating Punjabi influence in the Pakistani government.[19] Many Sindhis felt that they had been 'the ones who had given refuge to the central government ... this child who had not legs [*sic*] to stand on, no chair to sit and no papers to write', and here was the central government 'annexing' the capital without any payment of compensation.[20] In early June a meeting of the Sind Muslim League Council, under Khuhro's influence, passed a resolution condemning the 'grave and most deplorable' situation created by the decision to separate Karachi from Sind: the move was bound to alienate the respect and loyal cooperation of the province and the resolution instructed the Council to engage British constitutional experts to file an appeal against it on behalf of Sind.[21]

The agitated response of Sindhis proved to be more than just provincial politicking, however opportunistic the motives of politicians such as Khuhro may have been. By the end of the year, the province faced a particularly difficult problem in being able to present its budget, precisely because of the taking over of Karachi. Sind's financial position steadily deteriorated during 1948. The mass exodus of Hindus had had serious effects on its business life. Then there was the extraordinary expenditure on refugees, relief operations, repairs to roads and canals caused by flood damage, all of which placed a very heavy drain on the provincial treasury. Sind's financial future, as a small province with limited resources, depended very greatly on how adequately the centre eventually compensated it for its loss of Karachi.

By June, however, Khuhro had lost his job despite the continued support of a majority in the provincial assembly.[22] His successor as chief minister, Pir Illahi Baksh won the backing of Jinnah in return for an undertaking to follow a path of cooperation with the central authorities. Pro-refugee lobbies blamed much of the hardship faced by refugees on the 'provincial particularism' of Sind governments and so this was something which the new administration was now supposed to tackle. In Karachi, the deterioration in municipal cleanliness, public health services, roads and transport had all been very marked and it was not long before Karachi Corporation was also dissolved (in early July) for corruption and maladministration.[23] A special committee, appointed by the Pakistan-Sind Joint Refugee Council to compile refugee statistics for Sind, reported in July that more than 700,000 Muslim refugees had entered Sind by the end of May with nearly three-quarters of the newcomers settling in Karachi, the majority of the rest in the larger cities and only about sixty thousand on the land. Khuhro, through the Sind Muslim League, demanded separate Sind Cabinet ratification of the Council's decisions, placing the ministry, which was pledged to implementing them, in an awkward position, and the move was quickly condemned by the Pakistan Refugee minister, as 'meddling in administrative details'.[24] Meanwhile the provincial government had 'decamped to Hyderabad, the pre-British capital of the province'.[25]

Over-Spill Refugees from the Punjab

Khuhro's departure had important consequences for a third issue which was complicating centre-province relations in Sind and which again directly concerned the impact which the arrival of refugees was having on life in the province. This was how to absorb large numbers of 'overspill' refugees from the Punjab into the Sindhi countryside. By January 1948 there were still some nine hundred thousand refugees in camps in the Punjab, including nearly two hundred and fifty thousand in the open air. Relocating some of the overflow to Sind seemed a natural solution but, while discussions had started towards the end of 1947, action had been delayed partly because of the reluctance of refugees to uproot themselves again so soon despite the bitterness of the cold season.[26] Not surprisingly, many of them opposed the prospect of reassembling into foot convoys to start the lengthy journey southwards.[27] The task of transferring them to Sind, however, had also been affected by the reluctance of the Sind authorities to make space for them in the province, refusing to accept more than a limited number from the Punjab. This limit of one hundred thousand refugees was condemned by some commentators as 'un-Islamic'[28], but Khuhro made it very clear that Sind could not absorb more than this number – 'for every one Hindu that has left, two Muslims have come in' – and he argued against any further increase on the grounds of insufficient practical and physical resources.[29]

Conditions did not improve significantly over the following months. By April a severe outbreak of cholera in Lahore camps had increased tensions there with newly admitted East Punjabi refugee members of Punjab Legislative Assembly strongly critical of the government's handling of refugee resettlement and rehabilitation, complaining of lack of cooperation between central and provincial authorities, and threatening to withdraw their cooperation from the local ministry. It was clear that the handling of the refugee crisis there was beyond the capacity of the Punjab provincial government, and so it was decided that the central government should take control of the refugee problem and thereby oblige other provinces, particularly Sind, to absorb a greater number of the migrants. Thus Khuhro's departure meant that the ministry had become more amenable to the demands of the centre which were supported by figures such as those which had been released in July. Under these circumstances, the central government argued, Sind could surely accept further refugees, preferably resettled on the land. Newspapers such as *Dawn* voiced the concerns of refugee interests already established in Sind, condemning the enormous, unorganised influx into Karachi. In its opinion, besides straining the already overburdened accommodation and other essential services, refugees heading in such numbers here represented a waste of manpower urgently needed elsewhere, that is in rural areas.[30] Prime Minister Liaqat Ali Khan echoed this sentiment. One of the recurring themes in the speeches which he addressed to numerous public meetings during this period, was the need to 'replace provincialism by a spirit of Islamic unity, sacrifice and discipline ... and loyalty to [in other words, cooperation with] the new Government of Pakistan'.[31]

By late August, the central authorities could not afford to delay any longer. Tension in the Punjabi camps was running dangerously high, the West Punjab ministry appeared ineffective, and so on 27 August the Pakistan government declared a state of emergency which gave it the authority to resettle large numbers of refugees in Sind: two hundred thousand rather than the previously agreed one hundred thousand. Six thousand refugees a day were subsequently despatched to Sind. Their arrival there unfortunately coincided with the aftermath of serious floods which affected both Sind and the Punjab badly, adding to the numbers of homeless people and further handicapping agricultural production. In addition, there was a great increase in malaria in Upper Sind.

The Sind government was placed in a most uncomfortable position. On the one hand, refugee discontent in the Punjab had demonstrated the importance of securing the goodwill of the newcomers as a expedient measure if nothing else to avoid any repetition of the instability and violence which had begun to surface there. On the other hand, effective rehabilitation was a costly business and the Sind government clearly regarded the Rs 10 *lakhs* offered by way of financial support by the central authorities as inadequate.

By the end of October, the Punjabi camps had been cleared although there remained many refugees scattered in villages yet to be resettled in Sind. Eventually more than two hundred thousand had been transferred but the cost in terms of ethnic harmony had been high with inflamed latent provincial jealousy cranking up the tension between newcomer and local Sindhi peasants. Pro-refugee newspapers were keen to paint as positive a picture as they could of the refugees' arrival, full of praise for the resettlement arrangements, but equally their pages included more negative reports in the process of calling for greater unity and support. Apart from Sind's landed élite, who were bound to resent land passing out of Sindhi hands but who, by all accounts, had already managed to do well out of the evacuee property left by departing non-Muslims, another potential source of discontent was Sind's *hari* labour force. A major problem in resettling refugees with a rural background was that much of the land in Sind, as in the Punjab, which had been owned by non-Muslims had been cultivated by Muslim tenants. Tenant holdings accordingly now had to be reduced to make room for the refugees, but, to prevent matters from getting out of hand, the authorities made some improvements in tenancy rights. Rent reductions, for example, were introduced as a way of curbing potential dissatisfaction.[32] But these kinds of moves did not prevent conflict between 'local' tenants and the refugees, reports of which pepper in different forms the newsprint and official records of the period, ranging from physical confrontations between cultivators to fairly violent verbal reactions to decisions of the central authorities which concerned Sind. There is no doubt that anti-Punjabi feeling was common and to many Sindhis the terms 'refugee' and 'Punjabi' were still virtually synonymous, striking a chord with those who had already grown to resent the steadily increasing influx of outsiders, including many Punjabis, over the decades which had preceded partition. By the end of the 1940s, the stage was set for confrontation in the countryside and uneasiness in the cities where both sets of refugees, rural as well as urban, faced an uncertain future.

Conclusion

The 1950s turned out to be a period of tension in all parts of Sind. Refugees and local Sindhis found themselves in competition with each other while the position of Punjabi and Urdu-speaking migrants also started to diverge. The first decade following independence was punctuated by clashes between Punjabi interests and those of the refugees who came from other parts of India. The fact that the process of rehabilitation, whether on the land or in the cities, dragged on for years did not help. Sind was unlucky to be inundated with further waves of refugees long after the flow to the Punjab had dried up. The picture was further complicated by the seemingly inexhaustible manoeuvrings of Sind's faction-ridden élites whose political unscrupulousness was summed up by Khuhro's eventual turn-around *vis-à-vis* the centre when he engineered the Sind Legislative Assembly's acceptance of One Unit in the mid-1950s, a move long feared by many Sindhis whose suspicions about the intentions of the central authorities in this regard had surfaced as early as 1948. One Unit has to be seen, therefore, as an attempt not only to deal with sources of tension between East and West Pakistan but also an attempt to unify and control politically the country's fragmented western wing. But in this respect all the move really succeeded in doing was to paper over cracks considerably widened by issues such as the impact of partition-related migration.

Likewise, Sind's experience of handling refugees after independence and the lack of a coordinated response among the different layers of government to the crisis produced by partition serves as a further indication that 'Pakistan' remained a largely unfinished 'blueprint' in 1947 rather than thought-out and thought-through in terms of how its various pieces would fit together. Indeed, one of the biggest challenges facing Pakistan at the end of the 1940s was the problem of how to forge a working unity between its component parts. Today the problem still remains unsolved. In the task of nation-building, Pakistan has not been alone. Many other newly-created states have similarly grappled with how to define and sustain their national identity. From the Pakistani point of view, the results of the 1954 Bengali elections underscored the limitations of the political alliance which had brought enough Muslims together to secure the state's creation less than a decade earlier. But this and subsequent events in East Pakistan have tended to obscure the early signs of provincialism closer to the centre of power back in West Pakistan.

For a province such as Sind, which, despite the Bhuttos as prime ministers for various periods of time, has remained marginal in terms of exercising political power at the centre, the early centre-province bouts of the late 1940s and 1950s are significant. They point to the fact that, despite the deeply symbolic political break represented by partition, there has been a high level of continuity in the history of the region: pre-1947 suspicions of outsiders and the 'ethnic' clashes of the post-independence period form part of a longer continuum, complicated by the demographic upheavals of partition which the new Pakistani authorities were unable to address with any meaningful or lasting measure of success. The highly charged response generated by the arrival of refugees in Sind confirms that provincialism and ethnic issues have been integral to the politics of Pakistan from the beginning. Indeed, it could be argued that recent political events in Sind represent not the breakdown of ethnic relations so much as the culmination of years during which the rivalry and resentment, built up and stoked by the impact of partition on the province, were allowed to fester. Pakistan, in other words, is still bearing the costs of partition, whose legacy continues to cast dark shadows over the current political scene just as it helped to shape the contours of Pakistani life and politics in the 1940s.

Notes

1   See entry on 'Muhadjir' in *Encyclopaedia of Islam* (Leiden), New Edition, Vol. VII, pp. 354-356.
2   Telegram 835 (New Delhi), 845.00/9-1447, USNA.
3   Despatch no. 130, 845F.00/9-1547, USNA.
4   Despatch no. 206, 845F.00/10-2747, USNA.
5   A Pathan police constable ran amok and killed 3 Muslims, 2 Hindus and 1 Sikh on 3 September. This was then followed by 2 further deaths, see Despatch no. 121, 845F.00/9-947 USNA.
6   Summary of Political Developments in Pakistan during September 1947, Despatch no. 206, 845F.00/10-2747, USNA.
7   It was not until mid-December that any serious disturbances broke out, this time in the city of Hyderabad where curfew followed a flare up which was directly linked to the arrival of refugees from Ajmer whose tales of appalling suffering triggered off revenge attacks on local Hindus, see Disturbances in Hyderabad, Sind, Despatch no. 278, 845F.00/12-2947, USNA.
8   The announcement of the partition plan on 3 June had prompted some Hindu businessmen to transfer considerable funds to what would shortly become India, but on the whole, non-Muslims had stayed put in Karachi and further inland in Sind, see 'Promulgation of Sind Maintenance of Public Safety Ordinance, 1947', Despatch no. 142, 845F.00/9-2347, USNA, and Despatch no. 41, 845.00/7-847, USNA.
9   'Promulgation of Sind Maintenance of Public Safety Ordinance 1947', *loc. cit.*
10 Something of this 'dilemma' comes through in an episode in mid-September which led to the resignation of nearly all the remaining British Government officials in Sind. 'At the meeting (13 Sept. 1947), Khuhro is reported, despite his previous appeals to the populace to remain calm and preserve law and order, to have delivered a most inflammatory speech upon the atrocities committed by Sikhs and Hindus against Muslims in the Punjab and also in denunciation of the large number of Sikhs and Hindus who have been leaving Karachi literally by thousands ... [he] declared that a law was being drafted under which Sikhs and Hindus who left Sind would be able to take with them only the clothes they were wearing and a very few personal effects ... ' see Despatch no. 129, 845F.00/9-1547, USNA.
11 Well before partition actually became a reality, foreign observers had pointed out the fact that the 'average Sindhi [was] included to be provincial in outlook' and would not look upon 'the inflow of persons from other provinces, most of whom would take the best in Sind, [as] not an attractive prospect', see despatch no. 61, 845.00/7-2947, USNA.
12 For further discussion of the growth of anti-outsider sentiment in Sind prior to 1947, see Sarah Ansari, 'Political legacies of pre-1947 Sind' in D.A. Low (ed.), *The Political Inheritance of Pakistan* (Macmillan, 1991), pp. 173-193.
13 Despatch no. 18, 12 January 1948, 845F.00/1-1248, USNA.
14 United Kingdom High Commission (UKHC) Opdom 5 (15-21 Jan. 1948), L/WS/1/1599, IOL.
15 UKHC Opdom 6 (15-21 Jan. 1947), L/WS/1/1599, IOL.
16 UKHC Opdom 8 (22-28 Jan. 1948), L/WS/1/1599, IOL.
17 UKHC Opdom 10 (29 Jan.-4 Feb. 1948), L/WS/1/1599, IOL.
18 *Loc. cit.*

19   UKHC Opdom 42 (20-26 May 1948), L/WS/1/1599, IOL.
20   A. Jalal, *The State of Martial Rule: the origins of Pakistan's political economy of defence* (Cambridge, 1990), p. 89.
21   'Moslem Resentment in Sind: Separation of Karachi', *Manchester Guardian* (14 June 1948).
22   On 27 Apr., Jinnah dismissed Khuhro for 'mal-administration, gross misconduct of his duties and responsibilities, and corruption', UKHC Opdom 40 (13-19 May 1948), L/WS/1/1599, IOL.
23   UKHC Opdom 56 (8-15 July 1948), L/WS/1/1599, IOL.
24   UKHC Opdom 49, 17-23 June 1948, L/WS/1/1599, IOL.
25   Theodore P. Wright, Jr., 'Centre-Periphery Relations and Ethnic Conflict in Pakistan', *Comparative Politics* (Apr. 1991), p. 302.
26   UKHC Opdom 3 (3 Jan. 1948), L/WS/1/1599, IOL.
27   *Dawn,* 8 Feb 1948, p. 6.
28   UKHC Opdom 15 (Feb. 1948), L/WS/1/1599, IOL.
29   *Dawn,* 18 Jan. 1948, p. 8.
30   UKHC Opdom 53 (July 1948), L/WS/1/1599, IOL.
31   UKHC Opdom 46 (June 1947), L/WS/1/1599, IOLR.
32   *Dawn,* 24 Sept. 1948, p. 1.

Divided Landscapes, Fragmented Identities: East Bengal Refugees and their Rehabilitation in India, 1947-79 [*]

Gyanesh Kudaisya

Introduction

The partition of the Indian subcontinent in 1947 was followed by the forced uprooting of an estimated eighteen million people belonging to minorities who sought shelter across the newly-created boundaries in the two nation-states of India and Pakistan. When one considers the major communities that were uprooted from the regions which became a part of Pakistan and sought shelter in India – Sindhis, Sikhs, Bengalis, Punjabis, and North West Frontier Province Hindus – in aggregate terms the largest numbers were of those who came from East Bengal. Yet, it is ironical that accounts of partition have tended to be Punjab-centred and Bengal has not received the scholarly attention that it deserves. This chapter makes an attempt towards redressing this historiographic imbalance by looking at events that took place in Bengal following partition. It focuses on the predicament of the minority communities in East Pakistan (now Bangladesh) who were uprooted and forced to seek shelter in the truncated Indian province of West Bengal (Fig. 1). It considers the manner of the refugee exodus and the responses of the Indian federal and provincial governments to the challenge of refugee rehabilitation. A study is then made of the Dandakaranya scheme which was undertaken after 1958 to resettle the refugees by colonising forest land in an area far away from Bengal (Fig. 2). The difficulties experienced in resettling the refugees outside Bengal are examined and the complex interplay of identity and landscape, of dependence and self-help, that informed the choices which the refugees made in rebuilding their lives are discussed.

Partition marked the high point in the fragmentation not only of Bengal's landscape but also of the identities of its people. Several elements made up this identity: language, religion, climate, soil, customs, food. Prior to partition, the distinctions in the identities of people inhabiting the two states that were subsequently carved out of undivided Bengal were 'fuzzy'. The religious distinctions that existed were subsumed under the larger panoply of a Bengali

[*] A draft of this chapter was presented at the 9th International Conference of Historical Geographers (Pre-Conference Symposium) on 'Landscape and Identity' held in June 1995 at Singapore, and a shorter version appeared in the *Singapore Journal of Tropical Geography*, Vol. 17, no. 1 (1996), pp. 24-39. The permission of the Journal to reproduce some of the material is gratefully acknowledged.

Figure 1. Divided Bengal

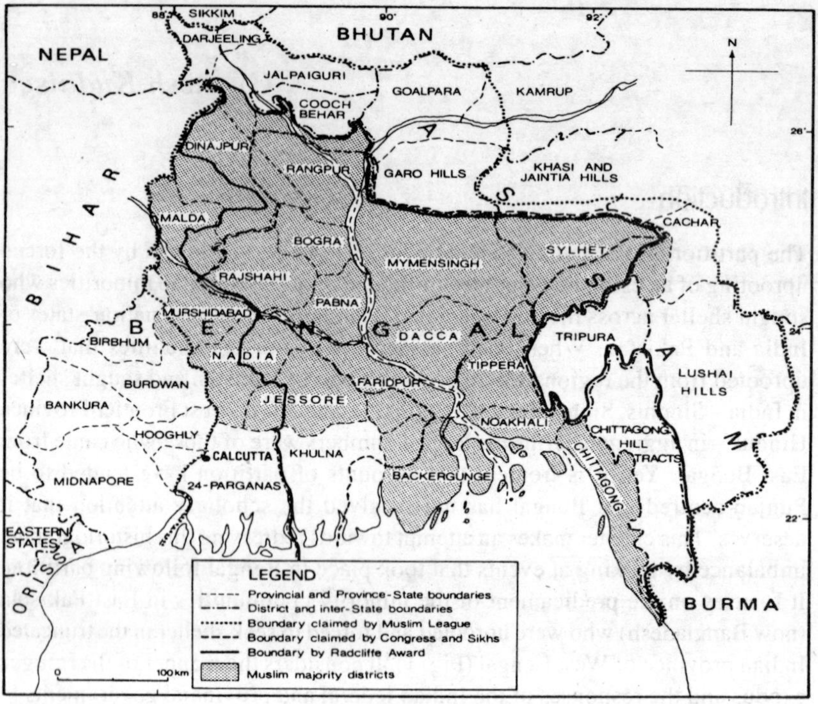

LEGEND
- - - - - Provincial and Province-State boundaries
-··-··- District and inter-State boundaries
·········· Boundary claimed by Muslim League
- - - - Boundary claimed by Congress and Sikhs
———— Boundary by Radcliffe Award
▓▓▓ Muslim majority districts

Source: Modified from O.H.K. Spate (1948)

cultural and linguistic identity.[1] Bengalis spoke the same language, although its usage and idiom in the west was closer to Sanskrit, while in the east it was embellished by Urdu terminology which was increasingly being preferred. There were, of course, differences in accents in the way the spoken word was used. Yet these linguistic differences were superficial, the two being dialects of the same language. In education, commerce and business, the medium of communication was the same Bengali language. In the eastern districts, Islamic influence was far greater due to a more dense concentration of Muslim communities – a fact that provided the subsequent basis and justification for the territorial division of Bengal.[2] Further, there existed a strong commonalty in terms of marriage and social customs, although in finer details there were some differences[3] Food habits and entertainment patterns were also characterised by a high degree of similarity. The caste and class structures were similar, though East Bengalis were engaged in certain occupations typical of their ecology. Ecological variation in the two regions was slight: East Bengal was riverine and received higher rainfall and was criss-crossed by canals and rivers which played an important part in people's lives. 'The whole of Bengal', observed the geographer Oskar Spate, 'has a common structural history and a very similar way of life based on rice'. In his view, Bengal 'had for some centuries possessed an historical entity' and was until the 1947 partition 'a linguistic and cultural unit focused on Calcutta'.[4] It was this distinctive cultural landscape which was celebrated in verse by the Bengali poet and Nobel laureate, Rabindranath Tagore (1861-1941), in his famous song *Amar Sonar Bangla* ('My Golden Bengal').[5]

Writing on the integrity of Bengal as a unified cultural landscape, the distinguished Bengali historian, Sir Jadu Nath Sarkar, observed on the eve of the partition:

> Here in the two halves of Bengal the population is absolutely one by race, language, and manner of life, they differ only in religion....Religion keeps the people of East Bengal internally divided, exactly the same way as in West Bengal by forbidding dinner, marriage and worship together. Both sects in both areas speak the same language, write the same alphabet, and have so long read and composed the same literature. The Hindus and Muslims of Bengali origin have lived together side by side in peace for so many centuries that it is now impossible to draw a clear cut geographical line dividing the Hindus from the Muslims.[6]

However, as the political mobilisation for a separate Muslim state gathered momentum in the late 1930s and 40s, the larger Bengali cultural and linguistic identity increasingly came to be fractured along sectarian and religious lines.[7] It is beyond the scope of this discussion to show how this process of fragmentation of identities took place in pre-partition Bengal, but when partition occurred in 1947 most people increasingly looked upon themselves as Hindus or Muslims first and Bengalis afterwards.[8]

This fragmentation of identities was accompanied by a division of the Bengal landscape by the partition of 1947. Let us consider the manner in which this division took place and the nature of the boundaries that were set up between the two Bengals. The Radcliffe Commission drew up a boundary line across undivided Bengal, which had a total area of 78,389 square miles, to create two separate entities – East Bengal which formed the eastern wing of Pakistan and West Bengal which became a province of independent India. The resulting 2,736 kilometres long boundary line cut across Jessore, Nadia, Malda, Dinajpur, and Jalpaiguri districts of Bengal and Sylhet district of neighbouring Assam. This boundary line was drawn arbitrarily, mostly ignoring factors such as communications and railway links, water channels, cultural and pilgrimage sites, location of industries and vital strategic factors. Partition left neither of the two Bengals a strong unit. West Bengal was left as a rump of about 34,000 square miles and a major portion of Sylhet was appended to it from neighbouring Assam to bolster its overall land size. It got a population of 24,320,000 out of which nearly seventeen per cent were Muslims. It became India's smallest and most overcrowded province, with a high degree of urban concentration around the Calcutta area.[9] With its enormous urban concentration on Hooghlyside, soon to be swollen by the tide of incoming refugees, West Bengal became a food-deficit area, its agriculture being qualitatively as well as quantitatively inferior to that of East Pakistan.[10] As far as East Bengal wasconcerned, the Radcliffe Award gave it an area of 54,501 square miles and a population of 41.8 million people (based on the 1941 census) which represented only forty per cent of the area, but almost sixty per cent of the population of the pre-partition Bengal and Assam provinces.

Figure 2 Major Bengali refugee resettlement sites

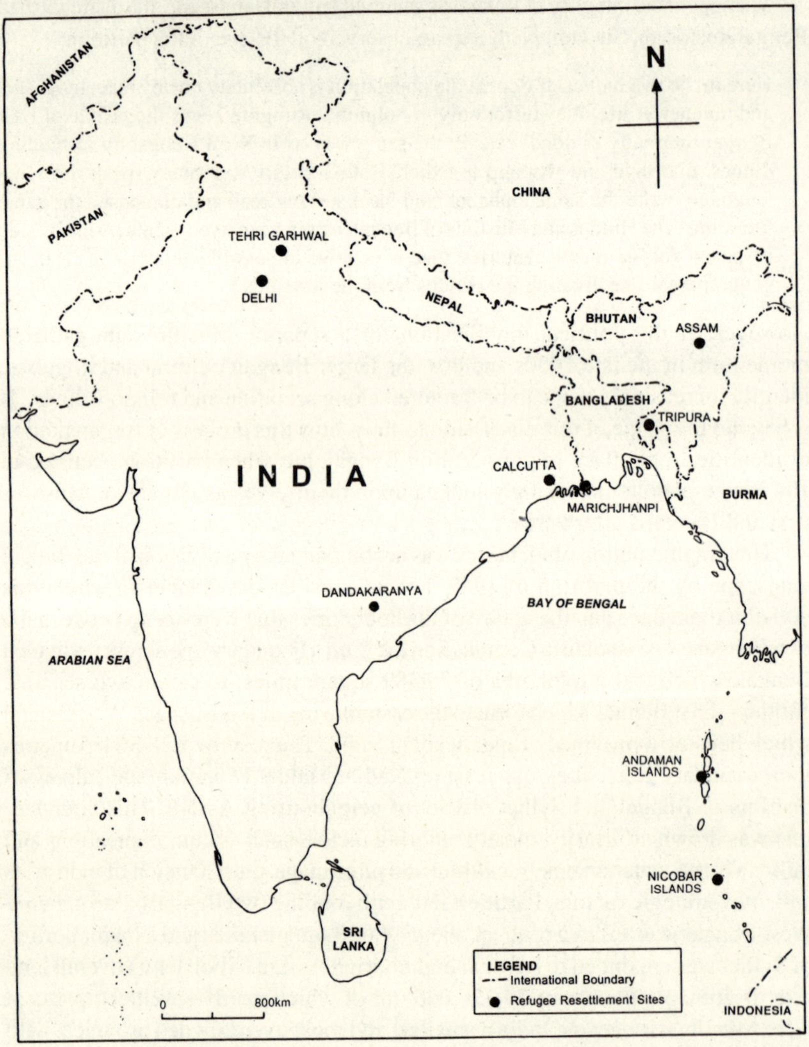

Source: Author's own

Refugees in West Bengal

Partition left 11.4 million or forty-two per cent of undivided Bengal's Hindu population in East Bengal. In 1947, at the time of partition, only 344,000 Hindu refugees came into West Bengal and the hope lingered among the minorities of

East Pakistan that they could continue to live there peacefully. However, these hopes were dashed as the East Bengal minorities increasingly experienced persecution and intolerance.[11] The year 1948 saw an influx of 786,000 people and in 1949 over 213,000 Bengali refugees crossed into India. In this context, it must be noted that the policy of the Indian government in Bengal aimed not at evacuating the minorities, as had been done so effectively in Punjab with the help of the military, but in negotiating with the Pakistani authorities for creating conditions of security, so that a mass exodus could be averted. While in Punjab the Indian government had facilitated an 'exchange of population', in the case of Bengal it wanted to prevent precisely such an exchange. Towards this end it took a number of initiatives. An inter-dominion conference was held at Calcutta in April 1948 where K. C. Neogy and Ghulam Mohammad, the rehabilitation ministers of the two states, made a joint declaration 'that they are determined to take every possible step to discourage such exodus and to create such conditions as would check mass exodus in either direction'. It was also decided, as a confidence-building step, to establish minority boards at the provincial and local levels in both the countries. Another inter-dominion conference met in Delhi in December 1948 to follow up on these measures.

These initiatives, however, failed to stem the tide and the refugees continued to pour into West Bengal. In early 1950 serious riots engulfed the whole of East Pakistan and the figures of incoming refugees again surged to alarming levels. To deal with the situation, a pact was signed in April that year between the prime ministers of the two countries. The Nehru-Liaquat Pact aimed at creating a sense of security among the minorities to discourage their exodus from either side by jointly reaffirming the right of equality in matters of citizenship. To some extent, the Pact made movement freer, reduced harassment by enforcement officials, and enabled people to bring in their movable assets. However, in reality it failed to create the much-needed sense of security among the East Bengal Hindus, who expressed the fear that the Pakistan authorities were so intolerant that 'the pact on which rests so much of hope in a dismal situation' may be 'reduced to a nullity'. Several months after the Pact was signed, a Minority Convention of East Bengal Hindus held at Mymensingh challenged the Pakistani authorities to declare their intent of 'whether the minorities are wanted here at all or not'.[12] The Convention, *inter alia*, demanded: special courts to punish culprits of communal violence; compensation for victims of riots; action against officials involved in the abetment of communal violence; stopping of requisition of Hindu homes by authorities; stopping of economic boycott of minorities; exemplary punishment for offences against women; protection and upkeep of Hindu temples; adoption of a rational and scientific educational policy; and finally a secular democratic constitution for Pakistan which would safeguard the rights of minorities. The minorities in East Pakistan, the Convention unequivocally declared, 'desire to live in the land of our birth with our honour unsullied and with our rights asserted'.

In West Bengal too, strong protests were raised against the harassment of Hindu minorities across the border and their continued influx into the province. The Pact was denounced as 'the hour of national humiliation' and 'surrender' to the 'dark and dismal forces of aggressive, anti-Indian and anti-Hindu communalism'.[13] The Bengal Hindu Maha Sabha launched a strong public campaign to highlight the plight of the East Bengali minorities by publicising evidence of attacks on Hindu properties and temples as well as crimes against women. The more secular Bengal Rehabilitation Organisation, which enjoyed the support of eminent public figures, such as the economist Radha Kamal Mukherjee and the scientist Meghnad Saha, also criticised the Pact which, it declared, 'has not at all helped to create confidence or a sense of security in the minds of the Hindus'. 'The clear rational object of the Government of Pakistan', in its view, 'is to establish a homogenous State based on Islamic Law by squeezing out the Hindus from their hearths and homes'.

The Pact thus failed in preventing an exchange of populations. The harassment of minorities to leave East Bengal continued but now took more invidious forms:[14] instead of actual violence, it was alleged that 'the Majority community are pursuing the methods of boycott of Hindu traders and artisans

and the Islamisation of Education' as 'weapons...in their armoury'.[15] In October 1950, J.N. Mandal, who had been the most prominent non-Muslim in Bengal to support the Pakistan movement and after partition naturally came to be seen as the spokesman of East Bengal Hindus, resigned from the Pakistan central cabinet.[16] Mandal, according to one account, 'felt horrified and completely bewildered' by the intensity of the 1950 riots and 'migrated to India in disgust, shame and sorrow'.[17] Samar Guha, a prominent political worker in East Bengal, conveys the sense of insecurity which the minorities there experienced:

A more frustrated and demoralised people could hardly be imagined than the non-Muslims of eastern Pakistan as they are today. Frozen in a morass of utter helplessness, only a ghost of their former self exists. Physically, in a state of perpetual insecurity, morally pulverised, spiritually having no value to claim as their own, socially routed, economically shattered and politically non-existent remnants of a formerly predominant non-Muslim Society are now maintaining a precarious existence in the eastern wing of Pakistan.[18]

In view of the prolonged conditions of insecurity, an estimated 1,575,000 people left East Bengal in 1950 to seek refuge in India. The following year another 187,000 refugees came and the figure of incoming refugees stood at 200,000 during 1952. This influx continued through out the 1950s and even beyond, with 76,000 persons coming to India in 1953, 1.18 *lakhs* in 1954 and 2.40 *lakhs* in 1955.[19] In the following year the number of incoming refugees again mounted to 3.20 *lakhs* when Pakistan adopted an 'Islamic' constitution.[20] The refugee influx fluctuated quite considerably, depending upon changing bilateral ties between India and Pakistan as well as upon community relations between Hindus and Muslims in East Bengal.[21] This process of gradual displacement continued throughout the 1960s.[22] In 1981 the government of West Bengal's Refugee Rehabilitation Committee estimated the number of East Bengal refugees within the state to be at least eight million or one-sixth of the population of the state.[23]

The East Bengal refugees looked upon themselves as the 'victims of partition' and regarded it, as Bengalis, to be their basic right to seek refuge in that part of Bengal which now lay in India. Having faced persecution and intolerance in East Bengal, they believed that it was their legitimate and rightful claim to seek rehabilitation within West Bengal which they now regarded as their natural habitat. Most of them, therefore, initially came to Calcutta which had always been the region's metropolis and the seat of the provincial government.

However, the West Bengal Government's response to the refugee influx was criticised for being 'tardy and half-hearted'.[24] It was also conditioned by the class character of the refugees. Among the first to leave in the late 1940s had been the Hindu upper and middle classes. Most already had contacts, through educational and kinship links, in Calcutta and could look forward to picking up professions and trades in their new surroundings. These groups were able to rent or buy properties in and around the Calcutta area with their own resources and did not really need to depend upon the government. In the 1940s, when it was mainly these groups who came into West Bengal, the authorities did not feel seriously burdened by the refugee influx. Although relief camps were opened, less than ten percent of refugees sought shelter there.

From the early 1950s onwards the authorities were faced with a different class of refugees who belonged either to the lower urban strata or came from the East Bengal countryside. This change in the character of the refugees aggravated the problem for the authorities, not just in terms of the sheer numbers who now made claims upon the government's resources, but also in the resourcefulness which they displayed in rebuilding their own lives.[25] As the 1950s dawned, the West Bengal government's 'refugee problem' increasingly became worse and came to assume crisis proportions. Accommodation in government-run camps became cramped and scarce, the dole queues grew longer and the sight of refugee families living on Calcutta's pavements became commonplace.[26] The provincial government found itself simply unprepared for such a crisis.

As a result the West Bengal government increasingly took the view that the refugees were not its sole responsibility but were rather a burden which ought to be shared jointly among the federal government and governments of the neighbouring states. Extensive deliberations were, therefore, held among officials to prepare plans for the dispersal of refugees outside West Bengal. The West Bengal case was that post-partition demographic changes and disruptions had made it the smallest and the most densely populated state within India, its population density rising by over twelve per cent.[27] Its regional economy, particularly the jute sector, had suffered great disruptions and it did not have the resources to bear the additional burden of relief and rehabilitation.[28] Moreover, the land-man ratio in West Bengal was already precarious and could endure no further agricultural colonisation or expansion. Muslim emigration as a result of partition had been negligible and, in any case, there was very little evacuee property which could be redistributed among the incoming refugees, as the majority of Muslims who had left West Bengal belonged to the poorer strata. The West Bengal government claimed that, in overall terms, it did not have the necessary resources at its disposal to take on the additional demographic burden caused by the refugee influx.[29] The responsibility for the refugees, argued the political leadership of West Bengal, must be equitably shared. This could be done by the federal government making adequate financial provisions, and by neighbouring states agreeing to host and resettle the refugees within their territories.[30] However, in spite of extensive official consultations, the plans for the dispersal of refugees outside West Bengal did not fructify. Certain states, in particular Assam, showed open reluctance to the proposal of hosting Bengali refugees.[31] The states of Bihar and Orissa showed some willingness, and there was also talk of resettlement in far-away areas like Hyderabad and Mysore. However, such talk was not matched by positive action and often it amounted to nothing more than lamenting the inherent difficulties involved in the dispersal of the refugees. The official discourse on the issue tended to be tinged with unjustified assertions about the 'inordinately parochial' character of the Bengalis and their unwillingness to be rehabilitated outside Bengal.[32]

Within West Bengal there developed a strong public campaign against turning the refugees out of the Bengali-speaking areas. A large and influential section of Bengali intellectuals and public figures criticised the official attempts at dispersing the refugees. They argued that the resources existed within West Bengal for the successful rehabilitation of all Bengalis who had sought refuge there after being persecuted in East Pakistan. In 1950 the Bengal Rehabilitation Organization formulated a detailed plan which claimed to have the potential to 'restore the economic and social life of the displaced community and to reconstruct the economic life of West Bengal'. The Plan expressed the optimism that 'refugee rehabilitation, scientifically planned and implemented, may give a new lease of life to the decadent, truncated state', and called for mechanised and cooperative farming through large scale land colonisation.[33] It was claimed that there existed 1.5 million acres of cultivable waste land within West Bengal which could be profitably used for agricultural colonisation and settlement of refugees. The Plan further suggested that possibilities existed for land colonisation schemes to be undertaken in proximate areas like Manipur, Bihar and Tripura. The economist Radha Kamal Mukherjee, in his introduction to the non-official Plan, estimated that 'the uncultivated land (excluding current fallow) amounted to 173 *lakh* acres in Assam, 64.5 *lakh* acres in Bihar and twenty-eight *lakh* acres in West Bengal'. He demanded that Bengali refugees should be settled in 'contiguous Bengali speaking areas'. He claimed that East Bengali farmers possessed 'the sturdy spirit of individualism, courage and enterprise' which was needed for land colonisation. It was, after all, 'the pioneer settlers', the forefathers of the refugees, 'who fought the tiger and the crocodile, and who overcame the hazards of the forest and the flood that created in East Bengal the granary of rice and jute in India'. It was their toil which, Mukherjee asserted, had made 'East Bengal one of the most flourishing gardens of Asia'.[34]

To address the problems faced by urban refugees, the non-official Plan envisaged the development of satellite towns and industrial centres within a radius of fifty miles from Calcutta to create auxiliary and small scale industries to generate the necessary employment opportunities for the refugees. These measures, it was claimed, would 'lead to a proper balancing and redistribution of population' and thus 'refugee rehabilitation and regional developments can aid each other'. Such a plan, it was asserted, 'will be much sounder economically than sending the refugees to distant and unfamiliar agricultural zones'. The authors of the Plan warned that, 'in the absence of planned integration between refugee rehabilitation and general economic progress of West Bengal we may sow the seeds of fresh cleavages and conflicts in a poverty and disease-ridden, truncated state, with a density of rural population and visible and invisible unemployment far greater than anywhere else in India'.[35] The proposal of sending the refugees outside West Bengal was denounced as 'banishment' and the strongest language was used to criticise the authorities:

> The present plan of rehabilitation without making classifications of different categories of refugees and haphazardly distributing them to different states of India, in an atmosphere not congenial to their health and spirit is sure to result in a large number of physical and spiritual deaths and even those who will survive will not be able to preserve their language and culture as Bengalis.[36]

In overall terms, the authorities were urged to take a humane view of the problem of refugee rehabilitation. The uprooted people, it was pointed out, 'represent one of the richest artisan and trading and intellectual groups of India' who due to the tragedy of partition 'have been suddenly rendered helpless and even destitute'. They need not be looked upon as a liability, it was urged, but should be seen as constituting a rich pool of human resource from which West Bengal could benefit immensely if only its government could harness this properly.

Squatters and Self-Rehabilitation

However, by the mid-1950s nothing had been done by the authorities towards formulating a long term plan for the rehabilitation of Bengali refugees within or outside West Bengal. Government efforts had not gone beyond providing relief to the incoming refugees.[37] In the absence of any meaningful plan for their rehabilitation, a large number of refugees started organising themselves in all kinds of 'cooperative' activities which aimed at establishing refugee colonies by encroaching upon vacant public land. The movement to forcibly occupy public lands and to build squatter colonies upon them (*'jabar dhakhal andolan'*) started in the late 1940s when groups of refugees began to take over public spaces for shelter.[38] Such groups usually worked under the cover of night when plots would be earmarked and thatched shacks were erected with amazing speed. Colony 'committees' thereafter supervised the laying and cleaning of drains and the provision of water supplies. This movement for setting up squatter colonies started from the eastern fringes of Calcutta in the late 1940s.

Squatter colonies represented a form of self-rehabilitation by the refugees. Typical in this regard was the Manohar colony situated in an area of fifty acres off Dum Dum Road near Calcutta. The colony exemplified initiative and enterprise; the refugees organised the reconstruction of all aspects of their lives on a co-operative basis. Upon arrival each refugee family was 'registered' by the colony's 'central committee' on the payment of a fee of Rs 10 per household. Plots were then allotted to enable each family to construct a hut. Hut-making was carried out as a collective activity. The day-to-day management of the colony was done by its central committee, which coordinated its activities with 'committees' of other squatter colonies in the vicinity.[39]

The squatter colony at Madhyagram, established twelve miles away from Calcutta, was another typical example of refugee enterprise. In this colony the 'committee' ran an upper primary school, and organised cooperatives of carpenters and weavers. Residents helped each other in building houses and making available locally produced goods and services at cheap rates. So successful was the Madhyagram enterprise that a press correspondent expressed the optimism that it had the 'chances of developing into a prosperous suburban town'.[40]

By the early 1950s squatter colonies such as Madhyagram and Santosh occupied a large part of the landscape of greater Calcutta. They stretched out from Kalyani in the north to Sonarpur in the south. Then in the 1960s the squatter colonies spread to the west bank of the river Hooghly, and not just Calcutta but its surrounding districts of Nadia, Malda, Jalpaiguri, West Dinajpur and 24-Parganas, were transformed by the enterprise shown by the refugees in establishing squatter colonies. As a result, what was previously a rural hinterland was transformed in less than two decades into a huge urban sprawl.[41] It is estimated that there are now 2,000 *bustees* or slums listed in the Calcutta Municipal area; counting Howrah the total exceeds 3,500, with some two million occupants. In the Calcutta Urban Agglomeration as a whole, the number of *bustee*-dwellers comes to more than three million people. It is reckoned that each square kilometre of space in Calcutta is occupied on an average by 28,571 people. Over 51 per cent of the people live in thatched or semi-permanent dwellings, while the poorest of the poor – those 25 per cent at the bottom of the social scale – occupy only 7 per cent of the city's land.[42] In all 49 per cent of the city's population lives in its slums. Out of these slum-dwellers, about 87 per cent are migrants, with the East Bengal refugees constituting a large part of the population.

While a large number of Bengali refugees opted for some form or other of self-rehabilitation, a sizeable section, especially those who had been engaged in agricultural occupations before being uprooted, found it difficult to make a new beginning and to reconstruct their lives. They did not possess any skill or capital and naturally craved for land for resettlement. These agricultural refugees came mainly from backward caste groups like Namasudras who were primarily engaged in paddy cultivation besides boating, fishing and carpentry. Colonial ethnographers describe the Namasudras as a non-Aryan caste which followed the Vaishnavite tradition of Hinduism.[43] It was the coming in the 1950s of these Namasudra agriculturists that aggravated the situation in West Bengal. The impoverished state of these refugees, their lack of money, contacts and skills and weakened physical state left them with no choice but to join the dole queues and seek shelter in government-run relief camps. Right from the beginning, the dominant political leadership of the ruling Congress party as well as the officialdom displayed an ambivalent attitude towards the incoming refugees. The West Bengal élites believed that the refugees were a tremendous economic liability and that their rehabilitation would make enormous demands upon the meagre economic resources of the province and jeopardise its prosperity and future. Moreover, they increasingly took the view that generous relief and compensation on the part of official agencies would act as a magnet and attract more refugees from across the border. Those crossing the border were perceived by them as economic migrants and not as minorities who were being forcibly displaced due to persecution and harassment.

Refugees in Dandakaranya

It was in this context that the Dandakaranya project was conceived as a long-term solution to the problem of rehabilitation of Bengali refugees. Its genesis lay in the consultations that took place in early 1956 at the Rehabilitation Ministers' Conference where, for the first time, it was officially announced that refugees would get state help and relief only if they opted for resettlement outside West Bengal.[44] A high-level committee was constituted to report on the feasibility of land colonisation schemes outside West Bengal for refugee rehabilitation. This committee reported in 1957 and in June that year its recommendations were accepted by the National Development Council. As a result, a special government agency called the Dandakaranya Development Authority (DDA) was set up in 1958. The plan contemplated the development of an area 78,000 square miles, known as Dandakaranya, in Koraput and Kalahandi districts of Orissa and Bastar district of Madhya Pradesh. This area lies in a low plateau ranging from six hundred to three thousand feet above sea level and is thickly forested. It is marked by hill ranges and rocky outcrops and its indigenous population is predominantly tribal. While the region as such is characterised by extreme backwardness, it is rich in unexplored mineral resources and forest produce. The plateau dominates the region's landscape and the two main rivers which criss-cross it are the Mahanadi, which crosses through its northern part, and the Godavari, which flows through the southern part. Although these rivers are perennial, only a small portion of their water is used for irrigation. In spite of its rich forest and mineral wealth, Dandakaranya had always been isolated due to its poor internal and external accessibility and the self-sufficient nature of its tribal inhabitants.

As Dandakaranya lies within the tropics, its climate is hot and humid. Over 80 per cent of the mean annual rainfall – about sixty to eighty inches – falls within one hundred days spanning June to September. This creates problem of unevenness of rainfall, thus making all agricultural ventures dependent upon the vagaries of the monsoon. The local brooks and streams are seasonal and dry up after the rains, and the region is deficient in underground water resources. Further, the soil quality is porous with a small clay content which makes it lacking in plant nutrients and, as a result, unable to sustain double-cropping. As Dandakaranya had a low indigenous population, the planners banked upon the availability of large tracts of virgin lands for colonisation by the Bengali refugees. In spite of the region's unpromising physical features, its low population density was a crucial factor in its choice as a site of refugee rehabilitation.[45]

Within the Dandakaranya region, four resettlement zones were established at Umerkote and Malkangiri in Koraput district and at Paralkote and Kondagaon in Bastar district. In these zones villages were earmarked for forty to sixty refugee families. Refugees were sent from camps in West Bengal by special trains to Raipur. From there they were taken to the Mana transit camp, and then to work-site camps where they had to work on land reclamation, road building works, etc. The idea was to get them used to hard labour before they took the plunge into full-scale agriculture. From the work-site camps they were finally taken to villages for 'permanent settlement'. Upon reaching the village each household was given a plot of roughly six and a half acres for cultivation and half an acre for gardening and a homestead. Further, loans were disbursed to facilitate their settling-in: these included a sum of Rs 1700 for house-building; Rs 1115 for the purchase of bullocks and implements; and Rs 150 for digging a well. In addition, a maintenance grant was also given for twelve months before the harvesting of the first crop.

From the late 1950s onwards, land colonisation was pursued vigorously in Dandakaranya. By 1965 significant progress had been made in achieving project targets, and the West Bengal leadership was optimistic that a solution to the 'refugee problem', at last, seemed to be in sight.[46] Over 270,000 acres of forest had been cleared and over 7,500 refugee families settled in over 184 villages that had been 'developed' by that year. These developments transformed the landscape of the region. As an official account put it:

> *Modernism* came with a bang and a clatter into this vastness. Monstrous engines roared into the jungle, ripping up earth, splintering giant trees that had defied a thousand storms as if they were match wood. The beasts of the forest fled helter-skelter, and the sleepy inhabitants of the villages snuggling among the clearings rubbed their eyes in wonder. What new breed of demons were these creatures belching smoke, filling the skies with their clamour?[47]

With the clearing of land came the refugee settlers, and by 1973 about 25,209 families had been moved to the region. However, out of these, only 17,217 families stayed back and the rest returned to West Bengal, having failed to make Dandakaranya their home. Out of these, 16,197 households were engaged in agriculture and 1,020 in non-agricultural occupations. By the early 1970s there existed 302 villages with 10,750 houses, and another 1,600 houses were under construction. In all 462 kilometres of main roads and 669 kilometres of link roads had been built. The total expenditure on the project had been Rs 53.70 *crores.*

Yet, in spite of this substantial expenditure, the project was beset with difficulties.[48] Foremost among these were the problems faced in persuading the refugees to go from West Bengal to Dandakaranya. A study suggests that 'the Bengali farmers, less mobile and more deeply anchored in the unique ecological setting of their deltaic homeland, perceived the distances involved as a great deterrent. From the very beginning they had little desire to move into the ecologically contrasted territory of peninsular India to reconstruct their life there'.[49] The refugees' perception of the distance of Dandakaranya from Bengal and their deep rooted reluctance to move out of Bengali-speaking areas impeded further resettlement.[50]

Another factor which seriously hampered the refugees' move to Dandakaranya was the persistent campaign by the Communists who urged them not to go out of West Bengal but to take to agitation to demand resettlement within Bengal. The influx of refugees and their concentration in and around the Calcutta area had transformed the configuration of politics in West Bengal. The cause of the refugees had been taken up very strongly by the Communists in West Bengal. Communist cadres encouraged the refugees to occupy public spaces for shelter, colonise land in the villages, resist the stopping of doles and the closure of camps by the government. They also opposed government plans for the dispersal of these refugees to neighbouring states. Several important studies have drawn attention to the close link between the refugees' agitations and the ascendancy of the Communists in West Bengal politics since the late 1960s. Donald S. Zagoria observes:

> In the urban areas of West Bengal, Communist strength does not appear to be based on any particular caste or community. Rather, one of the main bases seems to be the several million 'declassed' Hindu refugees who fled their homes in East Bengal after partition. These refugees constitute about one-fourth of the West Bengal population and a substantial portion of the Calcutta population. They apparently vote for the Communists overwhelmingly. Here, it would seem is a classic example of uprooted and declassed individuals supporting an extremist party in accordance with the model put forth by the proponents of the concept of mass society.[51]

A recent study by Prafulla Chakrabarty also presents very substantial evidence which shows that the political ascendancy of the Left in West Bengal owed a great deal to the refugees and their struggles for rehabilitation in the 1950s. Chakrabarty argues that, while the Communists provided the refugees with leadership in their struggle for rehabilitation, the refugees, in turn, became the striking arm of the Communists and provided them with the mass support which enabled them to entrench themselves in the city of Calcutta, of which the whole of the truncated West Bengal became merely a hinterland after partition. Chakrabarty maintains that it was the refugees who performed the 'vanguard function' in West Bengal of catapulting the Communists to power and that 'the refugee movement coalesced in a broad movement of the left and democratic process which reached a point of crystallisation during the general elections of 1967'.[52] As the refugees were largely centred around the Calcutta area, they tended to provide potential vote banks to the left parties. This is plausibly borne out by the electoral performance of the Left parties between 1951 and 1967, when it was the city of Calcutta, rather than the Bengal countryside, which was their stronghold – a trend which has been reversed since 1967.

However, Communist influence was just one of the factors in the refugees' reluctance to go outside West Bengal. This unwillingness to go to culturally unfamiliar areas for resettlement must be understood in terms of the state of the mind of the refugees themselves. The groups of refugees who were targeted for settlement in Dandakaranya were those who came to India in the mid 1950s and early 1960s. As mentioned earlier, most of these belonged to low caste Namasudra groups. Prior to their displacement these groups had suffered long spells of persecution and harassment. An observer in 1964 described the minorities on the eve of their displacement as being 'in a hopeless and hapless situation...They are dehumanised, demoralised and degenerated human beings, having been denied the right of citizenship and elementary human rights to live a peaceful social life....Worries are writ large on their faces'.[53]

Settlers' Experiences

The experiences of the refugees after being uprooted and upon their arrival in West Bengal were far from pleasant. They were forced to live in cramped government-run relief camps. There small sums were handed out to them as doles and they were given meagre family rations. In overall terms they were treated as no better than beggars.[54] No efforts were made to create employment opportunities to enable them to eke out a living. They were, at the same time, subjected to all kinds of pressure to agree to move out of West Bengal for rehabilitation in Dandakaranya. This pressure was coupled with threats by officials of stopping rations and doles and shutting down camps in an attempt to force them to go to Dandakaranya.

Lack of alternatives in West Bengal and persistent cajoling by the authorities forced a sizeable number of families to move to Dandakaranya in the late 1950s and throughout the 1960s. Once in Dandakaranya these settlers experienced a number of difficulties. An extraordinary account of the settlers' life is provided by S. K. Gupta who was in 1964 the chairman of the DDA for a brief tenure of ten months.[55] Gupta wrote a series of articles claiming that 'what I saw myself and learnt on further enquiry caused me profound disquiet. I have decided to share my disquiet with the public, not to cast reflections or start a polemic, but so that if things are what I believe they are, immediate action may be taken to set things right. Human distress on a large scale is much too serious a matter to be passed over in silence either to feed official complacency or to save reputations'.[56]

His private papers as well as his public writings provide a fascinating account of the untiring efforts made by the refugees to stand on their own feet as well as the flaws inherent in the Dandakaranya project which frustrated these efforts.[57] He observed that the 'emphasis of the DDA has been largely, if not exclusively, on agriculture', as almost 97 per cent of the refugee families were recorded as agriculturists. Although these families were given 'not an inconsiderable area for an agricultural holding on East Bengal standards', he expressed serious doubts about the quality of the allotted land and its potential to yield sustainable crops. In his view, it was not the quantity of land, but its quality which was important and this depended upon a number of factors such as soil texture, climatic conditions, irrigation facilities, seeds and implements used, and the farming skills and energy displayed by the settlers.[58] To begin with 'settlers had to make do with the worst quality of lands, hitherto regarded as uncultivable'. Soil surveys revealed that in the Pharasgoan sub-zone, for instance, '6 per cent of the plots were basically unfit for agriculture, 32 per cent were poor and submarginal, 53 per cent could be of medium quality if their moisture retention quality could be improved, and only 9 per cent were of good quality'. The overall finding of the soil surveys came as a revelation and Gupta discovered that 'lands are not ideally suitable for the production of a satisfactory paddy crop except where the soil is of a heavy texture and low in situation'. This was particularly distressing to agriculturists from East Bengal to whom paddy cultivation represented, not only a mode of subsistence, but an entire way of life.

The poor soil quality was aggravated by an absence of irrigation facilities which made agriculture 'a gamble in the rains'. Gupta recognised that 'irrigation in Dandakaranya is an absolutely imperative necessity without which any expectation of agricultural rehabilitation in the majority of cases will prove a mirage'. However, he lamented the 'DDA's preference for big and costly irrigation schemes and its complete indifference to minor irrigation'. The full irrigation potential of these big hydro-electric schemes could not be realised due to project delays and their non-completion. Inadequate irrigation facilities thus adversely affected agricultural yields. Gupta found from a detailed analysis of agricultural output between 1960-61 and 1963-64 that yields had been extremely poor. He discovered that 'in Paralkote about 50 per cent of the families were producing paddy which was less than what was needed for food and other requirements'. In one zone, he found that 'agriculture was so poor that people gave it up as a bad business' and sought alternate means of survival. He concluded that 'poor yields made it difficult to sustain an agricultural economy even on a minimum level of subsistence'. In such conditions the settler families desperately sought other sources of livelihood. 'Where casual labour was available people whose yield was poor eked out a sub-standard living somehow; where it was not, they starved', noted Gupta.

Poor yields affected the fortunes of almost each household. Instead of addressing this very serious problem, the DDA officials chose to lay the blame on the Bengali refugees by criticising their 'bad husbandry or laziness', their 'camp sluggishness' and their sentimental preference for paddy cultivation. Gupta's own experience in

Dandakaranya had, however, been quite different. He found that, 'there are undoubtedly a few slackers, especially among those who were not traditionally agriculturists, but by and large the cultivators are inherently hard-working when there is at all any prospect of wrestling a fair yield even out of reluctant soil'. He found the settlers 'receptive to suggestions and enthusiastic in work' and even willing to experiment with broadcast, rain-fed short duration varieties of paddy and other crops like groundnut, tobacco and mesta.

If the agricultural prospects for the refugees were bleak, the opportunities for alternative sources of employment were equally hopeless. 'In Dandakaranya', according to Gupta, the planners' 'imagination did not go beyond agriculture'. Non-agricultural rehabilitation was 'foredoomed to failure' as it was limited to providing a loan for starting a trade and some cash advance for building a house, both of which had to be made good within three months. Gupta observed: 'It is obvious that industries run by the DDA have been extremely amateurish, uneconomical, reckless about wastage of time and raw materials, and unconcerned about costs, with losses mounting up annually, with employment at a low level and sporadic because of occasional closing down of units, and with wages scandalously low for the large majority of employees'.[59]

In addition, there was growing evidence from early days that the Dandakaranya project was flawed in other respects too. No efforts were made, for instance, to generate urban or semi-urban employment. Nor was a master plan ever prepared for the region as a whole and the entire planning process was *ad hoc*. Infrastructural development proceeded slowly and even basic facilities like electricity were not made available to the settlers. Further, there was the slippage of project targets, especially in house building and road construction activities.[60] The shortage of drinking water in a large number of villages became a major grievance of the settlers against the DDA authorities. To make matters worse, the refugees were not given *patta* (title) rights to the land and the homestead which had been allotted to them. More seriously, the families which had moved into Dandakaranya discovered that they could not practice fish culture which was important to them. Further, the lack of medical facilities and the rudimentary public health services provided by the DDA led to frequent epidemic-like situations and consequently a high incidence of mortality among infants and children – factors which greatly unsettled the refugees in their new environment.[61] Within the region movement had to be mostly along jungle tracks and seasonal roads. There was also the imagery of the 'dark forest' (which is what Dandakaranya literally means), the fear of wild animals, and the unaccustomed topography of dark forested hills – all of which further deepened their sense of alienation. Dandakaranya increasingly appeared as a land of banishment rather than the haven of hope it had been made out to be by rehabilitation administrators. In Hindu mythology, too, it was to Dandakaranya that Lord Rama was exiled in the epic *Ramayana*.

Yet another factor contributing to the settlers' sense of unease was the adversarial relationship in which they found themselves vis-a-vis the indigenous *adibasi* (tribal) population. When the project was conceived, the planners did not take into account the ecological and cultural setting of the tribals who had for centuries lived in the region.[62] The very choice of Dandakaranya as a resettlement site within the heart of a tribal homeland showed a lack of regard and foresight on the part of policy-makers. The planners assumed that the settlement of agricultural communities like the Namasudras from East Bengal, who were well versed in paddy cultivation, would have a 'demonstration effect' on the so-called 'primitive tribals' of the region.[63] One study suggests that rehabilitation plans and their implementation by official agencies,

> ignored the inherently contradictory nature of tribal and peasant outlooks. The peasants had a vested interest in land while the tribals regarded the forest as a common resource. The settlement operations encroached on tribal lands and succeeded in driving the tribals out....The little tribal world of Dandakaranya had escaped centuries of social development and had survived as a partially closed ecosystem....The region came into limelight...when it was picked out, all of a sudden, as one of the potential areas for the resettlement of displaced persons.[64]

There is considerable evidence which suggests that the policies of the DDA were such that they 'destroyed the tribal social and economic formations without replacing them by a viable alternative basis for their rehabilitation'. In a study of seventeen villages, Ajaizuddin Ahmad reports the incidence of substantial land alienation and depopulation of tribal villages, with about 30 per cent decline in the tribal population.

Desertions and Return to Bengal

Thus long-standing grievances of neglect, apathy, and unsympathetic treatment against local agencies and officials contributed to the overall sense of alienation which the refugees experienced in Dandakaranya.[65] Desertions by refugee families from the project had started right from the beginning.[66] In 1965, 1,040 families left and the following year another 862 families. Between 1966 and 1972, 1,600, and between 1972 and 1978, another 10,923 families deserted the settlement.

In 1978-9, however, there occurred certain events which were almost apocalyptic as far as the Bengali refugees were concerned. Between January and June 1978 a wave of desertions took place from Dandakaranya, as a large number of refugees sold off their cattle and belongings to return to West Bengal where a Leftist government had recently returned to power, which they hoped would seriously take up the 'unfinished task' of their rehabilitation in West Bengal. Under the leadership of an organisation called Udavastu Unnayansheel Samiti about 14,388 families or one hundred and twenty thousand people sold off their belongings to return to West Bengal. Reporting this massive desertion of the Dandakaranya settlement, a news report described the process as 'migration in reverse gear'. The returning refugees, the report observed,

> present a picture of gloom at the Jagdalpur bus stand and at the Raipur railway station. Men, women and children in torn rags have a look of infinite sadness on their

faces. Heavy the sorrow, as the poet has said, that bows the head when love is alive and hope is dead. They say that their love for West Bengal is alive as their hope about Dandakaranya is dead. The refugees say that all their Dandakaranya days were dark and dreary... Refugees say they are deserting 'because of the humiliating conditions in which they lived.'[67]

But the refugees found to their utter dismay that the Left Front, which now controlled the reins of state power in West Bengal, turned its back upon them. 'The chickens have now come home to roost', was how the situation was described by an observer. The Left Front leadership looked upon these returning refugees as a potential liability who would damage the prospects of an economic recovery and divert scarce resources. The government attempted to stop the refugees' trek to West Bengal. The chief minister, Jyoti Basu, appealed to the refugees to go back. Interception points were set up *en route* to persuade and, if necessary, coerce the refugees not to persist in their journey from Dandakaranya to West Bengal. A large number attempting to re-enter the state were forcibly sent back. In August 1978 the West Bengal government claimed that it had succeeded in sending back 63,213 refugees who had 'deserted' Dandakaranya by 'persuading' them that their demand for resettlement in West Bengal was not realistic, and that their problems would be solved in Dandakaranya itself.

However, in April 1978, about 25,000 Namasudra refugees managed not only to return, but also set up a cooperative settlement on the island of Marichjhanpi which lay in the Ganga-Bramhaputra delta in the Sunderbans region in West Bengal. Marichjhanpi was reported to be an uninhabited thirty-nine mile long and eight mile wide island. There the refugees showed exemplary enterprise in creating a settlement of their own. They reportedly established fisheries, workshops, small-scale and cottage industries, bakeries, a dispensary and a primary school. They built roads, a water treatment plant to ensure the supply of drinking water, set up shops and tried, in as many ways as possible, to be completely self-reliant of all outside agencies.

The West Bengal government, nonetheless, looked upon the initiative of the refugees at Marichjhanpi unfavourably and was not inclined to tolerate the existence of their settlement. The refugees' initiative was declared an illegal encroachment on forest land in an area earmarked for the protection of endangered tigers. The government gave an ultimatum to the 'illegal' occupants of Marichjhanpi to leave the island by 31 March 1979. This was accompanied by intensive patrolling by police launches. When these warnings were not heeded, the authorities started an 'economic blockade' of the settlement on 26 January 1979. All movement of goods and people was stopped and even the supply of drinking water and essential food was not permitted. When the refugees tried to go to the mainland to procure food and drinking water, their boats were scuttled by police launches. The inhabitants of the settlement were tear-gassed, their huts were razed to ground, and their fisheries were destroyed in several encounters that took place between the police and the refugees.[68] Inevitably, violent clashes followed, leading to several deaths and a large number of casualties. While the police claimed that only two people died as a result of gun-shot wounds, there were reports that in all thirty-six refugees had been killed. The refugees themselves claimed that two hundred and thirty-nine died of eating food unfit for human consumption as a result of the police blockade of the island, one hundred and thirty-six died of starvation, one hundred and twenty-eight went missing in 'police action', one hundred and fifty were injured in baton attacks, five hundred were jailed and twenty-four women were subjected to 'humiliating abuse'.[69] Eventually, the West Bengal government ordered a forcible evacuation of the island in which a 1,500-strong police force took part between 14 and 16 May 1979. At last the Left Front government was able to claim that it had succeeded in 'freeing' Marichjhanpi from the illegal encroachment of 'deserters' from Dandakaranya.

Conclusions

With the suppression of the Marichjhanpi settlement and the forcible return to Dandakaranya of the East Bengali refugees, yet another chapter had ended in the refugees' continuing quest for rehabilitation. While the refugees could not succeed in holding on to the settlement, the message that resounded from Marichjhanpi was loud and clear: that state-sponsored rehabilitation of Bengali refugees had been nothing short of a farce, culminating in the appalling failure of Dandakaranya. A committee of the Indian Parliament, which investigated the project in 1979 after the Marichjhanpi violence, castigated the authorities for 'the callous neglect and unimaginative, lackadaisical and bureaucratic approach displayed by the DDA in handling problems of displaced persons and in executing the development projects taken up for their resettlement'[70] While there was confession of failure, the political will to meaningfully take up the unfinished challenge of rehabilitation was still lacking.

In retrospect, the conclusion seems inescapable that official policies in West Bengal did not go beyond providing relief for the refugees. This relief mainly took the form of providing temporary shelter in government-run camps and handing out doles and rations on a daily basis. Government policies clearly lacked a long-term perspective. Till the Dandakaranya scheme was formulated in 1957 as a panacea for all the troubles of Bengali refugees, nothing was done to colonise land for agricultural resettlement, or to create rural employment opportunities, or to provide training and vocational skills to absorb the refugees in new occupations. An overall developmental ethos was lacking in the government's approach to the problem of rehabilitation. Faced with such a situation, Bengali refugees across the social spectrum were forced to find their own solutions for rebuilding their lives. The several millions who poured into West Bengal in the late 1940s, 1950s and thereafter had to take recourse to self-rehabilitation. The upper and middle classes, who possessed capital, skills and contacts, were able to successfully rebuild their lives without depending upon official agencies. However, refugees from the poor strata and those from the countryside had no choice but to depend upon government agencies for succour and relief. When their expectations of help and support from the government were not adequately fulfilled, the disadvantaged refugees had no option but to find their own solutions. Squatting on public land and the setting up of slums in and around Calcutta was just one creative solution which they worked out, and undoubtedly it represented to them a method of self-rehabilitation. As it happened, it became the most widespread form of self-rehabilitation in West Bengal, and the most visible proof of this is to be found in the squatter colonies which are found everywhere in urban West Bengal.

An alternative for the Bengali refugees lay in their taking advantage of the opportunities that existed outside West Bengal. In their quest for rehabilitation, the refugees naturally showed a preference to be settled in Bengali-speaking areas. But if meaningful opportunities existed outside West Bengal, they certainly welcomed them. Several successful pockets of rehabilitation outside the province testify that the Bengalis could be as enterprising and mobile as any other displaced group. One example of this successful rehabilitation was in Tripura, where about eighty-eight thousand Bengali refugee families were able to settle down. Tripura could, in a way, be regarded as a cultural extension of the Bengal landscape, having been a part of undivided Bengal in colonial times. A second major rehabilitation site lay at a great distance in the Terai and Ganga khadar in the Uttarakhand region of Uttar Pradesh. Here, due to the initiative of the provincial political leadership, an ambitious scheme of land colonisation was undertaken to rehabilitate partition refugees, mainly from West Pakistan. Although Bengali refugees constituted a relatively small proportion of the beneficiaries of this scheme, nevertheless an estimated 4,000 families settled there.[71] The third area where Bengali refugees settled quite successfully was in the far-away Andaman and Nicobar Islands. Between 1951 and 1961, over 10,110 acres of forest land was cleared and 2,576 Bengali refugee families settled on the islands of Betapur and Neil in the Middle Andamans where they were able to integrate quite successfully with the local inhabitants.[72]

These examples of successful rehabilitation outside Bengal contest the stereotype embedded in official discourse which attributes the failure of refugee rehabilitation to the inherent parochialism of the refugees, their unwillingness to settle outside Bengal, and their lack of mobility and enterprise. In a recent study of contemporary East Bengali migration, Katy Gardner provides a fascinating account of the trials and tribulations that characterise migrant lives. In her account Bengalis are described as 'global migrants' and emerge as energetic, highly adaptable individuals who transcend cultural barriers to successfully carve out niches for themselves even in far away alien lands.[73]

Perhaps it may be appropriate here to address the question of 'ethnic' stereotyping which is so strongly embedded, not only in official discourse, but also in uninformed stories about the partition refugees.[74] The official history of the Ministry of Rehabilitation depicts the Bengali refugee 'as a creature apart' who is described as 'a bundle of apathy, impervious of the rehabilitation effort bestowed upon him'. He is caricatured as 'rebellious and obstructive' demanding 'the impossible–rehabilitation in West Bengal itself'.[75] On the other hand, the Punjabi refugee – also a victim of partition – is portrayed as having qualities of enterprise, resilience and self-esteem; someone too proud to depend upon others and willing to travel anywhere to seek a better life. 'Phoenix-like the displaced Punjabi farmer has risen out of the ashes', described M. S. Randhawa in his account of the Punjab refugees.[76]

I have elsewhere in this volume argued that the contexts of uprooting and refugee rehabilitation were strikingly different in Punjab and Bengal, and it is these differences, rather than the ethnic stereotypes, that need to be explicated. In Punjab the rehabilitation effort was successful precisely because the energy and creativity which the refugees displayed in rebuilding their lives could be harnessed by the state into patterns of rehabilitation that harmonised with integrated social development. The Bengali refugees too showed tremendous dynamism and zeal, but there was no matching effort on the part of the state to rehabilitate them. The 'failure' of refugee rehabilitation in Bengal was, in fact, the failure of the state: whatever rehabilitation took place in the province was largely self-rehabilitation by the refugees. On their part, the refugees made colossal efforts to rebuild their lives though, in the absence of any integrated planning, these inevitably entailed considerable social dislocation and environmental costs – the blame for which can hardly be fixed on them. It may also be observed that the exodus from Dandakaranya and the 'freeing' of Marichjhanpi are mere markers rather than terminal points in the Bengali refugees' continuing search for survival.[77] This struggle continues to this day, not only in the squatter colonies of Calcutta or the villages of Dandakaranya, but in the Sunderbans delta, the Assam valley and Tripura where, without any government assistance, the refugees have cleared forests, colonised agricultural tracts and created settlements based on cooperative enterprise and self-help.[78]

But what about Dandakaranya and the refugees' flight to Bengal? Why could the refugees, after all, not settle in Dandakaranya? Was it their cultural identity and their sentimental attachment to the Bengal landscape that proved to be the impediment? We have already seen the difficulties that Dandakaranya presented as a rehabilitation site. It is important to recognise that the refugees' overall experience of state-sponsored rehabilitation was alienating. The 'desertion' from Dandakaranya must be seen as a positive choice by the refugees towards self-rehabilitation, rather than enduring the endless humiliation and frustration which state-sponsored rehabilitation entailed. The withdrawal from Dandakaranya showed a search for self-rehabilitation and for dignity by the refugees. It represented, above all, their desperate attempt to build a home and to recreate a world which lay in shambles. The landscape on which this home was to be built was naturally conditioned by images of Sonar Bangla ('Golden Bengal'). 'This landscape was the work of the mind' and was imprinted in the collective memory of the refugees. The El Dorado which the Bengal landscape represented to them, and their desire for an abode within it signified, not so much a precise geographical location, but a state of mind.[79]

Notes

1   On these issues, see Richard M Eaton, *The Rise of Islam and the Bengal Frontier, 1204-1760* (Berkeley, 1993) and Rafiuddin Ahmed, *The Bengal Muslims 1871-1906: A Quest for Identity* (Delhi, 1981).

2   Sufia Ahmed, *Muslim Community in Bengal, 1884-1912* (Dacca, 1974).

3   Some of these issues are discussed in their complexity in Asim Roy, *The Islamic Syncretic Tradition in Bengal* (New Delhi, 1983).

4   Oskar R. H. Spate and A. T. A. Learmonth, *India and Pakistan, A General and Regional Geography* (London, 1954).

5   A translation of the full poem can be found in Paul R. Greenough, *Prosperity and Misery in Modern Bengal, The Famine of 1943-1944* (New York, 1982), p.9.

6   *Amrita Bazar Patrika*, 8 July 1947.

7   For an interesting discussion of these issues, see Leonard A. Gordon, 'Divided Bengal: Problems of Nationalism and Identity in the 1947 Partition', *Journal of Commonwealth and Comparative Politics*, 16 (1978).

8   For accounts of communal mobilization in pre-partition Bengal, see Joya Chatterjee, *Bengal divided: Hindu communalism and partition, 1932-1947* (Cambridge, 1994), Suranjan Das, *Communal riots in Bengal, 1905-1947* (Delhi, 1991), and Taj I. Hashmi, *Pakistan as a Peasant Utopia, The Communalization of Class Politics in East Bengal, 1920-1947* (Boulder, 1992).

9   Asok Sen and Alak Banerjee, 'Migrants in the Calcutta Metropolitan District 1951-71', CSSS Occasional Paper No.62 (Calcutta, 1983).

10 C.N. Vakil, *Economic Consequences of Divided India: A Study of the Economy of India and Pakistan* (Bombay, 1950).

11 Samar Guha, *Non Muslims Behind the Curtain of East Pakistan* (Calcutta, n d.) (probably 1950?).

12 Proceedings of Minority Convention held at Mymensingh, 12-13 June 1950, S. P. Mookherjee Papers, File No.160, Nehru Memorial Museum and Library (NMML), New Delhi.

13 N. C. Chatterjee in foreword to *The East Bengal Tragedy, the Delhi Pact and Thereafter* (Calcutta, Bengal Provincial Hindu Sabha, n d.).

14 For instance, see memorandum to Chairman, District Minority Board, Chittagong, by Mrs. Nellie Sen Gupta, M. B. Dutt and J. M. Rakshit, 19 June 1950, S. P. Mookherjee Papers, File No.160. This lists various instances of persecution and violence, molestation of women and police indifference in the district. Also see Rai Sahib Monomohan Das, Ex MLA, Kishoreganj, to Members of the Minority Commission, no date, citing cases of persecution of Hindu minorities, S. P. Mookherjee Papers, File No.160.

15 Face Facts, Calcutta: Bengal Rehabilitation Organisation: n. d. (probably 1950?), p. 27. Also see *The Tragedy of East Bengal Hindus and how to Resettle and Rehabilitate them (An Examination of the Working of the Indo-Pakistan Agreement)* (Calcutta, Bengal Rehabilitation Organisation: no date). Both these publications present detailed evidence to show an increase in crime against Hindus, in particular cases of abduction and rape, defilement of temples and attacks on properties.

16 See Mandal's letter of resignation to Liaquat Ali Khan, dated 9 Oct. 1950, cited in *Recurrent Exodus of Minorities from East Bengal and Disturbances in India* (New Delhi, 1965), appendix iv.

[17] Pravash Chanda Lahiri, *India Partitioned and Minorities in Pakistan* (Calcutta, 1964), p. 27.

[18] Guha, *Non Muslims Behind the Curtain of East Pakistan*, p. 23.

[19] Khushwant Singh, *The Unending Trail* (New Delhi, 1957), and his, *Not Wanted in Pakistan* (Delhi, 1965). A *lakh* is the Indian equivalent of 100,000 and one *crore* is made up of ten million.

[20] Government of India: Ministry of Rehabilitation: *Annual Reports, 1948-58* (New Delhi, 1949-59).

[21] Lahiri, *India Partitioned and Minorities in Pakistan*.

[22] There exists a serious problem with the accuracy of official data regarding migrations in Eastern India. Unlike Punjab where most people migrated between 1947 and 1949, there was no fixed period here as migrations started before partition and continued almost till 1970. Further, the concept of border in Eastern India was such that most refugees crossed on foot at countless unmanned points. No serious attempt was made to enumerate them and to ascertain the real magnitude of the refugee influx. However, official statistics, while not totally reliable, are certainly indicative of the overall trend. Official sources give the following figures of incoming refugees in West Bengal: 6000 in 1957, 64,898 in 1958, 7348 in 1959, 9712 in 1960, 10,847 in 1961, 13,894 in 1962, 16,295 in 1963, 693,142 in 1964, 107,906 in 1965, 7,665 in 1966, 24,527 in 1967, 11,614 in 1968, 9,763 in 1969, and 251,160 in 1970, Ministry of Rehabilitation, *Annual Reports, 1948-58.*

[23] Government of West Bengal, *Refugee Rehabilitation Committee's Report: 1981: 1* (Calcutta, 1981).

[24] See, for instance, the statement of Ashutosh Lahiri, General Secretary, All India Hindu Mahasabha, 27 Nov. 1948, Ashutosh Lahiri Papers, Subject File: 'Statements', NMML. Lahiri accused the authorities of adopting a 'policy of drift' and not facing the 'deep psychological question' that needed to be addressed about 'the fate of the Hindus in East Bengal'. He saw a 'proportionate exchange of populations' with Pakistan as 'the only way out'.

[25] For an account of prevailing attitudes in West Bengal to the refugees, see B. S. Guha, *Studies in Social Tensions Among the Refugees from East Bengal* (Department of Anthropology, Government of India Memoir No.1, Calcutta, 1959).

[26] Nilanjana Chatterjee, 'The East Bengal Refugee. A Lesson in Survival' in Sukanta Chaudhuri (ed.), *Calcutta: The Living City, Vol. II: The Present and Future* (Calcutta, 1990).

[27] The Bengal Rehabilitation Organisation acknowledged that after partition West Bengal's population density stood at 1200 persons per square mile, which was 'four times greater than the average density in the Indian Union, and the highest record in the world for an agricultural state'. See 'Summary of the Refugee Rehabilitation Plan Drawn up by the Rehabilitation Board formed by Bengal Rehabilitation Organisation' (Chairman: Radha Kamal Mukherjee), S. P. Mookherjee Papers, File No.38, p.10.

[28] Lahiri, *India Partitioned and Minorities in Pakistan, op cit.*

[29] See, for instance, speech by Mrs. Renuka Ray at Dum Dum Rajerghat Rehabilitation & Welfare Board, 7 Aug. 1953, Renuka Ray Papers, File No.27, NMML. In her speech Mrs. Ray declared: 'We have reached a saturation point...It is beyond the capacity and powers of this state to provide land for cultivators and even homesteads in urban areas for the newcomers'.

[30] B. C. Roy, *Towards A Prosperous India: Speeches and Writings of Dr Bidhan Chandra Roy* (Calcutta, 1964).

[31] On some of the difficulties faced in the resettlement and assimilation of Bengali refugees in Assam, see the report of Sri Prakasa, who had been personally deputed by Jawaharlal

Nehru to go to Assam to report first-hand the conditions there, see Sri Prakasa to Nehru, 14 Aug. 1953, in Ajit Prasad Jain Papers, Subject File No.1, NMML. Also see the views of K. Samaddar of Nowgong, Assam, in his letter to S P Mookherjee, 6 Aug. 1952, in S P Mookherjee Papers, Sub File No.165. On these issues, also see Nehru to Gopinath Bardoloi, Chief Minister of Assam, 29 May 1948 in Jawaharlal Nehru Selected Works (new series: henceforth JNSW), Vol. 6, p.118, and Nehru to Bardoloi, 18 May 1949 in JNSW, vol. 11, pp.70-2. Also see note by Nehru entitled 'Migration from East Bengal to Assam', 21 July 1948 in JNSW, Vol. 7, pp.67-8.

[32] See, for instance, *Statesman*, 29 July 1952.

[33] 'Summary of Refugee Rehabilitation Plan' by the Bengal Rehabilitation Organisation, S. P. Mookherjee Papers, File No.38, p 1.

[34] 'Summary of Refugee Rehabilitation Plan', p.4.

[35] *Ibid.*, pp.9-10.

[36] Radha Kamal Mukherjee, 'Introduction' to Manoranjan Chaudhary, *Partition and the Curse of Rehabilitation* (Bengal Rehabilitation Organisation, Calcutta, 1964), p.16.

[37] This was in sharp contrast to the situation in Punjab where the government had already distributed about 47 *lakh* acres of land for refugee resettlement. For a statement highlighting the sharp disparities in the official rehabilitation effort between West Bengal and Punjab, see Ranajit Roy, 'The Refugees: The Privileged and the Deprived' in his *The Agony of West Bengal* (Calcutta, 1971), pp.63-9. The disparities were clearly reflected in the expenditure on rehabilitation. For instance, the total expenditure on displaced persons from West Pakistan during the period 1947-48 to 1956-57 was Rs 236.88 crores (including grants, loans, compensation and expenditure on housing), while the expenditure on East Bengal refugees during the same period was only Rs 109.29 crores. See *Report of the Ministry of Rehabilitation* for 1956-57 (New Delhi, 1957), for a detailed break-down.

[38] Prafulla K. Chakrabarti, *The Marginal Men, The Refugees and the Left Political Syndrome in West Bengal* (Calcutta, 1990).

[39] *Statesman*, 3 Apr. 1950.

[40] *Statesman*, 18 May 1950.

[41] Partha Chatterjee, 'The Political Culture of Calcutta' in Chaudhury (ed.), *Calcutta: The Living City, Vol. II.*

[42] Raghab Bandhopadhyay, 'The Inheritors: Slum and Pavement Life in Calcutta' in *ibid.*

[43] Ramakrishna Mukherjee,*The Dynamics of a Rural Society* (Berlin, 1957), pp.101-6.

[44] *Amrita Bazar Patrika*, 29 Jan. 1956.

[45] For an early view of the scheme, see 'Dandakaranya Can Be Developed for Benefit of DPs' by a Special Correspondent in *Statesman* (New Delhi), 15 Aug. 1957, Independence Day number.

[46] See, for example, Padmaja Naidu, Governor of West Bengal, to S K Gupta, 23 Oct. 1963, expressing the hope that the Dandakaranya project will provide a lasting and meaningful rehabilitation solution for the East Bengal refugees, S K Gupta Papers, File Doc. DS: 'DDA – Official Documents', NMML.

[47] U. Bhaskar Rao, *The Story of Rehabilitation* (New Delhi, 1967), p.202, emphasis mine.

[48] S K Gupta to P.C. Sen, Chief Minister, West Bengal, 2 Sept. 1963, expressing his concerns about the state of affairs in Dandakaranya before taking up the Chairmanship of the DDA, and in particular his misgivings about the complicated structure of the DDA. S K Gupta Papers, File Doc. DS: 'DDA – Official Documents'.

[49] A. B. Mukerji, 'A Cultural Ecological Appraisal of Refugee Resettlement in Independent India' in Leszek Kosinski and K Maudood Elahi (eds), *Population*

Redistribution and Development in South Asia (New Delhi, 1985), p.110.

50 Note on 'Rehabilitation of Displaced Persons', by Shrimati Renuka Ray, MP, in Renuka Ray Papers, File No.2, n.d., NMML. The Note discusses in detail 'desertions' by the refugees and their 'tendency' to return to West Bengal and attributes it to 'psychological' factors.

51 Donald S. Zagoria, 'The Social Bases of Indian Communism' in Richard Lowenthal (ed.), *Issues in the Future of Asia: Communist and Non Communist Alternatives* (London, 1969), pp.97-124.

52 Prafulla K Chakrabarti, *The Marginal Men,* p.405.

53 Lahiri, *India Partitioned and Minorities in Pakistan,* p.74.

54 See, for example, the representation by Radhakanta Mandal, Shyambada Vaidya and Benode Kaviraj of Umarkote and Paighar resettlement zones to the Chairman, DDA, 10 Feb. 1964, complaining about the apathy of DDA officials, S K Gupta Papers, File DS: 'DDA – Official Documents'.

55 Saibal Kumar (S.K.) Gupta (born 1902), graduated from Calcutta University and joined the Indian Civil Service in 1923. He was District and Sessions Judge, 1931-47; Secretary to the West Bengal government 1947-50; and Chairman of the Calcutta Improvement Trust, 1950-60, a position which gave him a first-hand experience of the problems of refugees. Following his retirement, he was Chairman of the DDA during 1963-64. His private papers, recently acquired by the Nehru Memorial Museum & Library in New Delhi, provide rich material on several aspects of contemporary Bengal.

56 S. K. Gupta, 'Dandakaranya: A Survey of Rehabilitation I – The State of Agriculture', *The Economic Weekly,* Vol. XVII, No.1, 2 Jan. 1965.

57 'Memo on the Dandakaranya Development Project for the Rehabilitation of East Bengal Refugees' by Sri S K Gupta ICS (retd), no date, S K Gupta Papers, File No.Doc 13: 'Personal and Confidential File on DDA'.

58 On the difficulties involved in agricultural colonization in the Dandakaranya scheme such as rainfall variability, aridity, land reclamation, soil and hydrological problems, see B H Farmer, *Agricultural Colonization in India Since Independence* (London, 1974), especially chs 7 and 9. Farmer conducted in-depth fieldwork in Dandakaranya in 1963 and 1972 and his study provides valuable details about the project.

59 S. K. Gupta, 'Dandakaranya: A Survey of Rehabilitation II – Industries', *The Economic Weekly,* Vol. XVII, No.3, 9 Jan. 1965.

60 'Note on the Dandakaranya Project for the Use of the Estimates Committee by Sri S K Gupta, Chairman, DDA', no date, S K Gupta Papers, File No.Doc D11: 'Material supplied to Estimates Committee Vol I'

61 Confidential letter by Dr. S. Ghosh Dastidar, Medical Officer, to Director of Heath Services, Kondagoan, no date (late May/early June 1964?), S K Gupta Papers, File No.Doc D 16: 'Papers on East Bengal Refugee Rehabilitation'

62 Gupta was concerned as Chairman of DDA that the Dandakaranya region should not be swamped by Bengali refugees; he urged both the West Bengal Chief Minister and the Union Rehabilitation Minister to limit the proportion of refugees in relation to the tribals and to 'stop sending further people to Dandakaranya'. See his letters to P C Sen, 10 Jan. 1964 and to Meher Chand Khanna, 16 Feb. 1964, S.K. Gupta Papers, File Doc D16:'Papers on East Bengal Refugee Rehabilitation'.

63 The Dandakaranya region was largely inhabited by the Gonds who practiced shifting cultivation. The planners of Dandakaranya believed that Bengali cultivators could inspire the tribals to take to settled paddy cultivation. In the event, it was the Bengali farmers who learnt that tribal practices like sowing of sprouted paddy seeds, ploughing

of valley-bottoms rather than sloping fields and the use of early maturing varieties of paddy were far superior to those which the Bengali farmers practiced. B.H. Farmer observes: 'Ironically enough, farms established partly in the belief that the local tribal people were "poor cultivators" from whom little could be learnt (and who, indeed, needed instruction when they became settlers in the scheme) found themselves observing tribal agricultural technology and copying it in certain respects'. B H Farmer, *Agricultural Colonization in India,* pp.217-8.

[64] Ajaizuddin Ahmed, 'Regional Development Process and Redistribution of Tribal Population in mid-India' in Elahi and Kosinsky (eds), *Population Redistribution and Development in South Asia,* p.74. Ahmad further observes: 'The state policy on land redistribution, allocation of development funds and mode of payment of grants and loans was clearly discriminatory against the tribals. It was certainly disadvantageous to the tribals who faced an unprecedented influx of non-tribal elements on the one hand and the arrival of development agencies on the other. The organized encroachment on the forest land interfered with the normal tribal way of life. Considering the fact that the tribal mode of life and economy was intrinsically linked with the forest, the new conflict engendered by this systematic intervention was both economic and psychological...the [Dandakaranya Development] Authority's functioning within the tribal fastness of Bastar and Koraput created conditions which favoured the disintegration of the tribal mode of economy'. This view is endorsed by Farmer when he comments: 'In Dandakaranya colonization has meant the intrusion of an alien Bengali-speaking people into the former forest fastness of the Gonds, Koyas, and other peoples...There is no doubt that under the surface in Dandakaranya have long smouldered the fires of resentment at the intrusion of alien immigrants from the plains', Farmer, *op. cit.,* p.272.

[65] See S K Gupta's deposition before the Commission of Inquiry (Exodus of Minorities from East Pakistan) (N. Vittal, Secretary), dated 9 Nov. 1965, especially pp.1-26, S K Gupta Papers, File No.Doc D 16: 'Papers on East Bengal Refugee Rehabilitation'

[66] 'A Note on the Present Situation by Sri S K Gupta, Chairman, DDA', 2 Mar. 1964, S K Gupta Papers, File Doc: DS: 'DDA – Official Documents'. The Note analyses some of the reasons for the desertions from Dandakaranya. Also see S K Gupta to Mahavir Tyagi, Union Minister for Rehabilitation, 2 June 1964, enclosing his 'Note on Conditions at Mana Group of Camps after New Migration' in S K Gupta Papers, File Doc D16: 'Papers on East Bengal Refugee Rehabilitation'

[67] 'Exodus from Dandakaranya', *Secular Democracy,* Apr. issue, Vol. XI, No.VIII (1978).

[68] For one account of this highly controversial event, see Ross Mallick, *Development policy of a Communist government: West Bengal since 1977* (Cambridge, 1993), pp.97-103.

[69] *Statesman,* 14 May 1979.

[70] Indian Parliament, Estimates Committee Report, 30th Report, *Dandakaranya Project: Exodus of Settlers* (New Delhi, 1979), p.88.

[71] Parliamentary Proceedings (Lok Sabha) 14 Nov. 1957, p 555. For details of the Terai colonization scheme, see M.S. Randhawa, *A History of Agriculture in India,* Vol. IV (New Delhi, 1984), pp.51-61.

[72] Ashish Bose, 'Migration in India: Trends and Policies' in A S Oberai (ed.), *State Policies and Internal Migration, Studies in Market and Planned Economies* (London, 1983).

[73] Katy Gardner, *Global Migrants, Local lives, Travel and Transformation in Rural Bangladesh* (Oxford, 1995). Recent research shows Bangladeshis to be highly diasporic: remittances from overseas migrants contribute greatly to the economy, not only at the household level, but also nationally. In 1981, for instance, remittances

contributed 4.1 per cent of the country's GNP.

74 For an interesting discussion about ethnic stereotyping and unfair comparisons of Bengali and Punjabi refugees, see Taya Zinkin, 'Focus on the Bengali Refugee', *Economic Weekly*, Annual Number, Jan. 1957, pp.89-90.

75 U. Bhaskar Rao, *The Story of Rehabilitation*, pp.141-3.

76 M. S. Randhawa, *Out of the Ashes, An Account of the Rehabilitation of Refugees from West Pakistan in Rural Areas of East Punjab* (Bombay, 1954) p.111.

77 In 1981 the Government acknowledged that out of the 'official' figure of eight million displaced persons, over seventy per cent or 5.6 million still lived below the 'poverty line'. Government of West Bengal, *Refugee Rehabilitation Committee's Report*, p.50.

78 On the demographic upheaval caused by the gradual influx of population in the North-Eastern States and the resulting problem of ethnic reassertion, see Myron Weiner, *Sons of the Soil, Migration and Ethnic Conflict in India* (New Delhi, 1978), especially ch 3.

79 Simon Schama has in a recent work argued that landscape is perceived through the 'mind's eye'. He observes: 'For although we are accustomed to separate nature and human perception into two realms, they are, in fact, indivisible. Before it can ever be a repose for the senses, landscape is the work of the mind. Its scenery is built up as much as from strata of memory as from layers of rock'. See Simon Schama, *Landscape and Memory* (New York, 1995).

Remembered Villages: Representations of Hindu-Bengali Memories in the Aftermath of the Partition

Dipesh Chakrabarty

Memory is a complex phenomenon that reaches out to far beyond what normally constitutes an historian's archives, for memory is much more than what the mind can remember or what objects can help us document about the past. It is also about what we do not always consciously know that we remember until something actually, as the saying goes, jogs our memory. And there remains the question, so much discussed these days in the literature on the Indian partition, of what people do not even wish to remember, the forgetting that comes to our aid in dealing with pain and unpleasantness in life.[1] Memory, then, is far more complicated than what historians can recover and it poses ethical challenges to the investigator-historian who approaches the past with one injunction: tell me all.[2]

The set of essays I propose to discuss here turns fundamentally on this question of difference between history and memory. They were first serialised in the Bengali newspaper *Jugantar* from 1950 on and later collected together in 1975 in a book called *Chhere asha gram (The Abandoned Village)* under the editorship of Dakshinaranjan Basu, a journalist in Calcutta.[3] The names of the authors of the individual essays are not mentioned in the book, nor do we have any idea of their age or gender though one would suspect, from the style of writing, that with the exception of one, the essays were written by men. The authors recount their memories of their native villages' – sixty-seven in all – of East Bengal belonging to some eighteen districts. Written in the aftermath of the partition, these essays capture the sense of tragedy that the division of the country represented to these authors. This attitude was more Hindu than Muslim, for to many if not most of the Muslims of East Pakistan, 1947 was not only about partition, it was also about freedom, from both the British and the Hindu ruling classes.[4]

My aim is to the understand the structure of sentiments expressed in these essays. One should remember the context. There is no getting around the fact that the partition was traumatic for those who had to leave their homes. Stories and incidents of sexual harassment and degradation of women, of forced eviction, of physical violence and humiliation marked their experience. The Hindu Bengali refugees who wrote these essays had to make a new life in the difficult circumstances of the overcrowded city of Calcutta. Much of the story of their attempts to settle down in the different suburbs of Calcutta is about squatting on government or privately owned land and about reactive violence by the police and landlords.[5] The sudden influx of thousands of people into a city where the services were already stretched to their limits, could not have been a welcome event. It is possible, therefore, that these essays were written with a view to creating a positive emotional response in the city towards the refugees. The essays were committed to convey a shared structure of Bengali sentiment through the grid of which the irrevocable fact of Hindu-Muslim separation in Bengali history and the trauma surrounding the event could be read. The question of creating in print something of the sentimental and the nostalgic about the lost home in the villages of East Bengal was the task that these essays had set themselves. Not surprisingly, therefore, they drew on the modes in which 'the Bengali village', and in particular the villages of East Bengal, had already been seen in Bengali literary and nationalist writings.

There are then two aspects to this memory that concern us here: the sentiment of nostalgia and the sense of trauma, and their contradictory relationship to the question of the past. A traumatised memory has a narrative structure which works on a principle opposite to that of any historical narrative. At the same time, however, this memory, in order to be plausible, has to place the Event – the cause of the trauma, in this case, the partition violence – within a shared mythic construction of the past that gives force to the claim of the victim. Let me explain.

Consider what makes an historical narrative of the partition possible. An historical narrative would lead up to the event, explaining why it happened and why it happened at the time it did. Indeed, for historical analysis of the event of the partition, the event itself would have to be fundamentally open to explanation. What cannot be explained normally belongs to the marginalia of history – accidents, coincidences, concurrences that remain important to the narrative but which can never replace the structure of causes that the historian looks for. Conceived within a sense of trauma and tragedy, however, these essays maintain a completely different relationship to the event called partition. They do not lead up to it in their narratives, the event of the partition remains fundamentally an inexplicable event. The authors express a sense of stunned disbelief at the fact that it could happen at all, that they could be cut adrift in this sudden and cruel manner from the familiar worlds of their childhood. There is nothing here of the explanations of Hindu-Muslim conflicts that we are used to receiving from historians – no traces of the by-now familiar tales of landlord-peasant or peasant-moneylender conflicts through which historians of 'communalism' in the subcontinent have normally answered the question, Why did the Muslim population of East Bengal turn against their Hindu neighbours? Here the claim is that this indeed is what cannot be explained. The writers of these essays are all caught unawares by this calamity. One refrain running through this book is how inexplicable it all was – neighbours turned against neighbours after years of living together in bonds of intimacy and affection, friends took up arms against friends. How did this come to pass? This is the question that haunts the book. As the following quotes from *Chhere asha gram* will show, the event was not only seen as inexplicable, it was also seen as something signifying the death of the social:[6]

Dhirenbabu used to teach us history. ...He had been the Headmaster of our Jaikali High school for the last few years. ...Even a short time ago, I had heard that he was still in the village. I saluted his courage on hearing this. ...But, to my surprise,, he turned up in my office one day and told me about his plight. He and his companions were attacked by the friends of the very student who had advised him to leave while he still commanded respect. Eventually, he managed to extricate himself and his family in exchange of two hundred rupees, thanks to some mediation by his favourite student, and crossed the Padma to come to Calcutta. But the simple-hearted teacher from a village school remained in a state of shock - what was this that had happened? How did it happen? All these questions crowded his mind. The age of Ekalabya [a figure from the Mahabharata who cut off his own thumb as a payment to his guru] is now in the womb of a bottomless past, we all know that it will not return. But still it was unthinkable that in the land of the newly independent Pakistan, it is the guru who would have to pay the student .... Yet this happened and who can tell if this will not be the permanent rule in the kingdom of shariat?' (p.7)

Hindus, Muslims, Sikhs, Christians have always treated women with respect, what is this that happened today?' (Shonarang village, Dhaka district, p.57)

How could that land become somebody else's for ever! Just one line drawn on the map, and my own home becomes a foreign country!' (Binyapher, Mymensingh; p.66)

True, my home is in a country to which I have no relation. The house is there, the village is there, the property exists but I am homeless today. The suffering of somebody who has had to leave his home can only be appreciated by a person with a large heart. ... Man, the son of the immortal one, knows no happiness today - pleasure, security, peace, love and affection have also left the land with us. On all four sides exist the filthy picture of mean intrigues. Where have the images of the olden days – of happy and easy-going people and villages – disappeared? ...Who has stolen our good qualities? When will we be delivered from this crisis of civilisation? ...What happened was beyond the comprehension of ordinary human beings. By the time they could [even] form an idea [of the situation], the destruction was complete.' (Sankrail, Mymensingh; pp.88, 91)

Why was the innocence of the mind banished after so many days of living together? Why did the structure of the human mind change overnight?' (Sakhua, Mymensingh, p.101)

Who would have thought that the country would be engulfed in a such a fire? Brothers fight and then make up to each other but the common person had no inkling that the single spark of the day would start such a conflagration.' (Kanchabali, Barisal; p.122)

Who is the conspiratorial witch whose [black] magic brought death to the cordial social relations that were to be seen even only the other day? Why does man avoid man today like beasts? Can't we forget meanness, selfishness, and fraudulent behaviour and retrieve [the sense of] kinship?... Was our kinship based on quick sand, why would it disappear into such bottomless depths?' (Rambhadrapur, Faridpur; pp. 155, 156)

I am today a *vastuhara* in this city of Calcutta. I live in a relief camp. Some in this camp have contracted cholera. A *vastuhara* child died of pox this morning when I received a handful of flattened rice. I do not dare to approach the 'relief babu' who only gets into a rage if I try to say something. I do not ask, why this has happened. ...At the time of our leaving, I asked for [a loan of] the boat that belongs to the grand-son of Nurshvabi without realising that he also had turned against us. We tiptoed our way under the cover of darkness from Patia to Chakradandi. (Bhatikain, Chittagong, p.194)

And our Muslim neighbours? For eons we have lived next to them sharing each other's happiness and suffering, but did they feel the slightest bit of sadness in letting us go? Did it take only the one blow of the scimitar of politics to sever for ever the kinship that had been there from the beginning of the eras?'(Ramchandrapur, Sylhet; pp. 235 236)

On the day of the Kali puja we used to take care of the sacrificial goat, carefully feeding them leaves of the jackfruit tree and carrying them ... and stroking them all day. But we never felt any pain at the moment when we pushed toward death this creature that we had looked after with so much care all day. We were not old enough to explain then these contradictory qualities of the mind but today it surprises me a lot to think about it. [But] isn't that what has happened all over Bengal? (Bheramara, Kustia; p.293)

This very ascription of an inherent inexplicability to the event of the partition is what gives these essays their pathos. They are the helpless recall of a victim overtaken by events rather than of one in narrative control of them. And this, I suggest, is the first important distinction we have to note between history and memory (for the Bengali bhadralok) of the partition in Bengal. History seeks to explains the event, the memory of pain refuses the historical explanation and sees the event causing the pain as a monstrously irrational aberration. These are undoubtedly essays written in the spirit of mourning, part of the collective and public grieving through which the Hindus who were displaced from East Bengal came to terms with their new conditions in Calcutta. Yet we have to remember that this grieving was being publicised in print, perhaps in the cause of the politics of refugee rehabilitation in West Bengal in the 1950s that Prafulla Chakrabarti has written about in his book *The Marginal Men*.[7] This mourning therefore had the political task of garnering sympathy by speaking, at least in theory, to the entire readership of the Bengali press.

I

There are two Bengali words for 'refugee', *sharanarthi*, meaning, literally, someone who seeks refuge and protection – *sharan* – of a higher power (including God); and *udvastu*, somebody who is homeless but homeless in a particular sense, the word 'home' carrying a special connotation. The word *vastu* used here to mean 'home' is a Sanskrit word of Vedic vintage. Monier Williams defines it as meaning, among other things, 'the site or foundation of a house'.[8] In Bengali the word is often combined with the word *bhita* (or *bhite´*), a word derived from the Sanskrit word *bhitti* meaning 'foundation'. The idea of 'foundation' is then tied to the idea of 'male ancestry' so that the combined word *vastuvita* reinforces the association between patriliny and the way in which one's dwelling or home is connected to the conception of foundation. One's permanent home is where one's 'foundation' is (the subject of this imagination being, undoubtedly, male). The Bengali language has preserved this sense of distinction between a temporary place of residence and one's foundational home, as it were, by using two different words for a house: *basha* and *bari*. *Basha*, no matter how long one spends in the place, is always a temporary place of residence; one's sense of belonging there is transient. *Bari*, on the other hand, is where one's ancestors have lived for generations. Middle-class Bengali Hindus of Calcutta, when it came to ritual occasions to do with life-cycle changes (such as marriage), would often refer to the ancestral village in explaining where their *bari* was, while their *basha* might bear a Calcutta address.[9] *Bari* would also be exchangeable with the word *desh*, signifying one's native land.

An *udvastu* then – the prefix 'ut' signifying 'off' or 'outside' – was someone who had been placed outside of where his foundations were. And since this was not a desirable state, it could have only come about through some application of force and/or a grave misfortune. For the ability to maintain connections with one's *vastubhita* across generations is a sign of being fortunate, a fortune that itself owes something to the auspicious blessing of one's ancestors. This idea of 'home' was extended during the course of the nationalist movement into the idea of the 'motherland' where Bengal became the name of part of the world made sacred by the habitation of the ancestors of the Bengali people. To become an *udvastu* was then to be under some kind of an extreme curse. And if this curse had befallen somebody through no fault of their own, they deserved sympathy and compassion from others. This could indeed be the language of one's self-pity as well. But when a refugee spoke in this language of self-pity, he spoke, ostensibly, for the nation. 'I recall', wrote one contributor to *Chhere asha gram*, 'that about twelve years ago when a household in our village lost their only son,

Deben, my grandmother remarked in sadness, "What a pity, there is nobody left to light the lamp at Sarada's *bhite´* [this being an auspicious ritual of middle-class Hindu well-being].'" Today, every Hindu family in East Bengal, even if they are blessed with sons, is bereft of people who might have lit the lamp at their *bhite´*.[10]

To achieve this effect of speaking for the Bengali nation, the essays in *Chhere asha gram* have recourse to a particular kind of language, one that combines the sacred with the secular idea of beauty to produce, ultimately, a discourse about value. These are narratives that have to demonstrate that something of value to Bengali culture as a whole had been destroyed by the violence of the partition. The 'native village' is pictured as both sacred and beautiful, and it is this that makes communal violence an act of both violation and defilement, an act of sacrilege against everything that stood for sacredness and beauty in Hindu-Bengali understanding of what home was. There are four narrative elements that help achieve these ends. What gives the 'native village' its sacredness is patriliny, its ancestral connection. Worshipping of the land of the village was the equivalent of worshipping one's ancestors. The language of secular aesthetics is provided, on the other hand, by three different ingredients, all identifiably modern in character. They were: the idea (and hence the relics) of antiquity, connections the individual village may have had with recent nationalist history, and modern secular literary descriptions of the beauty of the landscape of rural Bengal. Altogether, this was a combination where sacredness was difficult to separate from questions of aesthetics. But one thing is clear: nothing in this combination had anything much to do with the Muslim pasts of Bengal. Muslims are mentioned in these essays; indeed, their depiction is critical to the depiction of an idyll, but their 'traditions' are not part of the sacred or of the beautiful. The following excerpts will demonstrate this.

The discourse of value I: ancestry. patriliny and the sacred:

I will refrain from framing these quotations which are self-explanatory. They all refer the reader to the narrative association between the sacred and patriliny. The figure of the mother, often evoked in describing one's sense of attachment to the land, is not a matriarchal conception.

> In this urban life humming with the sound of work, a message of greeting from a friend reached me one evening. ...He had just returned from [having spent some time in] the lap of the village in which we were both born. The question he asked as soon as we met was: 'I have brought this ultimate treasure for you back from *desh*, can you guess what it might be?' ...Eventually, he surprised all by handing over to me a clod of clay. This was from the soil of my *bhite´*, the 'Basu-house', sacred from the blessing of my father and grand father. This soil is my mother. The sacred memory of my forefathers is mixed with this soil. To me this was not just of high value – it was invaluable. I

touched this clod to my forehead. This is no ordinary dust. This clay is moist today with the blood that has been wrung out of Bengal's heart. (Bajrojogini village, Dhaka district, p. 1)

For seven generations we have been reared on the affection and grace of this land, perhaps our yet-to arrive progenies would have one day made this land their own. But that hope can only feel like a dream today. (Khaliajuri, Mymensingh, p.73)

An obscure ... village though it is, Gomdandi is a veritable part of historic Chattagram (Chittagong). ...In so far as can be gathered from history, it is observed that my ancestor Madhabchandra Majumdar, exasperated by the oppression of the *bargi* [Maratha raiders], left Bardhaman for Chattagram nearly two hundred years ago and founded a settlement there in the village of Suchia north of the river Sankha. Sometime later ...Magandas Choudhuri came to his farm in Gomdandi village and built a homestead there. ...*The village that is more-valuable-than-gold, where my forefathers had grown up for seven generations*, where is that village lost today? Where is Gomdandi today and where am I?(Gomdandi, Chittagong, pp. 195,197)[11]

But no friends stopped us and no Musalman neighbour told us not to go, the day we, driven by the need to save our honour and life and with no fixed destination, left for ever the sacred land of our place of birth where our forefathers for seven generations had had their *bhite´*. (Ramchandrapur, Sylhet, p.235)

We did not want to think that we might have to leave the village. Yet we had to leave and come away. Everybody did their last act of obeisance on the day of our departure – at the foot of the Tulasi tree [a sacred plant bringing well-being to the Hindu homestead], in the deity-room, even at the door of the cowshed. My old aunt would not leave the threshold of the deity-room, her tears and the sadness of the moment wetted my heart too. The village, associated with the many memories of my forefathers, was like a place of pilgrimage to me. On that last evening, I prepared myself for the departure with a respectful salute in the direction of the village, my mother. (Amritabazar, Jessore, p.241)

I wonder, will it not ever be possible to go back to the lap of the mother we have left behind? Mother – my mother-land – is she truly of somebody else's now? The mind does not want to understand. (Dakatia, Khulna, p.257)

The discourse of value II: antiquity, history and nationalism

It is understandable that the remembered village would derive some of its value from the associations it could claim with the nation's antiquity and anti-colonial struggle. The point to note is how unselfconsciously this association becomes Hindu. Nothing that the Muslims could take pride in feature in these accounts. Some excerpts follow:

The name of Bajrojogini is unforgettable in the history of Bengal ...this is the place of birth of [the] ancient scholar Dipankar Srigyan Atish. ...The historical village of Rampal next door – the seat of the Sena kings – is without any beauty today. I had listened to speeches by the Congress leader Surya Sen at the time of [the] non cooperation [movement].' (Bajrajogini, Dhaka, pp.3,5) Sabhar, my village, is one of the main centres of commerce in the district of Dhaka. In her breast she carries centuries of indestructible history, fading skeletons of ancient civilisations. ...It was here that the lamp of [learning] of Dipankar Srigyan was lit first, it was here that his education started in the house of the guru. Sabhar then was a city of supremacy, the capital of Raja Harishchandra, adorned with all kinds of wealth. (Sabhar, Dhaka. p.10)

Dhamrai, a place of pilgrimage. In the very ancient days the Sanskrit name was Dharmarajika. The modern name of Dhamrai was derived from the Pali name Dhammarai. Truly, the people of Dhamrai were mad about religion. But what is this result of so much cultivation of *dharma*? – The people of Dhamrai are themselves without a *dham* (place)! (Dhamrai, Dhaka, p.l9)

The well-known educationist Dr Prasannakumar Ray and the once-famous doctor of Calcutta Dr Dwarkanath Ray were both born in this village. It was in this village that Pandit Krishnachandra Sarbabhauma, a logician of yore belonging to the whole of Bikrampur and the neighbouring regions, lived in a thatched hut, teaching Sanskrit to the students of his *tol* [traditional school for learning Sanskrit]. (Shubhaddhya, Dhaka, p.42)

The history of my village is the history of peace. Its historical heritage makes it great. ...It contains the ruins of the Buddhist period. ...The successful women and men of this village come to mind. Some of the people from here have become famous professors, some ICS [officers], while some have gone to Europe as representatives of independent India. (Shonarang, Dhaka, pp.54, 59)

Banaripara occupies a special place in [the annals of] all the political agitations, from the Swadeshi movement of 1905 to the Non-cooperation and the Civil Disobedience movements. The contribution of this village in the freedom struggle of the country is truly great. The sixteen-year old youth, Bhabani Bhattacharya, who gave his life to the hangman for trying to kill the-then Governor [Mr] Anderson at a place called Lebong in Darjeeling in 1934, was an unselfish son of this village. (Banaripara, Barisal, p.108)
My village has remained blessed and sacred ever since it received the touch of the sacred feet of Netaji Subhashchandra [Bose]. (Gabha, Barisal, p.113)

It is said that it was during the reign of the emperor Shahjahan ... that the Bosu family settled here. Under the protection of Kandarpanarayan, the *Bhuians* of Chandradwip, a great and civilised society grew up in the neighbouring villages of Gabha, Narottampur, Banaripara, Ujirpur, Khalishakota and so on. (Kanchabalia, Barisal, pp. 118-119)

Many, instead of going to Navadweep, would come to the world-conquering pandit of this village, Jagannath Tarkapanchanan ...I have heard that some of the stone images and stone inscriptions of Nalchira have found a place in the Dhaka Museum. (Nalchira, Barisal, pp. 141-142)

Navadweep, Bikrampur, Bhatpara – the place of our Kotalipara is inferior to none among these jewels of the crown of Brahmanical knowledge in Bengal. (Kotalipara, Faridpur, p.148)

This young Brahman named Rajaram Ray features as a footnote to the history of Bengal. By the sheer force of his arms, Rajaram ... founded the settlement of this Khalia village. Gradually, his thatched hut was converted into a seven-winged palace. Only a fourth of that huge palace exists today. (Khalia, Faridpur, p.164)

I have mentioned the copper-inscriptions of Kumar Bhaskar ... discovered only two miles away from our village. The Kushari river described in those inscriptions still flows past our village. ...from this may be gauged the antiquity of the ... villages in this area. (Ramchandrapur, Sylhet, p.236)

Senhati is one of the famous villages of East Bengal. ...There is a saying that Ballal Sena made a gift of this village to his son-in-law Hari Sena. ...It was Hari Sena who named it Senhati. The book *Digvijava-prakasha* says that Lakshman Sena established a town called Senhati near Jessore ... Be that as it may, we do not need history now any more, Senhati today exists in its glory. I am a son of that village. That is what makes me proud. (Senhati, Khulna, p.248)

The village is self-sufficient. Its name is Ghatabari. The little river Atharoda flows past it. A few miles away is Bhangabari, the birth-place of the poet Rajanikanta Sen. Raja Basanta Ray is the person whose name is unforgettable in the history of this village. ...The ruins of his palace are still there in the village next door. (Ghatabari, Pabna, p.277)
What I have heard about the history of the village is this. Sati, the goddess, killed herself on hearing Daksha [her father] speak ill of her husband [Shiva]. ...One of the fifty-one pieces [of her body] fell on this obscure village Bhabanipur in north Bengal. (Bhabanipur, Bagura, p.303)

Let me tell you the history of the name Boda. Budhraja built a big fort and a royal palace over two square miles. With the passage of time, a temple was built at the fort, the temple of the goddess Budheswari. ...Gradually, the name was transformed in ordinary speech to Bodeswari, and from that came Boda. (Boda, Jalpaiguri, p.315)

The discourse of value III: The idyllic village. Bengali pastoralism and literary kitsch:

Apart from antiquity and the glories brought about by the village's participation in the life of the nation there is also a present pertaining to the village but it is an eternal present. The village lives in an idyllic present into which intrudes the beast of communalism. The writers of the essays in *Chhere asha gram* are not the first to create this idyllic picture of the Bengali village. The picture had been developing since the 1880s, the time when nationalist writers such as Bankimchandra Chatterjee and later Rabindranath Tagore and a whole host of others drew upon new perceptions of the countryside to create, for and on behalf on the urban middle classes, a powerfully nostalgic and pastoral image of the generic Bengali village. Thus the *basha/bari* distinction was rewritten into a much larger opposition between the city and countryside. I do not have the space to develop the point here but a few words may help set this document into its own context.[12]

The geographical name East Bengal' may have been of modern colonial and administrative origins but the languages and the ways of the people of the Eastern side - people usually called 'bangles' by their detractors on the west - were for long an object of amused contempt in the western side of Bengal. We know, for example, that the great Bengali Vaisnava leader Chaitanya of the fifteenth-sixteenth century reportedly once entertained his mother after his travels in the East by deliberately mimicking the manners of speech of the 'bangal'.[13] This tradition surfaces in Calcutta in the mid-nineteenth century when the city expands as European rule consolidates itself and people from the Eastern side begin to move to the city in large numbers.[14] It is significant that Bhabanicharan Bandyopadhay's text *Kalikatakamalalaya* (1823), while using the figure of the 'stranger to the ways of the city', does not make the 'stranger' speak in the *bangal* accent.[15] The *bangal*, it would appear, does not feature as the butt of jokes until well into the 1850s. By the 1860s, however, the *bangal* emerges as the standard laughing stock of the Calcutta stage, one of the most famous characters being that of Rammanikya in Dinabandhu Mitra's temperance-inspired play, *Sadhabar Ekadashi* (1866). Rammanikya is immortal for the following lines reporting his pathetic attempts to become one of the city's sophisticated. His self-pitying sentences would speak for a long time to the sense of marginality that migrants from East Bengal felt in a Calcutta dominated by the dandy descendants of the residents of the western half of the province:

I have eaten so much rubbish yet I cannot be like they are in Calcutta. What have I not done that is not Calcutta-like? I have gone whoring, made my woman wear fine *dhoti* [the normal sign of a widow], consumed biscuits from European houses, imbibed *bandil* (brandy), – yet in spite of all this I could not be *kalkatta*-like! What use is this sinning body, let me jump into the water, let me be eaten by sharks and crocodiles.[16]

Both before and after independence, this image of the man from East Bengal has supplied much of the urban humour of Calcutta. Sometimes, in fact, gifted artistes from East Bengal have used this to their advantage as in the case of the pioneering stand-up Bengali comedian Bhanu Banerjee who made a career in the 1940s and the 1950s selling precisely the accent Calcuttans loved to laugh at.[17] But some significant changes in the cultural location of East Bengal began to take place from the 1880s as an emergent Bengali literary nationalism started to work out, in the poetry and music of Bankimchandra Chatterjee, Rabindranath Tagore and others, an image of Mother Bengal as a land of bounty. Accompanying all this was the idea of a Bengali 'folk' situated in the countryside and evincing, as against the artificiality of the city of Calcutta, the qualities of the Bengali 'heart' (another category essential to the romantic nationalism of the period).[18] The village, as opposed to the city, became the true spiritual home of the (urban) Bengalis. The riverine landscape of East Bengal was as critical to this development as were new ways of seeing that landscape, including the influence on the Bengali imaginative eye of Sanskrit literature, of classical Indian music, and of European writings, paintings and the technology of the camera. Two major literary and intellectual figures should suffice as evidence, Tagore and Nirad Chaudhuri. Tagore's *Chhinnapatrabali*, a collection of letters written during the 1880s and the 1890s when his duties as landlord made him traverse East Bengal by boat, can be easily read as one of the first literary efforts in modern Bengali prose to describe the landscape deploying the idea of a Western and painterly perspective'.

Some people's minds are like the *wet plate* of a *photograph* [the italicised words are in English in the original]; unless the photo is printed on paper right away, it is wasted. My mind is of that type. Whenever I see a scenery, I think I must write it down carefully in a letter.[19]

Our boat is anchored on the other side of Shilaidaha in front of a sandbank. It is a huge sandbank – a vast expanse – no end in sight – only the river appears as a line from time to time – there are no villages, no humans, no trees, no grass ... turning the head to the east one can only see the endless blue above and down below an infinite paleness, the sky is empty and so is the earth, a poor, dry and harsh emptiness below and a disembodied, vast emptiness above. Nowhere is to be such *desolation* [in English] seen.[20]

I had sat outside barely for fifteen minutes yesterday when massive clouds collected in the western sky – very dense, disorderly clouds, lit up here and there by stealthy rays of light falling on them – just as we see in some paintings of storms.[21]

Nirad Chaudhuri's self-conscious discussion of the Bengali landscape and his experience of it in the 1920s, shows the same changes to be still under way a few decades on. Chaudhuri's discussion is extremely aware of the recent origins of the practice of seeing Bengal as beautiful. 'The curious thing was', writes Chaudhuri, 'that the Bengalis taken collectively showed no awareness of their natural environment, not even of their great rivers' and adds: 'Generally speaking, when modern Bengalis acquired a feeling for the beauties of nature they showed it by a vicarious enjoyment of those described in the source of their new feeling, namely, English literature. Thus English and Scottish landscapes in their imaginative evocation became the staple of the enjoyment'.[22] Chaudhuri's own experience of coming to grips with the landscape of Bengal shows the modernity of the landscape-question in Bengali history. Indeed, one could argue, nationalist perceptions of the Bengal landscape owed much to the labour of cultural workers such as Chaudhuri himself. He writes:

when I grew up I began to put this question to myself: does the Bengali landscape have any beauty...? I could not be sure. ...But one day I had an experience which I can regard as conversion in the religious sense. That was in 1927 during that very last stay at Kishorganj. I was always in the habit of taking long walks, and on that day I was strolling along the railway embankment northwards from Kishorganj. After I had gone about three miles I suddenly noticed a homestead with half a dozen huts to my left, which was silhouetted against the sunset. There was a long pool of water by the side of the railway line ... There was the usual pond before it... The whole scene was like one of Constable's landscapes, and I can confirm the impression after seeing the Constable country. ...I do not know if other Bengalis have felt like me, but for me it was like enlightenment bestowed in a blessed moment.[23]

It would be untrue to give the impression that this was all there was to the way the city/country question was given shape in Calcutta's urbanism. The nostalgic, folksy image of the village never died. In the early decades of the twentieth century, however, after the emotionalism of the Swadeshi days had subsided, 'realistic' novels such Saratchandra Chatterjee's *Pallisamaj* helped develop yet another stereotype of Bengali rural society. Bengali villages, so often celebrated as abodes of peace, now became the den of factionalism, casteist exploitation and malarial diseases, all making them deserving candidates for nationalist developmental work.[24] Yet the softer image, located in the lush water-washed landscape of East Bengal, remained and was celebrated, for instance, in Jibanananda Das's sonnets *Rupashi Bangla* [Bengal the Beautiful] written in the

1930s (though published posthumously in the 1950s and soaring in popularity during the 1971 liberation war of Bangladesh).[25] It is clear that by the time Bibhutibushan Bandyopadhyay's novel *Pather panchali* was published, in 1927, it spoke to a dearly held urban image of the 'generic Bengali village' – a place, true, marked by suffering, poverty and sometimes a meanness of spirit but yet the abode of some very tender sentiments of intimacy, innocence and kinship. This was the picture of the Bengali village as a modern cultural value. The exact geographical location of the village of Nischindipur, the village where the story of the novel unfolds, was not relevant to the way Bengali readers appreciated the story. As Suniti Chatterjee, the noted linguist, said of the novel: 'I have always lived in Calcutta but I have affection for the village. I feel that Nischindipur is familiar to me. Likewise, Apu and Durga's story seems to be our own, even though we have grown up in the city'.[26]

It is not surprising, then, that journeys – to East Bengal, to the countryside – should be a major feature of the literature dealing with the beauty of the Bengali landscape. For, quintessentially, that perception was urban. Tagore's eyes often frame the countryside through the window of his boat: 'Now, after a long time, being seated near the window of my boat [English in original], I have found some peace of mind. ...I sit in a reclining position by the side of this open window. I feel the touch of a gentle breeze caressing my head. My body is weak and slothful having suffered a prolonged illness, and this nursing by nature, calm and soothing, feels very sweet at this time'.[27] Travel, by boat, is a major motif in Nirad Chaudhuri's appreciation of the Bengali landscape as well:

Consciously, I never credited Bengal with beautiful landscapes. Yet when I passed through one or other of most commonly seen aspects of the Bengali landscape, for instance, a great river (and I have journeyed in boat and steamer on all the big three), the rice fields either in their green or in their gold stretching out to the horizon and billowing under strong winds, the bamboo clumps or the great banian tree, there was not one occasion when I did not lose my sense of being a viewer only and became one with these scenes like Wordsworth's boy.

I shall never forget one such occasion. It was 14 April 1913, that I was going from Goalundo Ghat to Narayanganj in the river steamer *Candor*. ...I had just read about Turner's paintings in a book. ...The glow of his paintings, visualised by imagination, seemed to lie on the wide landscape all around me.[28]

Tagore, of course, was a landlord visiting the countryside on business, and Nirad Chaudhuri, a salaried clerk in the city of Calcutta, visiting his family in East Bengal during holidays. But in either case, as in the case of so many other members of the Bengali bhadralok, it was a matter of accommodating the village and the country into the rhythm of an urban life, where the village and holidays stood in relationships of intimate association.

Chhere asha gram repeats these associations between urban life and images of the pastoral that informed the Bengali sense of a beautiful life which, it was said, was never theirs in the city. These themes appear in *Chhere asha gram* not as so many masterpieces of Bengali writing but as hackneyed expressions derived from Tagore and other sources, short cultural clichés, pieces of literary kitsch, aimed at the shared nostalgia of the city's bhadralok. In other words, this memory places the idyllic village squarely in the middle of the city-country' question. Here, too, the beauty of the village is often tied to travel by boat and to the rhythms of holidays in urban working or student-lives, the holidays coinciding with religious festivals. I reproduce again a long string of quotations to illustrate how profusely the sentiments appear.

> I remember the days of autumn. How long people would wait the whole year for this season to come. And what preparation! The people who lived afar were returning home. Everyday new boats would come and lay anchor on the banks of the Dhaleshwari. We boys would crowd the [riverside]. For a few days, Gangkhali was full of people. And everybody would renew their acquaintances. (Shabhar, Dhaka, p. 12)

> The steamers on the Narayanganj line would leave Goalundo ... and stop at Kanchanpur. The wind on the Padma would carry to our Station ghat the sound of the siren of departing steamers. And the sound would be heard in other villages across the Ilamora fields and the tanks of Aairmara. ...all the people of this district knew that their relatives who lived in exile in Calcutta were coming by those steamers. (Notakhola, Dhaka, p.47)

> We are educated, we have tasted the intoxication of the city. We have lost our caste. That is why we feel international. Without tap-water and machine-made bread nothing tastes good to our palate. ...The door of returning back to the village has been shut for ever in our lives. (Binyapher, Mymensingh, pp. 68-69)

> We had to take the ferry across the Jamuna after alighting at the Sirajganj ghat, and then take a boat to our village. I can clearly recall, even in darkness, the picture of the sun setting on the river. When the young sun, bright and bearing [the message of hope], appeared in the body of the sky, my head would automatically bow at its feet. I found life in the water of the river and youth in the sun... The taste of the gravy of rice and curried Hilsa fish that I used to have at the Sirajganj Hotel those days still lingers in my mouth like the taste of nectar... (Sankrail, Mymensingh, pp.89-90)

> My [village] Gomdandi, surrounded by the endless beauty of nature, had only green on all four sides. Whenever we could get over the seduction of the artificial environment of the city and find refuge in the green lap of the village, our mother, we would forget all the sadness and suffering of city-life.... Travelling on boats with white sails along the Karnaphuli in the month of

Bhadra and Aswin, when the river over-flowed both its banks, the exiles' minds would experience thrill at the very sight of the paddy fields ... (Gomdandi, Chittagong. p.196)

The puja[-holidays] are close. At the this time of the year, every year, the mind yearns to go to Shilaida[ha]. As soon as we got off at the Kustia station, our hearts would fill up with an immeasurable sense of joy. (Shilaidaha, Kustia, p.286)

I specially remember today the days of the Durga puja. Every year I would impatiently look forward to these days. A few days before the puja I would leave Calcutta for the village. The distance seemed inexhaustible. The moment I set foot on the village station after a long journey, I felt like a king. Who am I in Calcutta? I am only one among the innumerable ordinary men. In my village, the station-master at the very sight of me would ask with smile, 'So you have come back to *desh*?' (Phulbari, Dinajpur, p.306)

It was within this city/country division that the village appeared both as an ideal and an idyll, its idyllic qualities enhanced – in the experience of the writers and in their telling of their stories – by allusions to literature and festivals. Both of these allusions, as we have already seen, actually direct our attention to the city where this literature was produced and where the major Hindu festivals punctuated the annual calendar of modern work. But they also imaginatively endow the village with its 'folk' character, festivals being particularly important to the construction of the folk. The literary allusions are sometimes direct and sometimes buried in the very style of writing:

Whenever I could break the harsh and gloomy bonds of the city and placed myself within the affectionate and calming embrace of my mother-country, I would remember the truth of the great message of the Kaviguru [Tagore]. ...In a moment I would forget the insults, suffering and the weariness of the city... (Gabha, Barisal, pp.111-112)

Today I am a man of Calcutta. But I cannot forget her in the dust of whose sari-wrapped tender soil I was born. ...The moment I get a holiday, I feel like running away to that village three hundred miles away. I wish I could walk along the tracks of that dream tinged green village of Bikrampur and sing like I used to as a child: 'Blessed is my life, Mother, that I have been born in this land.' [Tagore] (Bajrajogini, Dhaka, p.4)

II

Where was the place of the Muslim – or indeed of people who were not Bengalis – in this idyll? Was this Bengali home – that the village was suppose to be – was it without a place for the Muslims? The language of kinship is one of the means by which the Other is absorbed into the idyllic and harmonious village. The

Muslims participated in the Hindu festivals and thus were narratively absorbed into the image of the eternal Bengali folk. The boatmen and other Muslims treated their Hindu passengers with civility, and are hence placed within the pleasures of the putative bonds of the village-life. Even the market-place is seen as an extension of this harmony. The imputed idyllic nature of this home only emphasises the inexplicability of communal violence and the sense of trauma that the violence produced.

> There was a woman who belonged to the Muslim community of a distant village. We called her Madhupishi [auntie madhu]. It was said that she had no family. She would often come to our house. We were apparently all she had – there is no counting of the number of times she would say this. Never did the thought arise in our minds that Madhupishi was Muslim. She would often bring for us presents from her house or fruits and herbs from the field. We would receive them with eagerness and joy. Not only this. A group of Bihari people, villagers from Bihar, ... had become people of this village, sharing our soul. ...Are they still there in my village? ... In our childhood we noticed that the Muslims' joy at Durga Puja was not any less than ours. As in the Hindu households, new clothes would be bought in their houses too. Muslim women would go from one neighbourhood to another to see the images [of Durga]. (Shabhar, Dhaka, pp.8, 13)

> The moment the college closed for the summer vacation, my mind would be restless to go to the village. Barisal is full of waterways. When would the steamer arrive at the Gaurnadi station? – with what anticipation I would look forward to it. As soon as I reached the ghat, Shonamaddi, the [Muslim] boatman, would smile his ever-familiar smile and say, 'Master, so you have arrived? Come, I have brought my boat. Of course, I knew that you would come today!' (Chandshi, Barisal, pp.131-132)

> The Goddess Kali was a live goddess in this region. People used to come from many distant villages to worship [her] ... for fulfilment of their desires. I have seen Muslim brothers make pledges [to the goddess] with folded hands. ...I cannot recall seeing an instance of devotion to Kali that was so independent of caste or religion. (Shonarang, Dhaka, p.58)

> 'Babu, so you have come back to the village?', asks the Muslim peasant out of an ordinary sense of etiquette... A strong pungent smell assails my nostrils as I approach the house of Syed Munshi. He works both as a kaviraj [an ayurvedic doctor] and as a teacher. ...He got calls whenever anything happened to small children in our village. There was no demand for 'visits' [fees] but often he would receive [gifts] of home-grown fruits and vegetables. Even today I consider them the closest of my relatives. For so long we Hindus and Muslims have lived together like brothers – we have always felt a strong connection with everybody.... But today? (Dakatia, Khulna, p.258)

In this idyllic home it is the Muslim of the Muslim League who erupts as a figure of enigma, as a complete rupture from the past, a modernist dream of 'junking the past' gone completely mad, a discordant image on a canvas of harmony. The following description of a Muslim man called Yaad Ali is typical.

> They used to build the image of the goddess on our chandimandap [the courtyard of a well-to-do Hindu household used for communal worship]. Close to the time of the pujas, three potters would be at work late into the night, working by the light of lanterns. Until the time they were overwhelmed by sleep, a crowd of children ... would sit there making many demands [on the potters]: 'Brother Jogen, could you please paint my old doll? ... My horse has a broken leg, Brother Jogen, could you please mend it?' 'You children, don't talk when it is time for work!' – Yaad Ali would scold the children from the other side of the courtyard. ...Don't you listen to these rascals Mr Pal, concentrate on painting, after all, this is all god's work', Yaad Ali would advise Jogen. But even before we left the village, we noticed that Yaad had changed. He is a leader of the Ansars now. He would not even say the name of a Hindu god, he now explains Islam beautifully! (Kherupara, Dhaka, pp.27-28)

The story of Yaad's transformation into an activist Muslim and the utter incomprehensibility of that phenomenon to the authors of the essays of *Chhere asha gram* give us a clue to the problem of this discourse of value within which the Hindu authors sought to place their Muslim brothers. These essays, being instances of public memory, eschew the low language of prejudice and produce instead a language of cultural value. The home that the Hindu refugee has lost is meant to be more than his home alone; it is the home of the Bengali nationality, the village in which in the 1880s nationalist writers had found the heart of Bengal. But in doing this they illustrate a fundamental problem in the history of modern Bengali nationality, the fact this nationalist construction of 'home' was a Hindu home. It is not that the Muslims did not share any of this language – after all, the national anthem of Bangladesh is a song of Tagore's that powerfully expresses the nostalgia I have discussed. The point is rather that for all of their talk of harmony between the Hindus and the Muslims, there is not a single sentence in the memories described in *Chhere asha gram* on how Islamic ideas of the sacred might have been of value to the Muslims in creating their own idea of a homeland or indeed how they might have helped create a sense of home for Bengalis as a whole. The Muslims did not do it, but nor did the Hindus. There are passages here that even saw – at a time when the Muslims of East Bengal would have been savouring their new-found independence (not always nicely) – Eastern Bengal as dead without a vibrant community of Hindus:

> The villages, markets, settlements of East Bengal are today speechless and without life, their consciousness wiped out by the horrors of the end of time

[kalpanta: the measure of a day in the life of the supreme Hindu god, Brahma]. In that land of 'thirteen festivals in twelve months' [a Hindu-Bengali saying], no conchshell is blown marking the advent of the darkness of evening, no ululation in the hesitant voice of the housewife is to be heard on Thursday evenings, the time for the worship of [the goddess] Lakshmi. The *ektara* [a musical instrument] is silent at the gatherings of the Vaisnavas, the string of the *gobijantra* [an instrument played by bauls] has perhaps acquired rust, while mice and cockroaches have probably built their worlds cutting into the leather of the drums of devotees of Harisabha [meeting place for Hindu devotional singing] (Kherupara, Dhaka, p.22)

In other words, without the sense of a Hindu home, East Bengal is simply reduced to an eerie emptiness!

This is where *Chhere asha gram* leaves us, with the central problem of the history of Hindu Bengali nationality. Hindu nationalism had created a sense of home that combined sacredness with beauty. This sacred was not intolerant of the Muslim. The Muslim Bengali had a place created through the idea of kinship. But the home was Hindu in which the non-Muslim League Muslim was a valued guest. Its sense of the sacred was constructed here through an idiom that was recognisably Hindu. What had never been thought about was how the Hindu might live in a home that embodied the Islamic sacred. It is in this sense that what spoke in public life of value also spoke, ultimately, of prejudice. In looking on the Bengali Muslim's ethnic hatred as something inherently inexplicable, their own variety of prejudice is what the essays is *Chhere asha gram* refuse to understand.

Notes

1   See Urvashi Butalia, 'Community, State and Gender: On Women's Agency During Partition', *Economic and Political Weekly*, 24 Apr. 1993; Ritu Menon and Kamla Bhasin, 'Recovery, Rupture, Resistance – Indian State and Abduction of Women During Partition', *Economic and Political Weekly*, 24 Apr. 1993; Veena Das, *Critical Events: Moments in the Life of the Nation* (Delhi, 1994); Gyan Pandey, 'The Prose of Otherness' in David Arnold and David Hardiman eds., *Subaltern Studies*, Vol. 8, (Delhi, 1994); Anne Hardgrove. 'South Asian Women's Communal Identites', *Economic and Political Weekly*, 30 Sept. 1995.

2   Friedrich Nietzsche, 'On the Uses and Disadvantages of History for Life' in his *Untimely Meditations*, R.J.Hollingdale (trans.) (Cambridge, 1989), pp. 57-124.

3   Dakshinaranjan Basu (comp. and ed.), *Chhere asha gram* (Calcutta, 1975). I am grateful to my friend Gautam Bhadra for drawing my attention to *Chhere asha gram* and for lending me his copy of it. I am grateful to him, Anthony Low and Anne Hardgrove for helpful discussions of the issues raised here

4   Ahmad Kamal. 'The Decline of the Musim League in East Pakistan, 1947-1954' (PhD thesis, Australian National Univ., 1989), Chapter 1; Beth Roy, *Some trouble With Cows: making Sense of Social Conflict* (Berkeley, 1994).

5   See Prafulla K. Chakrabarti, *The Marginal Men* (Calcutta, 1990).

6   The names in brackets at the end of each quotaion refer to the village and the district respectively. The page reference is given at the very end.

7   Chakrabarti, *The Marginal Men.*

8   Sir Monier Monier-Williams, *A Sankrit-English Dictionary (1899)* (Delhi, 1986).

9   See the discussion in Ronald B. Inden and Ralph W. Nicholas, *Kinship in Bengali Culture* (Chicago, 1977), p.7.

10 *Chhere asha gram.* p.30 (Dhamgar village. Dhaka district).

11 The italicised lines bear a literary allusion. They quote a well-known line from a nationalist poem on Bengal written by Satyendranath Datta.

12 I have discussed this question in more detail in a forthcoming essay, 'Nostalgia, Epiphany and the Cultural Training of the Senses'(unpublished). See also my 'Afterword: Revisiting the Modernity/Tradition Binary' in Stephen Vlastos (ed.), *Japan and the Invention of Tradition* (forthcoming).

13 Girijasankar Raychaudhuri, *Bangla charit granthe Sri Chaitanya* (Calcutta, 1949), p.89.

14 See S.N. Mukherjee, *Calcutta: Myth and History* (Calcutta, 1978).

15 This text is discussed in my, 'The Difference-Deferral of A Colonial Modernity: Public Debates on Domesticity in British Bengal' in David Arnold and David Hardiman (eds), *Subaltern Studies*, Vol. 8 (Delhi, 1994).

16 Dinabandhu Mitra, 'Sadhabar Ekadashi' in Kshetra Gupta (ed.), *Dinabandhu rachanabali* [Collected Works of Dinabandhu] (Calcutta, 1967), p.136.

17 Bhanu Banerjee made his first comic recording using *bangal* accent in 1941. Personal communication from his son Pinaki Banerjee.

18 See Tagore's essays on 'Loka Sahitya' (Folk literature) in *Rabindrarachanabali* (Calcutta, 1961), Vol. 13, pp. 663-734.

19 Rabindranath Tagore, 'Chhinnapatrabali' in *Rabindrarachanabali* (Calcutta, 1961), Vol.11, p.90.

20 *Ibid.*, p.8.

21 *Ibid.*, p.30.

[22] Nirad C. Chaudhuri, *Thy Hand. Great Anarch! India: 1921-1952* (London, 1987), pp.205, 207-8.

[23] *Ibid.*, pp.209-210.

[24] Saratchandra Chattopadhyay, *Pallisamaj* in *Saratsahitya samagra* (Calcutta, 1987), Vol.1, pp.137-84.

[25] See the discussion in Clinton B. Seely, *A Poet Apart: A Literary Biography of the Bengali Poet Jibanananda Das* (Newark, 1990), pp.89-90.

[26] Chatterjee quoted in Taraknath Ghosh, *Jibaner panchalikar bibhutibhushan* (Calcutta, 1984), p.38. It goes to the credit of the filmmaker Satyajit Ray that he could convey a sense of the generic Bengali village, essentially and literary and linguistic construction, through the visual medium.

[27] Tagore, 'Chhinapatrabali', p. 82. See also elsewhere in this book.

[28] Chaudhuri, *Thy Hand*, pp. 208-9.

THE INTEGRATION OF THE PRINCELY STATES: A 'BLOODLESS REVOLUTION'?

Ian Copland

> *At the far side of empire another country lay. Many new flags flew over it; many new men held authority in many parts of it; but, for all its unfamiliarities, it was still a country much like that which had already been travelled – a country populated by controllers and controlled.*
>
> A.P. Thornton, *Imperialism in the Twentieth Century*, xi-xii.

In August 1947 most Indians who thought and cared about such things fervently believed that their country stood on the verge of a golden era of material progress and social harmony. Half a century on it is still not clear how far their optimism was warranted. Although the economic indicators suggest that since going its own way India has achieved substantial progress, the academic fraternity has remained sceptical about many aspects of India's post-colonial record. Not surprisingly, the sharpest barbs have emanated from the Marxist left, for whom the years of independence have not been, except in West Bengal and to a lesser extent in Kerala, a politically fruitful time. But the critics are not only clustered on the left. Citing the endemic political corruption, the survival of pompous, 'imperial' forms of governance, the failure of land reform after 1948 to dislodge more than the top layer of the *zamindar* class, the persistence of poverty, and of oppression and discrimination against low castes and tribals, and a glaring mal-distribution of wealth, moderate and conservative Western scholars, too, have attacked the notion of a successful bourgeois revolution in India.[1] The consensus is that change since 1947 has been essentially of the *evolutionary* kind – or as Francine Frankel ironically puts it, 'gradual'.[2] This, of itself, has led to a re-think about the significance of August 1947 as a watershed event in Indian history.

However, the most direct attack on the singularity of '1947' has come from another quarter: from historians working on the micro-history of the transfer of power and its immediate aftermath. As a result of this research, it has become clear that the political settlement of 1947-50 was a very restricted one both in the strictly constitutional sense (large parts of the imperial Government of India Act of 1935 finding their way into the new constitution of 1950) and in the sense that it was thrashed out by a very small circle of élite and rather socially conservative politicians; that in 1945-7 a very considerable revolutionary groundswell among the student and labouring classes in the big cities of Bombay and Calcutta was allowed to wither on the vine by a Congress leadership desirous of 'quick and easy power';[3] and that, despite appearances, the transfer of supreme power to Indians in 1947 had little immediate impact either on the way India was ruled, or on the make-up of the governing class,[4] or on the established economic nexus between India and Britain.[5] Thus H.V. Hodson, author of *The Great Divide*, and one of the first scholars to make use of the official documentary record for the period, concludes his narrative with the Braudelian reflection that the transfer of power was 'but a passing scene' in the 'huge panorama of the rise and decline of [Indian] empires'.[6] In one context only, perhaps, does one still find 1947 commonly described as a revolutionary, watershed event, and that is in respect of the integration of the erstwhile princely states in the Indian union. According to the doyen of Bengali historians, R.C. Majumdar, integration 'was a great though silent revolution'.[7] Echoing States Minister Vallabhbhai Patel's own verdict in a speech to the Constituent Assembly, William L. Richter talks of a 'bloodless revolution from princely to republican rule'.[8] Not to be outdone, R.L. Handa dubs the integration of the states 'the world's biggest bloodless revolution'![9]

Two themes are evident here: first, that the integration of the states – at least in terms of its consequences – was a revolutionary process; and second, that it was essentially non-violent. Now some would argue with Gail Omvedt that genuine revolutions, by their nature, cannot be anything but violent.[10] But, putting this objection aside for the moment, what, in fact, do these two claims amount to? When the term 'revolution' is applied in a political context, it commonly signifies the overthrow of an entire order or system. At first sight this would seem to fit the case, since the effect of integration was not merely to end the separate existence of the princely states but also to topple the princes from their *gaddis*. But was the outcome really so clear-cut? If the integration of the states effectively spelled the end for the institution of monarchy did it also eliminate the idea of monarchy, so long entrenched in the popular mind? Did it, in crude terms, finish the princes as a dominant class? As for the notion that this was a 'bloodless' revolution, we can assume that its sponsors do not expect it to be taken literally. Nevertheless, the term carries explicit associations of peaceful transition and implicit ones of smooth, trouble-free transition. The suggestion is that the integration of the princely states was achieved without significant violence, or dislocation, or social trauma. Is this view truth or myth?

Sections III and IV of this essay address, in turn, the question of the nature of the transition that occurred in the states, and the issue of whether this amounted, in the terms we have posited, to a political revolution. First, though, we need to establish precisely what 'integration' entailed.

II

With the withdrawal of British paramountcy – a step formalised in the India Act of 1947 – about six hundred Indian kingdoms, large and small, became nominally autonomous. Fearing the consequences of Balkanisation, the Congress high command, in concert with the viceroy, Lord Mountbatten, persuaded the princes to surrender part of that independence by the signature of Instruments of Accession (IOAs) which bound them constitutionally to the new Indian dominion.[11] This may be thought of as Stage One of the integration process. However, while accession was in itself a considerable coup, for which Mountbatten has been rightly, if somewhat lavishly, praised,[12] its importance has been exaggerated. For a start, contrary to popular belief, Mountbatten did not achieve anything approaching the 'full basket' of accessions he had promised Patel by 14 August 1947. In addition to the two well-known cases of Hyderabad and Kashmir, at least a dozen other major states including Indore, Jodhpur and Radhanpur, and a host of smaller principalities, failed to return signed IOAs by the agreed date.[13] More importantly it did not, as Lord Mountbatten pretended to his superiors in London, resolve the 'great problem' of the princely states: that is to say their separate existence.[14] The settlement brokered by the viceroy merely required the rulers to give up their sovereignty over defence, foreign affairs and communications, and then without any financial obligation.[15] It did, as States Department Secretary V.P. Menon afterwards observed, 'secure in some measure the integrity of India', it did not, as he went on (somewhat tastelessly) to remark, represent 'in itself a final solution' to the princely problem.[16] Accordingly, as soon as power had been formally transferred, Menon and Patel began to plot its revision in favour of the centre.

Stage Two of the process – merger – was the result. As a party committed to democratic centralism, Congress had long subscribed to the belief that most of the princely states had no future as separate administrative units, and by the 1940s there was something of a consensus, endorsed privately by many of the bigger and more progressive *darbars*, that only those with a population over twenty *lakhs* and a revenue in excess of fifty *lakhs* should be allowed to survive. However it was understood, and assurances were given to this effect to the rulers, that the formula would not be applied rigidly, and that the essential test would be viability. As Menon told an officer of the U.S. embassy, the object was to aggregate the princely states into units large enough 'to maintain an efficient administration and to provide adequate social and health services'.[17] This fixed the spotlight firmly on the small states of Kathiawar, Central India and Orissa where services of this nature were conspicuous by their absence and where, to boot, there were signs of growing instability. In mid December 1947 princes belonging to the erstwhile Eastern and Chhattisgarh political agencies were summoned to a meeting at Cuttack and were there persuaded by Menon, in the course of an all-night sitting, to sign covenants integrating their states with the province of Orissa. In January 1948 a similar scenario was enacted at Rajkot where the Kathiawar states – also by and large small and resource-poor – agreed to join the union as the federated State of Saurashtra. After that it was the turn of the smaller Deccan and Gujarat kingdoms, which were merged with Bombay, and in March of the so-called Punjab 'hill states', which became part of a new centrally-administered unit called Himachal Pradesh.

Alarmed by the rapidity of these developments, which looked like the thin end of the wedge, a number of prominent rulers sought an interview with Patel in January 1948. Menon reassured them on the Minister's behalf 'that the principle of merger would not be applied to those states which had individual representation in the Constituent Assembly and which obviously had a future'.[18] Nevertheless it was. For a number of reasons: buoyed by their initial success, and the extraordinary ease with which it had been achieved; concerned about the strategic and logistic implications of an agglomeration of weak, independent states strung along what would become, in the event of an all-out war with Pakistan, 'the front line defence of the Indo-Gangetic Plains'; eager to clean up the administrative map of central India as they had done that of neighbouring Kathiawar; convinced that a unified Malwa had the potential to become 'a veritable granary' such as might, in time, compensate for the loss of West Punjab;[19] and mindful, perhaps, of the role that Yeshwant Rao Holkar had played in the princely resistance movement against accession, Patel and Menon orchestrated the merger, in April 1948, of Indore and Gwalior (and some twenty small states) into the Union of Madhya Bharat. This precedent was then extended to cover the incorporation of Udaipur (and later Jaipur, Jodhpur, Jaisalmer and Bikaner) in Rajasthan, of Patiala in PEPSU[20] and of Baroda in Bombay. By November 1949 only six of the 552 states that had acceded to India – namely Hyderabad, Mysore, Bhopal, Tripura, Manipur and Cooch-Behar – remained as separate entities within their old boundaries.[21]

Stage Three – which we might label 'democratisation' – overlapped with the aforementioned developments. Indeed, the process of constitutional reform in the princely states had, as we shall see, a significant pre-history. Nevertheless the transition to popular rule was given a big impetus by events in the provinces culminating in the 1947 devolution of power. As the Chairman of the Jaipur State Constitutional Reforms Commission, R.S. Hirianniya, noted in 1943, 'there has been a great awakening'.[22] Some rulers, convinced with Malerkotla's Nawab Iftikhar Ali Khan that 'the goodwill of the subjects is now the sole guarantee of the [continued] existence of the Rulers and their States',[23] took this new militancy in their stride; others tried, initially, to fight against it. But in the absence of British support, and with strong hints coming from New Delhi that 'timely concessions' to popular demands would not go unappreciated,[24] most *darbars*, in the end, came to accept the necessity for change.

So, with ever-increasing speed, the states took on the trappings of democracy. On 15 August 1947, independence day, Gwalior announced the appointment of a committee to draw up a democratic constitution; two weeks later, an elected cabinet took office in Cochin; in November, after negotiations with leaders of the local *praja mandal*, an interim government of popular ministers was formed in Kolhapur; in early December the Maharaja of Bikaner gave his assent to a reforms-package which, in the opinion of the American consul-general, went a very long way towards turning the state into a constitutional monarchy;[25] in April a popular ministry was formed in Bhopal; and in June, after several months of procrastination, the Gaekwar bowed to popular pressures and conceded a substantial measure of responsible government in Baroda.

Yet, swift though it was by pre-independence standards, this constitutional transition increasingly fell short of the expectations of the union government; and as early as December 1947 Menon began to consider the feasibility of requiring the rulers of states that had acceded to India to 'take practical steps towards the establishment of popular government'.[26] In turn, this line of thought fed speculation about integration as a way of reducing the number of intransigent *darbars*, and after a while the States Department saw how it could achieve both objects simultaneously by the simple expedient of getting the heads of the merged states to sign covenants binding them to act as constitutional monarchs. As a result, most people in what remained of princely India came to enjoy, by the middle of 1948, a large measure of responsible government, although, like their fellow citizens in the former provinces, they had to wait until 1951 to experience the full fruits of democracy.

Merger and democratisation together brought the states into line with the rest of the country as regards the manner of their governance; but one anomaly still remained. In their relations with the centre, the 'princely' unions continued to be cocooned by the IOAs signed by the rulers in August 1947, which restricted the extent of their accession to the Indian dominion to only three subjects, and then just for policy and legislation. Of course, the settlement of 1947 had commended itself to the princes precisely because of these features; and they had signed, for the most part, in the firm expectation that the union government could be relied on to keep its end of the bargain. However, for Menon and Patel, the paramount thing was the national interest, and it was becoming apparent that the special position enjoyed by the princely unions was hindering the government's program of national development.[27] At a summit meeting in Delhi in the first week of May 1948, the *rajpramukhs* of Rajasthan, Madhya Bharat, Saurashtra, Vindhya Pradesh and Matsya were induced to sign new IOAs ceding to the union the power to pass laws in respect of all matters falling within the federal and concurrent legislative lists included in the seventh schedule of the Government of India Act of 1935.[28] Again, the transition to the new political order was not instantaneous; it took time for the union government to translate its enhanced legal powers into actual legislation. Nevertheless, by 1950, enough had been achieved in the way of banking, labour and industrial reform for Transport Minister Gopalaswamy Aiyengar, himself a former princely bureaucrat, to claim that the economic life of the states had been 'revolutionised'.[29]

To reiterate: between August 1947 and May 1950 – that is to say, in the course of about twenty-one months – the union of India acquired sovereignty and administrative control over lands encompassing nearly half a million square miles (an area twice that of France) inhabited by over eighty-six million people; a territorial gain which, as Menon points out in his semi-official history, more than compensated Congress for the loss of parts of what had been British India to Pakistan.[30] On top of this, integration generated great changes in polity and society in the erstwhile states. It brought responsible government and paved the way for rapid industrial development and land reform and better public health management.[31] Conversely, it swept away hundreds of established political entities, some of them centuries old; brought down an entire political order, namely Indian monarchy; and in the process expunged a tradition going back to the *Mahabharata* and beyond. Here, surely, was one of modern history's more revolutionary episodes?

The principals in the drama certainly thought so. Patel's grandiloquent reference to a 'bloodless revolution' has already been noted. On the other side of the political divide, one newly retired *dewan* confessed to an English friend: 'the transformation [has been] so dramatic and drastic that I often wonder whether I am still living in the same world'.[32] Bikaner's Maharaja Sardul Singh, admonished by Patel for absenting himself from the opening of the Rajasthan legislature, retorted: 'ties of blood extending over the last five centuries have been severed by a stroke'.[33] Hindsight, though, allows for a more detached view. From this vantage-point the aforementioned events appear, at once, more turbulent and less revolutionary.

III

For one thing, merger and – especially – democratisation, owed much more than is generally realised (or admitted in Menon's account) to mass action. Between May 1946 and December 1948, at least twenty-one states[34] experienced sustained periods of popular upheaval involving flag marches, rallies, *hartals*, economic boycotts and (less commonly) acts of civil disobedience. And the biggest of them were of British Indian proportions. Within four days of the launch in May 1946 of the Jammu and Kashmir National Conference's 'Quit Kashmir' campaign one thousand party members had been jailed.[35] A year later ten thousand supporters of the Travancore State Congress signed up to undertake civil disobedience against the government of Sir C.P. Ramaswamy Aiyer which was planning to declare Travancore autonomous upon the termination of British paramountcy.[36] On 1 September 1947 a crowd of one hundred and fifty thousand gathered on the Bangalore *maidan* to hear Mysore Congress President K.C. Reddy's call for *satyagraha* to rid the state of 'foreign' advisers. State-wide strikes followed, including a total walkout by eleven thousand railway workers.[37] In Hyderabad, seven thousand college students flag-marched in August 1947 in support of the state's accession to India, while two months later thirty thousand cadres belonging to the Ittihad-ul-Muslimin demonstrated against it, clogging the roads around the residency where the negotiating team were staying with a 'seathing [*sic*] mass of humanity'.[38]

Moreover the majority of these outbreaks were extremely militant. Although the leadership of the popular movement in the princely states was predominantly urban, middle class and professional[39] it contained a significant leavening of left-wingers with links to the Congress Socialist Party,[40] and in states such as Travancore, Hyderabad and Manipur a sprinkling of full-blooded communists. Again, the very limitations of the All-India States Peoples' Conference (AISPC)-

affiliated *praja mandal* movement contributed to the militancy of the 1946-1949 upsurge, for when the popular deluge broke in regions such as Orissa where the AISPC was weak, control tended to gravitate into the hands of inexperienced youngmen and fierce *adivasis* from the forests.

Of course confrontation did not always end in conflict. Sometimes just the threat of imminent mass action was enough to prompt a change of mind on the part of the princely authorities.[41] But where, as in Travancore, Hyderabad and some of the Orissa and Punjab hill states, the demand for merger met with dogged and heavy-handed resistance, the popular movement assumed an intensity reminiscent of the Quit India struggle of 1942, but otherwise rarely attained by the major Gandhian campaigns in British India. In preparation for the agitation of September 1946, the Travancore Congress and its communist allies set up regional training centres for eight thousand party cadres, dug trenches around front-line villages, and built up a store of spears, sticks and knives. When the moment for action arrived, agitators disrupted bus and ferry services, ambushed police, cut telephone and telegraph wires and demolished several bridges.[42] Later the situation there was described, with scant exaggeration, as one of 'undeclared war' between ruler and subject.[43] In the Telengana region of Hyderabad state, communist bands 'numbering anything from five hundred to two thousand and armed not only with... rifles but with automatic weapons' assaulted landlords, took possession of unoccupied *darbari* lands and set up parallel governments in 'liberated' areas.[44] In Dhenkanal *praja mandalis* and tribals terrorised officials, occupied government buildings and surrounded the palace; while in neighbouring Nilgiri *adivasis* made off with grain from the fields of Hindu cultivators and looted village shops.[45] It was a similar story in Orchha, Chamba, Suket, Sawantwadi and Muli. Here were the makings of a real Indian revolution: which doubtless explains why the Congress government in Delhi was in general much less supportive of these movements than their leaders felt was appropriate for an avowedly democratic party.[46]

The second point that needs to be emphasised is that the succession struggle in the states was actually a rather violent affair. As we have seen, the *praja mandalis* were not averse, when the opportunity offered, to attacking police and officials; but the *darbars* gave at least as good as they got. It is often said, and widely assumed, that the princely states were militarily weak; and so they were compared with the British *raj* and its dominion successors. However most of them were quite capable of handling domestic unrest. Even Junagadh, which was by no means a large state, had in 1947 about 2,400 men under arms[47] while at the top end of the scale Hyderabad boasted an army of nearly divisional size. This, coupled with the relative absence in the states of judicial or legislative constraints on executive action, allowed the *darbars* to take a tough line with opposition; and many did so. As for the government in New Delhi, its methods were, in general, more subtle. Typically, Patel and Menon got their way with the rulers by hinting at the dire consequences that were likely to follow if they did not oblige. For example, in Menon's talks with the princes of Orissa and Kathiawar in December 1947 and January 1948, he made much of the popular pressure for change and suggested to them that they had a choice between coming to terms with the States Ministry (run by moderate and sensible men like himself and Sardar) or entrusting their fate to the tender mercies of *praja mandal* leaders with vivid memories of the insides of *darbari* police cells and jails. As the American ambassador commented dryly after the first of these sessions, 'the Embassy feels that the proposals of the Government...were placed before the princes in such a manner that they had no alternative [but] to accept them'.[48] Again, it was generally believed by the rulers that the States Department had dossiers on them which contained potentially incriminating information; and while this was probably untrue (witness Nehru's agitation when he discovered in 1947 that the Political Department was secretly burning files) the astute Menon did all he could to maintain the illusion. Yet when the situation required, Delhi also was perfectly willing to employ force to get its way. As is well known, the 'problem' of Hyderabad's non-accession was solved, finally, by the dispatch of an armoured brigade; while that of Junagadh was resolved by the imposition of sanctions and the unleashing of *jathas* of volunteers recruited by Menon with the aid of Gandhi's nephew Laxmidas. Indeed, Sardar Patel would have preferred to invade Junagadh too, despite the risk of war with Pakistan, and was only with difficulty talked out of this course by the joint chiefs, Nehru and Mountbatten.[49] Not so well known is the fact that during 1947 and 1948 Delhi sent troops or agency police to at least a dozen other states as well, including Bajana, Balasinor, Chamba and Tripura.[50]

However in the states, as in the provinces, it was the communal battleground that gave rise to the most sustained and lethal violence. Ironically, down to the 1930s, the states had not been much affected by communalism, but in retrospect this good record seems to have had less to do with public restraint or exemplary *darbari* policies, than with their constitutional backwardness and relative isolation: for once these artificial defences began to crumble in the 1940s, contamination spread rapidly, particularly in the northern Hindi-speaking states of Alwar and Bharatpur which had sizeable Muslim minorities and where the R.S.S. was active, and in the Punjab states which the Akali Dal saw as the nucleus of a Sikh homeland. Indeed a characteristic feature of the communal pattern in the states was the extent to which acts of violence were tolerated, if not actually encouraged, by the princely authorities.

Nevertheless it was the advent of independence (and its corollary, partition) which – in the states, as elsewhere in north India – turned what had been a creeping disease into a pandemic. In the months leading up to the transfer of power, thousands of frightened Muslim Meos from Gurgaon district in east Punjab sought shelter with their kinsmen in neighbouring Alwar. Inevitably, this migration exacerbated local tensions, and in August a cow-killing incident at a temple (which may have been orchestrated by the R.S.S. in combination with the Alwar branch of the Shuddhi Sangathan movement) touched off a communal conflagration which resulted in a number of deaths, some of them in quite atrocious circumstances, and the forced reconversion of at least ten thousand Meos to Hinduism. In September the riots spread to Bharatpur. Subsequent official enquiries established that, in both instances, the perpetrators had the backing of the state authorities, if not that of the respective rulers.[51] Meanwhile, in the states of Jind, Nabha, Patiala and Faridkot, which bestrode the major road and rail routes between east and west Punjab, organised gangs of Akali Sikhs ambushed trains and buses carrying refugees to Pakistan. Again, Muslims were 'killed in very large numbers', and again suspicion fell on the authorities, not least the Maharaja of Faridkot.[52] Sikhs, too, seem to have been mainly responsible for the 'reign of terror' in Gwalior and Indore during August and September, which saw a mass exodus of Muslim artisans and labourers to Bhopal and Hyderabad;[53] and for the still more terrible massacres perpetrated contemporaneously in the Jammu region of Kashmir, reports of which, filtering back to Punjab and the N.W.F.P., triggered the tribal invasion of 22 October and the Maharaja's belated accession to India.

It is impossible to say how many people died in communal clashes or in anti-*darbari* agitation in the princely states during 1947 and 1948; but the number was considerable. For instance, at least two thousand agitators were shot by police in the Shertallai-Punnapra-Vallayar area of Travancore in October 1946; and several hundred in Nilgiri, Talcher and Dhenkanal a year later; while as many as one hundred and fifty thousand Muslims may have perished in Jammu and the Punjab states and in Hyderabad following the Indian takeover in September 1948.[54] Crude as they are these figures obviously give the lie to the notion that integration was entirely an act of the pen, and never of the sword.

Thirdly, there is abundant evidence that the integrative process was not a smooth one. Although by and large the rulers resigned themselves after August 1947 to the impossibility of holding out against a government infinitely more powerful than their own, some dug their heels in and resisted every inch of the way. Bhopal, for example, simply refused to send delegates to the Constituent Assembly; while the Gaekwar managed to hold up the movement to democracy in Baroda for several months by the expedient of withholding his approval to the list of names for cabinet positions put up by the interim Chief Minister Dr. Jivraj Mehta and then flying off to Europe.[55] More effective however, than these small acts of defiance, was the resistance mounted by the rulers in concert with influential sections of the population. To be sure, by the end of the colonial period the princes were no longer looked upon as divinities in human form; but they remained, for the most part, immensely popular figures, respected and even revered by their subjects. In Datia a belated British attempt in 1946 to foist an unpopular *dewan* on the ruler sparked a state-wide *hartal* in sympathy with the royal family.[56] In July 1947 Nawab Hamidullah Khan was almost mobbed by up to fifty thousand tearful Bhopalis who had heard, mistakenly, that he planned to step down from the throne.[57] What is more, these sentiments were shared by influential leaders within the *praja mandal* movement such as Harekrishna Mahtab in Orissa and Jai Narain Vyas and Hiralal Shastri in Rajasthan, the latter a former tutor to the Maharaja of Jodhpur, Sawai Man Singh. As the AISPC's Sarangadhar Das remarked ruefully, after a visit to Orissa: 'I have always believed that feudalism has to be removed lock stock and barrel. But unfortunately I found towards the end [of my visit] that many of my [*praja mandal*] colleagues do not agree with this... view point'.[58]

Alternatively, a number of rulers were able to buy time and extract concessions by playing the old game of divide and rule. Even the democratic movement in the princely states was deeply fractured: particularly as between the *praja mandals*, which were mostly affiliated to the AISPC, and state branches of the Congress movement proper. And this internecine tension was heightened by the coming of responsible government and the vote. For instance, in Saurashtra politics after 1947 came to revolve to a large extent around the factional rivalry between politicians who had learned their trade in the state-based Kathiawar *praja mandal* school and those who had come to the fore by way of the district-based academy of the Gujarat PCC.[59] In PEPSU, a cut-throat tussle for ministerial office developed between the Punjab Riyasti Praja Mandal, the Akali Dal and the rural-based Lok Sewa Sabha of Jathedar Udhan Singh Nagoke.[60] Yet this contest among fellow travellers was soon dwarfed by another, more atavistic brand of competition based on ethnic differences. In Jodhpur and Bikaner, Rajputs and brahmans came together in defence of their patrimony against the upwardly mobile Jats. In Orissa, *adivasis* rallied against the dominance of caste Hindus; while in Kolhapur the Praja Parishad split down the middle in November 1947, partly on religious and linguistic lines.[61] Given these divisions, all the princes needed to do, in many cases, was to play the part of constitutional monarchs and allow loyalist groups to defend their interests by proxy.

Organised princely resistance to the merger process was thus widespread and, in the short term, pretty effective. Yet even after *darbari* resistance had run its course, things did not always go smoothly. The business of merger itself – which involved the overnight marriage of (in several cases) dozens of hitherto separate governments, each with its own laws and ways of doing things – caused a fair amount of administrative dislocation, and the transition was not helped by the paucity of qualified personnel in the smaller states. Moreover in Orissa, Vindhya Pradesh, and Rajasthan these difficulties were compounded by factionalism and corruption on the part of the newly empowered politicians. In some of the Orissa states, 'responsible' ministers treated the public fisc as their own property; by mid 1948 the biggest of them – Mayurbhanj – had regressed under the ministrations of its new popular regime from a position of surplus to one of virtual bankruptcy.[62] In Vindhya Pradesh, relations between Chief Minister Awadesh Pratap Singh and his ministers started to cool almost from the day of the government's inauguration in July 1948, and in March 1949 Singh dismissed four, claiming incompetence and disloyalty. About the same time, the Minister for Industries, Narmada Prasad Singh, was arrested following a police investigation and charged, *inter alia*, with accepting a bribe of Rs. 25,000 and taking kickbacks from a Lucknow dealer on the purchase of Chevrolet cars for official use.[63] Prasad Singh later confessed to Patel 'that the

Ministers, including himself, had proved thoroughly incompetent for the positions of responsibility that they held'.[64] However, grave as they were, these revelations were put in the shade by information uncovered by an enquiry ordered in July 1949 by the incoming Rajasthan Chief Minister, Jaipur's Hiralal Shastri, into the pecuniary dealings of the former ministry headed by his long-time Jodhpur rival Jaynarain Vyas. Vyas himself was found to have authorised improper payments by way of 'compensation' to relatives and corrupt former officials, to have defrauded the government by claiming refunds for 'rent' on a house allocated to him free of charge, to have placed government cars at the disposal of family and friends, and to have favoured members of his own community in making official appointments. The findings on two other ministers were no less damning.[65] Clearly the introduction of democracy to the princely states was not the painless experience that Patel, Menon and their nationalistic admirers would have us believe.

IV

Looked at from another angle, this saga of mismanagement opens up another line of reflection on the integration of the princely states as a revolutionary event. Revolutions are, by definition, points of demarcation, occasions when the existing order of things is dramatically transformed. Yet the foregoing discussion would appear to indicate that, at least as regards quality of performance, government in the former states under the new order was not all that different from the *darbari* one it superseded. Was this equally true of other features of the governing system? On balance the answer is 'yes'. For all the recasting of the constitutional superstructure which occurred in 1948-50, the informal conventions of governance, political behaviour, even the social composition of the ruling élite in the states, remained for a long time pretty much the same.

First, government in the erstwhile princely unions was infused with an authoritarianism quite at odds with the spirit of democracy. Perhaps responding to the expectations of a still largely traditionalist public, ministers and MLAs in the newly merged unions typically acted like royal courtiers. They held audiences, gave *darshan* to awed crowds of admirers, campaigned regally in fleets of cars accompanied by bevies of *khadi*-clad retainers, rewarded faithful client-constituents with jobs, schools and tubewells and generally cultivated an aura of power. 'It would not be an exaggeration', writes John Wood of post-merger Saurashtra politicians, 'to characterise them as potentates in their own district realms'.[66] Another scholar relates how she was mildly shocked to hear a group of petitioners address their local Congress MLA as 'maharaj'.[67] As Paul Brass reminds us, these traits are by now part of the common currency of Indian politics;[68] yet they may well have had their beginnings here, in the former states, where until a few years before, royal courts had been an actual part of the political landscape. In addition, decision-making under the new regimes was often extremely arbitrary: indeed, every bit as much as under their predecessors. We have already observed some examples of this behaviour under the Vyas administration in Rajasthan. To underline the point, it may be noted that two of the chief minister's more notorious political interventions occurred on his last day in office. Another was the Abdullah government's decision to abolish *zamindari* tenure in Kashmir without enquiry, consultation or compensation; something not done elsewhere in India.[69]

Second, parochial, state-based loyalties did not fade away with merger and continued long after 1948 to exercise a significant influence on politics in the unions. Throughout the life of the Vindhya Pradesh Union, for example, the axis around which political affairs turned was the age-old rivalry between the former agencies of Baghelkhand and Bundelkhand: regions defined, essentially, by the kinship networks of the locally dominant Rajputs. Likewise, the determining principle of politics in Saurashtra, according to Wood, was the mutual envy and suspicion of the ex-princely Kathiawari leaders for their 'mainland' Gujarati counterparts.[70] However, Howard Spodek has shown that this was counterpointed by a secondary feud within the Kathiawar region itself: between politicians from the former states of Nawanagar, Bhavnagar and Rajkot over the siting of the union capital,[71] a contest later replicated in Rajasthan where the selection of Jaipur as the state capital was stoutly resisted by politicians from Udaipur and Jodhpur. Finally in Orissa (and there alone, so far as I know) state-based parochialism remained strong enough into the 1950s to spawn a short-lived but quite successful political party, the Ganatantra Parishad.[72]

However, local nostalgia for the lost territorial order has been greatest in the ex-states merged with the provinces. In the unions, the merged units at least had the feeling that they were all in it together, partners in a common enterprise; but for those (generally isolated) groups of states which, for convenience sake, were joined to provinces, it was pretty much a case of the small swamped by the large. Of course, there was an attraction in that also, in that it held out the promise of access to better services and a larger political arena. But in many cases that promise has turned sour. An American political scientist who visited the one-time first-class principality of Kolhapur in the early 1970s found the politicians there filled with disillusionment and resentment towards the Congress party bosses in Bombay. And no wonder! In twenty-five years, not one Kolhapur-born person had managed to gain a top position either in the Congress party machine or in government.[73] Likewise there was much heartburning among Kathiawaris when Saurashtra ceased to exist with the creation of the new linguistic state of Gujarat; and nowhere more than among the citizens of Rajkot which, for over one hundred and thirty years had enjoyed a privileged existence as the region's capital but in 1956 was summarily 'reduced to the status of a district headquarters'.[74] For Kolhapur and Rajkot (and perhaps other states too) merger led, not to new benefits and political opportunities in a larger sphere, but to exclusion and progressive marginalisation. Ironically this bitter experience of the brave new order greatly strengthened the locals' sense of identity and their mythologising of the old regime it had replaced.

Last but not least, one finds a striking continuity in class terms (and even at the level of individuals) between the groups which ruled in the states during the late colonial era and those which took power after 1948. Even if it had wanted, for ideological reasons, to purge the states of their *darbari* heritage, Delhi simply did not have the skilled personnel of its own to replace them; thus, for the most part, the *darbari* bureaucrats were given new titles (*dewans* becoming collectors or deputy-collectors, other officials, *mamlatdars* and so forth) and left to get on with the job. This undoubtedly goes a long way to accounting for the continuity of policy that we noted earlier. Yet a *sine qua non* of the integration policy was the abolition of the monarchical system, and the pensioning-off of the rulers. Hence it is somewhat surprising to find that many of the princes, too, emerged from the 'revolution' of 1948-9 with much of their wealth and power still intact.

Part of this, again, was due to the wise pragmatism of the States Ministry which recognised that the rulers had the potential to be either a useful resource for the Indian state – for example, in the role of ambassadors – or, if alienated, a dangerous thorn in its side. Against the instincts of Gandhi and the expressed wishes of Nehru, Patel, with Menon's strong support, convinced the cabinet to let the rulers down lightly. They were given generous tax-free financial allowances linked to the revenues of their states. The basic formula, worked out in the course of Menon's negotiations with the Orissa princes in December 1947, was fifteen per cent of the first *lakh*, ten per cent of the next four *lakhs* and seven and a half per cent of all revenue over five *lakhs;*[75] but many of the more prominent princes managed to extract an even better deal. As well, the settlement with the government guaranteed them free lifetime medical care for themselves and their families, free electricity, exemption from customs duty, the right to go about with armed escorts, a state funeral with military honours and immunity from private prosecution in the courts.[76] As a special favour the *Maharajas* of Indore and Gwalior were permitted to continue to exercise the royal prerogative in regard to death sentences handed out by courts within their former domains.[77] Moreover, a number of princes were accommodated formally in the new constitutional setup as *rajpramukhs* and *uprajpramukhs* (posts akin to those of governor and lieutenant-governor in the Part A states). Certainly, the powers attached to these offices were much more restricted and defined than those they had previously exercised as autocratic monarchs, but they were still considerable. During the period from 1948 to 1950, when most of the unions were still without properly elected legislatures, the *rajpramukhs* had the job of appointing and removing ministers; and, even after this initial phase had passed, they retained a reserve constitutional power to assume the reins of executive government in the event of a parliamentary deadlock or a breakdown in law and order. Hence, when efforts to form a democratic ministry in PEPSU broke down in July 1948 on account of disputes between opposing factions, Rajpramukh Yadavindra Singh of Patiala was authorised by Delhi to take charge, and he remained pretty much in sole control of the state until January 1949. As the United States ambassador recognised, the *rajpramukhs* were more 'actual' than 'titular' heads.[78] Down to

1956, then, when the princely unions were abolished, the ex-rulers continued to enjoy not only personal privileges denied other citizens, but, in some cases, a very substantial measure of administrative authority.

However, the survival of the princes as a political force into the post-colonial period owed, in the long term, less to governmental largesse than to the rulers' ability to adapt to new challenges and in particular to compete efficiently in the hurly-burly world of electoral politics. At first, inured to a world of inherited authority in which the only substantial competition came from rival dynasties, they were reluctant to put their reputations on the line by engaging in open, public combat. Ironically, the first princes who ventured into the electoral domain did so at the behest of their former adversaries, the party leaders, who grasped, more quickly than the ex-rulers did themselves, what formidable political assets (wealth, charisma, high-level contacts, political experience) they actually possessed.[79] But once the ice had been broken this shyness quickly vanished. According to William Richter's calculations, forty-three members of princely families stood for state and national constituencies in the period 1957-60, fifty-one in the period 1961-66 and seventy-five in the period 1967-70. What is more, the princes have proved consistent winners, with a success rate at the polls, according to Richter, of around eighty-five per cent.[80] At the 1952 elections, for example, Hanumant Singh of Jodhpur not only won his home parliamentary seat handsomely, with over sixty-two per cent of the votes, in a head-to-head contest with Jodhpuri nationalist Jainarayan Vyas, but thirty-one state assembly seats into the bargain. In the 1962 Lok Sabha poll the Maharani of Jaipur set a new world record when she won her constituency by a margin of 175,000 votes![81] This popularity with the voters has, in turn, given the ex-princes great leverage within the legislatures; a number have gone on to serve as party leaders, as ministers, even as heads of state governments. Against all predictions and perhaps rather against the odds, scions of the old ruling class in the guise of MPs and MLAs have managed not only to maintain a political role, but in many cases a formal connection with regions their families once ruled as monarchs.

V

In his *Prison Notebooks*, the Italian Marxist philosopher Antonio Gramsci identifies a variation from the classic model of bourgeois revolution characterised by an incomplete social transformation delivered 'in small doses, legally, in a reformist manner', and by a limited tactical alliance between the nascent bourgeoisie and the existing dominant classes. He calls this variant 'passive revolution'.[82] What happened in the princely states between 1947 and 1950 closely fits Gramsci's paradigm. Too weak and too divided to challenge the hegemony of the princes and their governments directly, the *praja mandalis* settled for an accommodation with the dominant 'feudal' elements which gave them a share of political power but left the institutions and conventions of *darbari* rule, and the position of the traditional land-controllers, largely intact. As a result there was no overnight 'liquidation' of autocracy in the states. As late as 1950, a large number of people in the states were without the vote. Lacking legitimacy and experience, the 'popular' ministries set up during 1947-9 leant heavily on former *darbari* administrators for advice and support. Some proved venal and corrupt. Until 1956, the so-called Part B states remained wholly subservient to the overriding executive authority of the government of India. Meanwhile, the *Maharajas* themselves continued to wield influence in Indian politics: initially as *rajpramukhs*, and then, more widely, as mainstream politicians.

Yet if '1947' in the context of the Indian princely states was not the dramatic watershed that Patel and Menon claimed at the time, it was far from a non-event. Integration refashioned the political map of the subcontinent. It destroyed an ancient and venerable political tradition. It claimed thousands of lives and disrupted countless others. Moreover integration opened the door to further change. The post-princely regimes may not, initially, have been all that democratic, but they shared the centre's commitment to building a more humane and egalitarian society. In the 1950s spending on public health, education and community development in the erstwhile states rose sharply across the board. By the 1970s these new programs were starting to have a significant impact on literacy – up from around eleven per cent to over thirty per cent – and life expectancy which increased by nearly five years for males between 1961 and 1981.[83] Although the former princely territories as a body still lag behind the former British provinces in development (even today Rajasthan and Madhya Pradesh, the princely heartland down to 1948, are among the poorest parts of India), the gap is closing gradually.

Gramsci believed that genuine revolutions are rare events. This may be so. But it does not follow that the times between must be ones of stagnation. Whatever its surface features might suggest, change in society goes on continuously and inexorably. It is almost the only thing in history that we can be absolutely sure of.

Notes

1   The pessimistic view is presented in Francine Frankel, *India's Political Economy: the Gradual Revolution* (Princeton, N.J., 1978), and Ajit Roy, *Political Power in India: Nature and Trends* (Calcutta, 1975), esp. pp. 7-10. But note well Robert Stern's conclusion, based on the work of Gilbert Etienne, that 'smallholders' and 'even the landless' have benefited to some extent from the trickle-down effects of the 'green revolution'. Robert W. Stern, 'Bourgeois Revolution in India', in Jim Masselos (ed.), *India: Creating a Modern Nation* (New Delhi, 1990), pp. 421-2.

2   Frankel, India's *Political Economy, passim.*

3   Sumit Sarkar, *Modern India, 1885-1947* (Madras, 1983), p. 428; and Suniti Kumar Ghose , 'On the Transfer of Power in India, *Bulletin of Concerned Asian Scholars*, 17, 3 (July-Sept. 1985), pp. 31-2.

4   Scores of European administrative personnel (including the last viceroy, Mountbatten) stayed on for periods of a few months to several years; more importantly, both at the political level and within the senior public service, continuity of service was maintained among Indians. Thus British-trained officers were still in the majority in the I.A.S. as late as 1980; while it took thirty years for a non-brahmin to graduate to the Indian premiership.

5   B.R. Tomlinson, 'Continuities and Discontinuities in Indo-British Economic Relations: British Multi-National Corporations in India, 1920-1970, in W.J. Mommsen and Jurgen Oosterhammel (eds), *Imperialism and After: Continuities and Discontinuities* (London, 1986), pp. 154-7.

6   H.V. Hodson, *The Great Divide: Britain-India-Pakistan* (London, 1969), p. 542.

7   R.C. Majumdar *et. al., Struggle For Freedom* (Bombay, 1969), p. 784.

8   William L. Richter, 'Princes in Indian Politics', *Economic and Political Weekly*, VI, 9 (27 Feb. 1971), p. 538.

9   R.L. Handa, *History of Freedom Struggle in Princely States* (Delhi, 1968), p. 6.

10   Gail Omvedt, 'Gandhi and the Pacification of the Indian Nationalist Movement' in R. Jeffrey *et al* (eds), *Rebellion to Republic: Selected Writings, 1957-1990* (New Delhi, 1990), p. 65.

11   A small number – all, but one, Muslim majority states – signed with Pakistan.

12   See, e.g., Hodson, *op. cit.*, p. 388; R.J. Moore, *Escape From Empire: the Attlee Government and the Indian Problem* (Oxford, 1983), p. 347; E.W.R. Lumby, *The Transfer of Power in India, 1945-7* (London, 1954), p. 236; Philip Zeigler, *Mountbatten: the Official Biography* (London, 1985), p. 414; and M.N. Das, *Partition and Independence of India: Inside Story of the Mountbatten Days* (New Delhi, 1982), p. 261. For a more sceptical view, see Ian Copland, 'Lord Mountbatten and the Integration of the Indian States: A Reappraisal', *Journal of Imperial and Commonwealth History*, 21, 2, (May 1993), pp. 385-408.

13   'Accession of State to the Dominion of India', and C.C. Desai, Jt. Sec., States Ministry to Capt. R.V. Brockman, Priv. Sec. to the Gov.-Gen, 1 Nov., 24 Dec. 1947 and 15 Jan. 1948, India Office Records, British Library, London [hereafter IOL], PSV R/3/1/140; and Consul-Gen. Bombay to Sec. State Washington, 6 Feb. 1948, U.S. State Dept, decimal file 845.00/2-648.

14   Personal report No. 17 dated 16 Aug. 1947, Nicholas Mansergh *et al.* (eds), *Constitutional Relations Between Britain and India; the Transfer of Power 1942-7* [Hereafter *TP*] (London, 1970-83), XII, p. 768.

15   The cession of powers was formally spelled out in the IOAs. The financial aspects

were not, and, perhaps significantly, the Maharaja of Baroda's attempt to secure a collateral letter from Patel to cover this omission was cavalierly brushed aside. Baroda to Mountbatten, 10 Aug. 1947, and viceroy's personal report No.17, 16 Aug. 1947, *TP*, XII, pp. 643 and 767.

16 Speech to the rulers of Kathiawar, 17 Jan. 1948, V. P. Menon, *The Story of the Integration of the Indian States* (London, 1956), p. 174. Menon afterwards stoutly defended himself and Sardar Patel against allegations of duplicity. 'There was no question at the time that we would extinguish the States at all', he wrote in a letter of 1957. It is hard, however, to imagine that someone as intelligent and politically sagacious as Menon would not have seen that the three-subject accession formula was unlikely to last. See Menon to Mirza Ismail, 2 Mar. 1957, Mirza Ismail Papers, Nehru Memorial Museum and Library [hereafter NMML].

17 Ambassador, New Delhi to State Dept, Washington, U.S. State Dept, decimal file 845.00/12-3147; and note by Nehru on a conversation with the Nawab of Bhopal, Chancellor, Chamber of Princes, 21 Apr. 1946, Durga Das (ed.), *Sardar Patel's Correspondence 1945-50* [hereafter *PC*], (Ahmedabad, 1971-4), 3, p. 330.

18 Menon, *op. cit.*, p. 164.

19 Proposal for the formation of the United State of Gwalior, Indore and Malwa as summarised for cabinet by Menon (25 Apr. 1948), Mountbatten Collection, British Library, file 147. See also note by Menon for cabinet on the merger of the Gujarat states, 22 Mar. 1948, *ibid*, p. 146.

20 Patiala and East Punjab States Union.

21 Jammu and Kashmir still existed as a separate entity but after the tribal invasion of Oct. 1947 it became effectively a partitioned state. Sikkim and Bhutan likewise maintained an independent existence but these border states had always been treated as a special case.

22 Quoted in Bhawani Singh, 'Princes, Politics and Legitimacy, *Political Science Review*, Vol. 24, 3/4 (1988), p. 8.

23 Malerkotla to Maharaja Yadavindra Singh of Patiala, 22 Jan. 1948, Nawab of Malerkotla Papers, NMML, subject file 1.

24 Speech by N.V. Gadgil, Minister of Works, in the Constituent Assembly, 15 Mar. 1948, quoted in R.C. Majumdar *et. al.*, *An Advanced History of India* (London, 1967), pp. 995-6.

25 Consul-General Bombay to Sec. State Washington, 12 Dec. 1947, U.S. State Dept, decimal file 845.00/12-1247.

26 In conversation with the American Ambassador. See Ambassador New Delhi to Sec. State Washington, 10 Dec. 1947, U.S. State Dept, decimal file 845.00/12-1047.

27 Summary for Cabinet by V. P. Menon on the formation of the United State of Gwalior, Indore and Malwa, 25 Apr. 1948, Mountbatten Collection, file 147.

28 *The Sunday Statesman*, 9 May 1948; and U.K. High Commissioner New Delhi to Commonwealth Relations Office (17 May 1948), IOL, L/P&S/13/1848. The *rajpramukhs* – led by Saurashtra's elder statesman, and former Chancellor of the Chamber of Princes Digvijaysinhji of Nawanagar, did score one win. They persuaded Menon that the princely unions should not have to pay federal tax for up to fifteen years. However, this concession was later revoked on the recommendation of the Krishnamachari Committee of 1950-1.

29 Quoted in Menon, *op. cit.*, p. 227.

30 Menon, *op.cit.*, p. 468.

31 For what was done after integration in the former Punjab hill states, see Patel to A.V.

Thakkar, 17 June 1950, *PC,* 9, pp. 481-2.

[32] Kenneth Fitze, *Twilight of the Maharajas* (London, 1956), p. 87.

[33] Bikaner to Patel, 29 Mar. 1949, *PC*, 8, p. 501.

[34] Baroda, Bhopal, Bilaspur, Chamba, Cooch-Behar, Datia, Dhenkenal, Dhrangadhra, Gwalior, Hyderabad, Indore, Jind, Manipur, Mysore, Muli, Nilgiri, Orchha, Sawantwadi, Talcher, Travancore, Tripura.

[35] For a discussion of the aims and course of the Quit Kashmir movement see Ian Copland, 'The Abdullah Factor: Kashmiri Muslims and the Crisis of 1947' in. D.A. Low (ed.), *The Political Inheritance of Pakistan* (London, 1991), pp. 233-5; and Muhammad Yusuf Saraf, *Kashmiris Fight For Freedom*, pp. 672-7.

[36] Consul General Bombay to Sec. State Washington, 27 May 1947, U.S. State Dept, decimal file 845.00/5-2747.

[37] James Manor, *Political Change in an Indian State: Mysore 1917-1955* (New Delhi, 1977), p. 156; and Consul-General Madras to Sec. State Washington, 11 Sept. 1947, U.S. State Dept, decimal file 845.00/9-1147.

[38] Mir Laik Ali, *Tragedy of Hyderabad* (Karachi, 1962), p. 73.

[39] For an analysis of the structure and support base of two fairly typical north Indian *praja mandals*, namely those of Jaipur and Jodhpur, see Bhawani Singh, 'Princes, Politics and Legitimacy', in *Political Science Review*, 24, 3/4 (1988), pp. 1-20.. The burden of Bhawani Singh's argument is that the Jaipur freedom struggle was more broadly based, because there the *praja mandal* operated in concert with Jat leaders from the rural *kisan sabha*. But the basic point stands: both were essentially élitist, urban movements.

[40] On this aspect see Ian Copland, 'Congress Paternalism: the High Command and the Struggle For Freedom in Princely India, c. 1920-1940, *South Asia*, New Series, Vol. VIII, nos 1 & 2 (1985), pp. 121-40.

[41] D.B. Rosenthal, 'From Reformist Princes to Cooperative Kings I', *Economic and Political Weekly*, VIII, 20 (19 May 1973), pp. 907-8; and Consul-General Bombay to Sec. State Washington, 17 Jan. 1948, U.S. State Dept, decimal file 845.00/1-1748.

[42] Vanaja Rangaswamy, *The Story of Integration: A New Interpretation* (New Delhi, 1981), p. 214.

[43] *Free Press Journal* (Bombay) 19 July 1947.

[44] High Commissioner New Delhi to CRO London, 25 Mar. 1948, IOL, L/P&S/13/1204.

[45] Menon, *op. cit.*, p. 146.

[46] For a communist view of the Telengana 'betrayal': the thesis is essentially that Delhi delayed moving against the Nizam until the back of the Telengana movement had been broken by the state police and the para-military Razakar organisation. see P. Sundarayya, *Telengana People's Struggle and its Lessons* (Calcutta, 1972).

[47] Although some were equipped only with shotguns and muzzle-loading muskets. 'Appreciation of the Joint Chiefs of Staff of the Situation in Kathiawar, 2 Oct. 1947, Appendix D, Mountbatten Collection, IOL, file 90.

[48] Ambassador New Delhi to Sec. State Washington, 31 Dec. 1947, U.S. State Dept, decimal file 845.00/12-3147.

[49] Note by Rear-Admiral J.T.S. Hall, General R.M.M. Lockhart and Air-Commodore S. Mukherjee, 27 Sept. 1947, and notes by Mountbatten, 28 and 29 Sept. 1947, Mountbatten Collection, IOL, file 90.

[50] Karbhari, Bajana to Mountbatten, 7 Sept. 1947, Mountbatten Collection, IOL, file

90; memo. by CR Minister, U.K., 12 Sept. 1947, IOL, L/P&S/13/1848; Patel to K.C. Neogy, 7 Nov. 1947, *PC*, 5, p. 429; and 'Summary For the Cabinet On the Formation Of a Punjab Hill States Province' [by Menon?], 12 Apr. 1948, Mountbatten Collection, file 147.

51 Both *Maharajas* were forced to step down in Feb. 1948 pending the result of the investigations and separate charges that Alwar officials had provided sanctuary and assistance to Gandhi's assassin Nathuram Godse, who had stopped off there on his way to Delhi. The two rulers were eventually cleared of the charges of complicity but Alwar's pro-Hindu premier N.B. Khare was sacked and the two states were taken under the administration of New Delhi. Political Agent Jaipur to Crown Representative, 7 Aug. 1947, *TP*, XII, p. 571; Khare to Manilal Doshi, 13 Aug. 1947, N.B. Khare Papers, National Archives of India, p. 165; Ambassador New Delhi to Sec. State Washington, 17 Feb. 1948, U.S. State Dept, decimal file 845.00/2-1748; Nehru to Chief Minister Mysore, 26 May 1948, Nehru Papers, 1st instalment, p. 7; and interview between Dr. H.D. Sharma and Khare on 16 July 1967, Oral History Transcript No. 230, NMML, pp. 70-1.

52 Note by Lord Ismay on talk with Nehru, 3 Oct. 1947, Mountbatten Collection, file 90; Nehru to Pattabhi Sitaramayya, 3 Mar. 1948, Nehru papers, 1st instalment, p. 7; and Nehru to Baldev Singh, 17 July 1948, *Ibid*, p. 11.

53 Consul-General Bombay to Sec. State Washington, 27 Oct. 1947, U.S. State Dept, decimal file 845.00/10-2747. In this case the aggressors were Sikh refugees from West Punjab.

54 Estimates for Jammu vary wildly, and are confused by the mass migration which occurred after the massacres began, but comparisons of census records for Jammu and West Punjab between 1941 and 1951 leave about 200,000 people unaccounted for; some of these undoubtedly died in the holocaust. Again, Congress sources suggest that up to 12,000 Muslims may have been killed in 'Patiala alone'; while conservative estimates for Hyderabad range between 20,000 and 50,000. Figures for the Orissa states are fuzzy but Congress sources confirm that at least forty *adivasis* died as a result of police firing in Kharisan on New Year's Day 1948, the worst of some dozen similar incidents. Report by Sarangadar Das to Presdt. AISPC dated 2 Feb. 1948, AISPC, 129, Part I, 1947-8, NMML; Rangaswamy, *op. cit.*, p. 215; Alistair Lamb, *Kashmir: A Disputed Legacy 1846-1990* (Hertingfordbury, 1991), p. 123; R.J. Moore, *The Making of the New Commonwealth* (Oxford, 1987), p. 44; and W. Cantwell-Smith, 'Hyderabad, Muslim Tragedy', *Middle East Journal*, 4 (Jan. 1950), pp. 46-7.

55 On Bhopal see Patel to Nehru, 11 Jan. 1949, *PC*, 8, p. 482, and on Baroda, Menon, *op. cit.*, pp. 401-9.

56 Maharaja of Datia to Patel, 14 Nov. 1946, *PC*, 3, p. 376; and *National Herald*, 18 Nov. 1946.

57 Press communique, 14 Aug. 1947, IOL, PSV R/3/1/143.

58 Note by Das, 27 Nov. 1947, and report by Das on the merger of the Orissa and C.P. states, 2 Feb. 1948, AISPC, 129, Part I, 1947-8.

59 John R. Wood, 'British versus Princely Legacies and the Political Integration of Gujarat', *Journal of Asian Studies*, XLIV, 1 (1984), p. 73.

60 Menon, *op. cit.*, pp. 236-7. See also Sarangadhar Das, President Orissa SPC to M.P. Barghav, 12 May 1948 on relations between the Orissa states *praja mandals* and the Utkal PCC, AISPC, 129, Part I, 1947-8; and Rajbahadur Singh, Sec. 'Nagod

Congress', to Patel, 25 Jan. 1947 on the disruption caused to his organisation by cadres belonging to the Nagod Praja Mandal, *PC*, 5, p. 349.

61 The Parishad had two outstanding leaders, Madhavrao Bagal, a Marathi and member of the crusading Satyashodak Samaj, and Rutnappa Kumbhar, a Lingayat. The split in November 1947 had something to do with their competing designs on the premiership, but even more to do with underlying ideological differences related to Bagal's support for the creation of a Marathi-speaking province and Kumbhar's solicitude for his fellow Kannada-speakers. Presdt., N. Karnataka States Regional Council to Presdt. AISPC 24 Oct. 1947, AISPC, 45, Part I, 1946; statement issued by Kumbhar and seven other members of the WC of the Parishad, Nov. 1947, AISPC, 46, Part I, 1947-8; Kumbhar to Patel, 24 Nov. 1947, *PC*, 5, p. 455; and Rosenthal, 'Reformist Princes', I, p. 907.

62 Menon, *op. cit.*, pp. 150, 165.

63 Singh to Patel, 13 Apr. 1949, S.N. Mehta, Chief Minister's Office Rewa, to Menon, 22 Aug. 1949, and Rafi Ahmed Kidwai to Patel, 12 Sept. 1949, *PC*, 8, pp. 441-454.

64 Patel to Kidwai, 18 Sept. 1949, *ibid*, p. 454.

65 The ex-Justice Minister, Mathuradas Mathur, was accused of entertaining appeals from people he had represented in court, and of favouring friends and caste-fellows in the award of scholarships and in the matter of promotions; while the former Finance Minister was charged with 'dishonesty... and utter lack of responsibility' in his use of state cars, in obtaining fraudulent refunds on rent, in suppressing cases against black-marketeers, and in manipulating the allocation of licences for ration shops. Another former minister, Mohanlal Sukhadia, was also suspected by Shastri of graft, but the enquiry did not find enough evidence in his case to proceed with charges. Shastri to Patel, 11 July 1949, and list of charges put before the special judge, Rajasthan, Jan. 1950, *PC,* 8, p. 577, and 9, pp. 465-7.

66 Wood, *op. cit.*, p. 95.

67 Pamela Price, 'Kingly Models in Indian Political Behaviour: Culture As a Medium of History', *Asian Survey*, XXIX, 6 (1989), p. 566.

68 Paul R. Brass, *The Politics of India Since Independence* (Cambridge, 1990), p. 14. Brass adds the interesting comment that this may reflect the impact of princely traditions on contemporary Indian politics – which, if true, would reinforce our point about continuity.

69 For details see Sarvepalli Gopal, *Jawaharlal Nehru: A Biography* Vol. 2 (London, 1979), p. 20. Land reform was however part of the Sheikh's 'Naya Kashmir' blueprint of 1944.

70 Wood, *op. cit.*, p. 73.

71 Howard Spodek, 'Injustice in Saurashtra: A Case Study of Regional Tensions and Harmonies in India, *Asian Survey*, XII, 5 (1972), p. 424.

72 Afterwards assimilated into the Swatantra Party.

73 Rosenthal, *op. cit.*, pp. 995, 998.

74 Spodek, *op. cit.*, p. 420.

75 Note for Cabinet by Menon, 15 Dec. 1947, Mountbatten Coll., file 146. It was eventually agreed that payment of the privy purses should be guaranteed by the insertion of special clauses in the constitution. This was done in the summer of 1950 while Nehru was away in Indonesia. Gopal, *op. cit.*, pp. 18-19.

76 Frankel, *op. cit.*, pp. 80 and 80n. The latter privilege could be waived at the discretion of the government.

77 Menon, *op. cit.,* p. 227.

78 Ambassador New Delhi to Sec. State Washington, 4 Feb. 1948, U.S. State Dept, decimal file 845.00/2-448.

79 For example, after Chattisgarh was merged with Madhya Pradesh in 1948, its rulers were encouraged to enter politics and 'help make this democratic system a success' by the Congress Chief Minister, R.S. Shukla. William L. Richter, 'Traditional Rulers in Post-Traditional Societies: the Princes of India and Pakistan', in Robin Jeffrey (ed.), *People, Princes and Paramount Power: Society and politics in the Indian Princely States* (Delhi, 1978), p. 336.

80 William L. Richter, 'Princes in Indian Politics', *Economic and Political Weekly*, VI, 9, 27 Feb. 1971, p. 537.

81 Singh, *op. cit.*, pp. 12, 18; and Andrew Robinson and Sumio Uchimura. *Maharaja: the Spectacular Heritage of Princely India* (London, 1988), p. 58.

82 Antonio Gramsci, *Selections From the Prison Notebooks* (trans. Quintin Hoare and Geoffrey Smith), (New York, 1971), pp. 44-120.

83 *Asia-Australia Briefing Papers*, Vol. 1, no. 7 (1992), pp. 43-7; Research and Reference Division, Ministry of Information and Broadcasting, GOI, *India 1990; a Reference Annual*, pp. 14, 18, 52, 82-3; *Census of India 1991: Provisional Population Tables* (New Delhi, 1992), pp. 40-76; B.C.L. Johnson, *Development in South Asia* (Harmondsworth, 1983), pp. 37, 214-20. The figures quoted are averages for Rajasthan, Madhya Pradesh, Gujarat, Orissa, Karnataka and Kerala. These states loosely approximate to the territories formerly under princely rule.

BIHAR IN THE 1940s:
COMMUNITIES, RIOTS AND THE STATE

Vinita Damodaran

The 1940s saw important changes take place in India. Lord Linlithgow's declaration of war and his mistake of ignoring India's nationalist leadership had set the stage for the launching of the Quit India movement. In the popular unrest that followed in Bihar, rural communities renegotiated their relationship with the colonial state and effectively challenged its legitimacy. The violence of Quit India was not limited to the few weeks of August. The late 1940s saw further dramatic changes. The new Indian nation was being formed. At the level of élite politics the conflict between the Congress and the Muslim League had its impact at the popular level as rural communities reconstituted themselves and attempts were made to appropriate the nation state as a Hindu or Muslim entity. The riots immediately preceding partition and following it were the bloodiest the subcontinent had ever known. In the disorder that followed, communities were transformed and boundaries were redrawn through violence. It is possible to argue, as Franz Fanon has done in the context of the decolonisation of Algeria, that the disorder was created by the bloodthirsty and pitiless atmosphere, the generalisation of inhuman practices and the firm belief that people have of being caught up in a 'veritable apocalypse'.[1] The period of decolonisation and the discourse of the modern nation state thus provides a fertile ground for research.

Recent literature on the emergence of community has argued that communities are constantly being invented and reconstituted at particular moments in time.[2] With regard to nationalist collectivities Ernest Gellner argues that 'nationalism is not what it seems, and above all it is not what it seems to itself. The cultures it claims to defend and revive are often its own inventions, or are modified out of all recognition'.[3] Nationalist identities therefore have to be considered in their wider historical context.

This essay attempts to understand the historical conjuncture that led to the emergence of a specific community consciousness in northern India in the 1940s. How did communities constitute themselves? What were the strains at the popular level? Why did the cohesive nationalist activities of communities in Bihar in the early 1940s give way to the acute divisions of November 1946. It attempts to understand the violence that characterises the 1940s which created a whole generation of Indians 'steeped in wanton and generalised homicide with all the consequences that this entailed'.[4] Certainly the ways in which community identity came to be constructed and expressed in India seem to share common characteristics with Europe.[5] Most prominent of these, as Sandria Freitag has shown, have been the 'symbolic enactments of events and rituals that simultaneously delineated common values and drew on shared historical moments and locally significant cultural referents'.[6] From such common experiences have emerged perceptions, definitions and constructions of shared community. This process marked the period of transition from the colonial period and leading to a modern industrialised nation-state. It can be argued that the discourse of the nation-state in India and the language of modernity helped to construct the idea of a broader nationalist collectivity. However, such collectivities did not exist in a pure form. They fed on and competed with older, traditional identities of a communal, ethnic or regional nature. Social historians could usefully compare this process as it developed in Europe and South Asia.

Popular nationalism: The Quit India movement of 1942 in Bihar

What was the nature of popular consciousness in Bihar in the early 1940s? In August 1942 a mass movement of considerable dimensions broke out all over Bihar. The effects of an imperial war were being felt in India and, as the economic situation worsened, a Japanese invasion seemed imminent. In popular perceptions the weakening colonial state was held responsible for the developing crisis. In turn, such perceptions provided the context for a widespread mass movement against the state.

To the historian, the picture presented is one of fascinating complexity. Most of the primary sources talk of 'the fanaticism of the mobs that roamed the countryside'. Who were these mobs? We have been constrained in recent years by the pioneering studies of George Rudé and E.P. Thompson to avoid a loose usage of terms such as 'mob' or 'riot'.[7] With regard to the secondary works on the subject Max Harcourt and Stephen Henningham have both in some measure attempted to characterise the nature of popular action in Bihar in this period. Unfortunately their analyses suffer from several shortcomings. Max Harcourt has been justly criticised for the limitations of his 'middle peasant thesis' in connection with the Quit India agitation. He attributes the motive force of this agitation to a traditional smallholder peasant sector, squeezed by the high prices of 1942. Such an analysis, however, ignores the real complexity of the struggle and fails really to examine the 'faces in the crowd'.[8]

Stephen Henningham, on the other hand, is able to understand the more complex nature of the struggle. Unfortunately his exploration of the nature of popular action leads him to characterise it too neatly as a dual revolt, with the two streams relatively independent of each other: one of rich peasants and small landlords, and the other a subaltern rebellion of poor low castes. Henningham's dual revolt can be questioned on the grounds that he tends to underestimate the political character of the struggle and the context within which the struggle was waged. He notes that the revolt of the 'subaltern' stream was motivated mainly by the general economic crisis and the need to loot, while the élite movement had a conscious nationalist ideology. Most historians of popular movements (and this holds true of Henningham) have assumed that when rebels talk of the political, they mean the economic and social. It can be argued, however, that both streams within the movement which Henningham attempts to distinguish had definite political motives. Their actions cannot satisfactorily be defined in terms merely of the anger and disgruntlement of disaffected social groups. Instead there was a shared consensus among different social groups about the challenge that was being made against the colonial state. The Quit India struggle was thus a political movement, with a shared conviction among most participants that articulated both a political solution to distress and a political diagnosis of its causes.

In this context the nationalist vocabulary of the élite groups in the movement should not be seen as distanced from the ideas and visions of the common people. The objectives of the movement were interpreted in more than one way by different social groups, while its parameters were defined by certain common premises: such as the fact that the colonial state was conducting an illegitimate war, that it was responsible for the severe economic and social crisis in the country, and that its time had run out. The vision of an independent nation state held out hopes to the people. As Gareth Stedman Jones has noted in his reappraisal of the Chartist movement, 'to be successful, that is to embed itself in the assumptions of the masses of people, a particular vocabulary must convey a practical hope of a general alternative and a believable means of realising it, such that potential recruits can think within its terms'.[9] Only this type of notion can help explain why the anger and frustrations of these disaffected social groups should have taken the form they did, or why the political vocabulary of 1942 should have continued to express their changing fears and aspirations.[10] What I intend to examine in probing the popular action of 1942 in Bihar is the nature of the legitimising notion that informed the crowds of 1942. In a phase of rising prices and war requisitioning, the mass of the people rose to challenge state authority in the belief that they were supported by the wider community. This consensus was so strong that it overcame engrained motives of fear and deference to colonial authority. It thus presented an outright challenge to the state.

Reports made by district officials of the various districts on the outbreak of the Quit India movement in Bihar tell their own story. Accounts such as that of the Begusarai sub-divisional magistrate indicate that there was no clear planned strategy in the campaign.[11] The movement began with the processions and slogan-shouting of students and other local Congress activists. Later sabotage and looting with attacks on police *thanas*, the treasury and other symbols of state authority took place. In this second phase some form of popular consensus about the justice of challenging the state largely by attacking state property seems to have been at work. Both the urban and rural poor joined the movement at this stage. The type of duality in revolt suggested by Henningham, by which he characterised the upper castes as being mobilised over the issue of nationalism and the lower castes as being more interested in looting is not borne out by the evidence. The District Magistrate's report on Begusarai specifically notes that looting was not confined to any particular social group. Anybody who had an opportunity utilised it. Everyone, right through from upper-caste Bhumihars to poor labourers, took a prominent part in the looting spree.[12]

Several crowd actions served to highlight the complete breakdown of authority and the absence of fear at the popular level. These were the incidents at Fatwah and Pasraha and Ruihar which constituted perhaps the most severe kind of attack upon the colonial state. These were attacks on unarmed white men who, in the mass mind, represented the physical presence of colonial authority.[13] It is worth narrating at least one of these incidents here. At Fatwah on 13 August the Nineteen U.P. express train from Howrah stopped at Fatwah, near Patna, and then proceeded west, only to be stopped near a warning signal by a crowd that approached it, throwing brickbats. Two British officers, J.H. Smith and W. Short, were travelling in the first class compartment. In alarm one of the officers fired two shots from his revolver whereupon the crowd raised an outcry in the belief that a man had been injured by a shot.[14] The crowd beat on the window and within ten minutes the train was taken back to the station and an attack on the window was launched by a number of men from the surrounding countryside who were armed with sharp weapons like *khalas, pharsars* and *garasas*.[15] The officers were wounded while inside the compartment and, to save themselves from further attack, one officer emerged from the compartment hoping thereby to assuage the anger of the crowd. However, he was speared to death, as was his companion. Their two revolvers were then taken away and their bodies were dragged along the platform. After this they were placed on a *tum tum* (cart) and taken around the town before being thrown into the Poonpoon river. An interesting feature of the composition of the crowd on this occasion was that a majority of them belonged to the lower castes and were either Gope, Dusadh or Pasi.[16] While the ensuing prosecution mentions the crowd as being instigated to act by one Bihari *mahanth* it was, in fact the Dusadhs who had committed the act and then displayed the bodies around the town in a flagrant challenge to authority.[17] Once again the crowd seems to have been imbued with a notion of the legitimacy of their actions and motivated by a consensus and conviction that over-rode all fear and deference to authority. The resulting criminal case was registered only after much delay, on 26 August, and occasioned the compiling of a list of 'absconders' which gives a useful insight into the social composition of the crowd. Most of the 'absconders' were finally arrested only in June 1943. From their names it can be deduced that the majority of those accused were either Dusadh or Pasi.[18]

The colonial state was particularly disturbed by these incidents since, until mid-August 1942, the activities of the protesting crowds had focused on destroying government property rather than on killing Europeans. But by these actions, in contrast, the crowds had now shown themselves prepared to kill even armed white men. These attacks were important, for they were open attacks on the physical presence of colonial rule and constituted, one may argue, a final violent assault on colonial hegemony. No longer was the British *sarkar* a force both respected and feared at the popular level. Instead the whole apparatus of the colonial state could be challenged and humiliated. Moreover both upper and lower castes in the villages in question appear to have participated together in the attacks on Europeans, spurred on by a consensus that over-rode notions of fear. Not surprisingly, the British administration was particularly concerned to bring the culprits to book in these three cases and to reassert some measure of authority and legitimacy in the region. However, a more subtle form of resistance was then found to be at work. The Indian officers dealing with the cases postponed taking action sufficiently long for Richard Tottenham, the Home Secretary to the Government of India, to note that 'the progress of these cases was very slow'. In this fashion, the absconders were virtually allowed to go free until 1944.[19]

In examining the pattern of development of the Quit India movement in Bihar, it seems clear that in several areas local administration had retreated completely in the face of popular protest and parallel government. For nearly two critical weeks the British were taken completely unawares and took a considerable time to recover and restore the structures of policing and repression. Meanwhile sub-divisional officers helplessly reported many cases of popular governments having been set up with, in some cases, the active sympathy of lower levels of the local administration. In some cases, such as that of the Gope and Dusadh parallel government in Barh, the setting-up and functioning of a parallel government resulted in conflict at the popular level.[20]

Apart from these strains at the popular level, what is more important and, indeed, more interesting was the new and extended political participation of lower castes in general and their mobilisation, almost for the first time in the national struggle. In the Laskari canal subdivision it was reported in mid-August 1942 that most of the members of the crowds roaming the area were drawn mainly from lower castes.[21]

The low morale of the colonial administrative functionaries contributed to the complete breakdown of state power at the local level in late August 1942. It also revealed the extent to which, in the localities, the colonial state had always rested on flimsy supports. At the village level, the weakness resulting from the lack of penetrating institutions at the local level was confirmed when, in 1942, the *chaukidars* in many areas shifted their loyalties from the *raj*. In many areas they actually joined hands with the movement, and in Berh even became functionaries in a new Congress 'government'.[22] The upper echelons of the police services fared no better. The collector of Sitamarhi noted the inefficiency and panic of the police officers deputed to bring the Sahibganj police station under control. 'Some officers', he recorded, 'have become completely demoralised and are nervous about taking action'.[23]

The means of propaganda and the kinds of organisation that developed in the course of the movement are of some interest. Many independent underground organisations sprang up in the wake of the first disturbances. the Lal Kranti Sena and the Azad Dasta were the most important of these. These informal organisations were politically significant in keeping the Quit India movement alive well into 1944. They regularly organised minor raids on police stations and sometimes even on military depots for ammunition. Thus, while in North Bihar underground activity was firmly under the control of the CSP, which took the lead in the agitation in these areas, in south Bihar it stayed in the hands of several more shadowy organisations but particularly with the Azad Dasta and its breakaway groups.[24]

The Repression of the Quit India Movement in Bihar

The colonial state reacted to this grave assault on its authority and legitimacy with violence and repression. At first the pressures of the war effort had distracted the government from immediate action. However, when it came, the repression was heavy and crushing. The army was given a free hand and soldiers were sent out patrolling and burning villages. The Collector of Patna later wrote to the Chief Secretary of the Government of Bihar, on 2 October, that 'It is well known that during the process of coping with the situation, many forms of irregular action were taken by the military. There have been complaints that soldiers searched the house of one Ramnath Singh and took away jewels and gold ornaments'.[25] In Ruihar, where the pilots had been murdered, the troops vented their anger on the local populace particularly harshly. On 30 August a party of twelve British troops, accompanied by a clerk, raided the villages of Bengalia and Ruihar, while the men and women in the village fled their houses in terror. The troops then entered houses, breaking doors and meagre possessions like earthen vessels.[26] Henceforth the colonial state would rely completely on the army to maintain law and order, the institutions of the police and magistracy having shown themselves to be disloyal and demoralised.[27]

The repression was successful in pushing the Quit India movement underground. Despite this, however, the movement had successfully revealed the weaknesses of the colonial state and to some extent destabilised it. The state had few resources left to maintain control, and almost no support among its former interest-groups. The attitudes taken by *zamindars* who were covertly sympathetic to the movement had already been made clear: the state could no longer count on them. Similarly the colonial authorities had hoped for support from the business communities, on the basis that they depended on the law and order context provided by the state to carry on business activities. To some extent, this assumption was justified. Even during the mass movements of 1920 and 1930 the business communities had proved to be reluctant recruits into the national struggle and in 1930, as Sumit Sarkar has shown, these communities had successfully coerced Gandhi into accepting the Irwin pact so that normal business activity could continue.[28] In 1942 all such business considerations were pushed aside to support a movement which was seen to be the final assault on colonialism. Marwaris and *banias* now supported the movement quite openly and contributed funds to it. Among other groups, the mobilisation of the middle classes and the urban and rural poor in the struggle was, effectively, almost complete. In the end the *raj* remained buttressed only by the army.[29]

In many respects a profound change had occurred. The balance of power had shifted subtly, and the unquestioned authority the colonial state had exercised over various interest groups had been permanently eroded. Hitherto the colonial state had legitimised its rule by relying on effective support in local society from the *zamindars* and the merchant communities and by developing the service institutions of the state apparatus and the institutions of authority in the localities. Indeed a colonial hegemony had survived, through careful imperial strategy, well into the 1930s. Earlier mass movements in 1920 and 1930 had whittled it down, but it was the movement of 1942 which despatched the final blow. Ultimately the colonial state became extensively militarised once it was clear that the services, the institutions of authority in the localities, the *zamindars* and other interest groups had shifted their loyalties. Even in instituting punitive measures Houlton, the chief secretary to the Bihar government, noted that the police were slow in bringing the culprits to book and that local administrations were dragging their feet. Indian judges in courts dismissed many cases by reason of lack of evidence. Moreover, the mass movement had, in reality, not been crushed completely. Much of it went underground, where its embers continued to glow until 1944, causing immense difficulties to the administration. Once the Quit India struggle had so successfully revealed the weakness of the colonial state there could be no easy reversal.

The 1942 movement legitimised the use of violence in the public sphere. In challenging the colonial state as never before, the political arena opened up and the Indian nation was coming into its own. The erosion of legitimacy continued all through the period 1942-44 which saw incipient underground activity under the aegis of the Asad Dastas. However, this popular agitation not only challenged the state, it threatened and was to fundamentally affect the Congress organisation. A mass movement under an organised Congress leadership was one thing, while a disparate underground movement descending into violence in alliance with peasant dacoit gangs was quite another. At both the level of the imperial policy makers and the Congress leadership worries were expressed of a mass upheaval. The discourse of the new nation state was one of order, and uncontrolled popular unrest was regarded as posing a threat to the stability of post-colonial institutional structures of power and authority. Gandhi's views coincided with those of the new viceroy Wavell, who clearly realised the dangers of an underground Congress agitation continuing without any control and creating immense problems for any state, let alone the British, once the war was over. At the popular level the structure of the Congress was being transformed by peasant *dacoit* gangs and a popular socialist rhetoric was emerging.

Violence in the Countryside: the latter half of the 1940s

By the latter half of the 1940s therefore the situation was different. At the élite level a consensus was emerging between the Congress and the imperial policy makers. Gandhi's release in 1944 marked the first step towards the achieving of this political consensus. This was followed by the defeat of the Conservative Party in the British general election of May 1945. The consequent removal of Winston Churchill and Leo Amery from office was a particular relief to the Congress. This relief was further boosted by the hope that a Labour government might prove much more sympathetic than the Conservatives had been to nationalist aspirations.

In contrast, however, the economic situation in India was far bleaker. The post-war period was accompanied by rising inflation and a dramatic increase in unemployment, exacerbated by the demobilisation of over two million soldiers from the Indian army. These developments provided a fertile ground for discontent to flourish. They had the effect, too, of releasing pent-up passions and once more lifting the lid off the underground movement in Bihar, which had been simmering all through 1943 and 1944. It did not auger well for the Congress which had hoped for a smooth transition to power. In fact at the élite level, the political situation was becoming increasingly unstable. As the political arena opened up and the colonial state moved closer towards relinquishing power the confrontation between the Congress and the Muslim League became more embittered. Consequently, in this penultimate phase of the *raj*, the tide of popular passions ran high and threatened to drown even the new inheritors. The early 1940s had seen communities arrayed against the state in an attempt to question its legitimacy to rule, while the latter half of the 1940s saw communities arrayed against each other as attempts were made to incorporate the emerging Indian nation as a Hindu or Muslim entity. This was clearly a period of great upheaval and it affected groups on the cutting edge of change.[30]

By early 1946 a wave of popular action threatened to engulf Bihar. A period of intense political activity at the mass level, a series of agrarian upheavals and gory communal rioting followed the Congress acceptance of office. The period of turmoil stretched out in Bihar right through 1946 and 1947. In several Bihar districts communal rioting and agrarian unrest broke out within a short time of each other. Thus Gaya, Darbhanga, Muzaffarpur, Monghyr and Bhagalpur districts, all of which were major centres of Kisan Sabha activity, were also the most communally disturbed areas. The observations of a district officer in Monghyr in November 1946 make this point well. He noted that in one village an intense agrarian agitation was gathering force with both Hindu and Muslim peasants actively challenging the landlord. However, in contrast, in an adjacent village across the river, a gruesome communal riot over a trivial issue had left many dead.[31] How is one to explain this complexity?

When one examines the popular protest movements in Bihar in this period an interesting weave of different ideologies ranging right through from nationalism and religious communalism to class-based agrarian unrest can be observed. To date several historians have attempted to write about the historical context of the communal question. However, most of them have viewed it as being principally a product of élite manipulation and have concentrated in their analysis on élite-level politics. As a result no real attempt has been made to examine the internal dynamics of communal riots in the 1930s and 1940s or to study the nature of communalism in detail, on the ground.

It is difficult to identify simple causes for the particular configuration of communal and agrarian rioting that developed in Bihar in 1946. While in Bengal the communal upheavals in 1946 can apparently be explained quite easily, as Partha Chatterjee and others have done, in terms of the class divide between Hindus and Muslims, the situation in Bihar was probably more complex.[32] In the latter province, in contrast, there is little evidence to suggest that Hindus and Muslims fell into two distinct class categories in those villages where communal rioting was at its worst. While in some villages communal rioters seem to have come from outside, in many others resident lower caste Goalas, Kurmis and Dusadhs attacked their equally deprived Muslim neighbours. It is probably true that in Bengal it is possible to say that the main targets of attack for poor Muslims were the property of their class enemies. They attacked the absentee Hindu *Jotedars*, Marwari shops and idols worshipped in the houses of Hindu landlords. In Bihar the situation was quite different. Here sectarian conflict actually coexisted with class conflict and, in fact, it would be difficult to argue that class was the primary or only contradiction in the locality. Struggles between the communities, over such issues as cow protection and the playing of music before mosques, had created serious tensions between certain sections of Hindus and Muslims since the early part of the century. However, at that time the nature of the communal problem was still far less complex than that which had developed by the 1930s and 1940s. This change was contingent on a clearer political articulation, or crystallisation of perceptions, that came about at the provincial and national levels in the later period.

Clearly, therefore, the picture is a more complex one. It is true that mass upsurges occur at certain specific conjunctures in the historical process, and simplistic arguments cannot explain exactly when and why they happen. It is only by examining certain latent structures in social relationships and the nature of the conjunctures at which popular actions occur that we can understand or attempt to explain these upsurges. A main theme in this essay, therefore, consists in locating these latent structures as well as in examining the nature of popular actions in this particular period of transition.

This section will focus, among other things, on the popular movements in the context of decolonisation. Initially, however, it is necessary to mention briefly the basic economic background to the second Congress ministry and in particular to describe the lasting economic impact of the war on rural Bihar.

The Food Crisis and the Economic Situation

The beginning of 1946 saw the post-war economy in India in a crisis. All-India prices had registered their most alarming increase in 1943-1944 but had tended to settle in 1944-1945. They rose again steeply by 1945-1946, moving up by forty index points between October 1945 and November 1946. By June 1946 rice and wheat prices had shot up further and rice was selling at twenty to twenty-five rupees a *maund* in Bihar. Official calculations noted that Bihar would suffer a shortfall of eight and a half thousand tons of food grain.[33]

The food crisis was not the only problem the post-war economy had to contend with. Indian industry was also hit hard in the post-war period as demand slackened, having sustained itself during the war period with huge government orders. The return of demobilised soldiers added to the post-war burden.[34] They were unemployed and without any visible source of income. By January 1946 it was noted in Bihar that crime figures had climbed well above the average for the preceding four year period. Official reports asserted that the deteriorating crime figures were due to food shortages, the return of the soldiers and the steady reduction in war-work. The crime statistics for this period, confirm this increase.[35] It should be noted here that all the districts, except Purnea, Darbhanga, Ranchi and Singbhum, shared in the increase.[36] The crime rate reflected the growing impoverishment of the common people which had been exacerbated by the increasing loss of peasant land in the countryside.

The reasons for such a sudden increase in land transfers have not been sufficiently examined by historians. On close examination it seems that the changing economic situation from 1939 was closely associated with this development. Wartime inflation, food scarcity and high prices increased the market value of land. This made it attractive for the landlords to eject tenants, buy up their lands and settle it at higher rates of rent. The high prices had few beneficial effects on the poorer tenants. Forced to sell off their grain at harvest time to intermediaries (the grain trader or the rich landlord) to meet rent or debt obligations, the peasant was often unable to take advantage of the price increase. In many cases he was also forced to buy his food on the market, having sold off all the grain at harvest time. It was this impoverishment of the small farmers that forced them to sell their lands. The buyers in most cases were the traditional rural élite, that is, the landlords and the rich traders who had made money through war profits and speculative business.[37] By the 1940s the rural crisis was further exacerbated by the prospect of *zamindari* abolition. Tenants were threatened by the prospect of landlords buying up their lands and converting them into either *zirat* or *bakasht* to avoid losing their property. Weaker occupancy tenants were also threatened as the landlords compulsorily bought up their *raiyati* holdings to convert large areas of land in the countryside into sites for sugar mills, a tactic frequently used to circumvent *zamindari* abolition.[38] All these pressures on the rural community caused sustained agrarian rioting in large parts of both north and south Bihar by the summer of 1946. Thus on the eve of the Congress takeover of office the economic situation was a source of much discontent, both in the urban and rural areas. The takeover was immediately followed by a flurry of popular actions as different interest-groups started to agitate for their particular demands. The police went on strike first, demanding an increase in pay to keep up with rising inflation. This action was followed by working-class strikes in many factories and finally widespread agrarian agitation all over rural Bihar. With the Congress in office, it was widely hoped that popular demands would be met, and it was in such a context that popular aspirations and the hope of a better future climaxed in rural and urban rioting.[39]

The Congress in Bihar assumed office during a political and economic crisis. Prices continued to escalate in the early months of the Congress takeover and a scarcity of food grains quickly developed. The food situation was considered especially precarious in north Bihar and Chotanagpur.[40] The failure of the Congress in office either to tackle the food crisis or bring prices down resulted in widespread agrarian and urban unrest.

In this respect the Congress was clearly in difficulties. Subsequently, with the outburst of Labour agitation in urban areas and the gradual renewal of the *bakasht* struggle in the rural areas, the Congress ministry was forced increasingly to resort to the tactics of its colonial predecessor, in clamping down on agitation and introducing highly conservative legislation to ameliorate the situation. The application of this new reactionary approach made its greatest impact, however, in the context of agrarian struggles. It is to this impact that one may now turn.

The Land Question and the *bakasht* Agitation in 1946

In June 1946, a long drawn out struggle over *bakasht* land broke out once again in several districts in Bihar, the Congress legislation of 1938-39 having shown itself ineffective in stemming the onset of agrarian unrest. As outlined above, social pressures had been building up steadily in the countryside during the war years. A rapid increase in peasant disappropriation had taken place leading to the proletarianisation of large numbers of hitherto poor peasants due to alienation of land as the landlords sought to convert land into either *bakasht* or *zirat*.[41]

The result of these attacks on occupancy holdings and the increase in land transfers resulted in the dispossession of the tenantry and de-peasantisation on a large scale. Even where old peasants remained, the conditions under which they worked were substantially altered as a consequence of the land transfers. They remained as sharecroppers (*bataidars*), a position inferior to that of tenants. Many of these sharecroppers by the late 1940s had rights only to their homestead lands, averaging about 0.04 acres, which they obtained from the landlord rent-free in return for working on his land. In effect, therefore, they were being pushed into the ranks of landless agricultural labourers.[42] By the 1950s the number of landless families had increased from twenty-six per cent to forty-five per cent in some villages, an extraordinary rise by any standards.[43] In such circumstances attacks on peasant land and the consequent erosion of tenant rights could not remain unchallenged for long. As early as June 1946 a serious agrarian movement had erupted in several districts in Bihar. The timing of this unrest was directly related to the most recent attacks by landlords on tenancy rights, following fears of imminent *zamindari* abolition in 1945/46.

The struggle to reclaim *bakasht* lands affected many hundred villages in Bihar in 1946. Most villages had some *bakasht* land and in 1946 there were nearly twenty *lakh* acres of *bakasht* land in the whole province. The peasants cultivating these *bakasht* lands had few rights. The lands they tilled were given to them in plots in villages to cultivate either on high rates of cash rent (eight rupees or ten per *bigha*) or on produce-rent; the latter system being more prevalent. The *zamindars* frequently deprived the actual tillers of nearly eighty per cent of their produce through claims of rent and false loans. Peasants were also kept under constant threat of ejection and rarely managed to obtain any proper receipts from the landlord. Most of them were often compelled to work on the *zirat* lands of the landlord and forced to do *begari* without wages, while they had clear rights only to *bari* or homestead lands. In order to claim peasant holdings as their *bakasht* or *zirat* landlords had to evict long-term tenants. In Mokama it was reported that the landlords were anxious either to settle their lands at higher rents or to claim possession of the land, for if abolition of *zamindari* was undertaken then compensation would be paid only in accordance with the rent roll as shown by proper settlement. Landlords stood to lose both ways if they neither settled the lands nor retained *de facto* possession of it.[44] In many villages in June 1946, therefore, the landlords started preventing peasants from tilling their lands and claiming them as their *bakasht* land. The peasants reacted with anger and serious rioting broke out all over Bihar.

In Bhabuas subdivision in Shahabad struggles erupted in many villages.[45] By 4 July 1946, in Bhabua subdivision, the agitation had spread to seventy-five villages, involving twenty thousand acres of land in six police areas. As the *bakasht* disputes continued the landlords became increasingly worried and formed an association to resist trespass by the tenants and frequently clashed violently with their tenants as at Mokama. Such incidents of peasant protest and *zamindari* retaliation also occurred in several districts in the province. In examining the nature of the agitations some conclusions can be firmly drawn. With regard to participation, the struggles affected all sections of the peasantry, right through from the middle peasant cultivator to the small low-caste share-cropper. Low-caste poor peasants participated in the movement in a particularly significant way. Being weaker tenants, they were the first targets of the landlords. Many of these tenants were agitating for the restoration of their lands and for the re-establishment of their rights to the land. Other more radical claims were also asserted in the course of the agitation. These included the refusal of the peasants to pay more than the usual share of the produce to the landlord and the refusal to pay *nazrana* (or cash gifts) to the landlord. Landless labour also played an unprecedented part in the agitation and in some areas these groups used the opportunity boldly to demand more land from the landlords in return for *begari*.[46] Thus in many places the *zamindars* were now facing organised protests against *begari* and illegal extortion. Considerable community cohesion appeared in the course of the protest. Muslim peasants often joined hands with their Hindu neighbours in attacking their landlord. There is plenty of evidence in Monghyr, for example, to show this. The participation of women was also common, as in the peasant agitations in 1937-39, and there were many instances of women participating in peasant *satyagrahas* by lying in front of the plough. The involvement of women further bridged caste divisions.

Not only did lower-caste women agitate but upper-caste Bhumihar women came out of *purdah* to protest against their lands being taken away.[47]

In analysing the leadership and organisation of the 1946-47 struggles, it appears that the socialists and the Radical Democratic party were active in several areas and less in others. This involvement had antecedents in the Quit India agitations whose structures had never really died away. In the Darbhanga area the collector's reports frequently mention that Ramlochan Singh, the socialist leader who had been active in the Azad Dasta movement, was actively inciting the tenants. Another socialist who specialised in terrorising the petty *zamindars* in Warisnagar *thana* was Suraj Narayan Singh. Both these men were said to have a large number of followers and to have organised the local peasants to loot the paddy from the *bakasht* and *zirat* lands of the *zamindars*. In Chakdah village the communist leader, Bhogendra Jha, was also active in mobilising the *kisans* in the village against Amawan Raj.[48] In recognising the leadership of the Radical Democratic Party and the socialists in some of the struggles, I am not suggesting that the mobilisation of the peasantry was contingent on the intervention of these alone. On the contrary, the peasant in Bihar, as elsewhere, acted on his own volition and was the main maker of his own rebellions.

In the case of the *bakasht* land struggles, it was clear that the action was fuelled by the systematic attacks of landlords on tenant lands. Peasants were evicted from those lands and *zirat* lands were not a new phenomenon. In fact, landlords had been extending their *bakasht* and *zirat* lands since the rise in prices in the 1930s to take advantage of the price increase. In 1937-39 the peasantry had sought to protect themselves against the landlords onslaughts in an intense agrarian agitation under the Kisan Sabha. This was a period when the politics of nationalism and socialism had begun to penetrate the countryside on a significant scale and the experience of agitation and class struggle had built up the consciousness of the peasantry. Thus by 1946, when the landlords renewed their attacks on peasant holdings for fear of *zamindari* abolition, the peasants were more aware of their rights and more ready and anxious to defend them.

The peasant actions were not simply incoherent attempts to redress economic grievances. They were in every sense political. In undertaking to challenge his relationship with the landlord the peasant engaged himself in what was essentially a political task and a task in which the existing powe-nexus had to be turned upside down as a necessary condition for the full redress of any particular grievance. Engrained attitudes of fear and respect for the repressive authority of the landlord seem thus to have been overcome in these struggles to such an extent that, in many cases, the landlords actually feared to restore their authority in case of further peasant reprisals.

Communal Riots and Killings in Rural Bihar

The above account allows one to construct a comprehensive picture of peasant protest. Widespread agrarian agitation over the restoration of *bakasht* land and against the exploitative incursions of the *zamindars* was occurring in several districts in Bihar from the summer of 1946 onward. These peasant actions included both Hindu and Muslim peasants, who frequently made common cause against the *zamindar*.[49] On many occasions Hindu and Muslim peasants collaborated (in Monghyr, as well as elsewhere), in the forcible cutting of crops on disputed land.

In November 1946, however, a strange new dimension developed in the popular actions in rural Bihar: that of communal killing. Between October and December 1946 Bihar witnessed one of the worst communal outrages in its history. Four hundred thousand Muslims were affected in the districts of Patna, Chapra, Monghyr, Bhagalput and Gaya in rural and urban areas. By December 1946 fifty thousand Muslims from Bihar had migrated to Bengal in the wake of gory communal strife. All through November and December 1946 there was an annual configuration of both agrarian and communal rioting. Newspapers noted that, while parts of south Monghyr and Patna were smouldering with communal strife, just across the Ganges in north Monghyr Hindu and Muslim tenants participated together in a widespread seizure of the landlord's crops. In another village in north Monghyr Hindu and Muslim tenants captured twenty-five *bighas* of land.[50] In Chapra, after the fury of the communal riots, a new phase in the situation developed with the cutting of crops and the looting of properties by gangs of tenants, both Hindu and Muslim.[51] However, despite these instances of joint activity *vis-à-vis* the landlords, the rural areas in south Bihar continued to be rocked by communal carnage of the greatest magnitude.

Neighbouring Bengal had been smouldering since the great Calcutta killings and the disturbances in Eastern Bengal in August 1946. The ill-advised action of the provincial ministry to make political capital out of the matter resulted in it authorising the celebration of Noakhali day on 28 October, to mourn the death of Hindus in East Bengal.[52] This provoked the feelings of the communities against each other. Stabbings started in Patna town itself and by 31 October Bhagalpur further to the east succumbed to rioting and forty Muslims were massacred at Teragna station. By 2 November disturbances were widespread over north and south Bihar and a threat of related labour riots in the industrial areas of Jamshedpur and Dhanbad started to emerge. Tuker noted the difficulty the troops had in controlling four thousand square miles of violently troubled territory. The number of Muslims killed in this short and savage killing was seven to eight thousand men, women and children.[53]

The military reports of the Bihar killings give useful details of the riots. Bihar Sharif subdivision consisted of an area of eight hundred square miles with a population of seven hundred and fifty thousand, of whom ninety thousand were Muslim.[54] The greatest number of casualties were in the Hulsar circle in the western part of the subdivision, where the casualties amounted to two thousand five hundred killed. Here it was reported that at least two large villages and about one hundred small villages in the subdivision had been wiped out as a result of the mob frenzy that swept the province. The butchery of Muslims in

Nagarnausa area in the subdivision was one of the worst. Colonel Venning, who had moved into the area with some of his men, noted the extent of the destruction. He could hear the cries of the mob attacking the village and as he hastened forward, saw smoke rising from several burning houses. On reaching the village his party saw that a mob of between five and ten thousand were surrounding the village, burning and killing every Muslim they could find. They noticed that many of the corpses were in various stages of putrefaction so that it was obvious this attack had been in progress for several days.[55] The damage to property was heavy. Not only was the damage done during the riots, but a considerable amount of looting of the houses of those Muslims who had left the villages also occurred. It is perhaps a salutary comment on these events and on similar horrors of the period that no official enquiry was ever conducted into the rioting.[56]

Later, Gandhi visited the affected areas and demanded that information be collected on the riots in the areas he was to visit. Hence some picture of the nature and scale of the rioting can be pieced together. Gandhi was to note after he visited the riot areas that the extent of the killing in the riots in Bihar shocked him far more than the scale of the killing in Noakhali in Bengal. Some of these case studies of particular villages are especially useful in that they record the exact extent and the nature of the mob attacks on the Muslims.[57]

The District Magistrate recorded the following facts in respect of Andhari village (Fatwah police district) to be visited by Mahatma Gandhi. The population of Hindus before the riot was four hundred and sixty-two, while that of the Muslims was one hundred and sixty-eight. After the riot, the population of Muslims was recorded, straightforwardly, as 'nil'. Some had fled and many had died. Muslims from the neighbouring villages of Jaitya, Gazibigha and Nandechak had also sought shelter in Andhari village and two hundred to four hundred and eighty Muslims were thought to have been killed. The report also recorded that the majority of the people who took part in the attack were lower-caste Kurmis, Goalas and Dusadhs. The riot had been triggered off by a rumour that one Hindu of Bendauli village had been killed by the Muslims and this angered the Hindus. On 2 November 1946 Hindus in Andhari village were joined by other Hindus from the surrounding villages and began to attack the Muslim houses. Some of the Muslims then attempted to fire on the advancing mobs, while others resorted to the extraordinary measure of actually killing their women with own hands to prevent the attackers from dishonouring them.[58] The violence perpetrated on women both by men from within their community and from outside serves to underline the fact that communalism as an ideology affects women differently. Women are perceived as the site of tradition and honour of the community and consequently the violence is directed more forcefully against them by men both from within their communities and from without, with a view to either preserve tradition or defile it.

Such horror stories were repeated in several villages. In some villages there was evidence of complicity by the local élites in fomenting the riots. In Safipur and Khusrupur areas on 1 November 1946 a mob of five hundred Hindus (mainly Goalas) of the villages of Khusrupur, Shafipur and Harampur raided Shafipur village. They looted Muslim houses, set fire to thirty-six houses and killed four women. Sixty Hindus, mostly Goalas, were accused. However, one of the rioters was armed with a gun belonging to a *zamindar* called Deobi Babu and it would seem that the *zamindar* had encouraged and even supplied some weapons. Nearby, in Masaurhi village, it was reported that the looting of Muslim property was widespread. A distinctive aspect here was the direct involvement of the rice-mill owners in the village, for the crowd gathered on hearing the whistle in the mill.[59]

In examining the evidence on the dynamics of the riots a problem arises. Why did the rural areas of Bihar, which had been in the midst of agrarian upheaval since the summer of 1946, suddenly erupt into sectarian strife in November 1946? Such a massive outbreak of communal rioting had never occurred in the rural areas in Bihar, even during the cow protection movements in the period 1880-1917 which had given rise to the first substantial sectarian tension in the countryside. More significantly, the historian of 1946 in Bihar has to examine the specific configuration of agrarian and rural rioting that set rural Bihar alight. Can such a sudden and widespread outburst of mass action be explained away by the single factor of the manipulative activity of some élite leaders reaching down with a communal ideology and successfully building up sectarian strife in the countryside? Such an interpretation would be too simplistic and would ignore the social roots of populist actions. The sustained and intense mass actions in 1946 cannot be explained away by the machinations of leaders alone. Instead it seems essential to understand the history of sectarian relations before 1946 before examining the social context of 1946 and the strains and tensions of that specific historical juncture.

I have sought to argue that the communal violence of this period was specific to the historical context. This was a period of great upheaval. As the colonial state prepared to withdraw, and as a popular party assumed power, landlords intensified their exploitation in the countryside. The frustrations which resulted from the chronic competition for resources seem to have been exacerbated in the context of decolonisation. The consequences of this competition for scarce resources placed great strains on a colonial plural society. It affected groups on the cutting edge of change. Powerless to achieve their objectives through the institutions of the state or the Congress party Bihar's peasants had taken matters into their own hands. In seizing lands encroached upon by landlords they were violently asserting their rights.

That this reassertion of a class identity *vis-à-vis* the landlord also saw communities reconstituting themselves through communal violence was part of this process of change. As the colonial state prepared to withdraw, attempts were made to appropriate the new nation state as a Hindu or Muslim entity. In the context of sustained communal propaganda at the élite level the peasants of Bihar were able to revitalise familiar metaphors in their culture associated with the sacred. These were created in the sectarian tensions of the nineteenth and early twentieth century.

The beginning of sectarian tensions in the rural areas in Bihar can be located in that period, when there had been a massive outbreak of sectarian strife in the Bhojpuri region over the protection of cows in the 1870s. This movement, generated by the activities of the Arya Samaj in the region, acquired substantial support among both upper and lower caste Hindus in the villages. Eventually it had resulted in the institution of 'Kaurakshini Sabhas' in several places, specifically to protect cows. A leading part in the Gaurakshini agitation was taken by lower-status agricultural castes, Ahirs and Koeris, who joined hands with the *zamindars* to rally around the cause of the cow. Gyan Pandey has argued that the extended participation of these castes in the Gaurakshini *sabhas* represented an attempt to improve their ritual status and to use the cow protection movement as a vehicle of upward social mobility.[60] Though the motive force of these caste organisations was a challenge to the upper caste landlords, the *sabhas* also had strong links with the cow protection movement which was seen as a means of raising their ritual status.[61]

The anti-Muslim nature of the Kaurakshini *sabhas* had become clear as early as the 1890s, when the *sabhas* in Azamgarh (United Provinces) began to demand bonds from Muslim villages to the effect that they would not slaughter cattle under any condition. Muslim weavers were threatened with boycott and no one would buy their cloth nor would any *bania* supply them with grain. Two years later, during the Baqri-Id of 1893, severe inter-religious tension resulted in the Bhojpur region, and the call for revenge against those Muslims who had performed *qurbani* became widespread. The excesses of 1893 led to increased police vigilance and efforts to bring about agreement between local Hindu and Muslim leaders. This temporarily subdued the cow protection movement in the region. Nevertheless, a significant revival of the demand for cow protection in the eastern Bhojpuri districts in U.P. and Bihar took place in 1910, culminating in a massive outbreak of violence in Shahabad at the Baqri-Id of 1917.[62] Clearly, the cow had become a familiar metaphor and a sacred symbol in the culture of an emerging Hindu community.

It is not my intention to argue here that the bitter communal riots of the 1930s and 1940s were an inevitable outcome of these complex developments. The communal question in that period was also affected by the political articulation of the Muslim League and the Mahasabha in the 1930s and the jockeying for power at the élite levels of the Muslim League and the Congress. The political articulation of the Muslim League and the Mahasabha in particular fed on the suspicions and fears first nurtured in these early agitations and clashes. With the Congress in power in 1937-39 the Muslim League was able to build up the horrors of a Hindu *raj* and a sudden increase in incidents of rural rioting took place. Such a perspective helps to give a better understanding of the nature of the sectarian grievances and the rioting of 1946. The situation was markedly different in that it was a context of increased tension between the Muslim League and the Mahasabha and the jockeying for power at the élite level.

The manipulative possibilities of a communal ideology must also be taken into account. In fact there is much evidence which indicates the complicity of *zamindars* in fomenting the riots in several villages. One newspaper noted that, in Gaya, the president of the Congress committee had informed the ministry that the riots were the creation of the *zamindars*. They quoted evidence to show that the *zamindars* held conferences and made preparations for the rioting. The newspaper alleged, perceptively, that the *zamindars* were trying to defuse agrarian tension by lighting the communal torch.[63] This might well have been the case. In actively fomenting sectarian strife among the peasantry the *zamindars* hoped to turn attention away from themselves. Indeed, at a *zamindar* conference held at Patna under Maharaj Adhiraj of Darbhanga some *zamindars* actually suggested, quite openly, that it would be 'good' to make *kisans* and *khet majdoors* (agricultural labourers) fight among themselves. The landlords were not the only élite group actively fomenting the agitation. Traders and merchants were also actively involved in financing some of the operations. In Chapra it was proved that the key part in the riots was played by profiteers and black marketeers. In Masaurhi, in Patna, where thousands lost their lives, the local rice and flour mill proprietor organised the rioters. Here, mill sirens were used to collect and disperse the rioters. Clearly, the manipulative possibilities of communal ideology were starkly realised in the attempts made by the *zamindars* to use it to defuse the agrarian agitation.

The spread of communal propaganda in both urban and rural areas was also aided by the organisational build-up of Hindu communal bodies like the Hindu Mahasabha and the R.S.S. in Bihar. From 1942 onward, with the Congress leadership in jail and the Muslim League extending its influence, the R.S.S. could not have asked for a more suitable atmosphere in which to conduct their activities.[64]

The activities of the *zamindars* and the communal propaganda of communal groups do not, however, suffice entirely to explain the virulent spread of communal rioting in the countryside. At the level of peasant consciousness it is still difficult to fathom why sections of the Hindu peasantry, who had combined with Muslim peasants *vis-à-vis* the landlords, should suddenly have chosen to turn against them and use them as scapegoats for real or imagined grievances. While it can be asserted that the *zamindar*, the *mahanth* and the *bania* had fomented the agitation and in many cases encouraged the rioting, it would be incorrect to claim that the peasants in many villages who joined in the rioting were simply swept helplessly along in the tide. Instead it can be argued that different levels of peasant consciousness were at work and that the anti-landlord confrontation was not the only conflict perceived by the peasants. In the course of the Gaurakashini agitations suspicions and fears between the two communities had already developed. This sectarian conflict had remained alive in peasant memory. As I have already suggested, the tradition of sectarian conflict in south Bihar among the Ahirs, Koeris and Kurmis was not new. It had originated in their active participation in rioting to improve their ritual status, especially in Shahabad in 1917. Communal propaganda at the élite level in the 1930s and 1940s prayed on such fears and conflicts in local society and at the level of popular consciousness the contradictions in the localities remained many-sided.

Thus the scale and the nature of the communal rioting seems to have been affected by many factors. It originated in the spread of communal propaganda and the deliberate nurturing of 'hate' campaigns in the countryside. It was fuelled by the manipulative possibilities of a communal ideology, in so far as the *zamindars* were, in many cases, able to invoke sectarian hatred between Hindus and Muslims and foment communal rioting in order to defuse agrarian unrest. Unrest also fed on older traditions of sectarian conflict in many south Bihar districts. This was so in those areas where the cultivating castes of Ahirs, Koeris and Kurmis had attacked Muslims in the course of their Gaurakshini activities. These activities had built up an atmosphere of suspicion and fear which could be exploited subsequently when the opportunity offered itself. Furthermore, rioting provided an opportunity to indulge in the loot and plunder of Muslim houses. This was an attractive proposition for many poor low-caste Hindu families in villages pressed hard by the economic pressures of 1946. Only an understanding of all these different causes can help to explain the simultaneous emergence of agrarian and communal conflict in rural Bihar in 1946.

This essay has attempted to explore the nature of popular consciousness in Bihar in the period of decolonisation. It is clear that while the discourse of the emerging nation state in India helped to construct the broad nationalist collectivities as in 1942, this did not preclude the existence of competing identities of a communal or class nature at the popular level, as was manifested in 1946 in rural Bihar. This pattern of overlapping identities challenges many of our methodological assumptions about class, nation and ethnicity. I have sought to argue that this complex mosaic of competing identities was specific to the historical conjuncture of 1946. In the context of decolonisation and nation building plural societies are fraught with potential conflict. The frustrations, blunted expectations and divisiveness in these societies resulting from chronic competition for resources manifested itself in violence in Bihar as communities reconstituted themselves and boundaries were redrawn through violence. In the context of nation building the communal propaganda of the League and the Mahasabha fed popular fears and communities sought to incorporate the new nation state as a Hindu or Muslim entity. As boundaries were redrawn, it was as if violence had taken on a separate autonomy. As communal riots spread like wild fire all over northern India, the new communal theology justified the brutal killings and temporarily created a new morality.

Notes

1   F. Fanon, *The Wretched of the Earth* (London, 1983).
2   Benedict Anderson, *Imagined communities* (London, 1983).
3   E. Gellner, *Nations and nationalism* (Oxford, 1983).
4   *Ibid.*
5   See Natalie Zemon Davies, 'Rites of violence' in *Society and culture in early modern France* (London, 1975), pp. 152-187.
6   S. Frietag, *Collective action and community: public arenas and the emergence of communalism in north India* (California, 1989), p. 5.
7   George Rudé, *The Crowd in History* (London, 1985), E.P. Thompson, 'Moral Economy of the English crowd in the eighteenth century' in *Past and Present*, no. 50 (1971), p.79. Rudé, *op.cit.*, p. 10.
8   Max Harcourt, 'Kisan populism and revolution', in D.A. Low (ed.), *Congress and the Raj* (London, 1977), p. 323. He notes 'the overall picture, then, is of a kisan revolt led and loosely coordinated by a modernist élite, partly drawn from the village population and partly drawn from urban areas.' He also concludes that the crowd was composed of middle or high castes, a conclusion not borne out by my evidence which demonstrates the extended participátion of Dusadha, Ahirs/Goalas and Kurmis in the movement in large numbers. See also Stephen Henningham, *Peasant Movements in India North Bihar 1917-1942* (Canberra, 1982), Ch. 7.
9   Gareth Stedman Jones, 'Rethinking Chartism', in *Language of Class* (Cambridge, 1983), p. 96.
10 It was not simply the experience but rather a particular linguistic ordering of experience which would lead the masses to believe that their exclusion from political power was the cause of their social problems. As Gareth Stedman Jones notes, 'Consciousness cannot be related to experience except through the interposition of a particular language which organises the understanding of experience and it is important to realise that more than one language is capable of articulating the same set of experiences'. *Ibid.*
11 Freedom Movement in Bihar Papers (hereafter FMBP), file no. 45/1942.
12 While one can agree that looting might have been more economically advantageous. to the poorer sections one cannot conclude that they participated in the movement only for these reasons. Other actions of the lower castes, not involving loot, lead one to a different conclusion.
13 FMBP, file 519/43, Pasraha Report by J.G. Shearer; and see also file 323/43.
14 They believed that one of the men in the crowd called Bhola Dusadh, an ex-*chaukidar*, had been shot.
15 These refer to spears, knives and axes.
16 The Dusadhs were a low caste spread over northern and western India. Occupationally they formed the bulk of the village *chaukidars*, and many were poor labourers and also reared cattle for a living. See the Census Report of 1931 for the province of Bihar, p. 210.
17 *Mahanth* refers to a temple functionary. He was usually a landlord and owned many acres of land in the form of grants to the temple.
18 FMBP, file 519/43.
19 Ruhihar Case, R. Tottenham's rebuke to district officers in Bihar. FMBP, file 323/43.

20 The petition of the Mahtons noted that, following the outbreak of the violent disturbances on 10 August (involving arson and looting), some of the Gopes and Dusadhs in the village set up a *raj* government in Malpore and began to intimidate, molest and loot such of the inhabitants as refused to join them. They proclaimed, by the beat of drums, that the British *raj* had been abolished and *swaraj* had come. Accordingly they started to levy taxes which the Mahtons of the village refused to pay. See the petition of the Mahtons of the village. FMBP, file 75/42.

21 See Bihar State Archives (hereafter BSA), file 24/42.

22 At the village levels the Kanungo, the *patwari* and *chaukidar* were the *raj*'s main links to rural society. The *chaukidars*, as we have noted, were of low social status, yet were crucial figures in rural administration. their importance grew as government links to the local level became increasingly tenuous in the nineteenth century. Not only were the *chaukidars* a major source of information, but with the police so thinly stretched out, they were in effect the real force for law and order in the countryside. for the history of local control institutions see A. Yang, 'Between the British raj and the Saran raiyat, the development of local control institutions in the nineteenth and early twentieth century' in P.G. Robb (ed.), *Rural India* (London, 1983), p. 164.

23 Report of the District Magistrate of Muzaffarpur, FMBP, file 49/42.

24 Interview with Azad Dasta activist, Havildar Tripathi, Patna December 1986. See V. Damodaran, 'Azad dastas and dacoit gangs', in *Modern Asian Studies*, Vol. 16, 3 (1992), pp. 417-450.

25 FMBP, file no. 71/42.

26 It was alleged that in many cases local women had been molested. For details of the crackdown and repression, see FMBP, file no. 71/42.

27 There was even some attempt made by the socialists to infiltrate the army. But this effort had little success. See oral transcripts, Nilubhai Limaye and Madhu Limaye, Centre for South Asian Studies (hereafter CSAS), Cambridge.

28 Sumit Sarkar, 'The Logic of Gandhian nationalism: civil disobedience and the Gandhi Irwin pact (1930-1931)', *The Indian Historical Review*, Vol. III, no. 1 (1976).

29 However, one has to qualify this assessment of a complete mobilisation of the population in the 1942 struggle when referring to the views of the Muslim community, where clearly the Quit India movement had less support. Indeed, the Muslim League in Bihar had, in a resolution, actually asked Muslims to keep well aloof from the movement. Among the Muslim middle classes, by and large, this dictum was obeyed. Among the lower classes, however, as the Begusarai District Magistrate had noted, all social groups, including Muslims, had participated in the struggle.

30 As R. Brenner comments on modes of transition 'the element of indeterminacy emerges in relation to the different character and results of conflicts in different regions'. It is precisely in this zone of theoretical indeterminacy that real history becomes the battlefield of active human agents, consciously striving to change the given structure of social relations. In modes of transition there can be no final instance of structuralist determination. On the contrary if in the mode of production the economic is the determinant, in the mode of transition it is the political practice of struggle which is the determinant. Brenner, 'Agrarian Class Structure and Economic Development in pre-Industrial Europe', *Past and Present*, Vol. 70 (1976), p. 52.

31 Very little work has been done on the popular actions of this period. While A.N. Das has cursorily examined the agrarian agitation in Bihar in the 1940s, his work covers a wide timespan and fails to examine the agitation in any real detail or to understand

its links with communal outbreaks. See A.N. Das, *Agrarian unrest and socio-economic change in Bihar 1900-1980* (New Delhi, 1983).

[32] Partha Chatterjee, *The Land Question, Bengal 1920-47* (Calcutta, 1984), pp. 109-11. Sugata Bose, *Agrarian Bengal: Economy Social Structure and Politics, 1919-47* (Cambridge, 1986), p. 195, and Suranjan Das, *Communal riots in Bengal 1905-1947* (Delhi, 1991), p. 5

[33] *People's Age*, 23 June 1946.

[34] *Loc.cit.*

[35] Bihar police administration report (1945).

[36] Crime figures for Bihar; FR (Jan. (1) 1946); see also *Searchlight*, 19 Mar. 1946.

[37] In neighbouring Bengal the greatest land-ownership disaster for the peasantry was the famine of 1943 when, according to an estimate of the Indian Statistical Institute, 2.6 *lakh* families had completely lost their land and 9.2 *lakh* families had to sell part or whole of their holdings. B.B. Chaudhuri, 'The Process of Depeasantisation in Bengal and Bihar 1885-1947', *Indian Historical Review*, Vol. II, 1 (1987), p. 139.

[38] Ram Manohar Lohia's enquiry into the *bakasht* agitation revealed that nearly 50,000 acres of land in Bihar had been handed over to sugar mills.

[39] The new ministry was sworn in soon after the elections on 16 Apr. 1946. The ministers, including the prime minister, S.K. Sinha, came mainly from the Congress right wing. See FR (April (2) 1946). The list of AICC members from Bihar, however included more representatives from the left wing, seven members of the C.S.P. including Jayaprakash Narayan, Sheel Bhadra Yajee and two others from the Forward Bloc, and Sahajanand Saraswati from the Kisan Sabha. See *Searchlight*, 7 June 1946.

[40] FR (July (2) 1946).

[41] *Bakasht* lands were those on which the *zamindars* exercised more direct control over cultivation and, though occupancy rights could accrue here in certain circumstances, the *zamindars* normally cultivated the land through short term tenants or sharecroppers. *Zirat* lands were the homestead lands of the *zamindar* on which no tenant rights could accrue.

[42] Report of the Congress Agrarian Enquiry committee which was set up in 1949. See Rajendra Prasad papers, National Archives of India, file no. 89/49.

[43] Mitra and Vijayendra, 'Agricultural Labourers and Peasant Politics, Rural Proletarianisation in Purnea, Bihar', in A.N. Das (ed.), *Agrarian Movements in India*, p. 103.

[44] *Loc.cit.*

[45] *Bakasht* land disputes in Bhabua subdivision, BSA, file no. 336/46.

[46] For activities of landless labour see BSA, file no. 336/46.

[47] BSA, file no. 6 (vii) 47.

[48] In Chakdah the *raj* wanted to settle a piece of land with new tenants. This land had been used by custom as an area where the villagers would retreat to when the lands around Madhubani were submerged under water due to the Kamla floods. The villagers opposed this move by attempting to construct some huts on the disputed land. These were later pulled down by the sub-divisional officer and the *raj*'s men.

[49] According to the census of 1931, 83 per cent of the population of Bihar and Orissa were Hindus. The Muslims numbered about 4,284,306 and formed 10.1 per cent of the population. Their maximum strength was in the north of the province and grew steadily less as one travelled from the north to the south. The Muslims had a greater percentage of their population in towns, about 8.8 per cent as against 3.6 per cent for Hindus. As

a result the relative proportion of Hindus and Muslims in urban areas was 3.5:1 while in rural areas, excluding Purnea, there were eleven Hindus to every Muslim.

50   *People's Age,* 8 Dec. 1946.
51   *Hindustan Times,* 3 Nov. 1946.
52   Sir Francis Tuker, *While Memory Serves* (London, 1950), p. 184; and *People's Age,* 28 Oct. 1946.
53   Tuker, *op.cit.,* p. 182.
54   BSA, file no. 319/47.
55   BSA, file no. 319/47.
56   Nehru and Patel rushed to Patna as soon as the rioting erupted. Nehru noted in surprise that most of the rioters were ordinary peasants. He wrote 'In the affected areas, that is in Patna district, in a part of Monghyr district and in Gaya, there has been a definite attempt on the part of Hindu mobs to exterminate Muslims. They have killed indiscriminately, men women and children en masse. ...I have addressed some large crowds in the rural areas and I have no doubt that many of them had participated in this bad business. They were ordinary peasant folk of Bihar, very simple, unsophisticated and rather likeable. They shouted "Mahatma Gandhi ki jai"'. See S. Gopal (ed.), *Selected Works of Jawaharlal Nehru* (second series), Vol. 1, p. 63.
57   Mahatma Gandhi's tour program in Bihar Dec. 1946, in BSA, file no. 319/47.
58   *Loc.cit.*
59   BSA, file no. 319/47.
60   Gyan Pandey, 'Rallying around the cow, sectarian strife in the Bhojpuri region', *Subaltern Studies* (Delhi, 1982), Vol. II, p. 74.
61   Hetakur Jha has shown that in the 1920s the Goala caste *sabhas* were organising Goalas to challenge their uppercaste landlords and to refuse to do *begari* in Hilsa, Paithana, Islampur and other places. See Jha 'lower-caste peasants and upper-caste *zamindars* in Bihar 1921-25', *Indian Economic and Social History Review,* XIV, 4 (1977), pp. 550-4.
62   Gyan Pandey, *op.cit.,* p. 79. See also the *Shahabad District Gazetteer,* pp. 44-5.
63   *People's Age,* 22 Dec. 1946.
64   *Home Political,* 28 Apr. 1946 and 28 May 1946, See also J.A. Curran, *Militant Hinduism in Indian Politics* (New York, 1951), pp. 10-15.

Punjab and the Making of Pakistan: The Roots of a Civil-Military State

Tan Tai Yong

For most of its post-independence history, Pakistan's search for a stable party-based system of parliamentary democracy, which its Indian neighbour has apparently taken to so easily, has proven elusive. Since its creation nearly five decades ago, Pakistan has seen more than twenty years of direct military or quasi-military rule, and real political power has always been firmly entrenched in the country's powerful civil-military bureaucracy. The character of Pakistan's post-colonial state was shaped by two divergent, yet mutually reinforcing political processes in the first decade after independence.

The first was the failure and eventual collapse of the experiment with parliamentary democracy. Although the trappings of representative political institutions were evident at the creation of Pakistan, the intended democratic process failed to materialise. The country's two key political institutions: the law-making National Constituent Assembly and the Muslim League – the party which had successfully spearheaded the Pakistan movement and was expected to play a similar role to that of the Congress in India by providing the leadership and the organisational machinery to ensure and facilitate mass participation in the political structure – failed dismally. The National Assembly quickly degenerated into a forum for factional infighting and petty intrigues, while the Muslim League, precisely weakest in the areas which became the constituent parts of Pakistan, failed to develop into a national, democratic party capable of integrating the ethnic and regional diversities within a workable political structure. The second process, which developed in sharp contrast to the failure of political institutions, was the increasing concentration of state power in the hands of the bureaucracy and the army.

All this led to the eventual emergence of a powerful civil-military bureaucracy which was able to usurp state power in October 1958, and which remains the real force in Pakistani politics to this day.[1] While it is important to recognise that 'an interplay of domestic, regional and international factors' in the post 1947 period had allowed the bureaucracy and the military to dominate 'the evolving structure of the Pakistani state'[2], it can be suggested that the rise of a Punjabi controlled military-bureaucratic oligarchy, which was organised and powerful enough to wrest control of, and dominate, the post independent state of Pakistan, preceded the birth of the country. This essay argues that the groundwork for this 'organic collaboration' between a Punjabi-dominated bureaucracy and army and Punjabi landed families had been worked out and perfected in the past, in colonial pre-partition Punjab. It examines how developments in colonial Punjab during the first half of the twentieth century, especially related to its position as the principal recruiting ground of the Indian army, saw the rise of a well-entrenched and all-pervasive civil-military regime dominated by powerful landlords. This formation not only survived the disruptions and upheaval caused by the partition of the Punjab, but very significantly went on to form the formidable bastion of the new state of Pakistan.

Punjab and the Indian Army

By the end of the nineteenth century, the Punjab had became the major recruiting ground for the Indian army, supplying roughly half of all the soldiers recruited from India. The dominance of the Punjabis in the respective arms of the army was significant: just before the First World War Punjabis accounted for sixty-six per cent of all cavalrymen in the Indian army; eighty-seven per cent of the artillery; and forty-five per cent of the infantry.[3] These figures indicate the highest rate of military participation from a particular province ever experienced in colonial India. Yet paradoxically, while Punjabis dominated the Indian army, the military labour market in the Punjab was an extremely limited one. As British recruitment policies in India came to be informed by the 'martial races' doctrine, only a select group from the Punjab, mainly Sikhs, Muslims and, to a lesser extent, Dogras and Hindu Jats, were eligible for recruitment, while all other groups of Punjabis not considered of sufficient 'martial' qualities were automatically excluded. In their selection of recruits, the military invariably limited its choices to dominant peasants and aristocratic landowning types. For instance, over ninety per cent of the Sikhs recruited from the Punjab into the army were from the dominant Jat caste from central Punjab.[4] Similarly, recruitment of Punjabi Muslims was limited to those who belonged to tribes of high social standing or reputation – the 'blood proud' and once the politically dominant aristocracy of western Punjab. Consequently, socially dominant Muslim tribes such as the Gakkhars, Janjuas and Awans and a few Rajput tribes, concentrated in the Rawalpindi and Jhelum districts of the Salt Range tract of western Punjab, accounted for more than ninety per cent of Punjabi Muslim recruits.[5] In the upshot, the entire military labour market of the Punjab comprised a small group of landowning classes: Jat Sikhs from Amritsar and Lahore, and to a lesser extent, from Hoshiarpur and Ludhiana, and aristocratic Muslim tribes from the Salt Range tract, mainly from the districts of Jhelum and Rawalpindi, as well as a small proportion of Hindu and Muslim Jats from the districts of Rohtak and Hissar and Dogras from the Kangra hill district.[6]

The small size of the military labour market notwithstanding, the Punjab administration took special care to ensure that the military districts were constantly kept pacified. This concern was understandable, given that the province not only supplied more than half the combatants of the Indian army, but that in the villages where the army had traditionally recruited, an enormous number of men had, at one time or another, received military training. If the province came to be racked by unrest, the stability of the army could become adversely affected and a full-scale military revolt might erupt. It was not surprising, therefore, that the Punjab government was particularly sensitive to the conditions of its military districts. At the heart of its desire to maintain a contented rural population lay the fear of a rural-military revolt in the base of the Indian army. The passing of the Land Alienation Act of 1900 was intended to safeguard the 'martial peasantry' from rural indebtedness, while the repeal of the Canal Colonies Bill seven years later was clearly an attempt to placate the military classes in central Punjab. More specifically, the military labour market in the Punjab was secured by the 'prizes' that military service offered: regular pay, pension and other privileges such as free travel on railways. These made military service an attractive option, especially in districts where agricultural and economic opportunities were limited.

But military pay and pensions were sometimes insufficient in themselves to procure the services and loyalty of these military allies; often, the colonial state found that it had to resort to other means to encourage recruitment. Consequently, in a manner and on a scale not replicated anywhere else in India, the Punjab authorities made generous use of its landed resources for the purpose of strengthening its bonds with the military districts.[7] Large tracts in the newly-opened canal irrigated wastelands were reserved for allotment as *fauji* grants to soldier-settlers, pensioners, and ex-soldiers.[8] The bulk of the military grantees were settled in the four large canal colonies: Chenab, Jhelum, Lower Bari Doab and Nili Bar. The magnitude of the entire settlement exercise was phenomenal: in the canal colonies as a whole, the total amount of land allotted to military grantees was almost in the region of half a million acres.[9] The use of land as a form of reward was aimed not only at strengthening the appeal of military service, but also ensuring the loyalty of the military classes to the state. Ex-soldiers were eligible for grants only after completing twenty-one years of service, and grants were made on condition of continued loyalty. Grantees were usually chosen by the recommendations of their regimental commanders, and their military record was usually the sole criterion for eligibility for land grants. The promise of land was, therefore, a great incentive for prolonged and loyal military service.

In addition to lavishing state resources as rewards for their military allies, the Punjab administration and military authorities had to ensure that the military districts were properly monitored and managed. For this, the British had all along relied on the rural élites as military intermediaries and contractors. The tribal landlords of western Punjab were particularly well-suited to play the part of military intermediaries for the British government. They exercised considerable influence in their respective localities by virtue of their control of scarce resources such as land, water and credit, and through the domination of *biraderi* (kinship) networks. These were effective means by which tenants and kinsmen could be goaded into enlisting. Their military value had been evident at the very outset of British involvement in the Punjab. During the Anglo-Sikh wars, several chieftain families from the Punjab provided military assistance to the British. One such family was that of Malik Fateh Sher Khan, who provided four hundred horsemen to Colonel Herbert Edwardes during the Sikh rebellion at Multan in 1848.[10] During the 1857 rebellion, several Sikh and Muslim chieftains in the Punjab responded quickly to John Lawrence's call for soldiers by raising their own armed men and mounted levies to fill the ranks of the moveable column to Delhi.

To reward the military classes and the military contractors, the state provided pay and pensions and other prizes, most notably grants of land in the canal colonies opened in the 1880s. It was especially generous towards its rural intermediaries. Many of them, like the Mitha Tiwanas of Shahpur district, received large land grants and *jagirs* and were incorporated into the Indian army as honorary officers and appointed to civilian posts as honorary magistrates and sub-registrars in the district administration.[11]

Civil-military integration

The rural élite's military value was best exemplified in the First World War. During the war, the Indian army was substantially expanded to meet the demands of operations in various war theatres. As the bulk of recruiting for the Indian army had, by the turn of the century, come to concentrate mainly in the Punjab, the province came to bear the brunt of raising the necessary manpower needed to meet this expansion. The requirements of rapid mobilisation demanded by the War, however, showed the inadequacies of peace-time recruiting arrangements. These arrangements had been adequate for the needs of a small peacetime army which had been very selective of its recruits. But with the massive expansion of the army, the pre-war recruiting arrangements in the Punjab simply could not cope. Consequently, the entire bureaucratic structure in the province was militarised, as nearly all aspects of its activities were geared towards the provision of men and material for the war effort. To meet the crisis of manpower and to stimulate and facilitate recruiting in areas hitherto untouched by the army, the civil and military structures in the province, which had hitherto functioned separately of each other, coalesced into a formidable machinery, dedicated to generating canon fodder for the war effort.[12] During the war, recruiting areas were redrawn to correspond with the administrative divisions of the province. Each of the newly-constituted recruiting areas was under the charge of a divisional recruiting officer, a military officer who was expected to work very closely with his civilian counterpart in the divisional headquarters. In each district, a district recruiting officer was appointed by the civil authorities to function as a civilian link to the military recruiting staff. Under this system, the military function of recruiting was integrated into the civil administrative structure, thus providing the framework for the civil administration to assume direct control of recruiting operations in the province.[13]

This civil-military integration entailed not just the interlinking of the provincial civil structure with the military command, but very importantly involved the full support of the rural-military élites as well. The Punjab government decided that the most effective way by which the administration could assist in raising manpower during the war was to mobilise the landed élites to use their influence to persuade their tribal followers and tenants to enlist themselves. These rural notables not only functioned as military contractors, but were also instrumental in propping up an administration weakened by the departure of several officers and soldiers for the warfront. During the war, the rural notables – tribal chiefs, landlords, religious leaders, clan and caste leaders – demonstrated another dimension of their importance to the colonial state in the Punjab: that of intercessors and contractors in the all-important military districts of the province. The civil society in which they dominated was to a large extent militarised. Accordingly, they now constituted a rural-military élite whose importance to the state, and hence their position in the provincial polity, had been greatly enhanced.[14]

The process of mobilisation during the war thus laid the foundations of a militarised bureaucracy in the Punjab, whose administrative/military tentacles were able to reach every level of society and economy. The direct assumption of a military function by the Punjab government, and its intrusion into society on behalf of the military during the war, was to mark the beginnings of a quasi-military state in the Punjab.

This civil-military integration in the Punjab continued into the inter-war period, as the civil administration and the military authorities co-operated closely to ensure that the military districts were carefully secured against economic and political discontent. The maintenance of the military districts during the inter-war period was mainly achieved throughout the merging of the civil and military authorities in the province, particularly through the instrument of the District Soldiers' Boards.[15] Numbers of these boards sprung up all over the Punjab and their structural organisation facilitated civil-military penetration deep into the military districts. However, their viability as institutions of control and communication ultimately depended on the support and co-operation of the local élites. In districts where landlords and tribal chiefs were present and were willing to lend their support, such as in the western districts of the province, soldiers' boards tended to be very effective. In such districts, the rural élites became an integral part of the district's civil-military machinery. On the other hand, where there was an absence of a social or landed élite to provide the required leadership, as in the Sikh districts of central Punjab, soldiers' boards tended to be relatively weaker as institutions of control. This explains why, during the years 1922-24, when the Akalis gained some influence in the countryside through their claims to religious leadership, the loyalist elements among the Sikhs were effectively marginalised, and soldiers' boards generally failed to contain the spread of anti-government sentiments in the Sikh districts.[16]

Nonetheless, through the district soldiers' boards, which were associated with the interests of the military classes, the *sircar* in the military districts came to assume a dual civil and military image. The government came to be identified as a quasi-military state which was committed to preserving the interests of the military classes. This had an important socialising effect on the military districts as the military classes, especially among the Muslims in western Punjab – which became the mainstay of the military labour market in the Punjab following the army authorities' decision to restrict the recruitment of Sikhs as the result of the Akali movement – came to accept government by a militarised bureaucracy, or by the military itself as the norm rather than an aberration.[17]

Political entrenchment of the civil-military lobby

The position of the civil-military formation that had emerged out of the First World War in the Punjab was further reinforced by the political entrenchment of the rural-military élites in the provincial legislatures created by political reforms after the war. When post-war constitutional reforms created new opportunities for political power, the Punjab government sought to ensure that this power would be devolved to their traditional rural-military allies.[18] Their concerns were clear enough: to have future legislative bodies in the Punjab dominated by the urban classes could have certain adverse military implications. Successive Punjab governments in the past had successfully nurtured its military districts, on whose active co-operation the reliability, and ultimately, the security of India depended. Policies had been adopted that not only aimed at shielding the military districts from external political influences but, at the same time, protected the economic, social and religious interests of the military classes, thus keeping them contented.

But Punjab's role as the military bulwark of the *raj* could be seriously jeopardised if urban politicians were to be elected and became uncooperative partners in government, especially in dealing with the interests of the rural military classes. This concern was felt most strongly by O'Dwyer, the Lieutenant Governor of the Punjab. To him, it was a matter of the utmost importance that a province as militarily important as the Punjab be spared the fate of being run by an 'elected majority...of irresponsible politicians...in the legislature'.[19] Consequently, during the early stages of the constitutional reform process, while the Secretary of State and the Government of India were prepared to carry out the promise made in the August Declaration of 1917, O'Dwyer was intent on preventing the introduction of reforms in the province, prompting Motilal Nehru to accuse him of turning 'the Punjab into a kind of Ulster in relation to the rest of India'.[20] In a sense, one could see O'Dwyer attempting here to save the military districts of the Punjab from the urban politicians, just as Ibbetson had earlier saved the Punjab peasantry from the Hindu urban money-lenders through the debates on the Land Alienation Act of 1900.

But despite his strong objections, O'Dwyer was never really in a position to stop the momentum of change that had already been set in motion. Realising that he could not prevent the devolution of power to Indian hands, O'Dwyer decided that if political changes were to be brought about, then he would bring in the 'Old world to redress the New'.[21] If actual power was to be devolved into Indian hands, and if his government were to work with local politicians, it would be in the former's interests to ensure that such power passed to the government's allies in the province – the rural-military élites. His government accordingly submitted a set of proposals to the Franchise Committee in 1918, which clearly showed its intention to 'fix the terms of reforms' so as to marginalise the urban politicians and ensure the political entrenchment of the rural-military élites.

The Punjab government's proposals regarding the franchise were designed to establish a small, and overwhelming rural and conservative electorate in the Punjab. Its calculations about franchise suggested that the provincial electorate would consist of approximately 230,000 votes, of which 161,000 would be rural votes and only 70,000 urban. At the same time, the government tried to ensure that only the rural notables, landlords and dominant *zamindars* were eligible to vote. This was clearly aimed at creating a conservative electorate with a strong rural-military bias. The rural classes which the Punjab government intended to enfranchise were mostly beneficiaries of state patronage, whose interests were closely connected to maintaining the *status quo*. Most importantly, in a predominantly rural electorate those to be enfranchised were the very elements who were the mainstay of the Indian army, had supported the government during the war, and were in a position to maintain the military machinery of the province in the future. According to the calculations of the Punjab government, out of a projected total of 161,000 rural votes, more than 150,000 (above ninety per cent) would come from government officials, the military, rich landholders and peasant-proprietors.[22]

In November 1918, in an interview with the Franchise Committee, O'Dwyer explained the rationale behind the proposals of his government. He stressed that conditions in the Punjab were such that, in formulating a scheme for the reforms 'local conditions rather than logical precision or theoretical completeness were of primary importance'. He pointed out that the urban-rural dichotomy was a central feature of the Punjab, and it was the rural population that was predominantly important in terms of its numbers, the amount of revenue paid, as well as its overall predominance in the Indian army. According to O'Dwyer, the unique position of the Punjab as the major recruiting ground for the Indian army, as well as its location as the crucial military base for operations across the North West frontier, made it imperative for the government to ensure that the political power be devolved to its rural-military allies.[23]

The rural-military élites of the Punjab regarded the promise of constitutional reforms in the post-1919 India with a degree of trepidation. Prior to 1919, in return for their support of the military structure of the Punjab, their position in the province had been assured. To protect their interests they needed to secure a major share of the power to be devolved under the reforms, but they were apprehensive that representative power would not favour them. They knew that, as things stood, they were in no position successfully to wage an electoral contest against the better educated and organised urban politicians. Their influence as rural notables was essentially localised; each of them exercised influence only over his immediate caste, tribe or locality, and the source of such influence revolved around economic dominance and kinship ties.

These rural élites furthermore lacked an effective local structure with which they could mobilise popular support in the general elections. Their power and position were also state sponsored, and depended on state patronage. During the period preceding the reforms, fearing that their position in the provincial state structure would be usurped by the 'advanced politicians', the rural-military élites decided to make a collective effort to influence the reforms in their favour. They realised that the only way in which the process could be made to work in their favour was to use their influence in the administration and the military to pressure the British into acquiescing in their political demands for special provisions that would safeguard their interests. What emerged out of these fears and anxieties of this period was a loosely constituted rural-military lobby within the Punjab, which was able to use its importance in the rural administration and in the military as a leverage with which to stake a claim in the newly-emerging reformed political structure.

During the Secretary of State's tour of India in the winter of 1917-18, the rural-military élites in the Punjab, represented by two organisations – the Punjab Muslim Association and the Punjab Zamindar Central Association – submitted proposals on how the reforms should be implemented in the Punjab. Although organised on a communal basis, both associations shared a common concern: their objectives, like those of the Punjab government, were to secure special representation for landholders and to obtain a predominant share of political power for the rural-military classes. The proposals of the rural-military élites were very similar to O'Dwyer's, indicating the extent to which the interests of the colonial state and its rural-military allies had become integrated.

The Punjab Muslim Association, whose members were mainly heads of military families or were retired military officers who held honorary British ranks, emphasised the contributions made by Punjabi Muslims to the military, especially during the war, and expressed concern that the political reforms should not be allowed to adversely affect the special relationship between the Muslim rural classes and the state.[24] Its leader, Malik Umar Hayat Khan Tiwana, Honorary Lieutenant-Colonel and influential spokesman for the military classes in the province, submitted a memorandum to the Secretary of State in 1918 in which he warned that if political reforms were to replace British rule with a 'bania oligarchy', the outcome would be one of potential danger for the Punjab as a whole. He called for certain constitutional provisions to be made to ensure the protection of the landed and military interests which included, *inter alia*, the creation of a second chamber in the legislative council for representatives of soldiers and landholders and for the extension of the franchise to all soldiers.[25]

The Punjab Zamindar Central Association, originally known as the Jat Sikh Association, was also representative of the province's rural-military interests. About one-third of its members consisted of retired soldiers, many of whom had long connections with the military, and had assisted in recruitment during the war.[26] Like the Muslim Association, the Zamindar Association was concerned that constitutional changes should be made in such a way as to safeguard the interests of *zamindars* and peasant-proprietors, which had constantly supplied combatants to the army as opposed to 'the town bred educated people'.[27]

The terms of the Government of India Act of 1919 for the Punjab eventually incorporated much that had been proposed by the Punjab government and the province's rural-military lobby, while mostly rejecting the proposals made by the urban parties, which perhaps indicates how urban considerations had become marginal in the politics of the Punjab. The electorate in the province was a small and restrictive one, about three per cent of the total population. It was also heavily biased towards the countryside; of the total electorate, rural voters accounted for 423,192 and urban voters, 77,797.

One of the most important features of the 1919 reforms related to the provision for the military vote. In its original proposals, the Punjab government had recommended that only retired and pensioned Indian officers above the rank of *jemadar* should be enfranchised, while the rural-military representatives had demanded that the vote be extended to all ex-soldiers. It was finally decided that all ex-soldiers, irrespective of their rank, be given the vote.[28] Although the military vote generally formed a negligible portion of the electorate in other provinces, it constituted a very substantial element in the Punjab electorate, well beyond what the government had originally envisaged. In the upshot, the military vote in the Punjab was estimated to be 190,000, or 31.6 per cent of the entire provincial electorate.[29] The significance of the military vote in the traditional military districts in the Punjab such as Jhelum, Rawalpindi, Attock, Shahpur, Amritsar and Rohtak was even more pronounced. It is difficult to calculate with any accuracy the percentage of the military vote in any particular constituency, given the lack of definite figures of retired personnel in the districts. But if we assume that one-third of those recruited during the First World War were demobilised soldiers the proportion of voters with military connections in such districts would average over seventy per cent of the total district electorates.[30]

The real substance of the Punjab government's proposals, which had also been the main demand of the rural-military lobby, was that power be devolved to traditional allies to the exclusion of urban politicians. This was embodied in the Government of India Act of 1919. The terms and conditions of the Act were skewed very much in favour of the rural-military élites: more than 70 per cent of the rural voters in the Punjab were landlords, dominant *zamindars*, rural notables, minor officials and ex-soldiers, and their interests subsequently dominated the Legislative Council.[31] The significance of the first constitutional reforms for the subsequent political development of the Punjab cannot be underestimated. By providing for the overwhelming dominance of the landed and military vote in the Punjab electorate, the Act set the stage for the political domination of the very classes whose co-operation was always crucial for the Punjab's position as the military bulwark of the *raj*.

Subsequent elections in the Punjab under the 1919 Act, which took place in 1920, 1923, 1927 and 1930, all returned legislative councils which were dominated by the 'old world'. These councils comprised mainly landlords, peasant-proprietors, ex-army officers and only a sprinkling of traders and lawyers. The Punjab administration was comfortable with the councils, claiming that that 'it was the best instance of the right kind of provincial government, based broadly on the landlords, peasants, and soldiers'.[32] While loyalist in their basic political orientation, these rural-military élites constituted themselves into an informal lobby in the councils, aimed at promoting the interests of the landlords and landholding peasantry, the very stratum of agrarian society which had constituted the overwhelming bulk of Punjab's restricted electorate. High on the agenda of this rural-military lobby was the attempt to place the procedure of assessment for land revenue on a statutory basis, so that it could exert a direct influence in the council on the revenue administration of the province, particularly in the fixing of revenue. The lobby was also constantly on guard against any attempts by the government to raise taxes or canal rates, the two things which would work against its own as well as its rural supporters' interests. It was this rural-military lobby which towards the end of 1923 was constituted into the Punjab National Unionist Party and which, in turn, dominated Punjab politics right up to 1937 when a new set of reforms were introduced under the Government of India Act of 1935.[33]

With the entrenchment of the Unionists in Punjab politics, a paradoxical relationship seemed to have emerged between the government and its allies. Prior to 1920, the old aristocratic landlords and rural notables had been entirely dependent on the government's goodwill for the preservation of their special status. They had to show active loyalty, as they had during the war, to earn the state's patronage. Although successive Punjab governments had been careful not to alienate them and so lose their active support, these élites had seldom been in a position to dictate terms, and had virtually no direct influence on government policies. But changes following post-war reforms brought about, perhaps inevitably, a shift in this relationship. These élites were no longer entirely dependent on the state for their political position, but on the support of their electoral base. This meant that they had to cultivate their interests in the legislature, sometimes at the expense of official interests. Yet, despite their constant jockeying against the government for advantages in terms of land revenue and taxation, these élites realised that, in the last resort, their interests were still predicated upon the overall maintenance of British rule which they could not afford to challenge or jeopardise. The reforms had, therefore, brought about a new breed of collaborators who, although they emphasised their continued loyalty to the *raj*, were able to use their newly-found leverage to assert greater control over affairs which affected them and their constituents. It was an indication of this paradoxical relationship that, in the early 1930s, the Unionist Party was regarded by the British as an official opposition party within the legislative council, frequently voting against the government.

The political dominance of the rural-military élites, now symbolised in the Unionist Party, was not undermined by the political changes brought about by the Government of India Act of 1935. If anything, the rural-military élite-dominated Unionist Party emerged stronger than before. Out of the one hundred and seventy-five seats in the newly constituted Punjab Legislative Assembly the Unionist Party won ninety-five seats in the 1937 elections. The Congress, which had elsewhere, most notably in the UP and Madras, defeated erstwhile politically powerful landlord parties, was trounced at the polls by the Unionist Party, and could secure less than ten per cent of the seats.

This dominance of the Unionist Party was helped by a franchise which was only marginally altered. The 1935 Act did provide for a significantly extended franchise in the Punjab, from 745,000 in 1930 to 2.75 million in 1935 (from 3.1 per cent to 11.7 per cent of the provincial population). But, as in 1919, under the influence of the Punjab Government and the rural-military lobby in the council, the rural character of the legislative assembly and the provincial electorate was preserved. Of the one hundred and seventy-five seats in the Assembly, one hundred and forty-three were rural.[34] The qualifications for enfranchisement, although lowered in most cases, were not, however, radically altered. With the exception of special constituencies, the voting qualifications were still based on land and property ownership, land revenue or income payment, official appointments and titles.[35] Seventy-five per cent of the extended franchise provided by the 1935 Act was constituted by members of the agricultural classes, as defined by the 1900 Land Alienation Act.[36] Only seventeen per cent of landholders and fifty per cent of tenants enfranchised in the Punjab in 1935 belonged to non-agricultural classes.[37]

On the advice of the provincial government and the Army Department, the military vote was retained.[38] This vote, as mentioned earlier, formed a significant *bloc* in a number of constituencies and its proportion was a continually growing one, as soldiers who were pensioned or discharged from the army were automatically given the vote. The provincial electorate eventually approved for the Punjab was, therefore, still predominantly rural, with a strong conservative element, dominated by the landowning classes, whose interests were closely tied to the state. What all this implied was that the electoral base, on which the continued rural-military élite domination in the provincial legislatures prior to 1935 was predicated, had remained largely unchanged.

The terms of reforms, both in 1919 and 1935, thus fixed the political focus firmly in the countryside, strengthening the hands of the rural-military élites at the expense of urban politicians. What emerged out of the political development of colonial Punjab during the inter-war years was thus the political entrenchment of landlord politicians who were not only able to operate comfortably in a civil-military regime, but very much held it together. Once in government, the rural-military élites acted as the bond between the locality (the military districts) and the Legislative Council in Lahore, thus reinforcing the civil-military structure at all levels in the Punjab.

Punjab in the 1940s

Between 1939 and 1945 the Punjab was mobilised, once again, to support Britain in a major war in which India was only involved because she was a part of the British empire. This time, however, the initiative for mobilisation was undertaken by the Unionist-led government. In September 1939, almost immediately after the British had declared war on Germany, Sikander Hayat Khan, the Unionist Premier of the Punjab, issued a statement calling on the people of the Punjab to 'maintain their splendid traditions as the swordarm of India' by supporting the

British war effort.[39] In a manner reminiscent of O'Dwyer and his government during the First World War, Sikander and the Unionist ministry committed themselves to gearing the province for a massive contribution to the war effort. At the outbreak of War, Sikander and his ministers personally toured the districts to drum up enthusiasm for enlistment to the Indian army and, at the same time, to warn their detractors that the government would brook no opposition to its policy of co-operation in the War.[40] A provincial civil guard, comprising some thirty thousand men, was raised to prepare the province for full scale mobilisation as well as to help maintain law and order during the period of war.[41] Throughout the war years (even though Sikander died of a heart attack in December 1942), the Unionist government was fully behind the mobilisation process, during which more than eight hundred thousand combatants were recruited from the Punjab and Rs 25 *crores* raised through war loans and donations.[42] Rural notables eagerly supported the war effort, as they saw it as an opportunity to increase rural employment and raise the prices of agricultural products.[43] Hopeful of obtaining rewards of cash and land grants from the British, as many of them did in the First World War, the landowning élites actively encouraged recruitment in their respective districts.

As the war wore on, and the demands for troops remained high in the province already depleted of eligible recruits, the military, civil service and provincial arms of the *raj* once again coalesced into an integrated structure to direct recruitment operations in the Punjab.[44] During the First World War the mobilisation process had been co-ordinated by an integrated civil-military bureaucracy, with the assistance of the rural-military élites. In the early 1940s, the mobilisation process in the Punjab was similarly facilitated by a civil-military bureaucracy. But this time the process was smoothed by the conjoining of the bureaucratic edifice and a local political structure dominated by the rural-military élites.

At the end of the war, the Muslim elements within this larger rural-military élite pressured by the increasingly popular appeal of Pakistan, made a tactical shift from the Unionist Party to the Muslim League. And as Imran Ali points out, 'this swing provided the basis for maintaining major continuities.... [for] the Muslim landed élite chose to use the League as its vehicle for carrying over its authority into the post colonial period'.[45] In 1947, the military-administrative superstructure held together Western Punjab amidst the unprecedented violence and upheaval brought about by independence and partition. In post-independence Pakistan, as weak and ineffectual politicians squabbled, the organised and powerful bureaucracy quickly assumed control of the state machinery, with the army assuming a more civil role in performing non-military functions such as aid to the civil administration in maintaining law and order, control of communal riots, and the management of natural calamities such as floods, epidemics, food shortage and famines.[46] The primacy of this strong bureaucratic-military rule was made all the more conspicuous by Pakistan's uneasy relations with its neighbour, India. By the mid-1950s, the powerful Punjabi bureaucrats and army officers, whose alliance had already been perfected in the past, assumed total control of the centralised state apparatus, laying a firm foundation for the 'state of martial rule' in Pakistan.

Throughout the period of colonial rule, the Punjab had been closely associated with the Indian army. It was, for more than half a century, from about 1880 to 1947, the main recruiting ground for the Indian army. One of the outcomes of this close association was the militarisation of the administration of the Punjab, characterised by the conjunction of the military, civil and political authorities into a unique civil-military regime. This development was not replicated anywhere else in British India, nor indeed the empire. Military exigencies, namely the mobilisation and control of the province's important military districts during the First World War, brought about the integration of the civil and military structures of the province. This distinct nexus between the military and the state was maintained during the inter-war period as the provincial administration and the army co-operated closely to insulate the important military districts from external political influences. The closely integrated civil-military structure was then reinforced by the establishment of a local political structure dominated by rural-military élites, following constitutional reforms in 1920 and 1937. This civil-military regime remained essentially intact despite major political developments and upheaval in the 1940s, and was inherited thereafter by Pakistan. In the period after 1947, it was this powerful and well-entrenched civil-military alliance that took over the state apparatus and ensured the survival of the 'moth-eaten' and fragile state of Pakistan.

Notes

1   On these issues, see Omar Noman, *Political and Economic History of Pakistan since 1947* (Oxford, 1989); Hassan Gardezi and Jamil Rashid (eds), *Pakistan: the Roots of Dictatorship. The Political Economy of a Praetorian State* (Delhi, 1983), and Tariq Ali, *Can Pakistan Survive? The Death of a State* (Penguin Books, 1983); Ayesha Jalal, *The State of Martial Rule: the origins of Pakistan's political economy of defence* (Cambridge, 1991).

2   This argument is most convincingly developed in Jalal, *The State of Martial Rule*.

3   Annual caste returns compiled by Army Headquarters in India indicate that by 1900, Punjabis accounted for over fifty per cent of all native soldiers recruited from India. See 'Annual Caste Returns of the Native Army, 1800-1910', India Office Library and Records [henceforth: IOL], L/MIL/14/221-226.

4   H.D. Craik, Punjab District Gazetteer (PDG), Amritsar, 1914 (Lahore, 1914), Vol. XXA, p. 162.

5   Lt. Col. J.M. Wikeley, *Punjabi Mussalmans* (Calcutta, 1915), p. 125. .

6   See Annual Caste Returns, 1900.

7   For a full story of the use of the canal colonies in the Punjab for military purposes, see Imran Ali, *The Punjab Under Imperialism, 1885-1947* (Delhi, 1989).

8   *Ibid.*, pp.110-20

9   *Ibid.*, p.115.

10   See L. Griffin, *et al.*, *Chiefs and Families of Note in the Punjab* (Lahore, 1910), Vol.II, p. 179.

11   Andrew J. Major, 'The Punjabi Chieftains and the Transition from Sikh to British Rule', in D.A. Low (ed.), *The Political Inheritance of Pakistan* (London, 1991), pp.76-7.

12   This was largely achieved at the bidding of Sir Michael O'Dwyer, Lieutenant Governor of the Punjab from 1912 to 1919. See Michael O'Dwyer, *India as I Knew It. 1885-1925* (London, 1925).

13   'Notes on Recruiting Methods Employed in the Punjab' in Government of India (Home/Political), Feb. 1920, No. 373, National Archives of India.

14   A notable example was Umar Hayat Khan Tiwana, a prominent landlord from the Shahpur district of Western Punjab. At the outbreak of war, Tiwana volunteered for active service and was sent with the first Indian contingent to France. After serving there for fifteen months, he was posted to Mesopotamia on special duties connected with propaganda among Muslim troops. Tiwana was later promoted to the honorary rank of major, and served as an honorary recruiting officer in his home district of Shahpur. From his own estate at Kalra, he managed to get more than two hundred men enlisted during the war. For details of the family history of the Tiwanas, see Griffin, Lepel *et. al.*, *Chiefs and Families of Note in the Punjab*, Vol. II, pp. 168-93.

15   See T.Y. Tan, 'Maintaining the Military Districts: Civil-Military Integration and District Soldiers' Boards in the Punjab, 1919-1939', in *Modern Asian Studies*, 28, 4 (1994), pp. 833-74.

16   *Ibid.*, p. 859.

17   *Ibid.*, p. 874.

18   See Memorandum by Michael O'Dwyer on Constitutional Reforms, 10 Jan. 1918, in Annexure to Enclosure 22 of letter from Government of India, 5 Mar. 1919 and Enclosures of the Question Raised in the Report on Indian Constitutional Reforms in *Parliamentary Papers* [hereafter *PP*], 1919, Vol. XXXVII, p. 285. See also

O'Dwyer's autobiography, *India As I Knew It* (London, 1925).

19 Peter Robb, *Government of India and Political Reforms* (Oxford, 1976), pp.12-13

20 Motilal Nehru, *The Voice of Freedom: Selected Speeches of Motilal Nehru* (Bombay, 1961), p. 22.

21 David Page, *Prelude to Partition: The Indian Muslims and the Imperial System of Control, 1920-1932* (Oxford, 1982), p. 47.

22 For details see Proposals of the Punjab Government, *PP*, Cmd 141, Vol. XVI, pp. 668-9.

23 'Note of discussion with the Lieutenant-Governor of the Punjab', 7 Dec. 1918, in *PP*, 1919, Cmd 141, Vol. XVI, p. 677.

24 Address presented by the Punjab Muslim Association to the Viceroy and Secretary of State, 1918, in *PP*, Cmd. 9178, Vol. XVIII, pp. 478-9.

25 Memorandum on Indian Constitutional Reforms by Major Sir Umar Hayat Khan Tiwanaof Shahpur District, Punjab, July 1918, IOL,L/P&J/9/9.

26 Presentation by the Punjab Zamindar Association, and accompanying note by W.S. Marris, 20 Nov. 1917, in Montagu Collection, IOL, Mss Eur., D.523/35.

27 *Loc.cit.*

28 'The Military Service Qualification for Franchise' in Report of the Indian Franchise Committee (Lothian), 1932, in *PP.*, Cmd. 4086, Vol. VIII, p. 641.

29 Report of Indian Franchise Committee, 1932, *PP*, Cmd.4086

30 Roughly, in Rohtak the district proportion would approximately be 12,000 of 18,000 (sixty per cent); in Jhelum, Rawalpindi, and Attock, almost one hundred percent; in Shahpur, 9,000 of 17,000 (fifty-three per cent); Amritsar, 9,000 out of 18,000 (fifty per cent). For detailed figures, see M.S. Leigh, *Punjab and the War* (Lahore, 1922), pp. 59-60; and *Punjab Electoral Statistics and Maps*, 1920. (Lahore, 1921).

31 The electoral statistics of 1920 did not provide a separate count of the ex-soldiers vote in the districts. However, it can be assumed that the bulk of Punjab's ex-soldiers would already have qualified for the vote under the property or title qualifications. The numbers who actually only qualified under the military vote would thus be a small one. *Punjab Electoral Statistics, 1920.*

32 Note by F.L. Brayne, Seputy Commissioner, Gurgaon District, 1920 to 1927, Financial Commissioner and Secretary to Revenue Department, Punjab Government, 1939-40, n.d. in Brayne Collection, IOL, Mss Eur., F152/69.

33 The Unionist Party was, therefore, more a caucus of landowning rural-military élites in the Legislative Council than a formal political party with a creed, organisational grassroots support or an effective local hierarchy. It did not contest elections as a political party.

34 The territorial constituencies were divided communally, based on the Communal Award of 1932. The Muslims had eighty-four seats (nine urban and seventy-five rural), the Hindus under General Constituencies, had forty-two seats (eight urban, thirty-four rural) and the Sikhs were given thirty-one seats (two urban, twenty-nine rural). In addition, there were five special seats for landlords. See K. C. Yadav, *Elections in the Punjab, 1920-47*, (New Delhi, 1987), p.17.

35 Property and status qualifications of voters in the Punjab from 1937 included persons having passed primary and any other higher examinations; women being literate, widows or mothers of soldiers who died in the War, wife of a voter; owner/assignee/ lessee/tenant of land/Crown land with land revenue assessed at Rs.25 per annum; title holders; retired military personnel; government officials. For the urban vote, the qualifications were similar to the above except that in the place of land revenue and

ownership of land, the voter had to be paying an annual income tax of Rs.60 per annum or be in possession of immovable properties worth at least Rs. 4,000. Yadav, *Elections*, p.18.

36   See Report of Indian Franchise Committee (Lothian), 1931-32, in *PP*, Cmd. 4086, 1931-32, Vol. VIII, pp. 505-6.

37   *Loc.cit.*

38   'The Military Service Qualification for Franchise' in Report of the Indian Franchise Committee, 1932', in *PP*, Cmd. 4086, Vol. VIII.

39   Craik to Linlithgow, 13 Sept. 1939, Linlithgow Papers, IOL, Mss Eur., F.125/88.

40   *Loc.cit.*

41   Craik to Linlithgow, 20 June 1940, IOL, L/P&J/5/243.

42   Governor's Reports and Chief Secretary's Fortnightly Reports on the situation in the Punjab, 15 May 1945, in Political Department, IOL, L/P&J/5/248.

43   Ian Talbot, *Punjab and the Raj*, 1849-1947 (New Delhi, 1988), p.143.

44   Fortnightly Reports on the Political Situation in the Punjab, various dates, 1945.

45   Imran Ali, 'The Punjab and the Retardation of Nationalism', in D.A. Low (ed.), *op.cit.*, p. 47.

46   Veena Kukreja, *Civil-Military Relations in South Asia. Pakistan, Bangladesh and India* (New Delhi, 1991), pp. 46-59; Hasan-Askari Rizvi, *The Military and Politics in Pakistan, 1947-86* (Lahore, 1986), pp. 56-62.

G. D. Birla, Big Business and India's Partition

Medha Malik Kudaisya

In South Asian historiography, little attention has been given to the role of Indian big business in the processes that led to the partition of India. Ghanshyamdas (G. D.) Birla, one of the pre-eminent figures of big business, was a perhaps surprising supporter of the idea of partition from an unusually early date. He then had a good deal of influence on the attitude which big business took as independence loomed. As big business contemplated the prospect of partition, some significant figures amongst them set about calculating its implications, and came up with a variety of propositions which have not hitherto been much appreciated. This chapter tries to understand the process of India's partition in 1947 as seen by and from the standpoint of G. D. Birla and Indian big business.[1] The first part of this essay considers Birla's political background and his responses to partition from the late 1920s onwards. The second part then looks at the larger responses of big business to the prospect of partition, and finally the economic implications of partition for big business are analysed.

Before addressing the first theme of Birla and partition, it is important to understand certain underplayed aspects of Birla's early career and the formative political influences upon him. To most Indians and those familiar with India, Birla (1894-1983) as a public figure needs no introduction. He is perhaps best remembered as a builder of magnificent temples, as a philanthropist whose charities ran into millions, and as the man who sheltered the Mahatma and at whose house the great man was assassinated. However, Ghanshyamdas Birla as a historical figure is much more complex. Among other things he was a zealous reformer within his trading community of Marwaris; throughout his career he freely gave his patronage and money to Hindu causes; he was the single most important benefactor of the Indian National Congress, generously financing its many causes and campaigns against the *raj*. For over two decades, between 1927 and 1950, he remained one of the most influential spokesmen of Indian big business as well as its chief strategist. He led a dogged fight against British capital and was responsible for forging much of the solidarity which Indian big business displayed before 1947. For decades, he remained a strong critic of the economic policies of the colonial state. At the same time, he conducted one of the most successful Indian private enterprises of his time. His triumphs often lay in his varied roles as a lobbyist: in England pleading for great concessions for India; within the Congress working for right-wing solidarity; within wider nationalist politics promoting the constitutionalist viewpoint; and in business circles working for solidarity to fight foreign capital.

Philanthropy and Hindu nationalism

The general background of the politics of mercantile and business communities is now well known. From the work of Chris Bayly a good deal is known of the support given by mercantile groups to Hindu revivalist movements and early nationalist activity. Pre-dominant among these groups was the trading community of Marwaris, to which Birla belonged. From the beginning of the twentieth century, the Marwaris had been staunch supporters of Hindu resurgence movements across north India. Religious charity and philanthropy played a special role in their lives and were regarded as the path to prestige and stature within the community. Marwari philanthropy supported *go-shalas*, *akharas* for the physical training of Hindu youth, and helped Hindi language news papers. From about the 1910s, much of this support was given under the influence of the great patriarch of Hindu nationalism, Madan Mohan Malaviya.

To understand how the Birlas were placed within the Marwari community of Bara Bazaar, the commercial hub of indigenous business in Calcutta, we need to trace some of the early history of the family. The Birlas had set up business there only in the 1890s. They were late-comers in the world of Bara Bazaar, both in terms of prosperity and public prominence as compared to the more established *seths*. Like other Marwari traders, they were largely involved in speculation and trading in opium, silver, grain and Manchester cloth, although opium futures were the main stay of their early success. Philanthropy provided to the Birlas an avenue for upward mobility within the Marwari *samaj*. In the decade before World War I, they became the largest supporters of Hindu causes among the Calcutta Marwaris. It was in the field of philanthropy that the Birlas began to gain a stature which no other Marwari family could rival and which put them in the forefront of community leadership by the late 1910s. The huge profits made by them during World War I further extended their horizons and by 1920 the scale of their known philanthropy had exceeded 'Rs 25 lakhs in hard cash.' This charity earned the Birla family *sakh* and reputation among the Calcutta Marwaris.

From the early 1910s much of the Birla philanthropy was done under the inspiration of Malaviya. It was widely acknowledged that the Birlas were the largest donors to the Hindu University. In addition, the family supported a number of Hindu institutions. The restoration of Hindu temples, building of new ones, construction of *dharamshalas* and maintenance of cremation sites became an integral part of their charities. The Birlas continued to be Malaviya's principal benefactors until his death in 1946. [2]

G. D. Birla himself initially became closely involved with the politics of the Hindu wing of Indian nationalism. In the 1920s his politics were not those of Gandhi, but those of Lajpat Rai and Malaviya. From 1923 onwards, he supported Lajpat Rai whose over-riding concern after the collapse of the Non Co-operation

Movement had been to organise and then consolidate the Hindus of north India. Lajpat Rai's expenses figured prominently in Birla's ledger books of this period.[3] By 1925 Birla was closely identified with both Lajpat Rai and Malaviya, and in 1926 played a prominent role in the formation of their Independent Congress Party. Birla played a key role also in the 1926 Central Legislative Assembly elections, by providing election funds, and was himself drafted to stand for the Benaras-Gorakhpur constituency in United Provinces against the Swaraj Party, and was elected. Once he entered the Central Legislative Assembly his mentors, Malaviya and Lajpat Rai, wanted to groom him for the future leadership of the Hindu community. In 1927 he was offered the presidentship of the Hindu Mahasabha, a position he refused because of his business commitments.

Yet, by the end of the 1920s things had changed. In 1928 Lajpat Rai's death removed from the scene one of the strongest influences upon Birla. His links with Malaviya continued, as the two shared common concerns about reclaiming converted Hindu untouchables and building up the political strength of the Hindus. However, on the political plane Birla broke with Malaviya in 1931 when Malaviya opposed Gandhi at the second Round Table Conference (RTC). By this time Birla had moved closer to Gandhi and the nature of their relationship is too well known to be recounted here.

In August 1931 Birla accompanied Gandhi to the second RTC in whose deliberations he proved his worth when in September the pound sterling, to which the Indian rupee was tied, quite unexpectedly went off the 'gold standard'. He played the key role of an economic expert for the Indian delegation in its negotiations with the India Office.[4] By this time his family controlled over a dozen publicly listed companies with a paid up share capital of Rs 24,900,000. He owned the only major English daily published from the capital, the *Hindustan Times,* and had interests in two Calcutta papers. Personally close to several 'right-wing' Congress leaders, Birla was widely regarded as an insider in the Gandhian camp. Within his Marwari community, his pre-eminence was widely acknowledged. The larger business community recognised him as one of the founder members of the Calcutta based Indian Chamber of Commerce, and as the moving spirit behind the Federation of Indian Chambers of Commerce and Industry or FICCI, the apex level organisation of Indian big business.

Early ideas on separation

Against this background, one can place Birla's early ideas on partition. It is noteworthy that long before Jinnah or the Muslim League formulated the Pakistan demand (*vide* the Lahore Resolution of March 1940) Birla began to formulate ideas about re-drawing India's political map on the basis of separate religious communities. The first exposition of this idea can be found as early as October 1927 when during a discussion with Malaviya, Birla expressed his views on the re-drawing of provincial boundaries to create a distinct agglomeration of the Muslim-majority areas. He wrote:

Communal representation in Legislature should go, with reservation of seats for each community, and if possible redistribution of Provinces should be made. I do not know whether splitting the Punjab and Bengal would be liked by the people but I would personally welcome it. The West Punjab and the Frontier and Sind might be composed into one province thus giving a decided majority to Mohammadans in East Bengal and the West Punjab and the seats should be reserved on the basis of population.[5]

In such ideas lay the nucleus of Birla's thinking on the communal question. One can see that although Birla at this time was not an advocate of the division of the country into two nation-states, he believed in the need to redraw the political map of the country to create formations based on the principle of communal interests. On the basis of Ayesha Jahal's thesis, much of Jinnah's demand for Pakistan would seem to correspond with such ideas. [6]

During the 1930s he began to articulate his notion of partition with greater clarity and confidence. He saw the communal problem as a stumbling block towards political progress, and he felt that all constitutional advance was doomed until a workable solution to communalism had been found. Birla's analysis of the communal situation derived from his own personal experience of political developments during the 1920s and early 1930s. He viewed the problem against the background of agreements entered by leaders of different communities. He was convinced of the futility of such agreements with leaders of the minority community because these made an alliance something to be achieved by the 'highest bidder'. He had been personally involved with the funding of the Nehru Report and was witness to the bitter communal dissensions that led to the failure of the second RTC in London. These experiences convinced Birla that, 'as soon as a certain position had been gained, there was started a fresh agitation for another. While one section accepted the settlement made, another began denouncing it, and the section that indulged in denunciation came to be recognised as leader of the community'.[7] Birla was convinced that there could be no finality in such negotiations and agreements.

A staunch believer in constitutionalism, he was eager for the Congress to work the 1935 Act and was delighted when the party formed ministries in seven provinces. He was, however, sceptical of coalition ministries which, in his view, accentuated communal bitterness, instead of reducing tension and restoring confidence among the minorities. He predicted that coalition ministries in the Muslim-majority provinces of Punjab and Bengal would not lead to a lasting solution as 'the ministries will always pull their weight community-wise and in opposite directions'.[8] In other provinces where the Muslims were in a minority (besides Bengal, Punjab, Assam, NWFP and Sind), he went on to argue that, 'if power is given to them, it would mean that ten percent of the population would have the power of wrecking any measure they like'.

However, the larger question for Birla in the late 1930s was Indian control over the centre for which he wanted the inauguration of the federation scheme as soon as possible. He was extremely concerned that a lack of understanding between the Congress and the League should delay federation. For instance, in a letter to Gandhi in 1938 (addressed to Mahadev Desai) he wrote:

> I wonder why it should not be possible to have two Federations, one of Muslims and another of Hindus. The Muslim Federation may be composed of all the provinces or portions of provinces which contain more than two thirds of Muslim populations and the Indian states like Kashmir which is composed of Musalmans. Another Federation may be of Hindus and such states as are composed of Hindus.[9]

The Muslim League's propaganda campaign against the Congress's alleged 'Hindu misrule' further convinced him that conciliation was becoming difficult by the late 1930s. In essence the problem, in his view, boiled down to the impossible demands of the Muslim League. He was sympathetic to Muslim demands for safeguards on cultural and religious grounds but he believed that what was being asked for by the League was 'to be treated on equal basis' with vetoing power in the central and provincial legislatures. This seemed to him most unreasonable, almost a situation where '25% of the population should determine the course of political change'.[10]

In this period Birla persisted with his idea of two federations. So convinced had he become of the futility of attempts at communal settlement that he began to discuss with Congress leaders like C. Rajagopalachari the possible lines of division of provinces between 'Hindu India' and 'Muslim India.' He firmly believed that, as he put it, 'if we want to have a peaceful India, we must encourage this division and after that we will have no reservation of seats, no minority problem and no communal problem'.[11]

In the early 1940s Birla was impatient with the constitutional breakdown of the 1935 Act. He wanted the Congress to co-operate in the war effort, and not insist on complete independence, or what he called '16 annas of the Rupee', but to settle for dominion status. He wanted the Congress to settle with the League on the basis of the formula put forth in 1941 by C. Rajagopalchari. In December 1941 he persuaded his Bombay-based associate, Purshotamdas Thakurdas, to meet Jinnah while he himself took the initiative and met Liaquat Ali Khan, the prominent League leader. Birla followed up his talks with Liaquat by meeting Jinnah himself in September 1942. They reportedly had a 'good talk', but Birla came back with the strong impression that Jinnah 'could not clearly define the Pakistan' the League wanted.[12]

A confirmed Partitionist?

Although the Rajagopalachari formula did not gain strong support within the Congress, and Birla's hopes for an immediate settlement floundered, he was convinced that further progress was only possible after the Congress was able to face the paramount question squarely: 'Are we prepared to accept the principle of separation?' In early 1942 he took up the matter with Jawaharlal Nehru:

When you were in goal, I was seriously thinking of writing to you about the communal problem. ...Don't you think that we must take upon this question with greater determination [sic]? I cannot visualise how India will get freedom without unity. Although the third party is exploiting the situation, it cannot be said that the problem does not exist. I don't think it will be helpful simply to condemn 'Pakistan'. It is very difficult to see the objection to any separation if the Muslims as a community, really want it. ...Any partner in a business if he is not satisfied with the partnership, I suppose has the right to demand separation. The separation, of course, has to be on an equitable basis: but I cannot conceive how anybody could object to it. It is no doubt a very gigantic affair and may not perhaps, in practice, be found an easily workable proposition. But it is all the more necessary then that we should not show our reluctance in offering the solution on which the Muslims insist. I would, of course, make a condition that they will get only what is their due and, where we disagree, a machinery constituted for the purpose, will decide about the alignment of the new frontier and the exchange of populations if that be necessary. As you know, on a small scale this has been done in Turkey in the past.

If I were a Muslim, I would not accept Pakistan, because the separated Muslim India will have no iron and coal. But that is the look out of the Muslims themselves. ...I have no doubt that you have already, in your mind, analysed the pros and cons of the problem. But so far, somehow or other, I have not come across any strong argument against the separation. [13]

This letter to Nehru, let it be emphasised, was written in January 1942. It is clear that by the early 1940s Birla's perception of the way to deal with the communal problem had crystallised. From then on he was a confirmed partitionist. For him it was no longer a question of whether the Muslim League would be given Pakistan. The question centred around the terms under which Pakistan would be conceded and how an acceptable partition could be brought about. As he confided to Devdas Gandhi:

After all Jinnah is right in demanding separation. Of course, his Pakistan and my Pakistan would be quite different. Why can't we demand separation of the Hindu areas of the Punjab and Bengal and then have a new Hindustan. But, of course, there is no chance of it since neither the Congress nor the Government like it.

Given these views, Birla soon turned to analysing the economic implications of partition. In March 1940 he asked the FICCI Research Department to examine the implications of the Muslim League demand.[14] When the Research Department did not show much interest in doing so, he put together his own findings in the form of a pamphlet. There is evidence to suggest that it was widely circulated among public figures and businessmen who were asked to send their comments to Birla. Although the pamphlet had been ready for several years it was only in June 1947, the month Mountbatten announced the plan for partition, that Birla formally published his pamphlet which was entitled 'Basic Facts Relating to India and Pakistan'.

After the end of the war Birla was distressed by the long deliberations which took place between the Congress, the League and the viceroy. The victory of the Labour party in Britain in 1945 gave him hope that the process of the transfer of power would, at last, be speeded up. The ensuing constitutional negotiations about the future of a united India, however, filled him with apprehension. The Simla Conference confirmed his fears that a break-down between the leaders of the two communities was at hand. The lesson Birla learnt at Simla was that a negotiated settlement of the communal problem had reached a dead-end and the time had come for the Congress to fight the forthcoming elections to display its strength. The election results of 1946 came as no surprise to him as he was fully convinced of the popular support that the Muslim League now enjoyed. He saw in them the verdict that '80% of the Muslims are behind the League'.

It may be worthwhile noting that in the years between 1945 and 1947 Birla pinned his hopes on Sardar Patel, carefully distinguishing his politics from the rest of the Congress. In these years, it was Patel rather than Gandhi or Nehru who was steering the Congress, and it is hardly surprising that, despite Birla's close attachment to 'Bapu', he increasingly looked to the 'Sardar' for action. Their association had grown over the years, especially since the 1930s. In 1945-6 Birla was instrumental in the collection of funds for Patel for a variety of causes: for the 1946 elections and for the Congress Central Parliamentary Board. These collections were made at the behest of Patel himself. There is considerable evidence also to suggest that, in a general sense, Birla played an important role in advising Patel and the Congress leadership on economic issues in these years.

The formation of the Interim Government following the elections in 1946 initially excited Birla, although he, like other business leaders, felt that important economic questions were being neglected by the government whose obsession appeared to be with Jinnah and the Muslim League. However, on the entry of the Muslim League in the interim government, the crucial portfolio of finance was given to Liaquat, who then formulated the budget proposals for the Central Legislative Assembly in March 1947, and proposed a new business tax on profits and a graduated tax on capital gains. Birla felt that this constituted a concerted attempt by the League 'to kill the substantially Hindu industry', and he proceeded to lead the strong protest which big business lodged against the budget.[15] So effective was this protest that Liaquat Ali was forced to drop many of his tax proposals, and Birla was widely credited for this.[16] However, although big business was successful in spiking the guns of Liaquat Ali's budget, its overall experience of the interim ministry was disappointing. It accused the Muslim League of monopolising policy making in the economic sphere, because of its control over the crucial portfolios of finance and commerce.

By this time Birla could clearly see that communal politics had begun to affect the daily life of the two communities. He feared a total collapse of all economic activity in the cities. He was especially perturbed about Bengal which, in his view, faced the twin dangers of industrial strikes and communal rioting. He regarded Bengal as no longer a safe place for business or industry. Throughout the 1940s, he had, with great foresight, diversified his interests either to Gwalior or in the Bombay region. His only major industrial assets in Bengal by 1946 were his jute mills and the Textile Machinery Company.[17] Moreover he had begun to feel that Bengali Hindus were definitely unfriendly towards Marwari business and, as Marwaris were men of property, they were more vulnerable to communal arson, especially when their own Hindu brethren were not particularly co-operative.[18] To a business associate Birla later claimed with some degree of relief and satisfaction, that all he had in Calcutta were two thousand clerks. [19]

Following the Calcutta killings of August 1946 Birla felt that the time had come for the Congress to organise a national guard of volunteers to intervene on the side of law and order and the defence of property. His interest in Hindu self-defence went back several decades. Since the late 1930s he had consistently supported a Hindu para-military school – the Bhonsale Military School established in 1937 by Dr B.S. Moonje, the Hindu Mahasabha leader.[20] His elder brother Jugalkishore, moreover, supported the Mahasabha, and until 1940 V.D. Savarkar, its president, received a monthly grant of Rs 300 as a contribution towards the expenses of his presidential office in Bombay.[21] Some idea of the support given by Jugalkishore can seen by the fact that he contributed to this organisation Rs 25 *lakhs* out of its total assets of Rs 30 *lakhs*,[22] which included the Hindu Mahasabha Bhawan in New Delhi. Jugalkishore's funding of the Hindu Mahasabha had become something of a legend by the 1940s.

On the business front, the Birlas were better prepared to handle the trouble that followed partition than most businessmen. In Calcutta, for instance, the plant and machinery of their Textile Machinery Company were fully diverted by April 1947 to Gwalior.[23] However, there were two areas where they were still vulnerable: one related to the operations of the Birla-controlled United Commercial Bank in the Muslim majority provinces of Punjab and Sind and the other was a large cotton mill – the Sutlej Cotton Mill in Okara near Lahore. Bank branches in West Punjab and Sind had removed eighty per cent of their liquid assets to safer areas before disturbances broke out. Thus the bank was able to save a large part of its movable assets, although many of its premises suffered when the riots broke out.[24] Birla subsequently took up the issue of his bank, with that of other Indian banks in Pakistan, with the authorities, so that the banks could be compensated for their losses.[25]

That left the Sutlej mill as the only Birla concern that ran into trouble during the partition riots. It had a net worth of Rs. 3 *crores* in 1947 out of which Rs 2 *crores* were in stocks and Rs one *crore* was the investment in plant and equipment. It employed about four thousand workers. Trouble started in Okara in August 1947.[26] Soon after large scale riots began in Western Punjab, mill employees – most of whom were Hindus – fled. The mill was looted and declared evacuee property by the Pakistan government. Birla took up the matter with the highest authorities and by early October 1947, as a result of his lobbying, it was back to operating all of its shifts, [27] while he assured the Pakistan prime minister that 'we shall do our best to help the economy of Pakistan'.[28]

Big business rallies round Birla

By the early 1940s Birla was not alone among big businessmen in advocating partition as a lasting solution to the communal deadlock. Other business leaders rallied to his viewpoint. The political views of some other important businessmen reflected a similar desire for separation. For instance, Ramkrishna Dalmia openly claimed to be the first among business leaders to publicly support partition.[29] Another important businessman who held similar views was Homy Mody.[30] There is considerable evidence to suggest that in the early 1940s, the groundswell of opinion within big business was receptive to the idea of partition.[31]

In all this, it is important to understand the reasons why partition made good economic sense to big business as a class. For them, there were three principal considerations. First and foremost, the reason for big business' support for the idea of partition sprang from its long-term political strategy. Big business was astute enough to realise that the choice lay between accepting the partition of the country, on the one hand, or a loose federal structure in which the Muslim majority provinces would enjoy a large measure of autonomy. Clearly, if Jinnah had settled for less than Pakistan, he would have demanded greater autonomy for the Muslim majority provinces. For big business, however, a strong centre was absolutely crucial. They preferred a division of the country to any scheme of a loose confederation with a weak centre, nominally exercising control over strong provinces.[32] The second consideration arose from the enormous difficulties big business faced in the communally charged atmosphere of the late 1940s. Finally, business was anxious not to lose out on the opportunity that the post war years presented and that encouraged them further to accept the division of the country.

The case for a strong centre

Birla's particular genius lay in ensuring that business leaders realised that all schemes for a united India would inevitably be predicated on a weak centre, surrounded by strong provinces. He successfully convinced them that the League would accept nothing less than a weak centre with the real power concentrated in the provinces. As his *Eastern Economist* explained:

From the economic point of view the country needs a strong central Government. Politically while the Congress and Hindu opinion may be in favour of a strong centre, Muslim opinion can only be assuaged by a Federation which will limit the powers and aims of the Centre to very narrow and limited aims and grant all essential powers including residuary authority to the provinces. What is, therefore, politically practicable may not be economically satisfying or adequate.

All plans for a united India necessarily implied that political power would be concentrated in strong provincial governments to give the Muslim-majority provinces the autonomy the League demanded.

For big business the essentials of rapid industrialisation entailed economic planning, and fundamental to this was a strong centre and economic homogeneity within the country. It, therefore, envisaged a future in which the government at the centre would undertake the planned development of the economic infra-structure. Post-independence India, with a feeble centre, would 'wholly lack economic foundations' and autonomy to the provinces would 'effectively kill the economic unity of India, render planning almost impossible, bring about veritable inter-unit economic confusion and blast hopes for any reasonable increase in living standards for the common man'. Birla and his colleagues realised that large scale state enterprise would be needed for developing basic industrial infra-structure. They realised too that private enterprise would be unable to make investments in developing basic infra-structure, where returns were only possible after a long gestation period. The capital, technology and managerial resources needed for large projects to develop the basic industries could only be mobilised by the state.

On this there existed a remarkable consensus among business leaders like Purshotamdas Thakurdas, J.R.D. Tata, Kasturbhai Lalbhai, Shri Ram and Birla. It may even be said that planning for big business in these years was merely a euphemism for state enterprise. There had existed, as is well known, a close relationship between the Congress and FICCI on the need for economic planning, as was demonstrated by the work of the National Planning Committee of the Congress.[33] The clearest statement on the role of planning and state enterprise in independent India was, however, made in the 'Bombay Plan' for which Birla and his associates were responsible.[34] The fundamental assumption underlying the Plan, which was announced in January 1944, was that a single national government would be formed after the war.[35] Such a government would be constituted on a federal basis and its jurisdiction over economic matters would extend over the entire country. The plan represented a total economic blue-print by big business for independent India.

The most striking aspect of the 'Bombay Plan' was the central role envisaged for the state. It contemplated three kinds of state intervention in economic activity: government control, government ownership and government management. The state was to exercise control over the distribution of industries; minimise regional disparities; build up public utilities and basic industries; and undertake or subsidise non-remunerative private enterprise. While endorsing the plan, the prominent Calcutta businessman and former president of FICCI, N.R. Sarkar, declared that 'without economic unity and the absolute power of a central authority over economic matters, it will not be possible to carry through any rational plan of economic development'.[36] At the FICCI annual session of 1944 Birla proudly called the 'Bombay Plan' the 'non-official plan for the economic development of India,' and as things eventuated it became the basis of India's first Five-Year National Plan.

The 'Bombay Plan' did not mention the partition of the country. It would have been out of character for big business to indulge in political controversy. But the plan laid down the essentials of what independent India was to be in economic terms. And it always implied that a divided India was preferable to big business rather than a united India with a feeble centre and weakened by divisive elements. Further evidence of big business's preference for a strong central authority came with its support for the government's Industrial Policy Statement of April 1945 which laid the responsibility for most large-scale industries on the central government.[37] That big business was concerned that maximum powers should be given to the centre and that the Muslim League strategy of a loose federation should not be allowed to prevail is clear not only from the statements of the FICCI, but also from the concerns of individual leaders.[38]

That a strong centre was regarded as absolutely essential for future economic development by big business can be seen from the reaction of FICCI, which now represented more than ninety-seven Indian industrial organisations, to the Cabinet Mission proposals of May 1946. The mission essentially envisaged a weak centre which would have minimum powers under its control. It allotted only the three subjects of defence, foreign relations and communications to the union centre. The proposal of the Cabinet Mission alarmed big business and they were now galvanised into putting forth their views clearly and without mincing their words. The FICCI Research Department analysed the economic implications of the proposals and set out its critique in a paper entitled 'Economic Destiny and the Constitution'. Meeting in March 1947, FICCI criticised the Cabinet Mission Plan for the vagueness of its formulations regarding the central government's role. FICCI also passed a strongly worded resolution on the 'powers and policies of the Indian Union Government' in which it set out candidly that it was 'essential that the economic and industrial development of the country should be brought within a measurable distance of time through one common policy evolved and given effect by the Union government'.[39] Supporting the resolution, an important FICCI member declared that 'our only aim is and should be to maintain a strong Union centre as it is *sine qua non* with the prosperity and progress of our country'.[40]

A 'circumscribed' centre, as proposed by the League and embodied in the Cabinet Mission plan, was regarded by big business as 'a matter for disquiet'.[41] A month after FICCI passed its resolution, twenty-seven largely Bengal-based chambers of commerce meeting under the auspices of the Bengal National Chamber of Commerce, which included the Indian Chamber of Commerce, the India Sugar Mills Association and the Bengal Millowners Association, also put forth a similar view.[42]

Pragmatism of big business

The second reason for big business's support for partition arose from its hard core pragmatism. In practical terms simple considerations of public order dictated that a workable solution should be found to communal tensions which had begun to affect the economic fabric of the country. Rioting and communal disorders in the mid-1940s threatened the collapse of all economic activity, especially in Bengal. Birla articulated this anxiety when he wrote to Rajagopalachari in 1945: 'It is hardly necessary for me to draw your attention to the economic consequences of the disturbed conditions. ... In provinces like Bengal, Bihar, UP, production is seriously affected. Today you can't even build a house...serious labour shortages, coal shortages, no bricks, Muslim *mistries* don't come in Hindu areas and Hindu labour don't enter Muslim areas'.[43] Communal violence created fears of attacks on property to which businessmen in general and industrialists in particular were vulnerable. By late 1946 the economy reeled under the strain of civil strife and communal disorders.

In Bengal the situation deteriorated markedly after the Calcutta killings of August 1946. Businessmen complained about the impossibility of operating in a communally charged atmosphere. The very large Bengal Chemicals and Pharmaceuticals company, for instance, complained of absenteeism among labour because of communal outbursts, and they wanted armed military pickets stationed at their factories to provide safety for their staff.[44] A common complaint was of stocks being locked up because of an inability to open godowns and shops during disturbances, leading ultimately to huge losses.[45] The perception gaining ground among non-Muslim businesses was of communal bias among the city's police.[46] This was especially felt by Marwari businessmen who as a propertied group felt they were particular targets of violence. This led them to resort to methods such as the formation of their own defence committees to safeguard their lives and property in Calcutta. In these conditions they lent their powerful support to the on-going mass mobilisation which the Bengal Hindu Mahasabha was undertaking under the leadership of S.P. Mookerjee.[47] Marwari traders accordingly strongly supported the move to partition the province.[48]

A similar collapse of economic activity was witnessed in Punjab. For instance, in early 1947, the *Eastern Economist* reported that due to communal trouble Hindu and Sikh businesses were being closed down. It reported the flight of capital, nervousness in the stock-market, a down-turn in property prices, the mass exodus of labour from West Punjab and the closure of markets due to disturbed conditions.[49]

All these strains and pressures further propelled big business to seek an immediate and lasting settlement to the communal question. Business leaders were astute enough to realise that negotiations and pacts between leaders of the two communities scarcely ever worked and resulted only in a fragile peace. What made good economic sense to big business was to seek a long-term solution; partition came to be seen increasingly as the way forward.

Another important consideration for big business was the great economic opportunity which it saw in the post-war situation. A large number of business houses had reaped huge profits during the war years and were now looking for avenues for investment. However, the communal situation and the political uncertainty which loomed large in the expectation of an impending transfer of power frustrated their plans for expansion and diversification. The *Eastern Economist* viewed the situation as one where business-men were 'flooded...with more than sufficient financial resources' but were handicapped by the uncertainties of the times. A close study of the resolutions passed at the annual meetings of FICCI in the 1940s shows the concern at the government's neglect of economic issues. Homi Mody regretted in 1945 that 'matters of urgency' were being delayed because of the communal problem. Business leaders were impatient for constitutional advance and the communal deadlock was increasingly seen as a stumbling block.

The economic feasibility of partition

Given such an approach to partition, business leaders took steps seriously to analyse what partition would entail in economic terms. Two important leaders of big business who were closely associated with FICCI, John Mathai and Homi Mody, both from the Tata group, undertook a study in 1944 which they published a year later as *A Memorandum on the Economic and Financial Aspects of Pakistan*. They had originally submitted their findings to the Sapru Committee on Constitutional Reforms in 1944.

Mody and Mathai made their position clear when they stated that 'if a scheme which pre-supposed the political unity of India was not acceptable to the League and if the results of the forthcoming elections were to vindicate the Muslim League position, separation as a means of ending the political deadlock should not be ruled out'. They clearly declared that the priorities of the time were such that the communal deadlock should be settled immediately. 'As things stand at present,' they stated,

> the settlement of our political problems admits of no delay. Issues of greater consequences and urgency which may affect the future of India permanently are facing us, and it is of the highest importance that the present political deadlock should not be allowed to continue and that the direction of political affairs should, without further delay, be placed in the hands of Indian leaders who have the confidence of the country.[50]

In their study Mody and Mathai analysed in detail the economic consequences of the Pakistan idea. They assumed that Pakistan would consist of two economic zones, as set out by the Muslim League. They visualised two possible scenarios. In the first scenario, partition would be carried out according to the then existing provincial boundaries: all the Muslim majority provinces would form the new state. In the second scenario, boundaries would be re-drawn according to the contiguous Muslim majority districts of Punjab and Bengal. Mody and Mathai concluded that Pakistan would be a viable economic unit if partition was to occur province-wise. However, if the boundaries were to be drawn on the basis of Muslim majority districts, the position of Pakistan would not be a happy one.

They concluded that, in both the scenarios, there would be need for the two independent states to co-operate in the spheres of economy and defence. They emphasised that a large free trade zone was essential for the future development of the two economies. Mody and Mathai thus came to two major conclusions. If the objective was to maintain existing standards of living and budgetary requirements on a pre-war basis (excluding the provision for defence), partition, in their view, was feasible on economic grounds. But if the goal was to raise the general standard of living, then there existed the need for effective co-operation between the two states in areas of defence and the economy.[51]

Nonetheless, Mody and Mathai stated that they were prepared to recommend only a district-wise division. Their study emphasised the pre-eminent economic position of Calcutta in the division of the country. It concluded that, without Calcutta, the eastern zone of Pakistan would be poorly off. In view of the fact that the political situation was extremely uncertain in 1944 when the study was conducted, all Mody and Mathai could do was to visualise different scenarios. However, what they succeeded in doing was to establish the pre-eminent position of Calcutta in the minds of big business leadership and the vital importance of retaining it within India.

In June 1947 Birla published his own paper to which we referred earlier.[52] He showed that 'Hindu India' would have a 'larger population, larger area and larger resources and will in many respects be stronger' than Pakistan. The trade balance, he declared, would also be favourable to India since exports from India to Pakistan would amount to Rs 850 million and the imports from Pakistan would amount to Rs 700 million. The pamphlet demonstrated that, except in raw jute and water power resources, India would have a distinct advantage as compared to Pakistan.

He prefaced his study by the statement that a 'Hindu India' would be stronger than Pakistan but he acknowledged that even Pakistan could be 'strong and prosperous'. He advocated economic co-ordination for a higher rate of growth and concluded that 'it would be in the interest of both the parts to put up co-ordinated efforts in order that the whole of India may be able to achieve high economic prosperity, strength and dignity'. What distinguished Birla's pamphlet from Mody and Mathai's earlier study was that Calcutta was not even recognised as a possible issue of contention; it was assumed that the city would be a part of 'Hindu' India.[53] Birla took the position that, even without Calcutta, Pakistan would be economically feasible.

As it happened, the manner in which partition took place and Pakistan came into being took big business unawares. Their best hope had been that the two countries would co-operate in economic matters. But such hopes floundered in the face of the bitterness and violence that accompanied the partition. Nonetheless, the prior considerations which big business gave to the idea of partition left its indelible imprint on the consequences of partition. This can be seen in the fact that its aggregate cost to Indian big business was relatively small. With Calcutta remaining in India, there was little that big business lost due to partition.

For big business the stakes were less in Punjab, where their major industrial assets were the Shri Ram and Birla cotton mills at Lyallpur and Okra, the Mukund steel works at Lahore, the plants of Associated Cement Companies and the operations of the Narang group. This is not to suggest that big business did not appreciate the importance of the Punjab economy. It had anticipated the troubles and had been preparing in advance to cut its losses. A massive flight of capital from Punjab was witnessed in the months preceding partition. By May 1947 at least three to four premier banks and insurance companies had moved their headquarters out of Lahore, and the flight of capital was estimated to be above Rs 250 *crores*. Businessmen understood what this flight of capital meant for the soon to be formed state of Pakistan; one of them was reported to have remarked: 'After us the deluge. We are leaving Pakistan an economic desert'.[54]

The balance sheet of partition for big business

In total the cost of partition to Indian big business was minimal. In early 1948 after partition had taken place, FICCI initiated a study to ascertain what precisely had been the economic cost of partition. This study was conducted by G.L. Bansal, then Assistant Secretary in FICCI, and its findings were communicated to Shanmukham Chetty, the Finance Minister of India, who had been a past president of FICCI. Bansal's study entitled *India and Pakistan (An Analysis of Agricultural, Mineral and Industrial Resources)* drew an optimistic picture and concluded that in food articles, industrial raw materials and manufactured articles India's position 'is not only better off than Pakistan but is even superior as compared with that of the undivided India'. The per-capita production of all types of goods in the Indian Union was now thirty-six per cent more than it was before, while in Pakistan it was 18.5 per cent less. The study demonstrated also that the conclusions drawn by big business in the early 1940s had been vindicated, as India 'possesses almost all the resources for developing into a major industrial country of the world'.[55]

A number of indices reflected this. Over 90.4 per cent of the total industry of undivided India remained within India. In 1945 there existed a total of 14,677 industrial establishments in India, out of which 13,263 or 90.4 per cent remained in India, while Pakistan got only 1,414 or 9.6 per cent. Of the total industrial employment, India's share was 93.5 per cent, while that of Pakistan stood at 6.5 per cent.[56] In terms of basic infrastructure, it appears that India again had the edge. For instance, in electricity generation, India got 94.7 per cent of the total installed plant capacity in kilowatts, while only 5.3 per cent went to Pakistan (of this 4.8 per cent to West Pakistan and .5 per cent to East Pakistan). In the area of transportation, out of the total railways route mileage of 41,141 in undivided India, over 34,157 miles stayed within India and only 6,981 miles went to Pakistan.

This pattern was repeated in specific sectors of industry. In textiles, out of the total business establishments, 1,656 remained within India and 46 went to

Pakistan. In the case of engineering establishments, 1,734 remained within India, while 278 went to Pakistan. Out of the total of 108 jute mills in undivided India, none went to Pakistan. Of the 394 cotton mills, 380 remained in India, with less than 5 per cent going to Pakistan. Pakistan got only 10 of the 166 sugar mills. All the 49 paper mills of undivided India remained in India, as did all the 18 iron and steel mills. Thirty heavy engineering factories remained in India, while Pakistan got four.[57]

The FICCI study of 1948 reassured Indian big business that even in sectors where India had been left poorer by partition, the picture was not too dismal. For instance, even though India was deficient in food grains, in food articles it was better off than Pakistan. Even in raw cotton and raw jute, India could produce enough for her own consumption of cotton textiles and jute goods.

There were some temporary difficulties for big business. The jute industry in Calcutta, for instance, saw its supply of raw material threatened, as seventy per cent of raw jute production was in East Pakistan. But Indian industrialists were reassured that supply was likely to continue and India would continue to be the main buyer of East Pakistan's raw jute. Moreover, they felt that jute cultivation could be developed in Indian Bengal.[58] In any case by the late 1940s, jute was regarded as a sunset industry which had never recovered from its troubles of the depression years. Moreover, Bengal businessmen who had made their fortunes in the jute markets were now planning to move into new areas such as synthetic fibres. In general big business felt confident that the basic resources were in place to put India on the path of rapid industrial development with the future of private enterprise firmly secured, and thus weathered the experience of partition better than might have been thought.

Notes

1   This paper draws upon my larger work on G. D. Birla and Indian big business which is being revised for publication. See Medha Malik Kudaisya, 'The Public Career of G.D. Birla, 1911-1947' (PhD thesis, Cambridge, 1992).
2   M. Kudaisya, 'The Public Career of G.D. Birla', chapter 2.
3   Lajpat Rai to Birla, 30 Dec. 1928, Private Papers of G.D. Birla in the personal custody of the Birla family (henceforth BP). Series Important Files II (henceforth Series II), File L-7.
4   See M. Kudaisya, 'The Public Career of G.D. Birla', chapter 3 for details.
5   'Notes of Conversation with Malaviyaji on 17 Oct. 1927, Benaras'. by Birla, BP, Series Very Important Correspondence, File 10.
6   Ayesha Jalal, *The Sole Spokesman Jinnah, the Muslim League and the Demand for Pakistan* (Cambridge, 1985).
7   'The Present Impasse', Note given by Birla to the Viceroy's Secretary, n.d., BP, Series Miscellaneous, File 130.
8   *Loc.cit.*
9   Birla to Mahadev Desai, 11 Jan. 1938, in G. D. Birla, *Bapu: A Unique Association* (Bombay, 1977), Vol. III, pp. 142-144.
10 Interview with the viceroy on 11 Nov. 1939, BP, File 38.
11 Birla to Rajagopalachari, 12 Oct. 1938, BP, Series II, File H-10.
12 Birla to Padampat Singhania, 25 Sept. 1942, BP, Series II, File S-20. Jinnah later claimed before Nehru that Birla was in favour of Pakistan. See Birla to Nehru dated 3 June 1947, BP, Series II, File N-4.
13 Birla to Jawaharlal Nehru, 13 Jan. 1942, Jawaharlal Nehru Papers, NMML.
14 D.G. Mulherkar to Purshotamdas Thakurdas, 12 Apr. 1940, and Thakurdas to Mulherkar, 15 Apr. 1940, File 175/ 1936-40, Part I, Purshotamdas Thakurdas Papers, NMML.
15 So hostile was business reaction that stock exchanges closed down in protest. Important business leaders like Thakurdas and Tata rushed to Delhi to throw their weight behind Birla's campaign to scotch the budget proposals. It was widely believed that FICCI which launched a bitter attack on the budget was alongside preparing an alternative budget.
16 For details of business reactions to the interim government's budget see R. Chattopadhyaya, 'Liaquat Ali's Budget of 1947-48, The Tryst With Destiny', in *Social Scientist*, Vol. 16, no. 6-7 (1988). Also see Claude Markovits, 'Congress Policy Towards Business in the Pre-Independence Era', in R. Sisson and S. Wolpert (ed.), *Congress and Indian Nationalism : The Pre-Independence Phase* (California, 1988).
17 Birla to L.P. Misra, 26 May 1946, BP, Series Foreign Correspondence, File C-3.
18 Birla to Major Chatterjee, 2 Mar. 1947, BP, Series II, File C-1.
19 Birla to L.P. Misra, 26 May 1946, BP, Series Foreign Correspondence, File C-3.
20 B. S. Moonje to Birla, 28 Feb. 1947, BP, Series II, File M-21.
21 See V.D. Savarkar to Nirmalchandra Chatterji, 24 Aug. 1940 in File 53, S P Mookerji Papers, NMML.
22 'Arya (Hindu) Dharma Seva Sangha. Maharashtra Branch' notice in File 41, B.S. Moonje Papers, NMML.
23 Birla to J.K. Anderson, 24 Apr. 1947, BP, Series Foreign Correspondence, File 24 A-1.
24 R.S. Saraiya to Birla, 10 Apr. 1947, BP, Series II, File S-2.
25 Birla to Shanmukham Chetty, 24 Dec. 1947, BP, Series II, File S-12.

26 Wire from Birla to Sir Chandulal Trivedi, 22 Aug. 1947; also wire dated 23 Aug. 1947, BP, Series I, File T-15.

27 Birla to Shri Prakash, 21 Sept. 1937, BP, Series II, File S-24.

28 Birla to Wazir Ali, 16 Oct. 1947 and Wazir Ali to Birla, 10 Oct. 1947. BP, Series II, File P-2.

29 Ramkrishna Dalmia, *Some Notes and Reminiscences*, Bombay, 1948, p. 33.

30 In 1944-45 Mody declared: 'I am not in favour of ignoring the Pakistan demand. If our approach to the political power of India is to be realistic, we cannot afford to forget the events of the last two or three years'.

31 In this essay we are concerned with the politics of non-Muslim big business largely because of the lack of primary data on Muslim business houses. Although Muslim big business was not unimportant in our period of study, the largest conglomerations of business were non-Muslim. This is not to suggest that big business was all alonG.D.ivided on communal lines, but rather that communal politics had begun to play an important role in the considerations of big business by the 1940s. The reactions of big business are thus studied at an all-India level. Although regional differences were significant, by the mid-1940s there appears to be a commonality of views on important issues and it is these that came to have an over-riding importance in the politics of big business towards partition.

32 Claude Markovits first suggested this idea in a preliminary form in his 'Businessmen and the Partition of India', paper presented at IIM-Ahmedabad, Mar. 1989.

33 The research of Aditya Mukherjee and Raghabendra Chattopadhyaya demonstrates this quite clearly.

34 R.D. Tata recollects that it was Birla's initiative in Dec. 1942 that brought together the authors of the Bombay Plan. R.M. Lala, *Beyond the Last Blue Mountain. A Life of J.R.D. Tata* (Bombay, 1992).

35 Birla, Thakurdas, Tata *et al.*, *A Plan for Economic Development of India* (Bombay, 1944). Also see *Eastern Economist*, 28 Jan. 1944.

36 FICCI, *Proceedings of the 17th Annual Meeting held in 1944* (New Delhi, 1945)

37 Venkatsubbiah, *Enterprise and Economic Change. 50 Years of FICCI* (New Delhi, 1977), pp. 50-1.

38 For instance, see Purshotamdas Thakurdas to Birla, 4 July 1946., File 362, Purshotamdas Thakurdas Papers, NMML.

39 FICCI, *Proceedings of the 20 the Annual Meeting held in 1947*, Vol. III (New Delhi, 1948)

40 See speech by M.G. Lakshminarsu in *Ibid.*

41 For instance, see *Eastern Economist*, 17 May 1946. Also see 'The Cabinet Proposals II The Economic Aspect', *Eastern Economist*, 31 May 1946; also see *Eastern Economist*, 3 Jan. 1947.

42 Bengal National Chamber of Commerce to Rajendra Prasad, 1 May 1947. These chambers declared that in addition to defence, foreign affairs and communications which the Cabinet Mission had conceded to the centre, currency and exchange, customs and excise, generation of power, labour legislation, food policy and location of defence industry 'should all be under the jurisdiction of the Centre in the interests of India's economic development'.

43 Birla to Rajagopalachari, 12 Nov. 1945, BP, Series II, R-5.

44 Bengal Chemicals and Pharmaceuticals World Ltd. to S.P. Mookherjee, 2 Apr. 1947, Subject File 154 (Instalment II to IV), S P Mookerjee Papers, NMML.

45 This was an especially common complaint of traders. See for instance, Petition of 70

shop keepers of Chandney Chowk, Bow Bazaar, Calcutta to S.P. Mookerjee in Subject File 154 (Instalment II to IV), S.P. Mookerjee Papers, NMML.
46 Badridas Goenka to Birla, 6 Sept. 1946, BP, Series II, File G-8.
47 For details of the work of one particularly well organised defence committee on Upper Chitpur Road, see its 'Report on Work Done on 28th and 29th July 1947' in Correspondence with Defence Committee (Installment II to IV), S.P. Mookerjee Papers, NMML.
48 AICC Papers, File C14 (B) 1946, NMML.
49 'Punjab Letter', *Eastern Economist*, 25 Apr. 1947.
50 *A Memorandm on the Economic and Financial Aspects of Pakistan*, (Bombay, 1945). In Sept. 1945 they published their findings independently. The Economic Sub-Committee of the Sapru Committee consisted of Mody, Mathai and N.R. Sarkar. While the main committee headed by Sapru reported against the partition of India, Mody and Mathai disagreed with this recommendation and signed a note of dissent. They suggested partition on the basis of district-wise division of Muslim areas to form contiguous *blocs* in Muslim-majority province. They also advocated co-operation on economic and defence between the two new states. For this they proposed the setting up of an Inter-Governmental Council. *Constitutional Proposals of the Sapru Committee* (Bombay, 1946) pp. 343-5. N.R. Sarkar, the third member of the Economic sub-committee of the Sapru Committee disagreed with Mody and Mathai's recommendations. Sarkar declared that division, both province-wise and especially district-wise as proposed by Mody and Mathai would be highly prejudicial to Pakistan. Pakistan would have only five per cent of the mineral wealth of undivided India and even in oil, in which it was supposed to be in an advantageous position it would not have sufficient supplies. The division of India, he claimed, would be disadvantageous because of the economic interdependence of the countries which were 'almost inextricable bound up and interdependent'. District-wise division would not make Pakistan economically feasible and Sarkar concluded that Pakistan was not a practical proposition either economically or financially.
51 They conducted their feasibility study of Pakistan by considering: its budgetary position; its standard of living; and its defence requirements.
52 Birla, *Basic Facts Relating to India and Pakistan*, Eastern Economist pamphlets 5 (New Delhi, 1947).
53 There is evidence to suggest that Birla and other businessmen from eastern India put strong pressure on the Congress leadership on the need to retain Calcutta within India. The Congress in its memorandum before the Boundary Commission claimed that more than 91.55 per cent of properties in Calcutta were owned by non-Muslims and only 8.45 per cent by Muslims who constituted 23.59 per cent of the city's population according to the 1941 census. For details see 'The Congress Case as presented before the Bengal Boundary Commission', 26 July 1947 (published by the Secretary, Bengal Congress Central Consultative Boundary Committee) and 'Memorandum for the Bengal Boundary Commission: Submitted by the Provincial Hindu Mahasabha and the New Bengal Association'.
54 *Eastern Economist*, 16 May 1947. Punjab businessmen such as Sardar P. Sodhbans of the Indian Chamber of Commerce, Lahore, deplored the attitude of FICCI towards the province's partition. The Indian chamber of Commerce, Lahore, complained that FICCI did not pass any resolution on Punjab business and the president in his address did not so much as even mention the losses of Punjab business.
55 G.L. Bansal, *India and Pakistan (An Analysis of Agricultural, Mineral and*

Industrial Resources) (New Delhi, 1948).

[56] C.N. Vakil, *Economic consequences of divided India: a study of the economy of India and Pakistan* (Bombay, 1950), p. 247.

[57] For details, see M. Kudaisya, 'The Public Career of G.D. Birla', chap. 5.

[58] See Resolution moved by R.A. Poddar of the Bombay Yarn Exchange, Bombay in FICCI, *Proceedings of the 21st Annual Meeting of the Federation held on 28-29 March 1948* (New Delhi, 1948).

Index

ABOUT THE EDITORS

D.A. Low is a University Fellow at the Australian National University, Canberra. During a rich and distinguished career, he has been Smutts Professor of the History of the British Commonwealth (1983–94) and President of Clare Hall (1987–94), University of Cambridge; Director of the Research School of Pacific Studies (1973–75) and Vice-chancellor (1975–82) of the Australian National University; and Professor of History and Founding Dean of the School of African and Asian Studies, London (1964–72). Among his numerous publications are *Britain and Indian Nationalism, 1929–42, The Egalitarian Moment: Asia and Africa, 1975-80* and *Eclipse of Empire.*

Howard Brasted is currently Associate Professor in Indian and Islamic History, University of New England, Armidale, and Acting Director, UNE Asia Centre. His professional positions include Executive Director, South Asian Studies Association, and Editor of *South Asia* (both held since 1984). Apart from being widely published on topics ranging from the transfer of power in India, to Indian nationalism and the Indian National Congress, Howard Brasted has just completed, as part of a team, an AusAid Project on Child Labour in South and Southeast Asia which has just been published, and has begun another project: Muslims and Modernity in Asia.